THE PUNJAB UNDER IMPERIALISM,

1885–1947

IMRAN ALI

The Punjab under Imperialism, 1885–1947

PRINCETON UNIVERSITY
PRESS

Copyright © 1988 by Princeton University Press
Published by Princeton University Press, 41 William Street,
Princeton, New Jersey 08540
In the United Kingdom: Princeton University Press,
Guildford, Surrey

LIBRARY OF CONGRESS CATALOGING-IN-PUBLICATION DATA

Imran, Ali.
The Punjab under imperialism, 1885-1947 / Imran Ali.
   p. cm.
Bibliography: p.   Includes index.
ISBN 0-691-05527-0 (alk. paper)
1. Land settlement—India—Punjab—History. 2. Agricultural
colonies—India—Punjab—History. 3. Agriculture—
Economic aspects—India—Punjab—History. 4. Irrigation farming—
India—Punjab—History. 5. Elite (Social sciences)—India—
Punjab—History. I. Title.
HD879.P8I47 1988   338.954′552—dc19   87-34466
                                              CIP
                                       (Rev.)

This book has been composed in Linotron Times Roman

Clothbound editions of Princeton University Press books
are printed on acid-free paper, and binding materials are
chosen for strength and durability. Paperbacks,
although satisfactory for personal collections,
are not usually suitable for library rebinding

Printed in the United States of America by
Princeton University Press
Princeton, New Jersey

CONTENTS

LIST OF TABLES

IT COULD plausibly be argued that the experience of the Punjab under British rule proved to be qualitatively different from that of other parts of South Asia. The British came late to the Punjab owing to its geographical location, which was distant from their points of early contact with the subcontinent. They remained in the province two years short of a century, relinquishing it along with the rest of their Indian empire in 1947. The Punjab was at that juncture perhaps in a state of greater turmoil and human dislocation than any other part of South Asia. The sufferings of partition and indeed the continuing instability in this region since independence could be compared to the near anarchy experienced in the Punjab during the decades prior to British annexation. Between the Sikh interregnum that ended in 1849 and the emergence of Pakistan and India in 1947, the period of British rule seemed to be one not only of relative political peace and stability, but also of vigorous economic growth. The latter was largely premised on the subject of this study: the colonisation of newly canal-irrigated land. This process of agricultural expansion was extensive enough, and sufficiently pervasive in its impact and consequences, to mark out the Punjab from other provinces of British India as a "beneficiary" of colonial rule.

Such conclusions are not inaccurate, and they have had much currency in both official thought and scholarly assessment. Yet they require some qualification. If even a beneficiary remained an underdeveloped region, despite major economic change, then what reflection does this cast on the nature of imperialist rule, and on its consequences for its subject economies? Indeed, economic growth itself might have contained a certain "malignity" for the prospects of socioeconomic transformation in such regions. Such outcomes were very different from the more positive consequences of economic growth in those parts of the world that are now industrialised and affluent. That continued backwardness was entrenched because of, rather than in spite of, economic change, remains an intriguing problematic for research on the underdeveloped regions of the world. The present work tries to explain how one isolated subeconomy, that of the Punjab, could have experienced significant growth and yet have remained backward, or even have acquired through the very process of growth further structural resistances to change. The Punjab provides an instructive case study on the fortunes of a subject economy under imperialism.

The great agricultural colonisation schemes undertaken in the western Punjab during British rule turned this area into a virtual human laboratory, as castes, clans, and tribes from different parts of the province converged on the new lands. This ethos has left its mark on the character of the Punjab and its people. The restlessness born of migration is now a century old. This has unhinged the traditional moorings of village society, and freed people for intercourse with the wider world. The Pakistani Punjab, where these "canal colonies" are situated, still depends predominantly for its agrarian viability on the irrigation schemes initiated during the past century. This is truly a hydraulic society, where patterns of dominance and subordination are pervaded by the fact that the water that sustains cropping comes not from the heavens but through human agency and human control. The eastern parts of the old Punjab, now in India, provided large numbers of colonists to these tracts. But the Sikhs and Hindus among them, as well as among the indigenous western Punjabis, had to leave for Indian territory at partition. This undoubtedly compounded the problems of ethno-nationalism that have recently surfaced so violently in the Indian Punjab.

My work on the canal colonies has seen many changes of place and institution. It took its earliest form as an undergraduate dissertation at the University of Sussex. It became the subject of a doctoral thesis at the Australian National University, which was completed while I was teaching at the University of New South Wales. Revision of this work to its present form was undertaken while I was on teaching appointments at the University of Melbourne and lately at the Lahore University of Management Sciences. In a sense, my involvement with the canal colonies goes back much further, indeed to well before my birth, when my maternal grandfather, Nawab Sir Zulfiqar Ali Khan, undertook to construct a network of tubewells on a colony leasehold. His singular lack of success is documented here in the chapter on production. One can only hope that venture was not an ominous precedent.

This work has benefitted from advice and feedback from a number of people, too numerous to name individually. I am particularly indebted to my doctoral supervisor, Professor D. A. Low, for the many years of guidance and good counsel that he has given me. Dr. Margaret Case of Princeton University Press has throughout been most cooperative and supportive. Many people have helped in the completion of the manuscript: I wish to acknowledge in particular the assistance of Ms. Naveed Hasan. The primary research for this work was conducted mostly at the India Office Library and Records, London, and in Lahore at the Punjab Secretariat archives and the Board of Revenue. I am grateful to the staff of these centres for their help and cooperation.

Some conventions followed here may be briefly noted. In the case of references to assessment reports (ARs) and settlement reports (SRs), the years given in parenthesis are those of the Punjab Revenue and Agriculture Proceedings (PRAP) in which they appeared: more detailed references to these reports are contained in the Bibliography. With files from the Board of Revenue, the full title and file number are normally reproduced at the first reference, and thereafter only the number for further references in the same chapter. Unless otherwise stated, all officials referred to belonged to the Punjab Government. Correspondence to or from the financial commissioner was actually addressed to or by his senior secretary or junior secretary. However, for purposes of brevity, mention is only made to the financial commissioner (FC) in such cases. The names of certain districts and towns have changed since 1947: Lyallpur is now Faisalabad and Montgomery is now Sahiwal. I have retained the names of districts and localities as they were before 1947.

ABBREVIATIONS

AR	Assessment Report
AS	Army Secretary
BCGA	British Cotton Growing Association
BM	British Museum, London
BOR	Board of Revenue, Lahore
CO	Colonisation Officer
DA	Director of Agriculture
DC	Deputy Commissioner
FC	Financial Commissioner
FC(D)	Financial Commissioner (Development)
GOI	Government of India
IOR	India Office Records, London
KW	Keep With
LG	Lieutenant-Governor (to 1921, subsequently Governors appointed)
PCM	*Punjab Colony Manual*
PCR	*Punjab Colonies Report*
PG	Punjab Government
PRAP(A)	Punjab Revenue and Agriculture Proceedings (Agriculture)
PRAP(G)	Punjab Revenue and Agriculture Proceedings (General)
PRAP(I)	Punjab Revenue and Agriculture Proceedings (Irrigation)
PRAP(R)	Punjab Revenue and Agriculture Proceedings (Revenue)
RAS	Revenue and Agriculture Secretary
RODA	*Report on the Operations of the Department of Agriculture*
RPCC	Report of the Punjab Colonies Committee, 1907-1908
RS	Revenue Secretary
Rs	Rupees
SC	Settlement Commissioner
SO	Settlement Officer
SR	Settlement Report

THE PUNJAB
(at the transfer of power, 1947)

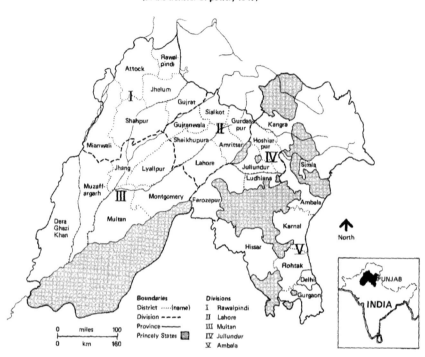

Boundaries
District ·····(name)
Division - - - -
Province ———
Princely States ▨

Divisions
I Rawalpindi
II Lahore
III Multan
IV Jullundur
V Ambala

| 0 | miles | 100 |
| 0 | km | 160 |

THE PUNJAB CANAL COLONIES

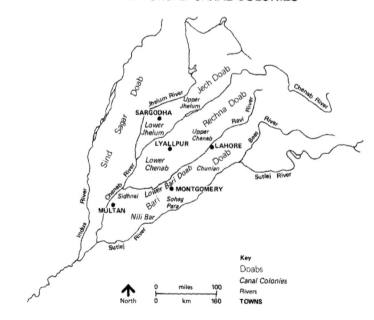

Key
Doabs
Canal Colonies
Rivers
TOWNS

| 0 | miles | 100 |
| 0 | km | 160 |

THE PUNJAB UNDER IMPERIALISM,
1885–1947

CHAPTER ONE

A New Agrarian Frontier

THIS IS the story of agricultural colonisation in the Punjab during the period of British rule. The Punjab, a province lying in the northwestern part of the British Indian empire, experienced rapid and extensive economic growth from the late nineteenth century onward. This resulted from the development of canal irrigation, accompanied by a process of migratory settlement in its western parts, in the area that came to be known as the "canal colonies." This part of the Punjab did not benefit, as did the eastern parts of the province, from monsoonal rains of sufficient strength to support settled agriculture. Cultivated lands, as a result, were confined to areas accessible to irrigation, which was derived either from groundwater sources through wells, or from seasonal canals utilising river water.

The laying out of an extensive network of canals based on perennial irrigation, with water drawn from the rivers through permanent weirs and headworks, has in the past century transformed this region from desert waste, or at best pastoral savanna, to one of the major centres of commercialised agriculture in South Asia. The sizeable in-migration from other parts of the Punjab that followed upon canal construction, and the ensuing extension in agricultural activity, has made the canal colonies a phenomenon of major importance in the recent history of this part of the world. For the British, under whose supervision they were founded, the canal colonies were the most potent of the many benefits that they believed their rule had brought to the people of this province. This new agrarian frontier could be held up as the crowning achievement of what they regarded as their benevolent participation in South Asian society. For the Punjabis themselves it became a major demographic outlet, with the opening up of the harsh lands of the western *doab*s posing a formidable challenge to their spirit of enterprise and initiative.

The Punjab had been annexed by the British in 1849. This event followed a century of turbulence that saw the collapse of the Mughal empire, a period of semi-anarchy during which confederacies based on peasant caste and tribal alignments fought for territorial control, and a feudal reaction within the warbands that resulted in the establishment of a number of petty princely states. It was the largest of these successor states, the adventurer Ranjit Singh's kingdom of Lahore, that the British overcame in 1849, thereby asserting their control over the entire province. British rule brought stability to the Punjab. Ruling groups, if they had desisted from provocation against British interests, were not replaced but confirmed as useful intermediaries between the state and the people. This partnership was consolidated with the Punjabis' vital intervention on the side of the British in the armed struggle of 1857-1858. The Punjabis went on to contribute manpower and logistic support for imperialism's conflicts on the northwest frontier, and also helped Britain to conquer and police far-flung overseas territories. Such cooperation continued throughout the period of imperialist rule, and with it the military became an important source of employment for Punjabis. About half the British Indian army came to be recruited from the Punjab; the British were fond of calling the people of this province ''the martial races of India.''

As soon as their administrative presence was established, the British undertook revenue settlements in each district. This regularised extraction from agriculture, which was by far the most important source of income for the state. Surveys were conducted to assess the revenue-paying capacity of each estate. Though state demand was generally fixed lower than the excessive rates imposed by previous governments, emphasis on ensuring efficient collection meant that the British extracted as much revenue, if not more, than their predecessors. Revenue assessments also served as a means of establishing proprietary status. They encouraged individualisation in property rights, which was a marked shift from the collective ownership by village communities and other complex forms of property that had existed in the pre-British period.

The process of individualisation created, probably for the first time, the prospect of alienation of land rights. With the increase in marketing of agricultural produce, aided by the development of road and rail transport, land came to have a monetary value. Agricultural owners realised that they possessed an asset that could be readily converted to more direct means of enjoying social expenditure and conspicuous consumption. After 1880 there was a considerable increase in land sales in the Punjab, but much of this alienation was forced rather than voluntary. As agriculturists entered more into the money economy, they fell deeper into debt to nonagricultural moneylending and commercial castes, though increasingly creditors also came from the ranks of the agriculturists themselves. Debt entailed mortgaging the only asset they possessed: their land. Unredeemed mortgages were converted to alienations by recourse to another institution introduced by the British, a civil and penal code. The new laws gave exceptional powers of manipulation to moneylenders, and turned law courts into arenas of agrarian conflict.

The British were greatly perturbed by these trends, which they regarded as undermining the position of the landowning ''agricultural castes'' on whom they relied for political support, revenue returns, and military recruitment. In 1900 they passed a remarkable piece of paternalistic legislation, the Punjab Alienation of Land Act. This forbade the passing of land from agricultural to nonagricultural castes, and allowed land transfers only within related agricultural caste groups in each district. This effort to shore up the landowning classes was followed in the remaining period of British rule by other legislative acts designed to protect agriculturists from inroads by commercial elements and the disruptive impact of market forces.

These processes suggest that the period of British rule in the Punjab was dominated by three major themes: political entrenchment, revenue extraction, and military requirements. These themes maintained their importance in the history of the region, even with the advent of significant changes in its economic structure. From 1885 on, the economy of the Punjab began to be reshaped by the unprecedented extension in agricultural production brought about by canal colonisation. In the western Punjab, the part that is now included in Pakistan, the emergence of a hydraulic society, combined with extensive irrigation schemes in the neighbouring province of Sind, has led to the establishment of one of the largest irrigation systems in the world.

The canal colonies resulted from the desire of the ruling authority to extend cultivation to the virgin lands of the western *doab*s. Existing irrigation systems were confined to tracts contiguous to rivers, but evidence of former habitations and earthworks in the slightly raised interfluves indicated the existence of irrigation networks in the past. The British had throughout evinced an interest in opening up the agrarian frontier in the west: from the early 1860s, not long after their annexation of the Punjab, they began to consider proposals for irrigation channels in the Rechna Doab. Several schemes were proposed before the final one for perennial irrigation from the Lower Chenab Canal took shape. This supplied irrigation water for what was to become the largest canal colony. Experience with colonisation had already been gained from smaller projects in the Bari Doab, namely, the Sidhnai, Sohag Para, and Chunian colonies, and later colonies emerged as the momentum of migration and settlement subsided in one *doab* and was taken up in another. In this way three other large colonies were founded: Jhelum, Lower Bari Doab, and Nili Bar, as well as two smaller ones, Upper Chenab and Upper Jhelum colonies.

There were nine canal colonies in all, and they absorbed the available lands of the Bari, Rechna, and Jech *doab*s. The westernmost *doab*, known as the Sind Sagar, lying between the Jhelum and Indus rivers, remained unconquered during British rule. Repeated projections for its colonisation failed to achieve fruition, owing largely to the unevenness of the terrain. It was not until the technology of the bulldozer was introduced after 1947 that the last *doab* of the Punjab was also colonised.

The historiography of this region is sadly underdeveloped (one reason for neglect being that the old Punjab province now comprises four different provinces in two nations, Pakistan and India), and there has been no overview of the emergence of hydraulic society in the western Punjab. Such a study, which is being undertaken here, furnishes a unique set of historical problems and involves areas of inquiry that have to date received little attention from scholars. There was established in the Punjab an entirely new society on barren wasteland, under the aegis of state authority but with the active involvement of the native population. The chief purpose of this study is to give this important experiment in social and economic engineering its due recognition in the history of the region. In so doing, light can be shed first on the nature of imperialist rule and second on the response and preparedness of the indigenous population in utilising the valuable opportunity for economic transformation that came its way.

The ramifications of agricultural colonisation are assessed here not from the perspective of economic theory but through the historian's craft. Lessons from the historical experience of one particular agrarian economy can provide insights into the wider problems of development and underdevelopment. The Punjab, like many other colonised economies, suffered the fate of retarded development and even underdevelopment. Yet this outcome was reached in the Punjab through a virtually unique process, one predicated on economic expansion rather than stagnation or decline. This theme of the coexistence of significant growth with continued backwardness is explored here to indicate that it may be as pervasive in its effects on the poorer economies of the world as the more generally acknowledged relationship between the lack of growth and economic backwardness.

The structure of this study follows certain themes that portray significant aspects of economy and society in the canal colonies. The emergence of each of the nine canal projects is traced in the chapter on colonisation, with an analysis of state policy, the different forms of land utilisation, and the social and regional composition of the recipients of land. In the subsequent chapters are discussed issues emanating from the colonisation process.

The chapter on entrenchment deals with the political benefits that accrued to the state from its control over the distribution of land, and also with the consequences of the differential access to colony land that social inequalities produced. The next chapter, on militarisation, examines the efforts of the state to channel colony land toward the fulfilment of military needs. The study then concentrates on aspects of production and distribution, enabling an assessment of the degree to which the potential for change was being realised. The chapter on extraction addresses questions relating to the state revenue structure, and to the social relations of production as revealed by patterns of cultivating occupancy. The next chapter, on pro-

duction, examines efforts at achieving agrarian improvement, and then surveys some broad features of cropping and cultivation in the canal colonies.
The insights gathered, and summed up in the final chapter, will reveal some
significant reasons for the simultaneity of growth and underdevelopment in
a society such as the Punjab's, whose failure to overcome economic backwardness now stands in stark contrast to the success of other regions, affluent and industrialised, in a world greatly polarised between rich and poor.

CHAPTER TWO

Colonisation

THE CANAL COLONIES

The process of agricultural colonisation commenced in the western Punjab from 1885, and it was to continue into the final years of British rule. The nine canal colonies developed in this period were situated in the interfluves west of the Beas-Sutlej and east of the Jhelum rivers. These tracts—the Bari, Rechna, and Jech *doab*s, lay between the Beas-Sutlej and Ravi rivers, the Ravi and Chenab rivers, and the Chenab and Jhelum rivers, respectively (see Table 2.1). The colonisation projects were based on the construction of a network of canals that took off from the rivers, with branches and distributaries spread over the flat, alluvial plains of the western Punjab. The canals were laid out primarily on uncultivated land, which was but sparsely inhabited by a semi-nomadic population of cattle graziers and camel owners. This made possible the migration into this area of people from other parts of the Punjab.

It was this element of colonisation, born out of the inadequate demographic resources of these *doab*s, that distinguished canal construction in the western Punjab from that further east. In other parts of northern India, such as the United Provinces, the canals constructed during British rule brought irrigation to already settled tracts.[1] They supplemented existing agricultural systems based on *barani* (rain-fed) cultivation, and did not therefore require any in-migration. In the western Punjab, owing to the insufficiency of rainfall, agriculture was far more dependent on irrigation, and traditional irrigation systems relied on wells and seasonal inundation, traditionally allowing cultivation only in tracts contiguous to rivers. The extensive interfluves, left elevated through river action, remained unirrigated. The irrigation network that emerged after 1885 was based on perennial canals that led off from river-spanning weirs and headworks. This rendered cultivable the upland plains that had hitherto remained inaccessible to the smaller-scale and technologically less sophisticated traditional

[1] The development and impact of canal irrigation in the United Provinces is examined in E. M. Whitcombe, *Agrarian Conditions in North India* (Berkeley and Los Angeles: University of California Press, 1972). Colonisation schemes undertaken in the state of India after 1947 are surveyed in B. H. Farmer, *Agricultural Colonization in India since Independence* (London: Oxford University Press, 1974).

TABLE 2.1. CANAL COLONIES IN THE PUNJAB

Name of Colony	Period of Colonisation	Where Situated		Name of Canal Work	Estimated Cost of Construction (Rs 000)
		Doab	Districts		
Sidhnai	1886-1888	Bari	Multan	Sidhnai	1,301
Sohag Para	1886-1888	Bari	Montgomery	Lower Sohag Para	1,803
Chunian	1896-1898 1904-1906	Bari	Lahore	Upper Bari Doab	a
Chenab	1892-1905 1926-1930	Rechna	Gujranwala, Jhang, Lyallpur, Lahore, Sheikhupura	Lower Chenab	53,072
Jhelum	1902-1906	Jech	Shahpur, Jhang	Lower Jhelum	43,613
Lower Bari Doab	1914-1924	Bari	Montgomery, Multan	Lower Bari Doab	25,086
Upper Chenab	1915-1919	Rechna	Gujranwala, Sialkot, Sheikhupura	Upper Chenab	43,596
Upper Jhelum	1916-1921	Jech	Gujrat	Upper Jhelum	49,770
Nili Bar	1926-b	Bari	Montgomery, Multan	Sutlej Valley Project	83,787

NOTES: a Chunian Colony obtained irrigation from a southern extension of the Upper Bari Doab Canal, which was constructed in the 1860s to provide irrigation to proprietary lands in Amritsar and Lahore districts.

b Not completed by 1940s.

SOURCE: *PCM*, pp 2-25; and Statement II-C in *Administration Report of the Punjab Public Works Department (Irrigation Branch)*, 1945-1946.

irrigation methods. The combination of migratory colonisation with the great dependence of cultivation on canal water supplied by a centralised authority created in this region a truly "hydraulic" society, such as could only exist in a diluted form further east because of the preponderate influence of *barani* agriculture.

Between 1885 and the end of British rule in 1947, the canal-irrigated area in the Punjab, excluding the princely states, increased from under

3,000,000 to around 14,000,000 acres. The great bulk of this increase took place in the canal colonies, which experienced thereby the greatest expansion in agricultural production in any part of South Asia under the British. The vast landed resources thus created in the canal colonies had a profound impact on economy and society in the Punjab. From the significant economic growth that ensued, the Punjab obtained its most promising prospects of economic development in recent history. The extent to which agricultural growth allowed the preconditions for successful development to emerge was greatly influenced by the nature of land utilisation in the canal colonies. "Colonisation," or the motives and methods involved in the settlement of these new lands, determined the character of the emergent society and the degree to which that society was capable of structural transformation from its existing state of economic backwardness.

The colonisation process was moulded by two forces: the state and the social structure. The former was important because it controlled land distribution: the canal colonies were situated in tracts designated as crown waste lands. This transferred ownership of these areas to the state, and allowed it to dispose of the land according to its discretion. Since the state also controlled the canal system and the water source, agriculture itself became dependent on the will of the ruling authority. The ownership of both land and water gave the central power virtual control over the means of production, thus greatly enhancing its authority over society. The role of the state was made manifest in the colonisation policy that provided the framework for land distribution in the canal colonies. State policy determined matters both great and small, ranging from the formulation of the general principles governing land distribution to the implementation of measures in the minute circumstances of the local arena. Here was an interventionist imperialism, extensively engaged in demographic and economic change.

The end product of state policy was the structure of landholding that emerged in the canal colonies. Colonisation had a major impact on people and society in the Punjab, since the manpower for agrarian growth came almost entirely from within the province. Existing stratifications and hierarchies in the Punjabi population were bound to be projected onto the new sphere. In rural society there existed extremes of wealth between large landowners on the one hand and poor cultivators and landless labourers on the other. Between these were intermediate layers of richer peasants and medium-sized landlords and, in addition, the urban-based strata of the bourgeoisie and working class. Only the last, constricted in size and preindustrial in nature, was unimportant to colonisation until colony towns came into their own.

Class divisions were not the only foci of socioeconomic distances: the caste system pervaded human consciousness and divided society into groups of superior and inferior status. The "superior" castes were also economically and politically dominant, for they followed elite occupations, and the means of production were concentrated in their hands. Because of their entrenched power, such groups were advantageously placed to exploit new agricultural and commercial opportunities. The extent to which existing inequalities in society led to an unequal sharing of resources is central to a discussion of the importance of the canal colonies to the Punjab.

Each canal project had its own distinct colonisation scheme, on the basis of which land was allotted to selected grantees or was otherwise utilised for purposes determined by the government. It is possible to examine the development of each colony in turn; this will be done as briefly as the many variations in colonisation policy and landholding forms allow. The attributes and implications of colonisation in the four larger projects require special attention: these were Chenab, Jhelum, Lower Bari Doab, and Nili Bar colonies.[2] There will also be discussion of the five smaller projects (those with under 400,000 acres allotted area): Sidhnai, Sohag Para, Chunian, Upper Chenab, and Upper Jhelum colonies.

The phenomenon of colonisation, leading as it did to the establishment of a large new society in hitherto barren tracts, involved a multitude of human decisions and activities. So variegated were the features involved that it is not possible to discuss several themes important in themselves but superfluous to the purpose here. Thus issues related to the actual construction of the canals and the problems of capital investment, labour utilisation, and administrative organisation entailed in such major public works will not be taken up. The nature of this work also precludes a discussion of the survey and demarcation work, the laying out of village and town sites, and the host of other administrative tasks necessary for land settlement, as well as the early experiences of the colonists, the vicissitudes they faced in breaking virgin soil, and their immediate social and economic problems in adjusting to the new environment. There is also little space to devote to the discussions among government officials that preceded the actual formulation of colonisation policy for each project. This is a dimension of "administrative prehistory" dear to many historians of colonial rule, but attention to it would greatly belabour the task at hand. Of course, the major considerations that affected state policy will be assessed, and the chief factors that governed colonisation identified.

The confines of the present work also preclude any detailed assessment of the hydraulic system of the canal colonies. Of its salient features, the essential ingredient was that of perennial irrigation from canals that provided water for cultivation during the entire annual cycle, and most impor-

[2] The full names of Chenab and Jhelum colonies were actually Lower Chenab and Lower Jhelum colonies, but they will be referred to by their shortened names here.

tantly for the spring (*rabi*) and autumn (*kharif*) harvests. The canals led off from the rivers through permanent weirs, with the main channel subdividing into branches and distributaries that covered the areas that were colonised as well as, in many cases, contiguous privately owned lands.

Many variations existed in the canal system, however. Sidhnai Colony was irrigated by a potentially perennial canal, that was, in fact, used only for the *kharif* harvest. The colony did not obtain a *rabi* supply, as all available water was taken away upstream on the Ravi River by the Upper Bari Doab Canal, which irrigated proprietary lands in Lahore and Amritsar districts. Thus, in effect, the Sidhnai Canal was a seasonal one, and the *rabi* crop, if sown, had to be matured through well irrigation. Sohag Para Colony was atypical because it was irrigated not by a perennial canal but by a seasonal inundation canal. This also provided canal irrigation for the *kharif* crop only; as in Sidhnai Colony, well irrigation was necessary for the *rabi* crop. In 1925, forty years after its construction, the Sohag Para Canal was converted to a perennial channel when it was incorporated into the Sutlej Valley Project. Chunian Colony was different again. No separate perennial canal was constructed for it; the colony was irrigated by an extension of the Upper Bari Doab Canal into crown waste land.

Chenab and Jhelum colonies each had its own perennial canal system, the waters of which were not shared with any other colony, and neither obtained water from any other canal network. This was true also of Lower Bari Doab Colony, except that water from its source river, the Ravi, was inadequate for perennial irrigation in this colony. To make large-scale irrigation possible, the Ravi supply had to be supplemented by water from the two western rivers, the Jhelum and Chenab. This was accomplished through the ambitious Triple Canal Project, which diverted water from the Jhelum to the Chenab and from the Chenab to the Ravi through two link canals. These link canals also irrigated state lands, and thus supported two colonisation schemes: Upper Jhelum and Upper Chenab colonies. Finally, Nili Bar Colony was irrigated not by one canal but by a series of channels designed to provide both perennial and seasonal irrigation. These formed part of the Sutlej Valley Project, which incorporated several older inundation canals in the area and also provided irrigation to the princely states of Bahawalpur and Bikaner. In this way one of the most extensive irrigation networks in the world was laid out in the Punjab's western *doab*s, whose parched terrain was now covered with man-made arteries carrying the elixir of canal water.

BY STATE FIAT

The nature and direction of state colonisation policy unfolded with the development of successive canal colonies. In such a large undertaking, spreading over several decades, the aims and objectives of the state can best be evaluated through examining the practice of colonisation. Official statements on objectives and guiding principles are inadequate and incomplete representations of the impact of the canal colonies on both state and people in the Punjab.

This province was certainly regarded in a favourable light by the British. Not only had the dominant elements of its agrarian hierarchy gone against their countrymen and taken the imperialist side in the struggle of 1857, but they had continued since to be completely loyal to British rule. The Punjab also supplied large numbers of soldiers to the British Indian army, giving this province a central importance in the political fortunes of imperialism in South Asia. The British believed that their rule, in turn, had brought peace and prosperity to the people of the Punjab, and especially to its agrarian classes. Of this beneficence they came to regard the canal colonies as the supreme example. The state's self-image of its role in agricultural colonisation was cast, therefore, in terms of benevolent and paternalistic solicitude, at least for those classes whose support was important for British rule. The officially stated aims for the largest project, Chenab Colony, could apply to the canal colonies as a whole:

1. To relieve the pressure of population upon the land in those districts of the Province where the agricultural population has already reached or is fast approaching the limit which the land available to agriculture can support.

2. To colonise the area in question with well-to-do yeomen of the best class of agriculturists, who will cultivate their own holdings with the aid of their families and the usual menials, but as much as possible without the aid of tenants, and will constitute healthy agricultural communities of the best Punjab type.[3]

To these may be added a third official objective, concerning an improvement in the standard of rural life. The administration intended "to create villages of a type superior in comfort and civilisation to anything which had previously existed in the Punjab."[4] Thus the state's explicit aims for colonisation were relief from population congestion, settlement of the land with the most efficient agriculturists, and improvement of rural living standards.

The real motivations of the governing authority went well beyond such objectives. A sequence of colonisation projects of such magnitude had far-reaching political and economic implications, and of these the British were fully aware. For one, land distribution won the loyalty of those so re-

[3] *Chenab Colony Gazetteer* (1904), p. 29.
[4] Report of the Punjab Colonies Committee, 1907-1908 (IOR: 10[3514]) (hereafter RPCC), ch. 1, para. 16.

warded. It also strengthened the status and authority of the social groups and classes selected for land grants, so that they in turn could serve more effectively as props to the ruling authority. Revenue was another important consideration. Canal projects were sanctioned only if their profitability was ensured, and few official decisions were made without extractive requirements in mind. As colonisation progressed, military needs emerged as a major factor, often overriding other aspects of governmental policy. Thus the benefits that the colonial state stood to obtain from a hydrologically oriented process of agrarian expansion were manifold and profound. They became clear not in any exegesis of official statements, but in the practise of colonisation as it gathered momentum in the Punjab.

The Earlier Colonies of the Bari Doab

The first colonisation project in the Punjab was Sidhnai Colony, located in Multan District. It was settled mainly in 1886-1888, and the total allotted area, after further extensions in the 1890s, was around 250,000 acres. For the utilisation of land, the government expressed the wish not to create large properties in which grantees would become mere rentiers, but to allot land to "small well-to-do agriculturists who will cultivate their own holdings."[5] The actual size of grants in Sidhnai Colony was influenced by the fact that canal irrigation was seasonal rather than perennial. Grantees of land had to construct wells to mature the all-important *rabi* crop, and for this they had to possess a certain amount of capital.[6] To attract such men, the minimum size of grants was fixed at fifty acres, which was up to four times as large as the smallest grants in the later, perennially irrigated colonies.

The next project, Sohag Para Colony, was situated in Montgomery District and was also settled in 1886-1888, with an allotted area of 86,300 acres. This colony too received only seasonal irrigation, so that landholdings had to be large enough to attract men with the capital to construct wells. The average size of shareholdings here was 55.5 acres. As in Sidhnai, the necessity for larger grants reduced the prospect of establishing a colony of self-cultivators. Surveys conducted a decade after settlement revealed that only 35 percent of the allotted area was cultivated by the actual grantees, whereas 65 percent was rented to subtenants.[7] Thus in both

[5] FC to DCs of Lahore, Amritsar, Gurdaspur, Hoshiarpur, and SOs of Jullundur and Ferozepur, 7 August 1885; in "Sidhnai Canal," BOR H/251/3 KW, p. 23. See also *PCM*, p. 4

[6] Initial settlement costs were estimated at Rs 1,000-1,200, of which the costs of wells alone was around Rs 500. The remainder was required for livestock, buildings, ground clearance, and initial consumption expenses. See DC, Multan, to Commissioner, Lahore, 25 January 1886; in BOR H/251/3 KW, pp. 58-59.

[7] *AR Lower Sohag Para Colony* (1899), para. 16. The average size of shareholdings of 55.5

colonies land was held by men who were either rich peasants or quite sub-stantial landlords. Even in these early schemes it was becoming clear that colony land was deemed too valuable a resource to entrust to the poor and landless sections of the peasantry.

Perennial irrigation, from which later colonies benefitted, brought greater flexibility in the variety of grants that could be created. By eliminating the need for costly well construction and maintenance, it made possible smaller-sized grants, while larger holdings could be awarded free of heavy development costs. Colonisation could thereby appeal to a greater mix of social elements, and this affected the next project, Chunian Colony. Situ-ated in Lahore District, the colony had an allotted area of 102,500 acres, and settlement took place in 1896-1898 and 1904-1906. Land in this colony was allotted under distinct categories whose names denoted the nature of the recipients or of the use to which it was to be put: peasant, civil, and military grants; some land was also set apart for auction sales. Smallhold-ings of 25 to 50 acres, now officially termed peasant grants, took up 78.45 percent of the allotted area, or 80,382 acres. The men selected for these grants belonged to peasant landholding lineages, and the government in-tended them to be self-cultivators.[8]

There were several reasons for this preference for peasant grantees, and such considerations were to recur in colonisation policy over the next five decades. The government felt that allotment of land to self-cultivators would prevent a rush of subtenants and labourers to the new tracts from neighbouring areas. This, it was hoped, would minimise social and eco-nomic dislocation to the agricultural communities of the western Punjab, whose class structure and economic viability the British did not wish to disturb.[9] Peasant settlement was also consistent with the need to relieve population congestion in districts where it threatened to cause economic, and consequently political, instabilities. Preference was given to obtaining grantees from districts where population densities had reached high levels. Paradoxically, this served to deter rather than enhance the prospects of so-cial change, for the possibility of migration obviated the need for technical innovation as a response to population pressure. Such priorities accorded well with the wish of the British to prevent agricultural colonisation from causing any major disruptions to the existing social structure.

A related factor that supported peasant settlement was the leaning of the

---

acres is derived from Table 2.7. See also "Printed Papers regarding Lower Sohag and Para Canals," BOR H/251/97.

[8] See "Colonisation of lands irrigated by certain extensions of Bari Doab Canal, Chunian Colony," BOR H/251/296; "Report by R. S. Tilok Chand on completion of Chunian Col-ony," BOR H/251/426; PRAP(G), August 1897, No. 26; and PRAP(I), March 1902, No. 21.

[9] PG to FC, 27 October 1885; in BOR H/251/3 KW, pp. 23-25.

British toward the concept of a strong self-supporting peasantry with a loyal and law-abiding disposition. They believed that both agricultural progress and political order could best be maintained by strengthening the position of the landholding peasantry. The dominance of such a class in the occupation of new land served to recreate existing landholding patterns in the Punjab, which was primarily a land of peasant proprietors. This tended to imbue colonisation with an inherently conservative character. Furthermore, it was not in the financial interests of the government to create large rent-receiving grantees, with their parasitical claims to an agricultural surplus whose division could be more rationally confined to the actual producer and the state.[10] Though a great number of larger holdings were created in the canal colonies, the bulk of land continued to be allotted in the form of peasant-sized grants.

Yet there was, even in these earlier colonies, evidence of other interests and goals that colonial rule wished to pursue. In Chunian Colony, about 11.75 percent of the allotted area, or 12,044 acres, was devoted to auctions. This entailed the sale of land at market prices, and hence an immediate return to the state of the capital value of colony land. The purchasers at these auctions were men of substance, belonging to landed, commercial, and professional groups.[11] In addition, an area of 1,937 acres was allotted to "military grantees": this was an early instance of a type of settlement that was to achieve much importance. There was also an allocation of 5,000 acres for "civil" grants, intended primarily as a form of reward for individuals and retired government officials whose services were considered sufficiently loyal and meritorious. These grants ranged in size from 50 to 250 acres; and since they were exempted from personal residence in the colony, the grantees generally functioned as absentee rentier landlords who practised little or no self-cultivation.[12] They could, thereby, make little positive contribution to agricultural development; but such considerations

---

[10] Another impetus for peasant settlement was the expectation that such grantees would be hindered from alienating their land. The fears of the state over unchecked land alienation came to the fore in a dispute that arose between the Punjab Government and the Government of India over the disposal of parts of Chunian Colony. The former wanted the land to be auctioned, as this was financially more profitable; but the GOI was unwilling to sanction this unless the powers of alienation of purchasers were restricted. The PG refused to accept this condition, as it would have brought down the price of land; and finally both agreed on peasant settlement, the political benefits of which continued in the future to outweigh the financial ones of land auctions. See PRAP(G): October 1896, Nos. 106-14; and December 1896, Nos. 78-79.

[11] PRAP(G), June 1896, Nos. 13-21; and PRAP(I), March 1906, No. 3.

[12] See "Civil grants of land in Chunian Colony," BOR J/3O1/794; "Grant of land to K. B. Allah Bakhsh Khan, Native Assistant to Political Agent to Sardar Ayub Khan," BOR J/301/732; and PRAP(I), March 1917, No. 247.

were outweighed by the political benefits derived by the state in appeasing men of this class.

Political considerations were also uppermost in the allotment of a grant of "latifundia" proportions in Sohag Para Colony. Fully 10 percent of the colony, an area of 7,800 acres, was allotted to one man, Baba Sir Khem Singh Bedi, who held considerable influence over the Sikh community. Bedi was the head of a family that enjoyed a holy, and indeed semi-sacred, status by claiming descent from the founder of the Sikh religion, Guru Nanak. Its spiritual standing made this family a powerful ally whose support could be invaluable. The Bedis had already demonstrated their loyalty to the British through their services during the struggle of 1857.[13] The colony grant further consolidated their alliance with imperialist rule. By providing families like the Bedis with land, the British not only dissuaded them from any thoughts of opposition, but also cemented both their loyalty and their authority by enhancing their economic power. A suitable land grant for the Bedis had been under consideration since the 1860s, but none had been forthcoming.[14] Before the canal colonies, such grants had to be on barren and unirrigated land, in which the element of reward was sizeably diluted by the potentially prohibitive development costs. Canal colonisation enabled the state to make viable and profitable land grants for which the capital outlay was made not by those rewarded but by the public treasury, and ultimately through their productive effort by the people of the Punjab. The transfer of resources to those aligned with the state structure made the canal colonies of immense political benefit to imperialism. Of this the Bedi grant was only a single illustration, albeit a spectacular one.[15]

In these three earlier colonies a number of trends were established in the utilisation of colony land. The major proportion of allotable area was devoted to the landholding peasantry, providing a continuity in dominant peasant occupancy from the old tracts to the new. Access to colony land was also extended to members of the landed and nonlanded elite, and a beginning was made to include the military in land settlement. An equally prominent, though highly negative, feature was the exclusion of the rural poor and landless from any occupancy share in the new landed resources. For them the roles of agricultural labourers and service menials that they

---

[13] For Bedi's family history, see *Montgomery District Gazetteer* (1933), Vol. A, pp. 107-108; and L. H. Griffin and C. F Massy, *Chiefs and Families of Note in the Punjab* (Lahore: Government Printing Press, 1940) (hereafter *Chiefs of the Punjab*), Vol. II, pp. 275-79.

[14] See "Lease of land to Baba Khem Singh in Tahsil Pakpattan," BOR J/301/48.

[15] After Khem Singh's death, his lands were divided among his sons and their heirs. Information on these estates is contained in the following Court of Wards records at the BOR: 601/1/21/112, 601/1/24/123, 601/1/24/155, and 601/1/24/212.

had inherited through generations of social inequality were not to be transgressed upon in this hour of economic reawakening.

Chenab Colony

The development of Chenab Colony created a new dimension for canal colonisation in the agrarian history of the modern Punjab. This was the largest of the canal projects, with an allotted area of over two million acres. The colony sprawled over the southern section of Rechna Doab, with the main canal subdividing into three great networks, those of the Rakh, Jhang, and Gugera branches.[16] These were colonised in succession during the years 1892-1905, with further extensions in the late 1900s and mid-1930s. In administrative terms, the colony took up Lyallpur District in its entirety, as well as portions of Jhang, Gujranwala, and Lahore districts (Sheikhupura District was created out of the colony portions of the latter two in 1921).[17] The Rechna Doab was well suited for large-scale colonisation. It was a level alluvial plain virtually unbroken by natural drainages, and a headworks suitably constructed upstream could render extensive areas commandable by canal irrigation. Just such a function was provided for Chenab Colony by the weir at Khanke.[18]

Colonisation was facilitated by the large area that had been appropriated by the government as crown waste land. By tradition in the Punjab, land that was barren or uncultivated was normally claimed by the state as its own property. In the Rechna Doab private ownership in land existed only in the riverine tracts, or *hithars*, which contained settled agricultural communities. The vast upland or interfluve, known as the Sandal Bar, was inhabited by a seminomadic pastoral people collectively called Janglis. The government did not recognise the claims of these tribesmen over their grazing areas as amounting to proprietary rights, and instead asserted its own ownership over this land. It was primarily on this crown waste that the canal network was established and settlement took place.[19]

[16] For the opening up of these branches, see *Chenab Colony SR* (1915), paras. 12-15. The total area of Chenab Colony was 2,757,046 acres or 4,308 square miles: *PCM*, pp. 11 and 13.

[17] Lyallpur was a new district formed in 1904 out of portions of Jhang, Multan, and Montgomery districts. It had four *tahsils*. Samundri, Lyallpur, Toba Tek Singh, and Jaranwala. For its formation see PRAP(G). June 1896, Nos. 49-58; July 1900, Nos. 10-49; November 1904, Nos. 23-28; January 1905, Nos. 15-29; August 1908, Nos. 36-60; and February 1912, Nos. 6-11.

[18] Proposals for the irrigation of Rechna Doab had been under consideration since 1862. It was not until 1890, after several proposals and revised estimates, that the construction of a perennial canal got under way. For the history of the Chenab Canal project, see *PCM*, pp. 6-10; and *Chenab Colony SR* (1915), paras. 38-45.

[19] Note by SC, 10 May 1900; in PRAP(I), July 1900, No. 17.

An enormous area had thus become available to the administration to dispense as it wished. Agricultural colonisation now became a large-scale affair, and the state could hold forth as a powerful possessor of valuable resources, with control of colony land and hydraulic management, giving it an authority over the populace that was unequalled elsewhere in British India. Moreover, with the visible economic benefits that these agrarian changes brought, the differential access of social groups to these new resources became a matter of great importance for the people of the province

In Chenab Colony there were three types of grants, distinct in both size and tenurial status. According to their official designations, they were called peasant (*abadkar*), yeoman (*sufedposh*), and capitalist (*rais*) grants. They ranged in size from half a square to two squares for peasant (one square = 27.7 acres), from two to five squares for yeoman, and from six to twenty squares for capitalist grants. The peasants had to remain as occupancy tenants of the state and could not acquire proprietary rights: "it was designed by altering their status to protect settlers from the consequences of their own want of thrift and foresight."[20] Thus the state intended to retain ownership of the peasant grants, thereby hoping to curtail the process of land alienation, which it regarded as a threat to rural stability. The yeoman and capitalist grantees could acquire proprietary rights after a qualifying period of five years; purchasers at land auctions could do so directly.[21] Differences existed also as to residential requirements: personal residence on the grant was compulsory for peasant and yeoman grantees, but not for capitalists and auction purchasers.

The colonisation scheme as officially formulated (see Table 2.2) shows that the government intended Chenab Colony to be settled predominantly with smallholders. An average of 80 percent of the land on the three major branches was allocated for peasant grants.[22] This reflected both the type of society that the British wanted to create in the canal colonies and the class of people whom they wished to appease. The backbone of the colony was to be a class of contented, landholding peasants. By origin, they were to be hereditary agriculturists belonging to landholding lineages: the very sections that formed the dominant peasant castes of rural Punjab. Develop-

[20] RPCC, ch. 1, para. 16. See also *PCM*, pp. 55-56 and 69-73.

[21] These larger landholders were also known as *nazarana*-paying grantees, because they paid an entry fee called *nazarana*, which was pitched at Rs 6 per acre for yeomen and Rs 10-20 per acre for capitalists, depending on the size of the grant: *Chenab Colony SR* (1915), paras. 7-8.

[22] Since they were developed at different times, the branches and extensions of Chenab Colony had separate colonisation schemes. For information see PRAP(I): July 1891, No. 19; and February 1892, No. 4 (for Rakh). See also BOR: J/301/526 (for Jhang); H/251/225 (for Gugera); and H/251/271 and 301/3/25/225 (for Extensions).

mental goals stood to be ill served by such political expedience, for the retention of the individualised peasant farm as the unit of ownership and production, while satisfying powerful social groups, could create structural constraints on agricultural innovation and change. The government had no hesitation in expressing its own preferences:

> It seemed essential to preserve the tradition of the Punjab as a country of peasant farmers. No other frame of society is at present either possible or desirable in the Province. . . . [T]he size of individual holdings has been fixed on a scale which will, it is hoped, attract the sturdy, the well-to-do, and the enterprising classes without excluding men of smaller resources or more broken fortunes.[23]

The rest of the land was to be allotted to yeoman and capitalist grantees. The yeomen too could belong only to the landholding agricultural castes, and were to be drawn from small and middle-level landlords. Their social composition was intended to be as follows:

> These Yeomen are simply the leading individuals among the peasant class—men who by wealth, energy or ability have raised themselves above their fellows without ceasing to belong to the agricultural population. . . . They were intended to attract a class which is not infrequently met in parts of the Province, *viz.*, the men who without attaining to the ranks of the richer gentry are still well above the ordinary level of the peasant land-owner. Naturally this class comprises some of the most intelligent and enterprising men in the agricultural community. They have good credit and resources, and if they can be attracted to the land should form most useful members of the new colony.

The capitalist grants could be allotted to men belonging to both agricultural and nonagricultural castes. These grants were intended both for those whom the British wished to reward for their political, military, or administrative services, and for those individuals with capital who would invest in improved farming and thereby help to raise agricultural standards. The government desired that:

> as far as possible, the grantees will be men possessed of means to devote to the improvement of land, Military Officers for whom the Government of India has ordered reward grants, and other gentlemen of good family and adequate resources. Most of the grants will probably be nearer the minimum than the maximum . . . capitalist farming in general is not a system suitable to the Punjab. But a moderate infusion of the capitalist

---

[23] RS to RS, GOI, 22 July 1891; in PRAP(I), July 1891, No. 19. The next two quotes are from the same source.

element is not without advantages. It supplies leaders for the new society. It gives opportunity to Government to reward its well-deserving servants, and to encourage the more enterprising of the provincial gentry. It attracts strong men who are able to command the services of considerable bodies of tenants. It furnishes a basis from which agricultural improvements may be hereafter extended. And lastly it enables Government to obtain a better price than might be otherwise possible for the ownership as distinct from the user of its lands.

The actual distribution of land in Chenab Colony deviated little from the colonisation scheme.[24] Table 2.2 shows that for the colony as a whole, capitalists received 7.0 percent of the allotted area and yeomen 8.2 percent, while peasant grantees made up the bulk of the allotment, with 78.3 percent of the area. The greatest discrepancy between policy and practice occurred on the earliest branch, the Rakh, where 30 percent of the land was reserved for yeomen and capitalists, but only 18.1 percent was actually allotted to them. It was found on this branch that there was no want of men to take up the peasant grants. A plethora of applications led to an allotment of over 60,000 acres in excess of the original allocation for the smallholders. By contrast, applicants of the right stamp for yeoman and capitalist grants were not forthcoming in sufficient numbers. Their hesitation increased as colonisation pushed further from existing lines of communication. Allotment fell short not only of the original allocation, but even of the area covered by successful applications. The government had little hesitation in allotting the deficit to peasant grantees, for even in these early days the yeomen and capitalists were proving to be unsatisfactory colonists. They were reported to be slow in developing their grants, they quarreled incessantly with their subtenants and among themselves, and they seemed more interested in immediate profits than in careful investment.[25] These factors induced the government to keep down the proportions of the larger grants on the later canal branches. Peasant tenure remained the predominant type.

For its size, Chenab Colony had a relatively simple pattern of land settlement. The landholding structure of the colony was designed to recreate and reinforce that of the province. There was a great emphasis on smallholders, though these had to belong to the landholding castes. A lesser share was allotted to the middling and larger landlords, and to a sprinkling of elite

---

[24] The BOR contains voluminous material on the actual settlement of Chenab Colony. For two of the largest of several files on the innumerable decisions and issues involved, see: "Chenab Canal," BOR H/251/16 A-F; and "Chenab Canal colonisation," BOR Printed 74, Revenue, Vols. I-III.

[25] Note by Commissioner, Lahore, 10 May 1893; in BOR Printed 74, Vol. II KW, p. 98; and F. P. Young, *Report on the Colonisation of the Rakh and Mianali Branches of the Chenab Canal* (Lahore: Government Printing Press, 1897), pp. 2-5.

TABLE 2.2. CHENAB COLONY: ALLOTMENT OF LAND

Type of Grant	Rakh Branch Acres	%	Jhang Branch Acres	%	Gugera Branch Acres	%	Extensions[a] Acres	%	Total Acres	%
Colonisation Scheme										
Peasant	280,000	70.00	500,000	91.0	544,000	77.7	—	—	1,324,000	80.2
Yeoman	60,000	15.0	25,000	4.5	35,000	5.0	—	—	120,000	7.3
Capitalist[b]	60,000	15.0	25,000	4.5	45,000	6.4	—	—	130,000	7.9
Police	—		—		6,000	0.9	—	—	6,000	0.4
Military	—		—		70,000	10.0	—	—	70,000	4.2
Total	400,000	100.0	550,000	100.0	700,000	100.0	—	—	1,650,000	100.0
Final Distribution										
Peasant	342,768	75.0	439,431	81.2	542,652	77.7	103,829	81.1	1,428,680	78.3
Yeoman	44,331	9.7	38,461	7.1	58,250	8.3	8,834	6.9	149,876	8.2
Capitalist	38,390	8.4	30,580	5.7	50,921	7.3	8,450	6.6	128,341	7.0
Miscellaneous	31,535	6.9	32,626	6.0	46,774	6.7	6,913	5.4	117,848	6.5
Total	457,024	100.0	541,098	100.0	698,597	100.0	128,026	100.0	1,824,745[c]	100.0

NOTES: [a] These extensions were the Bahlak, Bhangu, Nahra, Nupewala, Dangali, and Killianwala. The figures do not include three extensions opened up during 1926-1930: Pir Mahal, Khika, and Buralla.
[b] Includes auction purchasers.
[c] Does not include 81,464 acres of privately owned land that fell within the boundaries of Chenab Colony.

SOURCE: Imran Ali, ''The Punjab Canal Colonies, 1885-1940'' (Ph.D. Dissertation, Australian National University, 1980), Tables 2.3 and 2.4.

nonagriculturists. The landless poor remained landless; their association with the colony was limited to the roles of labourers and subtenants. The ruling authority did not wish to disrupt the existing structure of society, and was clearly averse to the idea of using colonisation to bring about social change. Indeed, its policies made the social structure more rigid. The British regarded Chenab Colony as one in which the interests of agriculture were held supreme.[26] This appeared all too true in the light of developments in later colonies. But if the interests of agriculture were to be served by an attitude of inherent conservatism, by a reluctance to transform a backward economy, by a wager on the strong, then this was only so in the context of imperialist aspirations, not progressive ones. Ultimately, it depended on the state structure whether it wished to utilise the potential of colonisation for economic development or distort it for purposes of its own survival. One of the roots of underdevelopment in the Punjab lay in the fact that the latter option was adopted. In no other case was this more apparent than in the next project that was taken in hand.

Jhelum Colony

With Jhelum Colony, settled between 1902 and 1906, there occurred a radical departure from the principles that had hitherto guided state land distribution policy.[27] A new force emerged in agricultural colonisation in the Punjab, and this was the reservation of large amounts of land for military requirements. The government had previously professed to have benevolent motives for colonisation: the relief of population congestion and the fostering of agricultural excellence. Similar goals were originally envisaged for Jhelum Colony as well, and a colonisation scheme was formulated and sanctioned by the administration along these lines. This scheme was replaced by another, however, based on the utilisation of the colony predominantly for military purposes.

Jhelum Colony had originally been planned for civilian colonists along the lines of Chenab Colony. Of a total allotable area of 540,000 acres,

[26] The following are two examples of the British view: "it does . . . seem to be true that nowhere in the world up to 1920 was there to be found so large a body of cultivators, so prosperous in proportion to the requirements of their lives, as the colonists on the Lower Chenab Canal," H. C. Calvert, *The Wealth and Welfare of the Punjab* (Lahore: Civil and Military Gazette Press, 1936), p. 22; and "The Lyallpur Colony is the richest tract in India, perhaps even in Asia," M. L. Darling, *The Punjab Peasant in Prosperity and Debt* (4th ed., London: Oxford University Press, 1947), p. 132.

[27] The colony was situated in Shahpur District, and had a total area of 1,531,000 acres, or 2,500 square miles. Its headquarters was the newly established town of Sargodha, for the founding and early development of which see PRAP(G): April 1901, Nos. 25-29; October 1901, Nos. 54-71; May 1902, Nos. 29-69; and September 1902, Nos. 1-12. See also *PCM*, pp. 15-17; and PRAP(I), February 1903, Nos. 1-8

about 75 percent, or 402,000 acres, had been reserved for peasant grantees. A further 44,000 acres each were reserved for military grantees and "civil" grants; the latter were analogous to the capitalist grants and were meant as a reward for persons who had served the government well. An allocation of 15,000 acres was made for land auctions, and of 5,000 acres for the Punjab police. In one important respect this scheme did differ from that of Chenab Colony: it was decided not to retain yeoman tenure, because such grantees had proved to be unsatisfactory colonists. Ironically, this very type of grant was to be revived under the new proposals.

Implementation of the original colonisation scheme had already progressed to the stage of selection of grantees in the hundreds by district officials, when this whole process was reversed by the change in policy.[28] The dramatic shift followed upon the proposals of a commission established by the Government of India to investigate the state of horse breeding in the country. This body, known as the Horse and Mule-breeding Commission, recommended that canal colonists in the Punjab should henceforth be required to maintain mares for breeding horses and mules for the army. The Government of India accepted these suggestions and prevailed upon the Punjab Government to impose such conditions of tenure in Jhelum Colony, with whose development the enquiries of the commission had conveniently coincided. The hitherto successful applicants had to be rejected, because with horse breeding a change occurred in the basis on which land was to be granted, and in the type of people who were to obtain land. The outcome of the Horse-breeding Commission's recommendations was that the selection of grantees now depended not on population densities and agricultural skills, but on the possession by applicants of mares suitable for breeding remounts for the cavalry.

The Horse and Mule-breeding Commission owed its appointment to concern expressed by army authorities in the 1890s about the state of horse breeding in India.[29] The British wanted their Indian empire to be self-sufficient in cavalry horses, rather than rely on external sources (Australia at this time was India's chief supplier of remounts). Despite much expenditure on horse breeding, little improvement had occurred in indigenous breeds. The commission was appointed to investigate the possibilities of improving the local supply of horses, and its recommendations had far-reaching repercussions. It proposed that future colony grants be allotted to

[28] For a discussion of the original scheme of colonisation and the discontinuance of yeoman grants, see PRAP(I): January 1900, Nos. 1-2; May 1901, Nos. 14-50; January 1902, No. 11; and October 1902, No. 17.

[29] See GOI, Military Department, Extract of Proceedings, 16 October 1900; and "Memorandum," containing a list of twenty-six subjects for enquiry by the commission, in PRAP(G), December 1900, Nos. 6-7.

men who would undertake to maintain brood mares. This would entail the selection of grantees with experience of horse breeding, such as men who already owned horses or who were retired members of cavalry regiments. The commission recommended that a breeding tenure be applied to an area (ordinarily half a square for peasant grantees) that would be allotted in addition to the ordinary grant as a reward for keeping a mare.[30]

The Government of India, and specifically its military department, accepted these proposals for Jhelum Colony, but it went beyond the commission's concept of such "service" grants. Believing that partial measures would be unlikely to succeed, it insisted that the service tenure be applied not to any additional half squares, but be made integral to the grant itself.[31] It overruled the Punjab Government's request to limit the scheme to one in which extra breeding tenures were added to a certain proportion of peasant grants. The breeding obligation not only became the basis on which grantees took up the land, but it was tied to their very source of subsistence. The army authorities also insisted that the scheme be imposed universally on peasant grants throughout the colony, and in this too they had their way. Furthermore, in order to maintain the grants as viable units for the production of young stock, it was decided that inheritance be limited to a single heir, a form of succession that was utterly alien to the Punjab. In proposing such an extensive involvement for the military, the state had to embark on measures that were bound to cause major distortions in agrarian custom and practice.

The comprehensive nature of the horse-breeding scheme proposed by the Government of India evoked a good deal of opposition from British officials in the Punjab. The most adverse reactions came from the more junior officers, who possessed practical knowledge of colonisation and its problems.[32] They questioned the Horse-breeding Commission's contention that service grantees would be easily available because horse breeding was popular in Rawalpindi Division, the area chosen to supply grantees for Jhelum Colony. This region proved, in fact, to be less heavily involved in horse

[30] See Report of the Horse and Mule-breeding Commission, 1900-1901 (IOR: Temporary 544); and PCM, pp. 132-33. See also President, Horse and Mule-breeding Commission, to Secretary, GOI, Military Department, 7 January 1901, in PRAP(G), July 1901, No. 26.

[31] The Government of India was afraid that any added plots would in time become dissociated from ordinary grants, through subdivision or alienation, and would then be insufficient to support horse breeding. It also felt that men already holding grants might not be tempted to undertake horse breeding in return for a small additional area. Land therefore had to be granted on none other than the service condition. See RAS, GOI, to RS, 10 October 1901, in PRAP(G), November 1901, No. 46.

[32] The views of Punjab officials on the proposals of the Horse-breeding Commission are contained in PRAP(G), August 1901, Nos. 39-53. For their response to the GOI's proposals, see PRAP(I), October 1902, Nos. 3-25.

breeding than other parts of the Punjab.[33] The commission seemed to have been misled by the fact that many leading men kept horses, and whenever high officials visited their districts they turned out in force to ride with them. Horse breeding was practised by men of means, who were well above the stamp of agriculturists normally selected for peasant grants.

Moreover, smaller landholders had little chance of acquiring the "branded" mares which alone were acceptable to the army for breeding cavalry remounts. Such mares now became a prerequisite for obtaining land grants, but they were limited in supply and their price began to rise steeply with the sudden demand for them. The new premium on horse flesh took it effectively out of the reach of the erstwhile candidates for the peasant grants, who now stood to be disqualified from obtaining land.[34] Horse breeding also required special skills and experience, and ordinary agriculturists seemed hardly likely to succeed in producing a specialised commodity like cavalry remounts. Such considerations, the officials argued, would necessitate the granting of land to men of a higher class, and to attract such men the size of grants would have to be kept large.

Nevertheless, the provincial administration accepted the centre's propositions, buckling under the pressure of considerations of strategic interest. The apprehensions expressed by the local officials now proved well founded. The minimum size of peasant horse-breeding grants was raised to two squares, or 55.5 acres. The recipients did not remain mere self-cultivators, but became rich peasants requiring subtenants or agricultural labour. The grantees selected under the original colonisation scheme were rejected because they did not possess branded mares, and an entirely new selection occurred from among those who now came forward with animals of acceptable quality. Thus, the move to military-oriented tenures also marked a less egalitarian basis of land distribution. The higher Punjab officials did not fail to provide rationalisations for this incursion of military imperatives, but in doing so they abandoned the cherished goals of population relief and agricultural excellence that had hitherto characterised col-

---

[33] Whereas the average number of *zamindars* to a horse or pony in the Punjab as a whole was thirteen, in Rawalpindi Division it was sixteen. Rising population and the scarcity of the late 1890s had also "compelled many of those who had brood mares to part with them, and having once given up an animal it is seldom that the practice is renewed": DC, Jhelum, to Commissioner, Rawalpindi, 23 December 1901; in PRAP(I), October 1902, No. 11 (and see No. 4 for statement of *zamindars* per horse/pony in each district of the Punjab).

[34] It was estimated that within a year or two, 10,000 such animals would be required for the colony. Yet there were only 7,000 "branded" mares in the northwestern Punjab, 13,000 in the whole province, and under 22,000 in all India. The consequence would be that "the small struggling farmer would have to wait at home. He is not the man who can be expected to keep a brood mare." See Commissioner, Rawalpindi, to SC, 6 January 1902; and also SC to FC, 11 January 1902; ibid., Nos. 8 and 7.

onisation. The financial commissioner felt no need to mince his words in passing sentence on earlier principles:

> The main object will now be an Imperial one, namely, to encourage horse-breeding and to create a reserve of horses fit for service with troops. It is difficult to combine the Imperial with the original Provincial aim. . . . As to the policy of the change, the land belongs to Government, and it is for Government to decide what use to make of it. If an Imperial purpose can be efficiently served my personal opinion is that the Provincial objects should not be allowed to stand in the way.[35]

Not only was the size of peasant grants enlarged with the introduction of horse breeding, but the yeoman (*sufedposh*) grants were also resurrected. These larger grants were allotted to members of elite rural families that were prominent for horse breeding in their localities. They were required to maintain five to fifteen mares at the rate of 1.5 squares per mare.[36] The British believed that such men would make more successful and enterprising horse-breeding grantees than the peasant colonists (though in the years to come these expectations were to be belied). In addition, eight large "stud farms" were also allotted, with a stipulation to maintain up to fifty mares. Seven of these farms were obtained by prominent landlord families of the northwestern Punjab, and only the eighth went to a professional horse breeder. The incorporation of the rural gentry into a landholding position in Jhelum Colony was a consequence entirely of the emergence of military priorities. It was the need for horse breeders that led to a reversal of the original decision not to have yeoman grantees, despite their poor performance in Chenab Colony. The British were no longer perturbed by the prospect in Jhelum Colony of a "comparatively small body of squireens and its numerous population of tenants holding at the will of a landlord."[37] Indeed, they showed a ready facility for justifying changing imperialist needs, to which the following logic was applied by the settlement commissioner:

> In its favour it might be argued that as the wealth of the Jhelum Colony will be concentrated in fewer hands it will possess more elements of progress than the Chenab Colony, where there will be a dead level of dull prosperity. . . . Perhaps we have in India too many peasants, prosperous and admirable though they are, and should now aim at raising a class of more wealthy and more intelligent land-holders, who might

[35] "Note on annexing brood-mare conditions to peasant grants in Jhelum Colony," by FC, n.d.; ibid., No. 16.

[36] CO, Jhelum Colony, to SC, 27 May 1902; and RAS, GOI, to RS, 17 October 1902: in PRAP(I), November 1902, Nos. 9 and 12.

[37] Note by SC, 23 March 1902; in PRAP(I), October 1902, No. 18. The next quote is from the same source.

combine with the virtues of the peasantry a higher standard of comfort and a greater readiness to make an advance in civilisation.

The final distribution of land in Jhelum Colony brought out graphically the dominant position of the military. Table 2.3 shows that 54.41 percent of the land was allotted for horse-breeding purposes, and a further 9.49 percent in grants to military personnel for purposes other than horse breeding. The original allocation for military grantees had been 44,000 acres, but the final allotment was over 75,000 acres. The increase was largely in grantees from cavalry regiments, as it was felt that they would make useful horse breeders. Men from infantry regiments were not allotted service tenures, and had to content themselves with grants of one square each. Of the rest, the "civil" grantees were originally allocated 44,000 acres, but received less than half that amount. This resulted from the shortage of land

TABLE 2.3. JHELUM COLONY: ALLOTMENT OF LAND, 1902-1906

Type of Grant	Acres	Percent
Horse-Breeding Grants		
Cavalry peasants	30,209	6.79
Cavalry yeomen	5,609	1.26
Peasants	159,790	35.91
Yeomen	15,495	3.48
Private stud farms	5,034	1.13
Army Remount Department	11,640	2.62
Regimental horse runs	14,356	3.23
Total	242,133	54.42
Other Military Grants		
Infantry	30,864	6.93
Other	11,377	2.56
Total	42,241	9.49
Other Grants		
Civil grantees	21,236	4.77
Jangli grantees	60,726	13.65
Other	10,130	2.27
Total	92,092	20.69
Miscellaneous	68,476	15.38
Total	444,942	100.00

SOURCE: *PCR*, 1922, pp. 11-12.

that occurred in the colony after horse breeding and other military requirements had been met.[38] A large number of "civil" grantees, as well as many of the rejected peasant grantees, did in the end receive land on the Chenab Colony extensions, but they had to wait for it for some years.[39] The only other nonmilitary allotment was the 60,926 acres allotted to the Janglis, or indigenous inhabitants of the Jech Doab. The grantees who were not horse breeders received land only after the horse breeders had been settled, and as a result they found themselves on the poorer soils. The Janglis, being the last to be settled, fared worst in the quality of land that they obtained, making their transition from a pastoral lifestyle to one of smallholding agriculture even more arduous and traumatic.

The contrast between Chenab and Jhelum colonies would thus appear to be most pronounced. The one was ostensibly devoted to agricultural goals, while the other was blatantly subordinated to military ones. It could be said that Jhelum Colony represented a major change in the attitude of the state toward agricultural colonisation. Such a characterisation, though not inaccurate, would obscure some significant convergences. In Chenab Colony, behind the facade of benevolence lay strong political considerations in the granting of land. The ruling authority sought to use its control over land and water to entrench itself by gaining the loyalty of the dominant classes in Punjabi society. In Jhelum Colony, it employed land and water to strengthen an institution equally vital for its survival: the military. Chenab and Jhelum colonies complemented each other; the deviation lay only in the different aspects of imperial needs that each served.

The innovations introduced by the state for achieving agricultural improvement in Chenab Colony and for meeting military needs in Jhelum Colony were to cause much friction with the colonists in the years that followed. The readiness of the state in abjuring its innovational role for the sake of political peace could be contrasted, however, with its adamant stand in maintaining its military requirements, even in the face of continued political agitation. Horse breeding in Jhelum Colony thus created deep problems, which will be discussed later.

Lower Bari Doab Colony

Lower Bari Doab Colony, where settlement proceedings began in 1914, was situated in Montgomery and Multan districts.[40] This project had a more

---

[38] FC to Heads of Departments, 17 June 1908; and FC to PG, 8 June 1909; in PRAP(G): July 1908, No. 32; and July 1909, No. 17, respectively.

[39] For information on "civil" grants, see "Allotment of lands on Jhelum Canal to Heads of Departments," BOR J/301/701; "Grants of land on Jhelum Canal to Public Works Department," J/301/764; and "Civil grants of land on Chenab and Jhelum Canals," BOR J/301/796.

[40] The colony lay in Okara, Montgomery, and Khanewal *tahsils*, the last being in Multan.

diverse and complex land distribution scheme than the other colonies. Since it was the only large tract to be colonised in the two decades from 1905 to 1925, it reflected a variety of trends in administrative thinking, and became the focus of a number of politico-economic needs. The two major considerations that governed the allotment of land in the colony remained tied to military requirements: horse breeding and land grants to military personnel. Areas were also reserved for the indigenous population, for the landed gentry, for peasants from congested tracts, and as compensation for losses of land from such causes as river action. A larger percentage of area was reserved for auctions than in previous colonies. The scheme included the reservation of land for the "depressed classes"—land intended for landless men who belonged to the lower castes. In addition, land was re-served for "special objects," which included horse runs for cavalry regi-ments, as well as some grants for purposes of agricultural improvement.

The colonisation scheme for the Lower Bari Doab was sanctioned by the government in 1914, and entailed the allotment of 1,192,000 acres. As settlement progressed, large areas of inferior land were encountered. The soil survey, from which estimates of allotable land were derived, had overstated the amount of satisfactory land available. As a result, the scheme had to be reduced in 1916 to under 900,000 acres, requiring a con-traction in area under each head of allotment (though the inferior soils were also allotted in later years).[41] Table 2.4 gives figures both of the estimates as originally sanctioned in 1914 and of the revised distribution of 1916. Cutbacks were necessitated for most categories of allotment, the major ex-ception being military grantees, the allocation for whom was significantly increased.

Though it did not monopolise colonisation, as in Jhelum Colony, horse breeding remained the dominant element in the Lower Bari Doab. The in-itiative for this came once again from the Army Department of the Govern-ment of India, which displayed increasing apprehension at the state of horse breeding in the country as the prospect of colonising further tracts drew nearer. The central government stressed the need to make India independ-ent of overseas supplies of horses, and to create a readily available reserve

---

Shaped as a long, narrow strip about 150 miles in length and 15 to 20 miles wide, and situated between the Ravi and the old deserted bed of the Beas, the colony had a total area of 1,638,000 acres (or 2,560 square miles), of which 181,000 acres were private proprietary lands. The 25-acre holdings here were called "rectangles" rather than "squares," the shape being deter-mined by the survey and demarcation conducted prior to colonisation. See *PCM*, p. 19.

[41] PRAP(I): March 1914, Nos. 12-13; December 1916, Nos. 7 and 13-14; September 1917, No. 4; and December 1919, Nos. 166-69. See also "Scheme of colonisation of Government Waste irrigable by Lower Bari Doab Canal," BOR H/251/476; and *PCR*: 1914, p. 44; 1915, pp. 32-34; and 1916, FC's Note.

of country-bred animals for an emergency. It pointed out that Jhelum Colony had become the most important area for imperial horse breeding in India, but the numbers produced were still inadequate to meet the annual requirements of British cavalry regiments stationed there. It therefore wanted as large an area as possible to be devoted to horse and mule breeding in the new colony.[42]

An Army Remount Committee, consisting of three army officers, was appointed in 1912 to make recommendations for a new scheme. It was decided not to impose horse breeding along the lines adopted for Jhelum Colony, owing to various political and administrative adversities encountered there. After considering several alternatives, the committee recommended a scheme devised by one of its members, the essence of which was to replace compulsion by competition.[43] It was proposed that ordinary peasant grants be allotted, but in addition a certain number of horse-breeding leaseholds, each of one rectangle, or twenty-five acres, be reserved in peasant villages. Grantees could then compete for these leases; horse-breeding would thus become a means of acquiring additional resources, thereby losing its element of compulsion. The lessee would not be staking his means of subsistence on his horse-breeding performance, but would have his own grant to fall back upon. It was hoped that even nonlessees would take up horse breeding in order to stand a better chance of qualifying for a leasehold if one became available. A time limitation on the leases would weed out unsatisfactory breeders and retain the competitive element.

Though pivotal to the scheme, it was this very aspect of competition that incurred the criticism of Punjab officials, especially those in touch with local conditions. They explained that it would create factionalism and conflict in village society, that vying in this manner for economic resources could destroy the harmony of peasant communities.[44] They spoke with intimate knowledge of the realities of rural society; and the following comment by the deputy commissioner of Montgomery was representative of their apprehensions over this latest form of military intervention:

[42] The Government of India expressed concern over the increasingly insecure foreign sources of cavalry remounts. In Argentina, Australia, Canada, and the United States the production of riding horses was said to be rapidly declining. See AS, GOI, to RS, 15 October 1912; in "Horse-breeding scheme for Lower Bari Doab Colony," BOR J/301/1101 A, pp. 5-6.

[43] See Report of the Remount Department Committee, 1912; ibid., pp. 7-18.

[44] One outspoken critic was a former deputy commissioner of Lyallpur, who painted a macabre picture of the factional infighting that the renewal of leaseholds would create. He wrote: "All these things . . . are the life and death of a village and it is the development of these situations that swells the coffers of the vakil and petition-writer and makes the Deputy Commissioner's hair grow grey before its time." See Note by G. F. de Montmorency, Personal Assistant to Chief Commissioner, Delhi, 13 December 1912; ibid., pp. 145-46.

I cannot but feel that the temptation offered by an unsuccessful competitor to make a fresh opportunity for himself by horse-maiming, bringing false complaints and other malpractices will be a strong one, and apart from this there is grave reason to fear that every vacancy in a Government rectangle, and one may be expected to occur each year, if not oftener, will be the signal for an outburst of intrigue, denunciation and bribery too appalling to contemplate with any degree of equanimity. . . . All these considerations will pass through the peasant's mind and leave him with the conviction that it is the best part of a wise man to make hay while the sun shines and put as little as possible into his leasehold and take as much as possible out of it. It may be that this price, the ill cultivation of 7,000 squares, is not too much to pay in view of the urgency of the demand for remounts, but be it a fair price or not there is a danger that it will have to be paid.[45]

Despite such criticisms, the government went on to implement the proposed scheme. The period of horse-breeding leases was fixed at ten years, with the possibility of renewal if the lessee proved satisfactory. A ratio of two peasant grantees competing for each horse-breeding lease was aimed at, though the actual proportions varied from village to village; a total of around 3,500 such rectangles were created. The prospect of open rivalry between incumbents and aspirants was not removed, even though it threatened to have a divisive effect on the corporate lives of peasant communities in the colony.

Next to horse breeding, the most important feature of the colony was the large area devoted to military grantees. The area initially reserved for them was 103,000 acres, to come out of the allocation for peasant horse breeders and "hereditary agriculturists."[46] With the outbreak of World War I, the area for military grantees was increased by 75,000 acres, to a total of almost 180,000 acres. The increase resulted from a magnanimous offer of more land from the provincial government, in view of the large number of Punjabi soldiers serving in the army. The offer was gratefully accepted by the Government of India, which was searching for ways of rewarding military war veterans.[47] Furthermore, it was decided that the entire allocation of 180,000 acres be reserved for the veterans rather than for military pensioners, as in earlier colonies. In reality, the latter too were accommodated,

[45] DC, Montgomery, to FC, 23 December 1912; ibid., pp. 149-51.

[46] For correspondence relating to military grantees in this colony, see PRAP(I), January 1915, Nos. 20-43; and "Land grants on Lower Bari Doab Canal to military pensioners," BOR J/301/1178.

[47] RS to RAS, GOI, 15 October 1914; RAS, GOI, to RS, 28 November 1914; and "Press communique," PG, 9 December 1914: in BOR J/301/1178, pp. 168-73.

on land allocated for civilian grantees, who were now increasingly constricted by the expanding absorption of land for military purposes. The British fully realised the great value of reserving such a large area for the war effort. The prospect of land grants stimulated recruitment, being in an agrarian economy one of the most attractive forms of reward. Other types of recompense, such as special pensions and cash *inams*, could not compare in value with colony grants. Other provinces in India could not offer such valuable resources for the gratification of military personnel, and this undoubtedly had considerable bearing on the fact that the Punjab continued to contribute more men than any other region to the British Indian army.

Further military needs were met from the allocation for "regimental farms and other special objects" (see Table 2.4). Two large horse-breeding grants of 7,500 acres each were allotted to two ex-army officers, Captain D. H. Vanrenen and Lieutenant Colonel E. H. Cole.[48] The medium-sized,

TABLE 2.4. LOWER BARI DOAB COLONY: ALLOTMENT OF LAND, 1914-1924

Type of Grant	Original Allocation Acres	Final Proposed Distribution Acres	%
Forests	40,000	30,970	3.50
Sale by auction	125,000	69,196	7.83
Regimental farms and other special objects	100,500	86,619	9.81
Horse-breeding peasants (including 180,000 acres for war veterans)	689,500	502,607	56.92
Hereditary agriculturists and compensatory	110,000	103,668	11.74
Depressed classes	30,000	20,000	2.26
Reward and reserve	22,000	10,000	1.13
Landed gentry	75,000	59,852	6.77
Total	1,192,000	882,912	100.00

SOURCE: PRAP(I): March 1914, No. 12, and December 1916, Nos. 7, 13, and 14.

[48] See "Application from Major James and Captain Vanrenen for grants of land to improve horse-breeding in the Punjab," BOR J/301/1053; and "Grant of land to Colonel Cole on Lower Bari Doab Canal," BOR 301/2/24/28. See also PRAP(G), June 1914, Nos. 1-39.

or *sufedposh*, grants were not retained for horse breeding in this colony, owing to their performance in Jhelum Colony. It was hoped that the two "latifundia" grants would prove more efficient, and this did indeed happen. The Military Farms Department received a large allotment of 20,000 acres, known as the Oat Hay Farm. This was perhaps the largest state farm in India, and although it was meant to provide fodder for army horses, it served actually as a commercial venture whose profits went to army funds. In addition, 18,000 acres were allotted as regimental horse runs.[49] Such grants were made in this and other colonies to cavalry regiments for the maintenance of young stock, though in reality they became profitable commercial ventures for these regiments.

Lower Bari Doab Colony also contained several types of grants designed to serve purposes other than military ones. Both political and developmental considerations served as the motivation behind a large number of such tenures. Under the former could be classed grants such as those to the landed gentry, to the landholding peasantry, and to the depressed classes and criminal tribes; and under the latter, grants allotted under a variety of tenurial conditions such as cattle breeding, seed farming, and cotton growing.

The area for "special objects" not taken up by military requirements was devoted to agricultural objectives.[50] Five cattle-breeding farms were created, covering a total area of around 15,000 acres. Their purpose was to encourage the livestock industry by improving the strain of two indigenous breeds, Hissar and Sahiwal cattle. These farms were allotted to five Punjabis, selected because they had adequate resources to finance and manage such large enterprises. A seed farm of 3,000 acres was allotted to a European cotton expert, H. T. Conville, on condition that he supply a certain amount of cotton and wheat seed to the Agricultural Department every year. To encourage the cultivation of improved varieties of cotton, and for the supply of fresh seed to colonists, a grant of 7,220 acres was made to the Manchester-based British Cotton Growing Association (BCGA). This was the largest grant allotted to a metropolitan commercial organisation in the canal colonies. After 1925, the BCGA was to expand greatly the area under its control by renting from the government large tracts under temporary cultivation leases in Nili Bar Colony. At one point it had under its management close to 70,000 acres under such terms, making it the largest land occupier in the canal colonies. Two fruit farms were also allotted, one of which, under an F. J. Mitchell, proved highly successful. A 2,000-acre farm was allotted to Sardar Jogindra Singh (a central minister for railways

---

[49] See "Government (Oat Hay) Farm, Okara," BOR 301/2/24/51; and "Disposal of land at present utilised as horse runs by certain regiments of Silladar cavalry," BOR 301/6/00/3.

[50] Grants made for this purpose will be discussed further in the chapter on production.

in the 1940s), which combined seed supply functions with the condition of cultivating with mechanised implements under the direction of the Agricultural Department. Within a few years of allotment, Jogindra was unable to fulfil the latter condition, one of the many examples in the canal colonies of the failure of mechanised and capital-intensive methods of agriculture.

The grants allotted for agricultural improvement had one factor in common: the government wished to achieve this goal not by direct involvement but through the agency of intermediaries. It did not itself manage land devoted to the improvement of seed, cattle, or agricultural implements, but saw fit to bestow this task on selected individuals. It thereby economised on the financial costs and organisational problems involved in managing such enterprises, and shifted these burdens onto the grantees. At the same time, it continued to derive its own profits by levying land revenue, water rates, and other cesses on these lands. Though it relieved itself of managerial obligation and financial commitment, the state placed the fortunes of these important initiatives in jeopardy, by entrusting them to the whims and abilities of individual grantees. In the years that followed, the lack of success suffered by many of these ventures was attributable largely to the failings of the grantees and to their inability to fulfil their responsibilities.

A similar policy of improvement by proxy was adopted to tackle the large areas of inferior land encountered in the colony, on which ordinary settlement was not feasible. The government did not attempt to reclaim these areas under its own management or from its own resources but instead divided them into smallholdings allotted on tenurial conditions that required the grantees to improve the land. By and large, the exercise proved to be futile, and the grants were eventually either resumed or converted into ordinary tenancies by allowing the improvement condition to lapse.

Certain types of grants in Lower Bari Doab Colony were neither military nor developmental in nature but were motivated by political considerations. The allocation of almost 60,000 acres to the "landed gentry" was intended for members of leading rural families: those who would have found mention in that compendium of the Punjab's landed elite, Griffin and Massy's *Chiefs and Families of Note in the Punjab*. This was the first occasion in which a sizeable amount of land was reserved specifically for this class, though individuals had received grants from the capitalist and civil categories in earlier colonies. The landed gentry grants were intended to strengthen old and influential families that had retained their hereditary influence and prestige among the rural population but that, unless assisted, were likely, the British feared, to suffer economic decline.[51]

The landholding peasantry of the Punjab received, as in other colonies,

[51] RS to RAS, GOI, 2 October 1913, Confidential; in BOR H/251/476 B, pp. 209-19. See also RS to FC, 19 March 1914; in PRAP(I), March 1914, No. 13.

the major share of allotable land. The allocations for "hereditary agriculturists," "compensatory grantees," and "horse-breeding peasant grantees," which together amounted to 68.66 percent of the total allotted area,
was reserved for this class.[52] However, included in the horse-breeding area
were the 180,000 acres for military grantees. This effectively reduced the
amount allocated for civilian smallholders to less than 50 percent of total
allotted area—the first time this had happened in any colony. The more
variegated nature of the colonisation scheme was responsible for this diminution, especially since greater proportions of land were being reserved
for the military, for auctions, and for the larger grantees.

Lower Bari Doab Colony contained, as well, grants for the nonlanded
poor, a class from whom land in the canal colonies had hitherto been withheld. These grants were allotted under the category "depressed classes and
criminal tribes," with a total allocation of 20,000 acres. The grants to the
"depressed classes" were allotted to men of lower castes who were either
Christian converts under the aegis of certain Christian missionary bodies,
or who were under the patronage of some Hindu or Muslim philanthropic
organisations. The "criminal tribes" grants were allotted to men who belonged to groups officially designated as "criminal and wandering tribes."
Efforts in the past to reclaim such people from their antisocial habits had
been almost completely unsuccessful. The British hoped that the attraction
of land might succeed where other reform practices had failed.[53]

In Lower Bari Doab Colony, the vast confirmation of military and political priorities could be contrasted to the relatively meagre efforts at agricultural improvement. It had become clear that agricultural colonisation
was to be structured in a way that served the political and military needs of
imperialist rule, and as a result strengthened the social structure that supported that rule. The granting of land to the rural elite, to ex-soldiers, to
the dominant peasantry involved the reinforcement of the strong, and by
implication the further emasculation of the weak.

Upper Chenab and Upper Jhelum Colonies

Contemporaneous with the settlement of Lower Bari Doab Colony were
two other projects, Upper Chenab and Upper Jhelum colonies. They entailed between them the allotment of 120,000 acres, though the canals that
fed them irrigated an even larger area of proprietary land. The two colonies

---

[52] Peasant grantees could now obtain proprietary rights after a tenancy of ten years. This
concession resulted from political developments discussed in the next chapter. See "Purchase
of proprietary rights in Lower Bari Doab Canal Colony," BOR 301/21/24/26.

[53] For allotment to these nonlanded elements, see "Grants of land to depressed classes in
Lower Bari Doab Colony," BOR J/301/1179; annual *Report on the Reclamation Department,
Punjab*; and annual *Report on the Administration of the Criminal Tribes in the Punjab*.

lay, respectively, in the northern parts of the Rechna and Jech *doab*s, north of the much larger Chenab and Jhelum colonies. The upper reaches of these *doab*s contained private lands, which now benefitted from irrigation from canals constructed primarily to take the waters of the Chenab and Jhelum rivers to the Ravi for use in Lower Bari Doab Colony, as part of the Triple Canal Project. The irrigation of crown waste land by these canals made possible the Upper Chenab and Upper Jhelum colonies.[54]

The land distribution schemes for these two colonies indicate that they were primarily utilised for meeting needs either created or not fully met in the larger colonies. Upper Chenab Colony had an allotable area of 78,800 acres.[55] Of this, the largest allocation was for "compensatory grants," comprising 24,200 acres. These grants were intended for men who had lost land through river action or waterlogging. The latter was becoming an increasing threat in the canal colonies. An area of 17,000 acres was reserved for "Jhelum grantees," meant for those originally selected for Jhelum Colony in 1900-1901, but who had failed to receive land owing to the introduction of the horse-breeding scheme. Military grantees received 3,000 acres, and "civil grants" for ex-government officials were kept to under 1,000 acres. An area of 15,000 acres was reserved for a "forest plantation," and 5,800 acres for "reserve and Chiragah."

In Upper Jhelum Colony, too, with an allotable area of 42,300 acres, a good deal of land was utilised to meet overflows from other colonies. An area of around 9,000 acres was allotted to former horse-breeding grantees of Jhelum Colony who had to vacate their lands owing to an expansion in the area of regimental horse runs.[56] Most of the 8,000 acres reserved for compensatory grants in this colony were allotted to two groups of people. One comprised agriculturists who had suffered from the construction of the Khanke weir of the Lower Chenab Canal, and the other were grantees transferred from Lower Bari Doab Colony because they wanted to be nearer their original homes. Similarly, 5,000 acres were reserved for military grantees, for whom land was either not available in Lower Bari Doab Colony or who preferred to be closer to home. A further 7,200 acres were reserved for a "forest plantation."[57]

[54] *PCM*, pp. 17-23.

[55] RS to RAS, GOI, 10 April 1912, Confidential; in "Draft of colonisation of Upper Chenab Canal," BOR J/301/434, pp. 29-33. See also PRAP(I): November 1913, No. 3; July 1914, Nos. 3-4; and August 1914, Nos. 24-25.

[56] See "Conditions applicable to horse-breeding tenants transferred from Lower Jhelum Canal to Upper Jhelum Canal," BOR J/301/1364.

[57] See "Scheme of colonisation of Government Waste irrigable by Upper Jhelum Canal," BOR H/251/475; "Compensatory grants—Upper Jhelum Canal," BOR J/301/1196; and PRAP(I), May 1917, No. 64.

In one case a new type of grant was initiated. A "preferential allotment" of 6,000 acres in Upper Jhelum Colony was reserved for individuals who had rendered services to the criminal administration. The grants were to be allotted to those who had distinguished themselves, or to the heirs of those who had lost their lives, by offering resistance to criminals or by assisting in the prevention, investigation, or prosecution of crime.[58] Here was an example of the use of colony land for the enforcement of law and order. Unlike the "police" grants of earlier colonies, these tenures were open to civilians as reward for assistance against "criminals," a term that could be extended to all those who opposed, for whatever reason, the established authority of the state. The British believed, quite rightly, that the prospect of a land grant would act as a better inducement than any other for obtaining the cooperation of the populace against such unlawful activity.

Nili Bar Colony

Nili Bar Colony, where settlement proceedings commenced in 1925 and continued until after 1940, was the last major colonisation project under British rule. Situated in Montgomery and Multan districts, the colony was part of the much larger Sutlej Valley Project, which provided perennial and nonperennial irrigation to both state and private lands.[59] Its colonisation scheme, given in Table 2.5, contained one radical departure from the two previous large projects, Jhelum and Lower Bari Doab colonies. Horse breeding played no part in the scheme—a product both of the general disillusionment with service tenures among government officials and of the fact that sufficient land had already been devoted to the breeding of military animals to make further allotments for this purpose unnecessary. Military interests, however, were by no means neglected, for 75,000 acres were reserved for army pensioners, which was over 9 percent of the total allotted area under perennial irrigation. The allotment to civilian peasant grantees of 250,750 acres was less than one-third of the total perennial area. This marked a further decline, already noticeable in Lower Bari Doab Colony, in the proportionate share of this class. But a further allotment of 230,400 acres was made in the nonperennial area to local inhabitants of Montgomery and Multan districts. Well-established local families who had leased state land in precolony days were catered to in the 40,000 acres reserved for "*Tahud Khahi*" lessees." Political considerations were also in evidence

---

[58] See "Grants of land on Upper Jhelum Canal for services rendered to criminal administration," BOR J/301/1154.

[59] The colony had an irrigable area of 1,000,000 acres perennial and 2,710,000 acres nonperennial, of which 864,000 acres and 350,000 acres, respectively, were crown waste, the rest being proprietary lands. See *PCM*, pp. 23-25.

TABLE 2.5. NILI BAR COLONY: ALLOTMENT OF LAND, AS SANCTIONED
IN 1926

Type of Grant	Acres	Percent
Perennial Irrigation		
Peasant grantees	250,750	31.17
Auction (including sale to civil officials)	362,250	45.02
Military grantees	75,000	9.32
Land for experimental, fruit, seed, and vegetable farms	2,350	0.29
Cattle farms	21,000	2.61
Borstal farm	1,000	0.12
Criminal tribes	5,000	0.62
Agricultural farms for graduates of Lyallpur Agricultural College	2,000	0.25
Tahud khahi lessees	40,000	4.97
Reward grants	36,750	4.57
Police grantees	5,000	0.62
Mandis	3,500	0.44
Total	804,600	100.00
Nonperennial Irrigation		
Janglis	230,400	88.48
Forests	30,000	11.52
Total	260,400	100.00

SOURCE: FC to Commissioner, Multan, 21 January 1926, in PRAP(R), July 1927, No. 4.

in the "reward" grants of 36,750 acres and in the "criminal tribes" and "police" grants of 5,000 acres each.

By far the most prominent feature of the scheme was the very high proportion of land reserved for auctions. This amounted to 362,250 acres, or 45 percent of the perennial area. Auctions were profitable for the government, for they yielded market prices for colony land, whereas the price at which grantees purchased their land was well below market levels. Thus, commercial and extractive considerations were uppermost in the provision of such a large proportion of the total area for auction sales. In contrast, the developmental grants, which had received an initiation in Lower Bari Doab, were not continued in Nili Bar.

It now became dramatically clear that agricultural development, as a conscious and deliberate aspect of state policy, was not to be one of the goals of colonisation. Several proposals that would have helped to improve the state of agriculture in the Punjab were considered for this colony, and some were even sanctioned by the government, but virtually none of these was implemented.[60] A scheme was proposed under which 3,000 acres would be utilised for experiments in sugarcane cultivation, and a further 20,000 acres set aside for cultivators who would supply a sugar factory with the necessary cane. But the governor of the Punjab, Sir Malcolm Hailey, refused to agree to the proposal, even on a reduced scale, and the scheme was dropped altogether.[61] The Agricultural Department wanted 20,000 acres to be reserved for a fruit orchard, on the produce of which a canning factory, and possibly even a wine factory, would be maintained. This proposal too was rejected by Hailey.

Some other proposals were provisionally sanctioned by the government, and they appeared in the colonisation scheme (see Table 2.5). An area of 21,000 acres was reserved for cattle breeding; from which two 3,000-acre farms were to be created, while the remaining 15,000 acres were to be allotted in peasant-sized grants on cattle-breeding terms. Later a third cattle-breeding farm of 3,000 acres was also sanctioned. A farm of 2,000 acres was planned for providing practical training to graduates of Lyallpur Agricultural College. In addition, an area of 2,350 acres was to be allotted to the Agricultural Department, of which 1,000 acres were for an experimental station, 500 acres for a fruit farm, 500 acres for a seed farm, and a total of 350 acres in the neighbourhood of market towns for vegetable farming. However, none of the above schemes was put into practice, with the exception of a 500-acre seed farm and a 50-acre vegetable farm. The cattle-breeding ventures, the graduates' training farm, and the experimental and fruit farms were all cancelled. This was the sorry state of developmental grants in a colonisation project of over one million acres.

In contrast to the developmental, claims of a political nature were amply met in Nili Bar Colony. The most prominent expression of this was, of course, the peasant grants. These tenures were reserved, as in other colonies, for the landholding peasantry of the Punjab, so that in this project too the landless stratum was excluded. Eligible for such grants were men whose land had been ruined by waterlogging and by diluvian and river ac-

---

[60] For information on these proposals, see FC(D) to RAS, GOI, 2 March 1922; Note by Executive Engineer, Montgomery, n.d.; and DA to FC, 17 May 1924: in "Matters requiring attention when the next colonisation operation is undertaken," BOR 301/1/C9/4, pp. 37 and 45-49.

[61] "Note on the colonisation of the Nili Bar" by Sir Malcolm Hailey, Governor Punjab, 21 August 1925, para. 7; in "Colonisation of Nili Bar," BOR 301/1/C9/3 B KW, p. 52.

tion, and those who inhabited congested tracts.[62] Grants of colony land that could compensate for natural or man-made disruptions to agrarian activity enabled the state to avoid, or at least to delay, tensions and conflicts in rural society.

Political considerations were also dominant in the case of the "reward," "police," and "criminal tribes" grants. The reward grants were meant for nonofficials who had rendered loyal services to the government. Land had been allotted for similar purposes in earlier colonies as well, and Punjabis had come to expect such grants as their rightful due for loyalty to the British. The police grants were a continuation of the "criminal administration" grants of earlier colonies, and were intended primarily for persons "who have been conspicuous in aid to the Police, or who have assisted Government in times of disorder or the like."[63] Also eligible for these grants were those in the police force or in other departments who had rendered assistance against crime at personal risk to their lives. The grants to the "criminal tribes," similar to the ones in Lower Bari Doab Colony, were made in the hope of reclaiming through settlement groups that displayed habitual criminal tendencies.

The extensive area reserved for auction sales, 362,250 acres or 45 percent of the perennially irrigated land, brought into greater prominence the extractive requirements of the state. In all canal colonies, revenue remained a prime consideration, and the government took care to ensure that each project was remunerative. This ethic extended from the minutiae of field assessment to the division of water resources between different colonies. But it was only in Nili Bar Colony that extraction was extended to the capital value of the land. In other colonies it was in this very respect that the state made a financial concession by allotting land to grantees who could purchase it at rates well below market levels. Auction sales had been confined to town sites and to very limited amounts of agricultural land. Only in Lower Bari Doab Colony had the auction area assumed some significance, amounting to about 70,000 acres. Even this appeared minute when compared to the proportions reserved in Nili Bar. Clearly, financial motives, which had been present in all colonies at the level of revenue, now came to the fore in the actual disposal of land.

The financial stringency faced by the Punjab Government in the postwar years lay behind the decision to convert to extractive priorities. The interest rate on loans required to finance the Sutlej Valley Project was raised from 4 to 6 percent by the central government.[64] This made it necessary to ensure

---

[62] FC(D) to Commissioner, Multan, 21 January 1926; in PRAP(R), July 1927, No. 4.

[63] Note by Hailey, 21 August 1925, para. 16; in BOR 301/1/C9/3 BKW, p. 56.

[64] For a discussion of the problems of financing the Sutlej Valley Project and Nili Bar Colony, see BOR 301/1/C9/3 A.

that Nili Bar should be more profitable than other colonies, in order to keep
up with the higher interest charges. Hence there arose the need to ensure a
rapid and profitable return on capital outlay, which the government believed would be provided by auction sales rather than land grants. The economic difficulties of the state could be largely attributed to its own reluctance, in previous colonies, to derive from its grantees an adequate price
for colony land. Purchase prices had been fixed at a fraction of market
rates, a political measure that served to bolster the economic position of the
intermediaries who obtained colony land. Resources were left in their
hands at the expense of the public coffer. When the government needed
money for the construction of the Sutlej Valley Project, it had to resort to
the drastic compensatory measure of reserving half the land for auctions.

The decision to leave such an extensive area to the mercy of market
forces had serious repercussions for the development of the colony. It
proved extremely difficult to dispose of so much land; this could only be
done by stages, for the market in land would have been undermined had
too large an area been put up for auction at any one time. To hold up land
prices, the government decided to sell an average of only 15,000 acres per
year.[65] The auctions made a promising start; but with the onset of the economic depression in the 1930s they came to a complete halt, owing to a
severe downturn in the price of land.[66] It was not until the 1940s that the
auctions picked up again, with a return of market confidence in agricultural
land. For the interim utilisation of this area, the administration resorted to
temporary cultivation leases, given out to individuals in both large and
small blocks. This led to great inefficiencies and bureaucratic corruption,
as well as much exploitation of subtenants by unscrupulous lessees.[67] The
prolonged mismanagement of colony land that resulted from years of temporary cultivation leases stood in stark contrast to the smoother and more
rapid settlement achieved in this and other colonies with allotment to grantees, especially self-cultivating smallholders.

Nili Bar Colony constituted the final phase of agricultural colonisation in

---

[65] Plots of varying size were to be put up for auction, in order to appeal to both capitalist
purchasers and men of more moderate means. The terms of purchase were 10 percent of the
sale price to be paid down, with the balance in five-yearly instalments, with simple interest at
8 percent on unpaid balances.

[66] With the fall in land prices, the government decided not to auction any further area till
the market recovered, rather than sell the land at unacceptably low rates. See *PCR*: 1930, FC's
Review; and 1931, p. 2. For more information on auction sales, see "Sale by public auction
in Nili Bar Colony of agricultural Crown land," BOR 251/8/C9/47 A-N; and Imran Ali, "The
Punjab Canal Colonies," (PhD dissertation, Australian National University, 1980) Appendix
I.

[67] Much information on temporary cultivation is contained in *PCR*, 1930-40; and "Leases
of temporary cultivation in Nili Bar Colony," BOR 301/11/C9/51 A-T.

the Punjab. It reemphasised the political and extractive themes in colonisation policy, and demonstrated that conscious developmental initiatives were very weak, if not altogether absent. In pursuing its political interests the state utilised land as it had done in other colonies, by making land grants to selected individuals. The system it introduced to realise its extractive goals was based on a different principle: the sale of land at auctions. This not only greatly extended the period of colonisation, but created serious disruptions during the course of the disposal of this area. The economic difficulties of the 1930s were largely responsible for the degree of dislocation, but its origins lay in state policy itself. The disarray in agrarian conditions in Nili Bar by 1940 presented a picture not of the successful completion of colonisation, but of its virtual breakdown. The unhappy consequences of the depression on the auction process in the 1930s highlighted the vulnerability of an agrarian economy to international economic crises. It was yet another reminder that exclusive emphasis on the agricultural sector was a source of weakness and not of strength, in a world in which economic development was becoming increasingly synonymous with industrialisation.

THE RECIPIENTS OF LAND

The pursuance of the state's land distribution policy was made possible, and indeed to a large extent engendered, by the cooperation of those groups who assumed a landholding status in the canal colonies. The social structure of the Punjab exerted its own influence on the shape and nature of canal colonisation, and more often than not this carried such weight that state policy had to adapt itself pliantly to its needs. In agricultural colonisation there took place a great saga of human migratory movements in the Punjab. Peasant lineages that had for generations been resident in particular villages and localities now provided in substantial numbers the manpower without which it would have been impossible to populate and develop the new lands.[68] Certain members of peasant families, and at times entire households, would depart from their ancestral homes to explore and exploit the new opportunities created by canal irrigation and agrarian extension in the western *doab*s. Canal colonisation was an exclusively Punjabi affair: it involved few, if any, from outside the province. Since its fruits were confined to people within the Punjab, it was bound to influence and affect a large proportion of the province's population. Not only were the lives of the in-

---

[68] For an analysis of local society in one such village in the Punjab, which also supplied migrants to the canal colonies, see T. G. Kessinger, *Vilyatpur 1848-1968: Social and Economic Change in a North Indian Village* (Berkeley and Los Angeles: University of California Press, 1974).

digenous people deeply touched, but the extensive migrations from other parts of the Punjab spread the impact of the canal colonies to well beyond their physical boundaries.

The social background and areas of origin of the settlers was a factor at least as important as state policy in shaping agricultural colonisation. As with the types of grants, the source areas of the grantees of land varied with each colony. This being a matter subject to government decision, different districts, or combinations of districts, were chosen for supplying migrants to particular colonies. As to social origins, a large number of subcastes, tribes, and clans were represented among landholders. This reflected the great ethnographic diversity of caste particularism, although in terms of general caste appellations there were some significant uniformities across colonies. For nonlanded occupational groups such as subtenants, labourers, and service and commercial functionaries, a heterogenous amalgam from most districts was inevitable. Many "menials," as they were called, followed their *sepidari* superiors to the canal tracts to recreate traditional ties of servitude.[69] The attraction of employment brought in others from both surrounding and distant areas. The benefits produced by agrarian growth were not equally shared by all, and the basis for variable gains was established with land distribution itself. One's prospects of obtaining land were very greatly determined by birth ascription, rather than any equality of opportunity or individual ability.

Certain features that were to continue throughout colonisation were already in evidence in the earliest schemes. In Sidhnai Colony, the government placed emphasis on obtaining grantees from the central Punjab. The districts of Lahore, Amritsar, Gurdaspur, Hoshiarpur, Jullundur, and Ferozepur were selected for this purpose.[70] It was conceded that a certain amount of land would have to be reserved for the inhabitants of the local Multan District, but preference was given to men from the nominated districts. British officials were convinced that central Punjabis were the most skilled and efficient agriculturists in the province, and they believed that a colonisation project would have greater chances of success with men of proven abilities.[71] In Sidhnai, though numerous applications for land came

---

[69] Descriptions of the *sepidari*, or *jajmani*, systems are covered quite extensively in the literature on social anthropology. See especially Zekiye Eglar, *A Punjabi Village in Pakistan* (New York: Columbia University Press, 1960); McKim Marriot (ed.), *Village India* (Chicago: University of Chicago Press, 1969); and Louis Dumont, *Homo Hierarchicus* (London: Wiedenfeld and Nicholson, 1970).

[70] FC to DCs of Lahore, Amritsar, Gurdaspur, Hoshiarpur, and SOs of Jullundur and Ferozepur, 7 August 1885; in BOR H/251/3 KW, p. 23.

[71] An incentive of five acres or so per follower was provided to village leaders and influential men in the selected districts, who were asked to bring forty or fifty well-to-do cultivators

in from Multan District and from men of means for larger grants, the government held on to the idea of attracting peasant colonists from the central Punjab. After some initial hesitations, induced by the remoteness of the tract and the hostility of the indigenous population to the introduction of strangers, applications for land from the selected districts did begin to materialise. Once the reputation of canal irrigation became well established, with the efforts of some early settlers from Amritsar proving successful, applications from prospective grantees flowed more freely.[72] Thereafter, with its profitability proven incontestably, colony land was to be highly sought after by Punjabi agriculturists.

Official intentions of settling Sidhnai Colony with a strong component of central Punjabis were only partially realised. The distribution of land by districts, given in Table 2.6, shows that over 40 percent of land was allotted to men from the home district, Multan. Colonists from Lahore and Amritsar districts did participate substantially in the allotment, and together obtained as much land as the Multanis. Districts in the central Punjab more distant from Sidhnai Colony, such as Jullundur, Ferozepur, and Hoshiarpur, supplied far fewer settlers. With colonisation such a novelty, people were not prepared to stake all and move over such large distances, though this reluctance disappeared as more colonies were established. Migration from ancestral homes to colony tracts was to become very much a "spirit of the age" for the rural population of the Punjab.

The distribution of land by castes for Sidhnai, as shown in Table 2.6, reveals a pattern that was to recur in later colonies. This was the virtual monopoly over colony land of castes that ranked high in economic position and social status. The land was allotted to "dominant" castes: to groups that already enjoyed a landholding status in their home districts. The non-landed rural poor, belonging to the service and "menial" castes, did not figure in land distribution. Jats obtained three-quarters of allotted land, and this illustrated the class rather than simply the caste aspect of colonisation. The term "Jat" is of such wide application among proprietary groups in the Punjab as to be almost synonymous with *zamindar*, or landowner.[73] Numerous proprietary clans all over the province adopted it as a form of general identification, to indicate more their position in society than any kinship or ethnic affinities. Other holders of land in Sidhnai were also of the "dominant" ilk. Kambohs and Arains were important proprietary landholding castes of the Punjab. They too were hierarchically superior to the

---

with them, each grantee being promised fifty to sixty acres: Report by DC, Multan, n.d.; ibid., p. 200.

[72] See ibid.; and PRAP(I), September 1889, Nos. 1-5.

[73] The classical discussion of the castes of the Punjab is Denzil Ibbetson's chapter on the subject in the 1881 Census: see D.C.J. Ibbetson, *Punjab Castes* (Patiala, reprint 1970).

TABLE 2.6. SIDHNAI COLONY: LAND DISTRIBUTION BY DISTRICT, CASTE, AND COMMUNITY

	Muslim		Hindu and Sikh		Total	
	Number of Grantees	% of Allotted Area	Number of Grantees	% of Allotted Area	Number of Grantees	% of Allotted Area
District						
Multan	607	37.32	73	4.21	680	41.53
Lahore	236	14.63	192	12.60	428	27.23
Jhang	60	3.69	12	0.76	72	4.45
Peshawar	12	0.73	—	—	12	0.73
Rawalpindi	6	0.40	11	0.65	17	1.05
Bahawalpur	12	0.71	—	—	12	0.71
Amritsar	220	13.71	4	0.28	224	13.99
Gurdaspur	96	5.79	—	—	96	5.79
Muzaffargarh	20	1.19	—	—	20	1.19
Others	36	2.39	17	0.94	53	3.33
Total	1,305	80.56	309	19.44	1,614	100.00
Caste						
Jat	1,012	62.15	188	12.22	1,200	74.37
Syed	58	3.49	—	—	58	3.49
Shaikh	27	2.07	—	—	27	2.07
Afghan	38	2.27	—	—	38	2.27
Rajput	14	0.75	—	—	14	0.75
Kamboh	109	6.77	2	0.14	111	6.91
Arain	34	2.19	—	—	34	2.19
Miscellaneous	13	0.87	119	7.08	132	7.95
Total	1,305	80.56	309	19.44	1,614	100.00

SOURCE: "Sidhnai C," BOR 4/251/3 KW, p. 217.

service castes, and were reputed to be strong and efficient agriculturists. Syeds, Shaikhs, Afghans, and Rajputs had an even more elite status, for they composed the gentry: elements ranging from local landlords to landed magnates. They were generally noncultivators, but they had as their hereditary occupation the enjoyment of the fruits of agriculture. This concentration of new landed resources within the upper layers of society established a trend that was to become more pronounced as the story of colonisation unfolded further.

In Sohag Para Colony, as in Sidhnai, the government wished to choose men of the best agricultural stock, and of a reliable and law-abiding disposition. That this again resulted in the selection of members of dominant landholding castes is shown in the allotment figures for this colony (Table 2.7). The most marked feature was the large area allotted to Jat Sikhs: 30,000 acres or 38 percent of total allotted area. The average size of their shareholdings, at around sixty acres, was also substantially larger than the average for the other peasant castes, such as the Arains, Kambohs, and Mahtams. These grantees belonged, therefore, to the richest sections of the Jat Sikh peasantry; and with such substantial areas per shareholder, they should more truly be regarded as petty to middling landlords. The smaller holdings of the Arains (who held about 6 percent of allotted area) was in keeping with their tradition of more intensive farming and market gardening, and of their ability to make more out of a smaller area than other castes. The Kambohs (8 percent of allotted area) were also a well-established agricultural group, belonging to the central Punjab. The Mahtams (also with 8 percent) were a people indigenous to the local Montgomery District. Among the variety of occupations they followed were cattle thieving and other forms of crime, which tended to lower their social standing. But many Mahtams were established agriculturists, and some even claimed to be fallen Rajputs.[74] Grants to these people undoubtedly consolidated their more peaceable instincts, at the cost of their less law-abiding proclivities.

TABLE 2.7. SOHAG PARA COLONY: LAND DISTRIBUTION BY CASTE AND COMMUNITY

Caste	Community	Number of Grantees	Percent of Area	Average per Holding (Acres)
Jat	Sikh	484	37.90	60.73
Arain	Muslim	121	5.90	37.81
Kamboh	Hindu	51	2.89	43.86
Kamboh	Muslim	97	5.30	42.38
Mahtam	Muslim	156	8.33	41.40
Khatri	Sikh	37	4.52	94.70
Khatri (Khem S. Bedi)	Sikh	1	10.06	7,798.00
Others		310	25.10	62.79
Total		1,257	100.00	61.69[a]

NOTE: [a] Average per holding, excluding Baba Sir Khem Singh Bedi = 55.53 acres.

SOURCE: Derived from Statement V, "Abstract of Tenures in Sohag Para," in *AR Lower Sohag Para Colony* (1899).

[74] H. A. Rose, *A Glossary of the Tribes and Castes of the Punjab and North-West Frontier* (Lahore: Civil and Military Gazette Press, 1914), Vol. III, pp. 49-51.

In Table 2.7, "others" comprises very largely tribes indigenous to Montgomery District, such as Wattus, Bilochis, Joiyas, and Dhudhis, and Muslim Jats and Rajputs, all of whom held one village each in the colony.[75] The high average area per shareholder for such grantees indicates that their social origin was that of landlords, or at best very rich peasants. The Khatri Sikhs (4.5 percent of allotted area) were kinsmen and followers of Baba Sir Khem Singh Bedi, to whom the large personal grant of 7,800 acres was allotted in the colony. Their large units per shareholder also reveal their rentier and landlord rather than self-cultivating role.

Where did these Sohag Para grantees come from? The Mahtams and the tribes included in "others" were inhabitants of Montgomery District, whereas the Khatri Sikhs, along with Khem Singh Bedi, belonged to Rawalpindi District. With the exception of the latter, the government had wanted to confine allotment in this colony to *zamindars* from the home district. This proved to be a mistake, for settlers in sufficient numbers were not forthcoming from Montgomery, which turned out not to possess the surplus population required for colonisation. Land was then made available to selected agricultural castes from neighbouring overpopulated districts. The largest number of grants finally went to Lahore (241) and Amritsar (126), followed by Montgomery (112).[76] This reflected the demographic reality that the southwestern region of the Punjab was unable to provide the manpower for large colonisation projects, whereas the central areas did have the surplus population to do so.

The next project, Chunian Colony, was unique in that its peasant colonists belonged to the district, Lahore, in which it was itself situated. Lahore had sufficient surplus population to absorb the area available in this colony, and grantees were drawn largely from riverain villages along the Ravi and Sutlej, which were suffering most from population congestion. The colony was settled in two stages, known as the southern and northern blocks. In the former, the great majority of grants were once again allotted to colonists who belonged to hereditary castes of agricultural owners, chiefly Jats, Kambohs, and Arains.[77] As in Sidhnai and Sohag Para, landless elements were not considered for colony grants.

By the time the northern block came up for settlement, the state had acquired, in the form of the Punjab Land Alienation Act of 1900, a legal and universal basis for differentiating between agricultural and nonagricultural castes. The primary function of the act was to try and halt the expro-

---

[75] PRAP(I), August 1891, Annexure E to Nos. 7-12. The statement gives details of the area allotted, number of holdings, and proprietary caste for each estate in Sohag Para Colony.

[76] SC to FC, 21 June 1898; in PRAP(R), January 1899, No. 26. See also *PCM*, pp. 87-88.

[77] "Report on the colonisation of new villages in the Chunian Tahsil," by Assistant Commissioner, Kasur, 22 March 1898; in PRAP(G), June 1898, No. 18.

priation of agricultural owners by moneylending and trading groups.[78] To administer this protective and paternalistic measure, lists of "agricultural castes" were drawn up for each district of the province. The government then adopted this categorisation for an even more telling purpose: it became the basis for eligibility for land grants in the canal colonies. For land distribution after 1900, the administration did not need to nominate specific groups, but could simply rule that in each selected district the agricultural castes, and those castes alone, were eligible. Thus the Act of 1900 served not merely to confine land alienation within related caste groups of agriculturists but it also established for access to colony land the basis for the inclusion of agricultural owners, and the exclusion of the nonlanded stratum of the Punjabi poor. This measure was put into practice in Chunian Colony, with the stipulation that the agricultural castes of Lahore District were all eligible for land grants.[79] It was implemented in all further land distribution measures, except in the rare and specific cases in which the nonagricultural castes were granted eligibility for smallholdings. The larger grants always remained more accessible to the richer nonagriculturists, who even in a smaller project like the Chunian were able to obtain land through auctions and "civil" grants.

Chenab Colony, the largest project, requires a more detailed consideration of the social and geographical origins of the grantees of land. The basic distinction between immigrant and indigenous grantees continued in this colony, the former receiving 64.6 percent and the latter 35.4 percent of total allotted area. The indigenous grantees were those who belonged to Jhang, Gujranwala, and Montgomery districts, whereas the immigrant grantees came from districts other than these three.

In selecting the districts from which immigrant peasant colonists were to be obtained, the state adhered to its two principal objectives for Chenab Colony: to provide relief from population congestion, and to procure the most skilled agriculturists. These requirements led it to select seven districts: Ambala, Ludhiana, Jullundur, Hoshiarpur, Amritsar, Gurdaspur, and Sialkot.[80] These districts were situated firmly in central Punjab (only Sialkot lay west of the Ravi River), and this was the region the British believed to contain the best agriculturists. By a seemingly fortunate coincidence, these districts also contained at the time the highest densities of population

---

[78] For the land alienation debate among British officials, and the passing of the act, see P.H.M. van den Dungen, *The Punjab Tradition* (London: George Allen and Unwin, 1972); and N. G. Barrier, *The Punjab Alienation of Land Bill of 1900* (Durham: Duke University, 1966).

[79] DC, Lahore, to Commissioner, Lahore, 3 October 1901; in PRAP(I), March 1902, No. 21.

[80] PRAP(I): July 1891, No. 15; and April 1898, No. 11.

in the province. In the coming decades colonisation resulted in a significant population shift toward the western Punjab, with densities in the canal colony districts multiplying through migration, while those in the central Punjab remained relatively stable.

The choice of the central Punjab as a supply area for grantees was also influenced by the fact that it was the homeland of the Sikh population, with its strong representation in military service and its previous history of political volatility. Its record of struggle against the Mughal empire and early resistance to British incursions created an urgent need for its pacification, to ensure the prospects of a stable rulership.[81] The canal colonies proved a useful outlet for the demobilised Sikh soldier-peasantry, which had run rampant over the province with the collapse of Mughal rule, and which could only inadequately be reabsorbed into the military structure of British India. This central region contained, as well, strong Muslim and Hindu Jat lineages, whose political support and revenue contributions were also important to the state. Colonisation not only brought new resources to such groups, but it also relieved the tensions of overpopulation. It was an effective means of avoiding instability in rural society.

Colonists from the seven selected districts obtained the predominant share of land—well over 90 percent of the area—allotted to immigrants in Chenab Colony. In terms of the whole colony, they obtained around 60 percent of the allotted land, an area of over one million acres. There was, therefore, little deviation from the policy of confining immigrant landholders to these seven districts.[82] Apprehensions were expressed that the predominantly Muslim districts of the northwestern Punjab were being neglected and would have cause for dissatisfaction. It was decided that, rather than share in the present scheme, they would provide grantees for the forthcoming Jhelum Colony, which would be closer to their homes.[83] Thus

---

[81] For a discussion of the political and economic structure of the Punjab prior to the phase of agricultural colonisation, see Indu Banga, *Agrarian System of the Sikhs* (New Delhi: South Asia Books, 1978); and A. J. Major, "Return to Empire; The Sikhs and the British in the Punjab 1839-72" (PhD dissertation, Australian National University, 1981).

[82] For the distribution of grantees by community and district of origin, see *Chenab Colony SR*, paras. 65-83. There were two minor exceptions to the general rule: the first an allotment of 15,200 acres to men from congested tracts of Lahore, Gujrat, and Jhelum districts; and the second an allotment of 6,900 acres to cultivators affected by river and diluvian action, which was shared among Lahore, Hoshiarpur, Jullundur, Bannu, Sialkot, and Gujranwala districts. See "Proposed grants of land on Chenab Canal to *zamindars* from congested tracts in districts other than the eight congested districts," BOR J/301/604; and "Grants of land on Gugera Branch to persons of non-selected districts who have lost their lands by diliuvian or *chos* action," BOR J/301/616.

[83] The financial commissioner, S. S Thorburn, had written: "The Mussalmans of the Western Punjab are very depressed, think themselves neglected, are in a dissatisfied state and have some reason for their dissatisfaction. They all produce good recruits and belong to sturdy

Chenab Colony contained a very large number of non-Muslim landholders. When the canal colonies fell to Pakistan in the partition of 1947, these settlers had to return to the east. Though the British had no way of knowing that their actions would contribute to tragedy half a century later, through their policies they did accentuate the demographic and economic disruption that the transfer of power was to bring to the Punjab. It is not unlikely that the massacres of 1947 were induced, in the case of Sikhs and Hindus, at least in part by the prospect of losing valuable and extensive landed resources in the western parts of the province.

The social composition of the immigrant grantees was determined by the desire of the government to procure skilled cultivators. Accordingly, it was decided that the peasant grantees should be hereditary and landholding agriculturists. They were to belong to the castes of Jat, Saini, Arain, and Kamboh: all designated as agricultural castes under the Land Alienation Act.[84] This measure yet again excluded the landless poor. The government decided that yeoman grantees also had to belong to the agricultural castes. Capitalist grantees could be nonagriculturists, but by the very nature of the grant they could only be elite ones.[85] Hindu (including Sikh) and Muslim grantees obtained a roughly equivalent amount of land, each around 31 percent of the total allotted area. In caste terms, the predominant recipients were the Jats, with 675,580 acres, or 36 percent of the entire colony. Arains and Kambohs also obtained sizeable areas (10.7 and 3 percent, respectively). The substantial area allotted to Rajputs (3.3 percent) was representative of the more elite colonists, who obtained yeoman and capitalist grants. Much of the area under the category "miscellaneous" (6.8 percent) also went to elite castes such as Brahmans and Khatris among the Hindus, and Syeds, Qureshis, and Mughals among the Muslims. The figures give clear proof of the monopolisation of colony land by castes dominant in rural society, further increasing their economic and political power.

The "indigenous" grantees, by contrast, did not fulfil either of the two objectives for the settlement of Chenab Colony. Neither did they come

---

fighting tribes. It will be good policy to offer these districts small allotments." See Note by FC, 22 January 1898; and also RS to FC, 29 April 1898, in PRAP(I), April 1898, Nos. 7 and 11.

[84] The two most vivid descriptions of the manner of selection of peasant grantees were provided by: "Note for selection of colonists for Jhang and Bhowana Branches," by CO, Chenab Colony, n.d.; and "Memorandum describing method of selection of colonists for Chenab Canal from Amritsar District," by SO, Amritsar, n.d.: in BOR Printed 74, Vol. III, pp. 957-60.

[85] For lists of applicants for the larger grants, their caste and area of origin, their landholdings and capital, and final outcome of the applications, see: "Applications for Yeoman grants on Chenab Canal," BOR J/301/382; and "Capitalist applications for land on Chenab Canal—Gugera and Buralla Branches," BOR J/301/650.

from congested districts nor could they in the great majority of cases be regarded as efficient, self-cultivating agriculturists. The allotment of land to them was a response to the disruption caused by canal irrigation to the lives of the people of the Rechna Doab. These grantees comprised two elements: the seminomadic pastoralists of the plain, who were called Janglis, and the settled agriculturists of the riverain, called Hitharis. These people ultimately received the very sizeable area of 663,000 acres, or 35 percent of total allotted land. Initially, however, the government had no plans to make such an allotment. The grants grew out of the need to compensate: the Janglis for the world they had lost, and the Hitharis for the environmental impact of canal irrigation on their riverain lands.

The pastoralists of the Sandal Bar, as the upland plain of the Rechna Doab was called, were faced with a revolution in their lifestyles when their grazing areas disappeared under canal irrigation. They were pushed out of their old homes, and their land was taken up by strangers, whom they regarded as usurpers.[86] Their loud protestations, combined with a sudden increase in crime (especially cattle theft, to which they felt much affinity), as well as the all too obvious loss of their means of subsistence, forced the government to allot land to these Janglis. Those who could produce evidence that they had paid the grazing tax, or *tirni*, in precolony days became eligible for land grants.[87] This effectively restricted access to land to the owners of cattle, who composed the dominant elements in Jangli society. The lower strata of the Janglis, which had traditionally been servile to the cattle owners, had no option but to seek a livelihood as landless labourers with their former masters or with immigrant grantees. Even in a situation of environmental transformation, the existing Jangli hierarchy was preserved. In the end the Janglis received the substantial area of 448,000 acres, or about 24 percent of the total allotment in the colony.[88]

Even so, they retained a strong sense of grievance, and not without justification. Though their leading men received larger grants, most Janglis

[86] F. P. Young, *Report on the colonisation . . .* , p. 24; and Deva Singh, *Colonisation of the Rechna Doab* (Lahore: Punjab Government Record Office Publication No. 7, n.d.), pp. 23-24. For a description of the Janglis, see *Chenab Colony SR* (1915), paras. 86-93.

[87] The attestation of Jangli status was a complicated affair, causing the administration much trouble and the applicants anxiety and grievance. The prospect of land grants brought forth a much larger number of claimants than the amounts of land allocated were able to absorb. See Note by SC, 23 March 1900, in PRAP(I), June 1900, No. 4; and *PCR*: 1898, paras. 7 and 11; 1899, para. 2; 1900, para. 13; and 1901, para. 8. For a history of the *tirni* system, see *Chenab Colony SR* (1915), paras. 138-41.

[88] For further information on land grants to Janglis, see *Chenab Colony SR* (1915), para. 84; "Grant of land to Janglis and Hitharis in Sheikhupura District," BOR 301/3/17/71; and "Allotments to nomads and locals in the new extensions of Pir Mahal, Khikhi and Buralla, Lyallpur District," BOR 301/3/25/217.

were allotted land at the rate of half a square, or about 14 acres, per family. This was half the size of grants to immigrants, and it allowed for little more than subsistence farming. With little or no previous experience with cultivation, they had suddenly to conform to the demands of smallholding agriculture and the market economy. In the years that followed, many became successful agriculturists, but others remained the most backward of colonists, stranded on their minute grants, with their cattle little more than a liability, and bewailing the days of their lost freedom.

One section of the Janglis, the Biloch tribes, owned camels rather than cattle. They acknowledged the cattle owners as their superiors, but found themselves with colony grants twice as large as those allotted to their betters.[89] This was because the Biloch possessed in the camel an animal of much importance for military transport. Afraid that canal irrigation might lead to its disappearance from these parts, the British introduced "service" tenures under which the Bilochis obtained land on condition that they continued to maintain their camels. This contrasted starkly with the complete lack of any provisions for the upkeep of the Janglis' cattle, which was of much greater agrarian significance but which suffered a serious decline. The Bilochi service grants, since they predated the horse-breeding schemes, represented the first effort to turn the peasant in the western Punjab into a military servitor. They will be discussed in a later chapter.

Chenab Colony had also another type of indigenous grantee, the Hithari landowners. The development of canal irrigation had adverse consequences for the agricultural communities of the riverain tracts.[90] The canals reduced the supply of water in the rivers, and this disrupted the inundation irrigation systems that had traditionally existed in the *hithar*. Well irrigation was also adversely affected, through a decline in the subterranean water table. New employment opportunities in colony areas tempted away labourers and subtenants, which hurt the local landlords who were not self-cultivators.[91] To minimise the dislocation of the *hithar*'s agricultural economy, the government undertook two types of compensatory measures. First, canal irrigation was substantially increased for proprietary lands. By 1915, 85,000 acres were commanded by canals, and by the late 1920s this stood at 143,000 acres. Second, colony grants were given to Hithari landowners: the smaller ones received peasant and the larger landlords yeoman and capitalist

---

[89] For a discussion of these grants, see RPCC, ch. 11, section A; and also the chapter on militarisation below.

[90] For a description of the Hithari tribes, see *Jhang District Gazetteer* (1908), pp. 42-60.

[91] *Report of the Indian Irrigation Commission, 1901-1903*: Part II, ch. 14, p. 31; and "Evidence," Vol. IV, Punjab, pp. 3-4. See also PRAP(I): July 1900, No. 17; and December 1900, No. 36.

grants.[92] Most of the land for Hitharis was allotted to elite landowning groups, such as Aroras, Rajputs, Syeds, and Qureshis; these grants were intended to preserve the existing structure of Hithari society during a period of rapid economic change. So as not to remove these men of influence from their old homes, the Hithari grantees were, as a further concession, even exempted from personal residence. They continued to reside outside the colony, and merely rented out their grants to subtenants. In the years to come, they proved to be the worst of colonists, for as absentee landlords they played only a negative role in the colony.

Patterns established in Chenab Colony were followed for subsequent colonies as well. Both "indigenous" and "immigrant" elements continued to be catered to, and the state retained the policy of allotting peasant and most other types of grants only to members of the "agricultural castes" as notified under the Land Alienation Act.

In Jhelum Colony, this pattern survived despite the incursion of military tenures. Though the basis for allotting grants changed from agricultural skill and population pressure to the possession of a suitable mare, the social composition of the grantees remained confined to landholding groups.[93] The horse-breeding grantees could come from none other than the agricultural castes, and indeed as owners of horses they belonged to the more advantaged sections of this stratum. With grants of fifty-five acres, the peasant horse breeders could aspire to much more than subsistence agriculture. And the larger, or *sufedposh*, grantees were chosen from families of landed magnates that had gained a reputation for horse breeding. These were also prominent and influential families of their localities, holding such rural offices as *halqadar, inamdar*, and *zaildar*.[94] Such grants carried with them the political aspect of bringing the rural gentry closer to imperialist rule through recourse to military services. One class of allottees that did not obtain horse-breeding grants were the Janglis indigenous to the Jech Doab. Officials felt that these erstwhile pastorals, only lately relieved of their nomadic freedoms, lacked the discipline to become suitable service grantees. They did receive 60,700 acres in the colony, but since they were

---

[92] For land grants to the Hitharis, see "Compensatory grants on Chenab Canal for the neighbouring districts affected by it," BOR J/301/619. There is also much information in PRAP(I) 1897-1905 on this subject.

[93] "It goes without saying that none but true agriculturists should be chosen as peasant grantees. The orders of Government restrict the choice to hereditary land-owners or occupancy tenants. . . . It is, of course, politic, no less than it is just, to make our selections amongst the great landholding tribes": FC to SC, 8 July 1901; in PRAP(I), October 1901, No. 12. See also "Selection of agricultural tribes as Peasant colonists on Jhelum Canal," BOR J/301/700.

[94] For lists of *sufedposh* horse-breeding grantees, see "Allotment in Jhelum Canal Colony of land to selected Peasants and Yeomen for maintenance of brood mares," BOR J/301/684 KW.

the last to be settled they had to accept the most inferior lands. This low priority, along with the diminutive size of their grants—fourteen acres or so per family—further diminished their prospects of a successful transition to settled agriculture. It was those aligned to military wants that were the favoured colonists.

The adoption of military priorities did cause a significant shift in the supply areas of grantees for Jhelum Colony from that originally intended. Five districts of Rawalpindi Division had been selected for the provision of grantees: Gujrat, Hazara, Jhelum, Rawalpindi, and Shahpur. Smaller allotments were to be made to Gujranwala and Sialkot districts.[95] Thus the northwestern areas of the Punjab were now to benefit from the canal colonies; they had hitherto not participated significantly in the colonisation process. These districts were retained for the revised scheme based on horse breeding, but dramatic changes occurred in the share of each district. These deviations were caused by a reversal in the methods by which colonists were chosen. Selection of horse-breeding grantees was taken out of the hands of district officials, for local knowledge of population congestion and agricultural expertise was no longer required.[96]

Instead, the colony official, W. M. Hailey, was ordered to tour the selected districts, inspect mares and the credentials of their owners, and make his selections accordingly. The distribution of grantees by districts was not predetermined but depended on the number of men who came forward with acceptable mares. Hailey found that there was a rush of applicants from Gujrat, Sialkot, and Gujranwala districts. As a result, these more central areas received grants greatly disproportionate to the amounts originally intended for them.[97] Shahpur, the home district of the colony, also received a substantial number of horse-breeding grants, but Jhelum only a moderate number, while Rawalpindi and Hazara obtained very few. Thus horse breeding caused a major shift in districtwise allocations in favour of the more settled central regions, to the great disadvantage of the poorer submontane tracts of the trans-Jhelum area.

The social origins of the military grantees in Chenab and Jhelum colonies was also limited along caste lines. Ex-soldiers obtained around 80,000 acres in each of the two colonies, and the recipients had to belong to the agricultural castes.[98] Soldiers who came from nonagricultural castes were ineligible for these grants. The areas to which these military grantees be-

[95] FC to RS, 29 March 1901; in PRAP(I), May 1901, No. 14.

[96] Many of the original and unsuccessful candidates for grants were found land in the Chenab Colony Extensions, and from the 17,000 acres reserved for them in Upper Chenab Colony.

[97] See reports by W. M. Hailey in BOR J/301/684.

[98] PRAP(G), July 1904, No. 39; and *PCM*, p. 104.

longed also tended to be the districts that supplied civilian grantees in these colonies: that is, the well-tried central regions of the province, and to a lesser extent the northwestern districts. These rules were relaxed for Lower Bari Doab Colony, where 180,000 acres were reserved not for military pensioners but for veterans of World War I.[99] Political expediency was followed in granting eligibility to combatants even if they belonged to the nonagricultural castes. Military grantees who were noncombatants still had to come from the agricultural castes, which ensured that the price of land for nonagriculturists would be levied in blood. The supply areas for the war veterans were also widened; they could come from any part of the Punjab, and even from the North-West Frontier Province and Kashmir. Such deviations in colonisation practice were designed to stimulate war recruitment, just as soldier settlement in general was meant to increase the attractions of military service. The prospect of obtaining such grants undoubtedly induced many a Punjabi to regard a military career as the best means of improving his social and economic standing. The more liberal social and regional basis for the selection of ex-soldiers was continued in Nili Bar Colony, where 75,000 acres were reserved for them.

No such concessions were made in the case of civilian colonists, for whom possession of colony land remained a matter of birth. In Lower Bari Doab Colony, once again, all civilian peasant grantees had to belong to the agricultural castes. The allocations (see Table 2.4) for ''hereditary agriculturists,'' ''compensatory grantees,'' and ''horse-breeding peasant grantees'' (except nonagriculturist soldiers) were reserved for this class. Under the category ''hereditary agriculturists,'' grantees were obtained from tracts suffering from population congestion, chiefly in Amritsar, Gurdaspur, Hoshiarpur, and Jullundur districts. They belonged largely to the Jat, Arain, Saini, and Kamboh castes.[100] Under the category ''compensatory grants,'' allotments were made to two types of agricultural owners: men from Delhi territory whose lands had been expropriated for the construction of the new capital, and men who had lost their land through diluvian and river action.[101] The ''landed gentry'' of the province were also provided for in this colony, as were to some extent members of the nonlanded ''depressed classes''; these grants will be discussed later.

In Nili Bar Colony, provision was made for both immigrant peasant grantees and for local inhabitants (those belonging to Montgomery and Multan districts). The latter obtained grants on nonperennially irrigated

[99] For discussion among officials for the liberalisation of older restrictions, see BOR J/301/1178, pp. 13-251; and PRAP(I), September 1915, Nos. 14-51.

[100] See ''Lower Bari Doab Canal—Grants to Peasants from congested districts,'' BOR J/301/1185.

[101] See ''Lower Bari Doab Colony—Compensatory grants,'' BOR 301/4/24/9.

land to the extent of 230,400 acres and, in addition, old lessees of state land got a further 40,000 acres under the *Tahud Khahi* allocation (see Table 2.5). The more elite local inhabitants also obtained ample opportunities for gain from the temporary cultivation leases given out on the areas reserved for auction sales. Indeed, such leases ran much longer than intended when the auction process faltered with the collapse of land prices during the depression: another example of new land adding to existing inequalities.

The peasant grants in the perennially irrigated area of the colony were confined, as in other colonies, to the agricultural castes. Many grants were of a compensatory nature. Men whose lands had been ruined by waterlogging or by diluvian and river action, or those who inhabited congested tracts, were eligible for these peasant grants. The sufferers from waterlogging came from Gujranwala, Gujrat, Sheikhupura, and Sialkot, all being districts in the canal colony zone. By the mid-1920s, canal irrigation had begun to create hydraulic imbalances on an extensive scale. Especially damaging were the Upper Chenab and Upper Jhelum canals, which cut across the *doab*s and natural lines of drainage, thus causing high rates of seepage. The resulting waterlogging and salinity brought ruin to a number of canal colonists, but this dislocation was to a large extent ameliorated by the allotment of compensatory grants in Nili Bar Colony. By 1929, over 70,000 acres had been allotted to sufferers from waterlogging from the four districts.[102] A potentially dangerous cause of tension and conflict was thus avoided, for the despoilation of the livelihood of those affected was attributable to artificial causes: the hydraulic works that the state itself had created. A large number of grants were also given in compensation for lands lost by river action. These grantees were drawn from several districts, and though their dispossession was caused by natural disasters for which the government could not be blamed, their ensuing discontent could have led to disloyalty. The compensatory factor in land distribution made it possible to solve particular disruptions and grievances, for which remedies might not have been available but for colony land.

Peasant grantees in Nili Bar Colony were also drawn from tracts suffering from population congestion. Although a proportion of the grants were to be allotted to men from the central Punjab, the government decided that residents of tracts that had so far received little or no canal land should also be selected, provided that such men were skilled agriculturists and promised to make good colonists. This enlarged the supply area for peasant

---

[102] See "Note on selection of colonists for Nili Bar Colony from waterlogged tracts in Gujranwala District," by DC, Gujranwala, 15 February 1928; in "Selection of Peasant grantees for Nili Bar Colony," BOR 301/2/C9/188 B, pp. 11-13. See also statement of allotment in "Canal administration, Waterlogging. Damage to land by waterlogging in Village Thatta Asalatke, Gujranwala District," BOR 251/39/00/78, p. 21.

grants, and thereby extended over a wider region the benefits that accrued to the state and the agricultural castes from colonisation. In addition to the central Punjab districts of Amritsar, Gurdaspur, Hoshiarpur, Jullundur, and Ludhiana, peasant grantees were drawn from congested tracts in Attock, Ferozepur, Gujrat, Jhelum, Muzaffargarh, and Shahpur districts.[103]

Sale by auction, that ubiquitous feature of Nili Bar Colony, proved to be a far more difficult method of land disposal than allotment to grantees. In order to hold up prices, the government was forced to offer only a limited area for sale at any one time. It decided for Nili Bar to put up an average of 15,000 acres per year, in the hope of selling the entire area in twenty to twenty-five years.[104] Economic crises accompanying the depression of the 1930s played their own disruptive role in bringing the auction process to a halt. A buoyant start, with high land prices, was made in 1926, and by 1929 an area of 38,100 acres had been sold. Then prices collapsed with the onset of the depression, and in the next ten years the government disposed of only 3,800 acres.[105] Even in the three years 1939-1941, only 15,200 acres were sold, evidence of the prolonged and retardative effect of the depression on an agrarian economy such as this. Thereafter sales picked up more rapidly, though a high overall deficit remained up to the final years of British rule. In two decades total auction sales amounted to 118,700 acres, only one-third of the area reserved for this purpose.

The social composition of the auction purchasers in Nili Bar Colony appears in the records in terms of "Tribes" ("Agriculturists" and "Non-agriculturists"), and "Communities" (Hindu, Sikh, and Muslim). With tribes, in the sales before the depression, the agriculturists dominated over the nonagriculturists, and bought land at particular auctions in proportions varying from two-thirds to nine-tenths of the area sold. Land at this time was disposed of largely in smaller plots, and the purchasers were mostly smaller *zamindars* from other canal colonies. This reflected the prosperity of agricultural owners, and especially of colony grantees, after a period of

---

[103] For investigations and discussions on areas that could supply peasant grantees for Nili Bar, see BOR 301/1/C9/4, pp. 1-27; and "Recruitment of Peasant cultivators from Punjab for Bahawalpur State," BOR 301/2/0/140, Notes pp. 5-54.

[104] The process of auction sales in this colony is comprehensively covered in "Sale by public auction in Nili Bar Colony of agricultural Crown land," BOR 301/8/C9/47 A-N.

[105] Another effect of the depression was to undermine the ability of auction purchasers to keep up with their instalment payments. Large arrears became outstanding, and though this initially led to the confiscation of much auctioned land, the government had in time to make several concessions in the face of a widespread liquidity crisis, in such matters as interest and instalment rates, indemnities, and reductions in areas purchased. See "Nili Bar Conference held on 12 January 1937," BOR 301/14/C9/102; and "Memorandum. Relief granted by Punjab Government to agriculturists owing to agricultural depression," n.d., in BOR 251/59/00/20 on this subject.

high crop prices in the mid-1920s. For the limited areas sold in the 1930s, buyers were merely men from within Nili Bar Colony who wished to extend their allotments by taking on adjoining areas. In the sales from 1939 onward, much higher proportions of land were bought by nonagriculturists. This reflected the especially adverse effects of the depression on agricultural owners, and the greater economic strength of commercial groups. From 1943, after a few years of high agricultural prices, land sales occurred in roughly equal proportions between the two groups. In terms of communities, the detrimental effects of the depression were also visible. Hindu buyers, mostly nonagriculturists, never purchased more than a third of land sold at auction prior to 1930, and at times their purchases were down to 10 to 16 percent of land sales. Yet after 1938 they never purchased less than 45 percent, and at some auctions bought over 60 percent, of the total land sold. Muslims and Sikhs, being mostly agriculturists, bought a smaller proportion of land after the depression than before it.

The opening up of the canal colonies also created a substantial movement of population toward the western Punjab. This occurred not only with the recipients of land, but included also the many other occupational groups that migrated into this region to take up employment. Immigration resulted, in the decades after 1890, in a significant demographic shift in favour of the canal colony districts, as shown by Table 2.8. The variation in the province's population from 1891 to 1941, from 18.6 to 28.4 million, represented an increment of 52.36 percent. The increase in this half century in districts with canal colonies was well above the provincial average. Jhang, Multan, Shahpur, and Sheikhupura all rose by over 100 percent, Montgomery by 219 percent, and Lyallpur by a massive 2,215 percent. Lahore District, with Chunian Colony, increased by 88 percent, though growth in the city of Lahore accounted for much of this. By contrast, population increase in all other districts except two, Ferozepur and Mianwali, stayed below the provincial average, and many districts were unable to reach even half this average figure.

A general and substantial increase in all districts showed up with the 1941 enumeration. This resulted partly from political factors, as each religious community sought, with impending communal divisions, to increase its own proportionate strength. If this upward bias for 1941 is kept in mind, a picture of even greater stagnation of population for noncanal colony areas emerges. Partly as a result of migration to the colonies, and partly through mortality from plague and influenza epidemics, most Punjab districts suffered population reverses in the first two decades of this century. The canal colony regions were the only ones that experienced unbroken demographic growth. The dramatic jumps in particular districts with the emergence of colonisation programmes can also be seen in such cases as Lyallpur in

TABLE 2.8. PUNJAB: VARIATION IN POPULATION, 1891-1941

| District | Number of Persons (000) | | | | | | Percent Variation |
	1891	1901	1911	1921	1931	1941	1891-1941
Ambala	865	817	691	681	743	848	−1.96
Amritsar	993	1,024	881	930	1,117	1,414	42.38
Attock	448	464	519	512	584	676	50.72
Biloch Trans- Frontier Tract	6	24	29	27	30	40	578.28
Dera Ghazi Khan	428	472	500	469	491	581	35.71
Ferozepur	886	958	960	1,099	1,157	1,423	60.60
Gujranwala	661	740	606	624	736	912	37.96
Gujrat	806	792	788	824	922	1,105	37.03
Gurdaspur	944	940	837	852	971	1,154	22.20
Gurgaon	760	843	730	682	740	851	12.00
Hissar	776	782	805	817	899	1,007	29.75
Hoshiarpur	1,011	990	919	927	1,032	1,170	15.71
Jhang	402	426	525	571	665	882	104.21
Jhelum	514	501	512	477	541	630	22.48
Jullundur	908	918	802	823	944	1,127	24.20
Kangra	763	768	770	766	801	899	17.87
Karnal	863	885	801	829	853	995	15.31
Lahore	899	1,004	1,000	1,130	1,379	1,695	88.63
Ludhiana	649	673	517	568	672	819	26.19
Lyallpur	60	586	836	968	1,167	1,396	2,215.37
Mianwali	287	302	341	358	412	506	76.40
Montgomery	417	430	482	686	1,000	1,329	219.07
Multan	621	700	801	879	1,160	1,484	138.96
Muzaffargarh	494	528	569	568	591	713	44.33
Rawalpindi	534	559	548	569	634	785	47.12
Rohtak	780	834	715	772	806	956	22.63
Shahpur	478	488	645	720	821	999	108.85
Sheikhupura	401	523	540	634	696	853	112.46
Sialkot	962	933	872	878	980	1,190	23.80
Simla	36	39	38	45	37	39	6.85
Total Punjab (British Territory)	18,653	19,943	19,579	20,685	23,581	28,419	52.36

SOURCE: *Census of India*, 1941, Vol. VI (Punjab), pp. 8-11.

1891-1911, Shahpur in 1901-1911, Montgomery in 1911-1931, and Multan in 1921-1941. One reason why percentage increases in colony districts appear so large could be that their initial populations were low, compared to the more highly populated central and eastern districts. Nevertheless, these rises represented sizeable growth in actual numbers, with areas like Lyallpur, Montgomery, and Multan reaching populations of well over a million each, and figuring by 1941 among the most populous of the Punjab's districts—a major transition from their relative obscurity half a century earlier.

In terms of population densities, as well, the canal colonies had a profound impact on demographic levels in the western Punjab. Percentage rises well above the provincial average (47.6) for 1891-1941 were recorded in the districts of Jhang (106.0), Lahore (89.8), Lyallpur (2,540.0), Montgomery (236.2), Multan (141.3), Shahpur (109.0), and Sheikhupura (112.6). All other districts, with the exception of Attock, Ferozepur, and Mianwali, were below the Punjab average, reflecting again the effects on provincial population of the movement of people into the canal colonies. Once again, low initial densities in the western Punjab led to dramatic percentage increases with colonisation; the more densely populated districts to the east, like Amritsar, Jullundur, and Ludhiana, retained the greatest concentration of people throughout this period. However, by 1941 the western *doab*s could no longer be regarded as the sparsely peopled tracts that they were in the nineteenth century. It was in them that population change occurred most steadily and rapidly, whereas demographic levels in other districts tended to stagnate (especially if the 1941 figures represent some degree of overenumeration). Census statistics need not be seen as entirely accurate; but they do represent trends realistically, and these reflect strongly the importance of the canal colonies as the region with the greatest demographic growth, and consequently economic expansion, in the Punjab—if not, for that matter, in the entire subcontinent.

CHAPTER THREE

Entrenchment

AGRICULTURAL colonisation had a profound impact on the position of both state and people in the Punjab. The state, for one, enjoyed special authority in a hydraulic society such as the canal colonies. Not only did it control the source of agriculture—canal water—but it had complete rights over the manner in which the land was to be disposed, to whom land was to be allotted, and the type of tenurial rights that were to prevail. This position of strength accrued essentially from its ownership of land in the canal colonies, these areas being categorised as crown or state waste lands. By incorporating a very great number of Punjabis into the process of agricultural colonisation, either directly as grantees of land or indirectly in terms of increased opportunities for commerce or agricultural labour, the British stood out as potent benefactors. Their rule, undemocratic and imperialistic though it may have been, could be regarded by the beneficiaries of land as a benevolent despotism. The impact of this control of the British over landed resources became evident in the differences between the strength of the nationalist movement in the Punjab and the rest of India, a contrast observable even at the eve of independence on the subcontinent. The greater strength of the state, its "entrenchment" in society, arose out of its pivotal role in this region of hydrological agriculture.

Access to colony land affected the distribution of economic and political resources among the people of the Punjab. Those who obtained land strengthened their position in society, and were the real beneficiaries of agricultural colonisation, while those who were excluded from this new resource suffered a relative weakening of their status. Benefits accrued equally to the commercial elements that traded in agricultural produce and to the members of the bureaucracy that managed this hydraulic society. The class of subtenants and agricultural labourers, though it played a vital role in the canal colonies, failed to achieve economic and social mobility, for it was denied control of the means of production. Its increased vulnerability, stemming from the deprivation of proprietorial and occupancy access to colony land, contrasted strongly with the enhanced dominance of the well-placed groups that acquired land. These differentials in the terms of trade between social classes are also embodied in the concept of "entrenchment."

The impact of agricultural colonisation on the social structure of the Punjab is best examined through the participation of each of the major classes that were involved. These were the landholding peasantry, the landlords, the bourgeoisie and the rural poor.[1] The first part of this chapter traces the role of each class in these newly settled lands. The second part deals with the more direct use of colony land by the state for the maintenance of political and social stability. Such were its consequences that the retardation of nationalism in the province could not have been unrelated to the deference for political "order" that land distribution wrought.

THE DOMAIN OF CLASS

The Landholding Peasantry

The landholding peasantry was regarded by the British as the backbone of Punjabi society, and its support was believed to be essential for the maintenance of British rule. This insight came from a judicious grasp of both history and self-interest. The political alienation of the dominant peasantry was known to have had dire consequences for the state in the past, as with the Mughal empire in the eighteenth century.[2] In the Punjab the violent opposition of landholding groups, especially those that came together under the Sikh religion, had weakened and eventually overcome Mughal rule.[3] The British realised that the allegiance of this class was essential for political stability. Militarily, too, this stratum was of much importance, for recruitment to the army occurred predominantly from its ranks; and the Punjab provided more soldiers to the British Indian army than any other province. The state also relied for its income on this more than any other class, for the mass of agricultural land was under peasant possession and it yielded the major proportion of land revenue. British concern for the preservation of the landed peasantry was embodied in the Land Alienation Act

[1] This is, of course, a simplified categorisation of class divisions. For a fuller discussion of the problems of representing social stratification in South Asia, see Andre Beteille *Studies in Agrarian Social Structure* (Delhi: Oxford University Press, 1974); Saghir Ahmad, "Peasant Classes in Pakistan," in K. Gough and H. P. Sharma (eds.), *Imperialism and Revolution in South Asia* (New York: Monthly Review Press, 1973), pp. 203-21; and Saghir Ahmad, "Social Stratification in a Punjabi Village," *Contributions to Indian Sociology*, New Series, 4 (1970), 105-25; and Hamza Alavi, "Kinship in West Punjab Villages," ibid., 6 (1972), 1-27.

[2] Agrarian revolts against the Mughal empire are discussed in Irfan Habib, *The Agrarian System of Mughal India* (Bombay: Asia Publishing House, 1963), pp. 317-50.

[3] This was well known to British officials. In Griffin and Massy's *Chiefs of the Punjab*, in the histories of many individual families, especially Sikh ones, is described the rise of dominant peasant groups against Mughal rule. A similar story is retold for local regions in *tahsil*-level assessment reports: see, for example, *AR Hafizabad and Khangah Dogran Tahsils* (1904), ch. 2; and *AR Wazirabad Tahsil* (1911), paras. 11-19.

of 1900, the protective measure that tried to overcome the threatened expropriation of this class by commercial and moneylending groups.

The dichotomy between "agricultural" and "non-agricultural" castes brought about by the Land Alienation Act proved to have far-reaching consequences for agricultural colonisation. For the peasant grants (14-55 acres in size) in the canal colonies, the government maintained with rigid conformity that allotments should be made only to members of the "agricultural castes": those who already held land and were hereditary agriculturists. The "non-agriculturist" service and labouring castes, which made up the landless stratum of the rural population and were commonly termed *kamins*, or "menials," were excluded from access to land grants. The Jats, who comprised the most important and numerous landholding caste in the Punjab, obtained the largest amount of land in the canal colonies. Other groups that figured prominently were Arains, Kambohs, Sainis, and Gujars, all "agricultural castes." The caste and social origins of colony landholders have been discussed in some detail in the previous chapter. The present chapter will be more concerned with the position and status of these grantees in the period subsequent to their settlement on the land, for major changes occurred that had not been originally envisioned.

The amount of area made over to the landed peasantry was vast indeed. Well over 3,000,000 acres were allotted in the form of peasant grants: it was chiefly through the absorption of these smallholdings that the landed peasantry found its place in the canal colonies. The proportion of land devoted to such grants never fell below 50 percent in any colony, and exceeded 80 in some colonies. The recipients of these grants were not only selected on the basis of their social origins, but they were also settled in villages with others of their own caste, and preferably from the same district, so as to preserve homogeneity and social harmony.[4] Where possible, entire canal distributaries were reserved for men of similar or kindred castes, while a cardinal principle of colonisation remained that men of different castes should not be mixed in the same village.[5] Members of the dominant castes of the Punjab were settled in this manner over extensive tracts, to make up what became reputedly the most prosperous peasant community in South Asia. In an area where production for the market was well advanced, the emphasis placed on caste signified a strengthening of traditional forms of social organisation.[6] This seeming anomaly characterised the very nature of agricultural colonisation in the Punjab.

[4] "Note on selection of colonists for Jhang and Bhowana Branches," by CO, Chenab Colony, n.d.; in BOR Printed 74, Vol. III, pp. 957-58.

[5] For examples for Chenab Colony of grantees from distinct castes or districts settled along separate distributaries, see *AR Upper Jhang Branch* (1909), ch. 3, para. 2; *AR Lower Gugera Branch I* (1911), para. 12; and *AR Rakh Branch* (1913), para. 21.

[6] Not only was land distributed on the basis of caste, but distinguishable social, economic,

Indeed, events were to show that the extent of this entrenchment of the landholding peasantry went well beyond the limits set by the state at the time of colonisation. The allotment of land to peasant grantees had been made under well-defined terms of tenure, which were drawn up in a statement of conditions that the grantees had to accept when first taking up the land. The grantees were obligated to fulfil these conditions, under the supervision of the administration, thereby establishing between the two a much closer relationship than that which had traditionally existed. The greater involvement of the state with society was intended to provide the preconditions for a more innovatory role for the former. However, this increased contact contained an explosive mixture whose outcome proved to be counterproductive for developmental goals.

One of the major structural features of the peasant grants was that the state intended to retain ownership of the land in its own hands. Peasant grantees were to remain as occupancy tenants and were not allowed to acquire proprietary rights. It was as the owner of land that the state obliged its tenant grantees to meet their conditions of tenure. These extended over a number of aspects of village and agrarian life, and were designed to effect several improvements in living conditions and agricultural practices. In matters such as sanitation, home sites, and arboriculture, the administration reserved the right to supervise the maintenance of minimum standards, and by the very logic of this any defaults became liable to punitive action.

The grantees were also subject to regulation over more important matters, such as residence in the colony, succession, and alienation of land. Residence of grantees in colony villages was regarded as a prerequisite for their success as colonists. Absenteeism had adverse social and economic effects, for it converted grantees from producers to rentiers, who imposed parasitical claims on output but contributed little or no productive effort themselves. Furthermore, the regulation of succession was necessary if the grants were to be saved from rapid subdivision, and thus be retained as viable units of production capable of generating a marketable surplus. Similarly, the power of alienation, though already subject to the restrictions imposed by the Land Alienation Act, could be further regulated and controlled if the grantees were occupancy tenants rather than proprietors.[7] By

---

and even physical attributes were ascribed in official thinking to each of the major caste groups that obtained land. As an example, see *Chenab Colony SR* (1915), paras. 60, 70, and 72.

[7] The need to restrict the alienation of land from "agricultural" to "nonagricultural" castes was regarded by the British as essential for political and economic stability. This consideration influenced colony tenures. "We were led to this conclusion from our experience of the danger of allowing to peasant cultivators the power of alienating their land by sale and mortgage, which had in many parts of the Punjab resulted in the passing of a large area of land from peasant proprietors to rent receiving landlords and thus given rise to what seemed to us a grave economic evil, not without political danger." See Reply by FC, n.d., in "Punjab Canal Colonies Committee," BOR H/251/403, Answer No. 1.

deciding to remain as the landlord over the peasant grants, the state retained an institutional role that empowered it to supervise and bring about various facets of agricultural improvement. This important innovation was introduced in the earlier canal colonies, but an adverse reaction to this situation from the colonists forced a reversal in policy after 1912.

Tensions increased when the government tried to formalise its position and place it on a permanent basis. The means to accomplish this lay through legislative enactment. In 1906 it introduced in the Punjab Legislative Council a Bill for the Colonisation of Government Lands (known in abbreviated form as the Colonisation Bill).[8] This was designed to supercede the Government Tenants Act (Punjab) of 1893, under the aegis of which tenancies had hitherto been allotted, but which was found to be inadequate for dealing with several aspects of colonisation. Most importantly, the necessity to provide power to officials to enforce the conditions of tenure by summary or executive process, and without recourse to civil courts, had been overlooked in the existing act. This functioned as a constraint on officials in implementing the observance of tenurial conditions. The practice increasingly adopted to enforce compliance was the imposition of punitive measures on defaulting grantees. Such measures were without a proper legal basis, however, for they were not sanctioned by any legislation. They usually took the form of fines but in the more serious cases consisted of the temporary, and at times even permanent, confiscation of grants.[9] They were highly unpopular with the colonists, who regarded them as a further exaction on their already stretched resources. They were also believed to be arbitrarily and inequitably applied by an ever corrupt subordinate bureaucracy (which was Punjabi rather than British in composition).[10]

The grantees felt great antipathy toward the many regulations and requirements to which they had to conform. Officials argued that such rules were indispensable for maintaining an ordered society. This appeared especially necessary in the early years of settlement, when new tracts were being rapidly developed, and only standardised procedures could prevent

[8] For the debates on the Colonisation Bill and its eventual passage in the provincial legislature, see Punjab Legislative Council Proceedings; 25 October 1906, and 21 and 28 February 1907.

[9] See "Confiscations of lands on Chenab Canal," BOR J/301/850; which deals with a number of individual cases of confiscations.

[10] "They [fines] were employed to promote the policy of Government generally, to correct faults, remedy defects and stimulate effort, and the evil lay less in the system itself than in the opportunities it afforded to the parasite horde of underlings to satisfy dishonest and selfish ends": *Chenab Colony SR* (1915), para. 23. For further information on fines and other punitive measures, see "Running file on instructions to and proceedings of Colonies Committee, Punjab," BOR H/251/416, pp. 242-86; RPCC, pp. 134-39; and letter of "Pro bono Publico," in *Tribune* (Lahore), 16 February 1907.

an anarchy of deviant practices. However, the grantees had been unfamiliar with such rules and regulations in their old homes, and they now felt little tolerance for these sanctions on their freedom. Especially irksome was the more intrusive role of the administration, a necessary complement to the supervision of these stipulations. To a degree, the recalcitrance of the grantees was warranted, for the implementation of tenurial conditions invariably entailed more bureaucratic involvement, and a further series of exactions by subordinate officials.

Conservatism was another and less justifiable reason for the landholders' hostility, for the conscious and deliberate efforts at agricultural innovation marked a move away from customary practices. The grantees were averse to adopting both the state of mind and the practical measures required for improvement.[11] The dominant peasantry which the state had entrenched with land grants was quite capable of prospering through commercial agriculture. To these ends it readily absorbed the new resources made available in the canal colonies, and undertook the difficult task of bringing barren wastes under the plough. But it also displayed an incapacity to make more fundamental sacrifices, and thereby contribute to economic "progress." The fact that administrative action could not be disentangled from the renewed tyranny, at every opportunity, of petty officialdom further compromised the prospects of agrarian innovation. In order to free themselves from the onerous obligations they had accepted on taking up the land, the grantees undertook a political agitation in 1907. This was sparked off by the Colonisation Bill of 1906, and it eventually succeeded in obtaining the institutional adjustments that they desired.[12]

The Colonisation Bill of 1906 created great controversy in the canal colonies, for it threatened to consolidate the very relations with the state from which the grantees sought relief. The bill was opposed in the Punjab Leg-

[11] The official portrayal of the failure of colonists to "modernise" their attitudes and behaviour was one of injured sensibility: "So far from relying implicitly upon the ordinances of Government, according to their wont and tradition in the old districts, the colonists showed themselves unprepared for the most elementary forms of discipline and inclined to cavil at the most transparent measures for their welfare. . . . All this disaffection was but the price of efficiency: in creating, or attempting to create, ideal conditions the Colony officers found themselves at variance with public opinion, which expressed itself emphatically in favour of ancestral custom. It was not the fault of Government, or of the Colony officers, that their efforts for the public weal were so deliberately misinterpreted." See *Chenab Colony SR* (1915), paras. 22-23.

[12] The political personalities and organisations involved in the 1907 movement are discussed in some detail in N. G. Barrier, "Punjab Politics and the Disturbances of 1907" (PhD dissertation, Duke University, 1966), see especially ch. 4, pp. 168-217. A useful collection of documents relating to the Colonisation Bill is contained in S. R. Sharma, *The Punjab in Ferment* (New Delhi: S. Chand, 1971).

islative Council by the nonofficial members, and even the most loyal of
these, Malik Umar Hayat Khan Tiwana, spoke out against it. It was passed
in the Council with the support of the official members, however, and was
then sent to the centre for the Governor-General's assent. At that level it
was vetoed, one of the rare instances of this kind in the constitutional history of British India.[13]

For in the meantime, the canal colonies had erupted in a major political
agitation against the bill. The movement gathered such momentum that it
threatened to undo all the beneficial effects for British rule that colonisation
had bestowed. The agitation took the form of several meetings held in the
canal colonies, with speeches and resolutions protesting against the injustice of the new measure.[14] The Punjabi press was also vociferous in its
criticism of the administration, while prominent politicians, among them
Lala Lajpat Rai and Ajit Singh, were also drawn into the agitation.[15]

Threatened with a combination between urban and rural elements, and
fearing even, in their wilder fancies, the conspiratorial hand of Russian
agents, the British recoiled at the prospect of alienating a constituency so
important to their rule. They expeditiously reversed the commitment to agricultural development that had brought matters to such a head. The seri-
ousness with which the agitation was taken was shown by the refusal of the
governor-general to give his assent to the bill and by the appointment of a
commission to conduct a thorough investigation into conditions in the canal
colonies. Thereafter, the colonies returned to their usual political placidity,
for the agitation had achieved its desired goals. Not only did it succeed in
aborting the Colonisation Bill of 1906, but in the longer term it changed
the balance of forces between the state and the grantees, in favour of the
latter.

As a consequence of the movement of 1907, the government made major
concessions to the colonists, and these had profound implications for the
future of the canal colonies. A high-powered body known as the Colonies
Committee was appointed to look into the grievances of the colonists and

[13] See N. G. Barrier, "The Punjab Disturbances of 1907: The Response of the British Gov-
ernment in India to Agrarian Unrest," *Modern Asian Studies*, I, 4 (1967), 353-83; Punjab
Legislative Council Proceedings, 28 February 1907, pp. 22-23; and *Tribune*, 1907: 2 and 13
March, 30 May, and 6 June.

[14] For reports on political meetings, and articles and editorials on the 1907 agitation, see
Tribune, 1907: 12, 15, and 25 January; 1, 2, 7, 15, 16, 19, 22, 24, 27, and 28 February; 16,
20, 24, 28, and 29 March; 11, 23, and 30 April; 1, 11, 17, and 24 May; 1 and 19 June; 4
September; 16 and 26 October; and 7 November.

[15] For extracts from vernacular newspapers, such as the *Zamindar*, *Paisa Akhbar*, and *Pun-
jabee*, see ibid., 1907: 2 February; 14 and 23 March; 21 April; and 8 May. See also "Punjab
Native Newspaper Reports" (IOR), 1907-1908, Vol. XX, pp. 14, 26, 31-33, 36, 70, 96, 120-
21, 124-25, and 150.

to review the whole question of colony administration. Members of the committee travelled through the canal-irrigated tracts and sought the views of a number of people. They investigated the various issues that had brought the administration into contact with the colonists, such as tenurial conditions, the nature of revenue assessments, and the role of the subordinate bureaucracy. The committee also examined a number of specific problems that had caused friction, among them the management of village sites, grazing areas, arboriculture, and sanitation. In its report, the committee made several proposals that were largely incorporated into the legislation finally adopted to administer the canal colonies. This new measure was called the Colonisation of Government Lands Act (Punjab) of 1912 (or, more simply, the Colonisation Act). It was to have a profound bearing on the status of the peasant grantees and on their future relationship with the state.[16]

Perhaps the most important repercussion of the events of 1907 was the decision to allow proprietary rights to peasant grantees. They could now purchase these ten years after obtaining occupancy rights, or fifteen years after the date of settlement. The Colonies Committee had strongly recommended such a transition in status, arguing that occupancy tenancy should only exist for a limited term and be regarded as no more than a "period of restriction and guidance" to prepare the colonists for the role of proprietors. It conceded that proprietorship was preferable to tenancy because it bestowed a higher social status on the grantee. In justifying the new status for peasant grants, it made an ingenious appeal: "According to ancient custom, the reclamation of waste and unappropriated land is recognised throughout northern India as giving a title to proprietary rights, and in giving lower rights Government will be open to the charge of conceding less than is due by ancient custom."[17] The committee held that the grant of proprietary right "would be an immense stimulus to the progress of the development of the colonies," but gave no arguments to support this assertion.

There appeared no reason to believe that the economy of the Punjab would be strengthened by the grant of proprietorship to peasants. Indeed, the consolidation and perpetuation of individualised smallholdings was more likely to act as a constraint on the emergence of agricultural capitalism, and thereby retard rather than accelerate the process of economic

[16] For the debates on the Colonisation Act in the provincial legislature, see Punjab Legislative Council Proceedings: 16 December 1910, pp. 72-77; 1911, Vol. II, pp. 200-201; and 1912, pp. 99-103.

[17] RPCC, pp. 18-19. The report stated further: "The term 'tenant' involves, as compared with 'proprietor,' an idea of insecurity or inferiority. In the Punjab . . . the contrast suggested to a colonist between the position of a proprietor and that of a tenant is particularly strong."

change. In deciding to grant proprietary rights the state was reneging on its role as an agent of improvement, for as proprietors the grantees were no longer subject to any special conditions of tenure. In political terms the decision was a judicious one, for it further consolidated the collaborative network between imperialist rule and the landowning classes. For both, it led to greater entrenchment in society by further securing the position of groups already dominant in the social structure, a status which the state was seen to have provided.

The price at which peasant grantees could acquire land also represented a major concession on the part of the state. The Colonies Committee had, in the heat of the moment, recommended the extremely low rates of Rs 3.75 per acre for Sidhnai and Sohag Para colonies, and Rs 5 per acre for Chenab and Chunian colonies. The rates finally adopted by the government were not much higher: Rs 5 per acre for uncultivated and Rs 10 per acre for cultivated land in Sidhnai and Sohag Para colonies, and Rs 12.5 per acre in Chenab and Chunian colonies (proprietary rights were withheld from Jhelum Colony because of the preponderance of horse-breeding tenures). These prices were a fraction of the prevailing market rates for land realised at the periodic auctions that were held in the canal colonies.[18] Thus, the peasant grantees not only obtained ownership of the land, which they had not expected at the time of colonisation, but they did so at very concessionary rates. This represented a transfer of economic resources to the landholding classes, for by paying below market rates they deprived the public coffers, and thereby the people of the Punjab, of equitable capital returns from colony land.

Concessionary rates were also adopted for the later projects. In Lower Bari Doab, Upper Chenab, and Upper Jhelum colonies, peasant grantees were charged half the market price prevailing at the time of allotment (rather than at the time of purchase, which in itself was a significant concession), with a maximum of Rs 100 per acre.[19] In Nili Bar Colony, the price of purchase fixed by the government reflected the general rise in land prices in the mid-1920s, but it still fell considerably short of prevailing market levels: Rs 100 per acre if paid within a year, rising to Rs 240 per acre if paid in 40 years' time.[20] Further concessions were made during the eco-

---

[18] In the early 1900s, ten years before the decision to grant proprietary rights, average prices at land auctions were over Rs 100 per acre. In 1913 the average price at auction of 1,500 acres in Upper Chenab Colony was Rs 313 per acre, and rates of Rs 150-300 were commonly assumed for colony land at this time. See PRAP(I), August 1900, Nos. 1-7; and PRAP(G), April 1899, Nos. 23-30, and November 1913, No. 33.

[19] PRAP(I), July 1914, Nos. 9-11; and "Purchase of proprietary rights in Lower Bari Doab Colony," BOR 301/21/24/126.

[20] "Nili Bar Colony—Purchase of proprietary rights by Crown tenants," BOR 301/21/C9/30.

nomic difficulties of the 1930s, to try and alleviate the liquidity problems faced by the landowners. The burden of purchase payments was eased in such matters as the scale of instalments, arrears, and accumulated interest charges. Minimal land prices and solicitude during adversity gave the dominant classes further proof of the benevolence of British rule, and constituted yet another step in entrenching their position and that of the state. Moreover, the fear of losing the political adherence of such groups led the British to make even further concessions.

With the grant of proprietary rights, the government lost control over succession to peasant grants. Prior to 1912, it was in a position to control and regulate the rules of inheritance, for the peasant grantees were its tenants. It had done so by restricting succession to direct lineal heirs of grantees, and in the absence of these by reserving the right to select a single male heir from the female line. This was a move away from customary law, for it excluded the host of collateral relations who could claim inheritance in the absence of agnate descent. These deviations from the traditional laws of succession had proved highly unpopular with the grantees, and the issue figured prominently in the agitation of 1907. As a result, the matter was investigated by the Colonies Committee, and was discussed widely within the government. The final proposals, embodied in the Colonisation Act of 1912, made major concessions on the rules of succession. For grantees who acquired proprietary rights, the act allowed customary laws of succession to prevail. These varied with different castes, but the government itself imposed no further regulation on them, in the case of proprietors. Even for grantees who had not acquired proprietary rights, and who were still state tenants, the act allowed customary laws in the case of inheritance subsequent to succession from the original grantee.[21]

Thus the state conceded virtually all rights of regulation over succession, and allowed colony tenures to become subject to customary laws. This threatened to bring about the rapid subdivision and diminution of these smallholdings, a factor that had plagued traditional agriculture and acted as a major constraint on agricultural development. Except, significantly, for horse-breeding grants in Jhelum Colony, where military needs were to be served (and where the practice was continued despite the 1907 agitation), the British did not contemplate primogeniture for peasant tenancies. By giving up even the powers of sanction that it originally possessed, the government removed all checks on partibility. The situation boded ill for the prospects of achieving a ''higher level of civilisation,'' especially since the impetus for a reversion to traditional forms of succession had come from the colonists themselves.

---

[21] On the issue of succession to tenancies, see *PCM*, pp. 65-69; *Chenab Colony SR* (1915), para. 29; and RPCC, pp. 22-25.

Once proprietary rights had been conceded, the government could no longer insist on residence by grantees in their colony villages. Prior to the agitation of 1907, personal residence had been regarded as vital for the success of a colony grant.[22] Absenteeism defeated the very purpose of land settlement, and bred a parasitic class of rent receivers. But permanent residence in the canal colonies was unbearable for many grantees, and they sought ways of evading this requirement. This brought them into conflict with the administration, which in turn retaliated by imposing fines and other punitive measures on defaulters. The residence issue was one of the major grievances of grantees in the agitation of 1907, and its *raison d'être* was removed with the decision to concede proprietary rights. Here, too, the government gave in on a matter that might have made it unpopular, but which had undeniable benefits for agriculture. After 1912, residence could only be insisted upon in the initial period when grantees were government tenants, but once they had acquired proprietary rights there was no further hold on them. Again, it was the grantees who exerted an influence for the worse, and the state gave way without many qualms, not wishing to antagonise its beneficiaries.[23]

It can be seen that fundamental economic and political factors were responsible for the landholding peasantry becoming the largest recipient of land in the canal colonies. Such large tracts could not have been opened up without peasant colonisation, and the section of the peasantry that possessed the productive capacity to meet the new demand could not have been attracted to the canal colonies except with the promise of secure rights of tenure. It would also have been politically unwise to neglect this important class and make over an inordinate proportion of colony land to any other stratum of society. By making the landholding peasantry its chief beneficiary, the state built for itself a sound base of political support, and it also consolidated the position of elements in village society that were already dominant.

[22] "It was held to be essential that the new colonists should actually reside on the land to be granted to them, as general experience . . . has proved that a healthy development of agriculture can be expected only from a resident population; and we desired to avoid the many evils that were certain to arise if the lands came into the hands of absentee landlords, whose only interest in it would be to draw as high rents as possible from the actual cultivators." See Reply by FC, n.d., in BOR H/251/403, Answer No. 1. See also *PCM*, pp. 72-79; and RPCC, pp. 27-29.

[23] The achievements of 1907 represented a form of successful "class action" by the landholding peasantry. Similar activity has been discussed for South Asia for a subsequent period: see T. J. Byres, "The New Technology, Class Formation and Class Action in the Indian Countryside," *Journal of Peasant Studies*, VIII, 4 (1981), 405-54. For the local springboard for such action, see Hamza Alavi, "Politics of Dependence: A Village in West Punjab," *South Asian Review*, IV, 2 (1971), 111-28.

The Landlords

The larger grants in the canal colonies, those above fifty acres or so in size, were allotted to two groups of people: the landlord class and the bourgeoisie. The term "landlord" refers here to those landowners in the rural Punjab who did not personally cultivate the land but subsisted instead on rental earnings from tenants or the proceeds of cultivation by agricultural labourers. Such a class would include men who held land in only one village as well as those who wholly owned several villages. Despite substantial economic differences among them, these landowners formed a distinct class, for they occupied a similar position in the process of production and distribution. The economic role of the landlord class was also distinct from that of the landholding peasantry, for the latter relied primarily on self-cultivation. In caste terms, too, the larger grantees in the canal colonies belonged to elite castes to a far greater extent than peasant grantees. Whereas the latter belonged to castes such as Jat, Arain, Kamboh, Saini, and Gujar, the larger grantees tended to hold Rajput, Qureshi, Syed, and, to a lesser extent, Khatri status. There were, of course, several Jat and Arain families in the Punjab with substantial landholdings, and for this reason a number of Jats and Arains did receive the larger grants. In general, in both the economic and social sense, the larger grantees of rural origin belonged to a distinct stratum of society, and they formed a distinct class of colony grantees.

The landlord class was allotted grants in most canal colonies. These holdings differed in name and size from one colony to another. In Sidhnai and Sohag Para colonies, grants of fifty acres and above were common, and were allotted in order to attract men with capital. Sohag Para Colony also contained the large grant of 7,800 acres to Baba Sir Khem Singh Bedi, the head of an eminent Sikh family. This allotment was one of the largest to an individual in any colony. Landlords also received land from among the civil grants of Chunian and Jhelum colonies, and on a much larger scale as capitalist and yeoman grantees in Chenab Colony. They were the exclusive recipients of the horse-breeding yeoman (*sufedposh*) grants in Jhelum Colony, where they were also allotted landed gentry and stud farm grants. In Lower Bari Doab Colony, the landed gentry grants were allotted to members of the rural elite, normally those whose families were mentioned in Griffin and Massy's *Chiefs and Families of Note in the Punjab*. Landlords also participated in auction sales, which took place in most colonies, and were particularly extensive in Lower Bari Doab and Nili Bar colonies.[24] Men from this class also obtained reward grants (many of which were for help with recruitment to the army) and grants to military officers.

[24] Landlords were in fact advantageously placed for land purchases in these two colonies,

The size of grants to landlords varied greatly: from 75 acres (as with yeomen in Chenab Colony) to several thousand acres (as with Khem Singh Bedi). The capitalist grants in Chenab Colony ranged between 150 and 600 acres, most being closer to the lower figure. The landed gentry grants ranged between 150 and 350 acres. Land in the canal colonies being a scarce resource, the size of grants had to be kept down in order to make room for a greater number of people. The amount of land allotted to an individual provided a rough reckoning of his social status, though with time the size of grants tended to contract. A capitalist grantee in Chenab Colony could have more land than his peers allotted landed gentry grants a couple of decades later. Though rural landlords obtained much less total area than the landholding peasantry, this did not constitute any discrimination against them, but merely reflected the landholding structure of the Punjab as a whole. In aggregate, the upper strata of rural society absorbed a sizeable area of colony land, which represented an extensive involvement of this class in agricultural colonisation.

Both small and large landlords were allotted land in the canal colonies. The yeoman grants in Chenab Colony were intended for the smaller and middle-level landlords. An important socioeconomic group was tapped by these grants: men analogous to the "primary *zamindar*s" of Mughal times.[25] These were landholders who retained much influence at the local level, for they were resident among the rural population, and many belonged to the castes tapped for the peasant grants. This stratum could be relied upon by the state for help in maintaining political control and authority, for it provided official and semiofficial functionaries at the level of both single villages and groups of villages. Such considerations were kept in mind for the choice of these grantees: "Broadly speaking in deciding whether a man answered to the definition of a yeoman, Deputy Commissioners were to be guided by much the same principles as would determine the eligibility of a man for the post of lambardar or zaildar."[26]

---

owing to the provision of "private treaty" sales. This enabled them, along with ex-government officials, to purchase land by private agreement with the government, rather than through attendance at auctions, which was regarded as too demeaning for men of such status. See "Register of applications for purchase of land by private treaty on Lower Bari Doab Canal at full market value," BOR J/301/1261.

[25] S. Nurul Hasan, *Thoughts on Agrarian Relations in Mughal India* (New Delhi: People's Publishing House, 1973), ch. 3, pp. 30-40; and Hasan's article in R. E. Frykenberg (ed.), *Land Control and Social Structure in Indian History* (Madison: Wisconsin University Press, 1969).

[26] *PCM*, p. 116. Another description was: "Yeoman grantees comprised those who, without attaining to the ranks of the richer gentry, were still well above the ordinary peasant class. They were recruited from good *zamindari* families with considerable ancestral holdings in the old districts, a class rich in credit and resource and including men of undoubted intelligence

While this social group was important to the state for its collaborative role, it also possessed a great potential for instability if it decided to exercise opposition to the ruling authority. Land grants in the canal colonies were as effective a measure as any for ensuring that the prospects of loyalty would be enhanced, and those of dissension weakened. During the twentieth century, intermediary groups in several provinces moved into opposition to British rule. Two of many such examples were the *pattidars* of Gujrat and the Nayars of Kerala.[27] Such disaffection did not emerge in the Punjab: presumably the maladjustments and unfulfilled ambitions that could foster it were absent. Canal colonisation enabled influential rural elements to seek new vitality within the agricultural arena, and this either removed or counteracted the causes of discontent that existed elsewhere.

The political implications of the grants to yeomen applied with equal force to the other categories of grants allotted to the landlords of the Punjab. The yeoman horse-breeding grants in Jhelum Colony were allotted to members of families prominent in their local regions both for the extent of their landholdings and for their services to the administration. The men came from families that contributed *zaildar*s, *ilaqadar*s, *inamdar*s, extra-assistant commissioners, honorary magistrates, and divisional and provincial *darbari*s. In diverse ways, these families were tied into the functioning of imperialist rule, and the rewards for this proved in the Punjab to be considerable.

Similarly, among the capitalist grantees of Chenab Colony, those of landlord origins were selected not only because they promised to provide the capital required to develop the land (an essential condition for these grants), but also because they were men of influence in their home districts. It was no coincidence that the vernacular term officially used for capitalists was *rais* grantees—and *rais* actually means a man of high status rather than a capitalist, the term for which would be *sarmayadar*. However, the terms *sarmaya* or *sarmayadar* did not even appear in official glossaries or in standard reference works for revenue administration.[28] The British did not really intend to have on these grants a class of ''capitalist'' farmers, but

---

and enterprise.'' See *Chenab Colony SR* (1915), para. 7. For yeoman applications for land, see BOR J/301/382 A-F.

[27] Robin Jeffrey, *The Decline of Nayar Dominance* (Brighton: Sussex University Press, 1976); and David Hardiman, *Peasant Nationalists of Gujrat, Kheda District, 1917-1934* (Delhi: Oxford University Press, 1981). See also, for a discussion of the leadership roles of agrarian intermediaries, E. Stokes, *The Peasant and the Raj* (London: Cambridge University Press, 1978).

[28] This is true of J. M. Douie's *Punjab Settlement Manual* (4th ed., Lahore: Government Printing Press, 1930), of the *PCM*, and of H. H. Wilson's *Glossary of Judicial and Revenue Terms* (2nd ed., Delhi: Munshiram Manoharlal, 1968). The terms also did not appear in any of the glossaries of settlement reports and assessment reports consulted.

wished instead to use the land for allotment to landlords (whose ability to undertake progressive farming will be discussed presently). The expectations of the rulers from the capitalist allocation were defined as early as 1891:

> It supplies leaders for the new society. It gives opportunity to Government to reward its well deserving servants, and to encourage the more enterprising of the provincial gentry. It attracts strong men who are able to command considerable bodies of tenants.[29]

The capitalist grants, though they continued to have an admixture of non-landed elements, became primarily an outlet for landlords. By 1898 these priorities could be bluntly stated:

> we are agreed that no good purpose is served by establishing non-agriculturist capitalists, pure and simple, as large landlords. Successful bankers, contractors, shopkeepers, manufacturers, money-lenders, and even civil employees of Government, who have amassed capital during their service, have no claims to State consideration when State lands are being colonised. We think, in future, if Government decides to auction some land that will be opening enough for such men.[30]

Whereas the middling landlords had received sizeable areas as yeoman and capitalist grantees, it was not till Lower Bari Doab Colony that the landed elite of the Punjab benefitted from the canal colonies to a significant extent. Hitherto, members of the more notable rural families had received the odd individual grant, but in Lower Bari Doab Colony an area of 75,000 acres was reserved specifically for this class, under the name of landed gentry grants. The government felt that the opportunity should not be allowed to pass for extending the benefits of agricultural colonisation to a stratum so important to its interests. The concern of the British for the landed elite, and the political motives that underlay these grants, found the following expression in 1913:

> This class in comparison with others is declining in wealth and influence owing to various causes, such as the recurring partitions in each generation of ancestral lands and in some cases even of jagirs, the simultaneous rise of a prosperous middle class, and the growing wealth of the peasantry as a whole. But its members are still—and if properly handled should continue to be—an important political asset, and a great support to the district officer and to the administration generally in dealing with the rural classes. Little has been done for them in various colonisation

[29] RS to RS, GOI, 22 July 1891; in PRAP(I), July 1891, No. 19.
[30] Note by FC, 22 January 1898; in PRAP(I), April 1898, No. 7.

schemes compared with what has been done and what it is proposed to do for the peasantry, and the present scheme offers one of the few opportunities still left for assisting them and strengthening their position.[31]

The landed gentry grantees were selected from all five administrative divisions of the Punjab, but the distribution was an imbalanced one. The allocation for these grants by district and division shows that most of the grants were allotted to men from the western Punjab. Of the 2,300 rectangles distributed, 1,406 were allocated for districts that were included in Pakistan at the time of independence in 1947, and only 894 to the districts that fell to India.[32] These proportions reflected the greater incidence of larger landholdings in the western part of the province, smallholdings being more characteristic of the eastern part. The distribution of these grants was one indication of the greater strength of the landlords as a class in the Pakistani rather than the Indian part of the Punjab, and indeed in other parts of India.[33] As a result, they were able to impose their interests on the politics of Pakistan to a much greater extent than they did in India. Land grants in the canal colonies provided them with an asset of commercial importance, and this helped to preserve them from economic decline.

It is not possible to compile a complete or even a comprehensive list of the larger grantees. The government itself never undertook such a task, nor did it have a separate official establishment or record series dealing with the larger grants.[34] The histories of several individual families who ob-

[31] RS to RAS, GOI, 2 October 1913, Confidential; in BOR H/251/476 B, p. 209. Owing to shortage of land, the area actually allotted was 60,000 acres, but further land was found in the Renala extension and in other colonies. The landed gentry grants were five to fifteen rectangles in size, and personal residence was not required, because the administration needed the services of these men of influence in their home districts.

[32] The entire Rawalpindi and Multan divisions, and Lahore, Sialkot, and Gujranwala districts in Lahore Division were included in Pakistan at partition; and the remaining districts of the Punjab went to India. Of the 2,300 rectangles for landed gentry grants, 20 were allotted to the Bugti chief of Baluchistan. The remaining 2,280 rectangles were distributed between the five administrative divisions of the Punjab as follows: Ambala (250), Jullundur (396), Multan (422), Lahore (502), and Rawalpindi (710). For more detailed figures for these grants, see Imran Ali, "The Punjab Canal Colonies, 1885-1940": Table 3.1 gives the allocation by districts, and Appendix II lists the names of several individual recipients.

[33] There were, for instance, no land reforms in Pakistan along the lines of the *zamindari* abolition reforms that followed close upon independence in India, and subsequent efforts have been ineffective and half-hearted. See N. Sandaratne, "Landowners and Land Reform in Pakistan," *South Asian Review*, VII, 2 (1974), 123-36; and P. C. Joshi, "Land Reform and Agrarian Change in India and Pakistan since 1947; I-II," *Journal of Peasant Studies*, I, 2-3 (1974), 164-85 and 326-62, respectively.

[34] Imran Ali, "The Punjab Canal Colonies," Appendix II contains a list of names of larger grantees collected from various sources. A number of BOR files contain lists of applicants for such grants, providing information on caste origins, positions held, available capital, and

tained such grants are given in Griffin and Massy's *Chiefs of the Punjab*, and they reveal the extent to which these recipients of land cooperated with British rule. Aid to the district judicial and revenue administration, participation in local government, military service, and active work against any political agitations that occurred (the Khilafat and Akali movements were two examples) provided the background to these grants. The bulk of the landed gentry grants were allotted during and just after World War I, and the extent of their contribution to the war effort was a major consideration in the selection of these grantees. The number of recruits that a person brought forth, the number that he personally financed, and his contributions to the War Loan and other war funds all influenced his prospects of obtaining a land grant.

The state not only made over colony land to the larger estates of the Punjab, but it also came to their aid at times of adversity. Estates owned by families deemed to be of political importance were taken under the protection of the Court of Wards, in the event of their falling into debt or being badly managed, or for reasons such as family dissensions or the minority of the owner. The estates were then managed under the supervision of the relevant deputy commissioners, and were normally released from the Court of Wards only after the more outstanding problems had been resolved. The decline and at times the dissolution of these estates, stemming from ineptitude or economic adversity, was averted by the timely aid of the administration.[35] It is doubtful whether many of the large estates would have survived the pressures and vicissitudes of modern times had the state not interceded on their behalf.

This function assumed unique proportions during the 1930s. The economic depression led to heavy indebtedness among the larger estates, and threatened at a stroke to do away with many of them.[36] Civil suits instituted by the creditors, who mainly belonged to the Hindu commercial castes, would have led to the breakup of these estates through insolvency. Some properties were heavily indebted even before the depression, indicating that these large holdings were vulnerable to insolvency even under more stable

---

source districts for subtenants. For Chenab and Jhelum colonies, see BOR J/301: 650, 684, 802, and 909.

[35] Officials frankly acknowledged that certain estates would be faced with extinction unless brought under the Court of Wards. For example, FC to Commissioner, Multan, 1 July 1921; in "Management of estate of Walidad Khan Sial of Jhang District," BOR 601/1/26/63, p. 77.

[36] The drastic fall in rental incomes, resulting from reduced agricultural prices, seemed the primary cause of the sudden indebtedness of many large estates. A 1931 survey for canal colony land revealed the widespread inability of lessees and subtenants to continue rental payments at previous levels: "Rent for colony lands held by estates under Court of Wards," BOR 301/22/00/3.

economic conditions.[37] The affected estates were brought through the crisis by recourse to the Court of Wards. Some were contracted in size, but it appears that none suffered dissolution.

These estates were salvaged through a variety of measures on the part of the administration. Their management was improved; and the more excessive patterns of consumption of the owners were curtailed, many being placed on fixed allowances. Settlements of various types were arrived at with creditors: debts were written off through part payments, redemptions on loans were deferred and interest rates reduced, lower scales of instalment payments were negotiated, threats of civil suits were averted,[38] and certain lands of the estates were even leased to the creditors at favourable rates as a form of payment.[39] Where necessary, carefully selected parts of properties were sold off.[40] In cases where their affairs were in sound condition, further land was purchased, often in the canal colonies;[41] and other types of investment were made, such as loans to other estates or purchase of government bonds.[42] Many of the above transactions would not have been possible without official intercession: certainly the estate owners seemed to lack the requisite entrepreneurial ability to manage their affairs as judiciously as the administration did.

However, the criterion for such protection from the state remained the political importance of the family. In cases where this was seen to have

[37] For example, "Estate of Malik Sher Muhammad Khan, Jagirdar of Mitha Tiwana," BOR 601/1/19/13. The Leghari estate had a debt of over Rs 100,000 when taken under the Court of Wards in 1927: "Management of estate of Nawab Jamal Leghari, Tumandar, in Dera Ghazi Khan District," BOR 601/1/29/71.

[38] For examples of favourable loan adjustments with creditors, see "Management of estate of Syed Nasiruddin Shah etc. of Jahanian Shah, Shahpur District," BOR 601/1/29/93; and "Management of estate of Baba Hardit Singh Bedi of Montgomery under Court of Wards," BOR 601/1/24/155.

[39] The *chak* of Burhanpur in Lahore District was leased to creditors of the Faqir estate: "Management of property of Faqir Syed Najmuddin of Lahore," BOR 601/1/12/70.

[40] A particularly judicious and complex scheme of selective sales was arranged for the Vahali estate, which owned 3,300 acres in Chenab Colony alone: "Management of Vahali estate of Jhelum District," BOR 601/1/20/147. Similar measures were undertaken for two Bedi estates, of Gurbakhsh and Harbans Singh, BOR: 601/1/21/112 and 601/1/24/123.

[41] Between 1927 and 1931, thirty rectangles and several shop sites were purchased in Nili Bar Colony for the Kalabagh estate. This was under Court of Wards during the minority of its owner, Amir Muhammad Khan, the autocratic governor of West Pakistan in the 1960s: "Management of estate of late Nawab Ata Muhammad Khan of Kalabagh, Mianwali District," BOR 601/1/23/24.

[42] Colony land and government bonds were purchased and loans extended to other estates for two minors: Syed Abid Hussain (1915-1936), "Management of Shah Jiwana Court of Wards estate, Jhang District," BOR 601/1/26/44; and Amir Abdullah Khan (1926-1934), "Management of estate of late Hayatullah Khan of Tarkhanwala, Shahpur District," BOR 601/1/19/55.

declined, or proved to be inadequate, the estates were not taken under the Court of Wards, even when the affected families were faced with serious economic problems.[43] Through such methods of succour, and a selectiveness born of political pragmatism, British imperialism aided the continuation of the agrarian-based power of the landed elite. The lesson was not lost on this class, and the following remarks of one of its members in 1932 may well have expressed a collective appreciation:

> We are all very grateful to you for bringing our entire property under the management of the Court of Wards and hope that under the fine supervision of our benign Government, the whole property will remain intact, and make gradual progress.[44]

Nowhere was the consolidation of elite groups through colony land more apparent than in the *doab*s in which the canal colonies were situated. Much strain was placed on the landowning groups of these areas by the advent of canal irrigation, which attracted away manpower and physically disrupted the older irrigation systems. Rather than allow the existing social stratification to be subverted by new economic forces, the government endeavoured to maintain the position of the indigenous elite. In the case of the Chenab riverain, efforts were not only made through the Court of Wards to secure the viability of the more eminent families but the landlords of the riverain tracts were also allotted grants in Chenab Colony as compensation for any disruption they might have suffered from the perennial canals.[45]

Such compensatory measures were also adopted for other colonies. In the Jech Doab during the second half of the nineteenth century, state lands had been leased to several individuals in both small and large plots, many for services to the administration or as a mark of favour.[46] Land from these leased areas, including the larger holdings known as the "Shahpur long leases," came under irrigation from the Lower Jhelum Canal in 1902. After investigations in each case, the lessees were allotted canal-irrigated land roughly equivalent to the area of their leaseholds that they had brought under cultivation.[47] A number of lessees were also allowed to purchase

[43] The heavily indebted Hajipur estate was released from Court of Wards in 1934, when the deputy commissioner of Dera Ghazi Khan District reported that the owners had lost considerable influence and importance since their conversion to Shiaism: "Management of estate of Shahnawaz Khan Serai of Hajipur, Dera Ghazi Khan District," BOR 601/1/29/53.

[44] Kanwar Dhanwant Singh Bedi to FC, 4 July 1932; in BOR 601/1/21/112 A, pp. 78-79.

[45] See, for example, for the leading families of the Sial tribe, BOR: 601/1/26/63, 601/1/26/108, 601/1/26/119, and 601/1/26/138.

[46] For information see "Reports of long leases of Government Waste Lands in Shahpur District," BOR J/301/486; and PRAP(G): August 1894, Nos. 15-18; April 1896, Nos. 22-49; November 1897, Nos. 40-78; March 1900, Nos. 35-42, and October 1900, Nos. 16-25.

[47] See "Grants of land on Jhelum Canal to holders of leases in Shahpur District," BOR J/

proprietary rights on the rates fixed in the original leases. These terms were originally intended for barren land, with purchase prices pitched at Rs 2-5 per acre. They proved to be highly concessionary under the changed conditions. Thus the Shahpur lessees reaped a windfall, obtaining perennially irrigated land at a pittance. Since many of the lessees were men of influence in the western Punjab (some belonged to the Nun-Tiwana clan, of whom more presently), the state was not averse to alienating resources to them.[48]

In other areas, too, leaseholds proved profitable to incumbents. In Lower Bari Doab Colony old leases of state land, called *tahud khahi*, were converted to colony grants on the basis of the amount of land brought under cultivation.[49] Similar measures were adopted in Nili Bar Colony, where 40,000 acres were reserved for the *tahud khahi* lessees.[50] In addition, local notables were allotted grants for several other purposes, and were given temporary cultivation leases on canal-irrigated land, often at concessionary rates.[51] At times this occurred in connivance with the subordinate bureaucracy, without the knowledge of British officials—a practice that was unearthed on some scale in the Chenab Colony extensions in the 1930s.

It was in the treatment of the "private canals" of Shahpur District that British efforts to preserve the existing class structure were most visible. These canals were inundation channels situated in the riverain tract of the Jhelum River, and were owned and managed by individuals on land leased to them by the government from 1860 onwards.[52] At the termination of the

---

301/728; and PRAP(I): June 1902, Nos. 29-36; September 1902, Nos. 43-48; May 1903, Nos. 9-13; October 1903, Nos. 8-12; April 1905, Nos. 3-9; and June 1907, Nos. 1-4.

[48] The Nun-Tiwana clan obtained seven large leaseholds, which they later purchased and irrigated with private canals. The total area of the leaseholds was approximately 21,350 acres, of which the largest was Kalra at 9,240 acres, owned by Umar Hayat Tiwana. See DC, Shahpur, to Commissioner, Rawalpindi, 31 March 1894; in BOR J/301/728, pp. 18-38.

[49] See "Montgomery Tahsil—List of Government lands held on farm or leased wells," BOR J/301/437; "Disposal of leases in Lower Bari Doab Canal area," BOR J/301/1112; and PRAP(G): May 1915, Nos. 7-26; and November 1915, Nos. 18-26.

[50] For names and holdings of these lessees, see untitled BOR 301/4/C9/8. Conversion to colony grants was normally at 150 percent of area developed or cultivated, after official investigation of each leasehold. In the race for land, irregularities were rife, as with "a well within the depths of the jungle, bound under the terms of the lease to be kept in use, but for years unused and the haunt of several families of pigeons, has been cleared and set to work a few hours before the arrival of the inspecting officer, to whose gullibility there is evidently supposed to be no limit." See *PCR*, 1926, p. 80.

[51] Two examples, for help in army recruitment and administration, were the forty rectangles allotted in Lower Bari Doab Colony to Farid Khan, the influential *zaildar* of Khanewal; and twenty-two squares in Upper and Lower Jhelum colonies to Chaudhry Fazal Ali, head of the Gujar tribe of Gujrat. See their files, BOR: J/301/1365 and 301/21/27/71. For temporary cultivation leases made to several eminent individuals in the Chenab Colony extensions of Khika and Buralla, see BOR: 301/11/25/107 and 301/11/25/137.

[52] The first private canal on state-leased land was constructed around 1863 by Sahib Khan Tiwana, the great-grandfather of Khizr Tiwana, the last premier of the Punjab under British

leases, these men were allowed to purchase the leased areas, as well as continue with water management, so that they came to enjoy ownership of both land and water. They were also allowed to sell water from their canals to other cultivators, a concession that gave them much economic and political power, for they became "waterlords" in addition to being landlords. All except one of the eight private canals in Shahpur District were owned by members of the kindred Nun and Tiwana families.[53] These two families had rendered loyal services to the British from the time of the struggle of 1857. They continued to do so up to the final days of British rule in India, when Khizr Hayat Khan Tiwana, as premier of the Punjab, went against the tide of Muslim nationalist sentiment by continuing to lead a pro-British, anti-Muslim League provincial government. The Nun and Tiwana families received large amounts of land in the canal colonies, and became during the period of British rule a significant landholding force in the northwestern Punjab.[54]

For Shahpur District from the early 1900s, the Irrigation Department had drawn up plans to substitute irrigation from these seasonal private canals with perennial irrigation from the Lower Jhelum Canal.[55] This would have entailed the construction of a new canal branch, to be known as the Shahpur Branch, a project that was welcomed by the cultivators of the riverain both because of the more stable and efficient irrigation system and the relief from overlordship that it promised. The private canal owners were opposed to the new branch, for it would have put an end to their special water rights.[56] The government was prepared to compensate them for losses of capital and income, but despite several years of negotiations no agreement could be

---

rule. With the success of Sahib Khan's venture, other Nun and Tiwana notables took out leases: "As a fact after 1863 all the local world knew what an El Dorado lay in a block of land irrigible by canal from the left bank of the Jhelum": Note by Commissioner, Rawalpindi, 5 April 1894; in BOR J/301/486, pp. 17-18.

[53] The eighth canal was owned by the Pathan family of Isa Khel, for whom see Griffin and Massy, *Chiefs of the Punjab*, Vol. II, pp. 341-48; and "Management of estate of M. Nawaz Khan of Isa Khel, Mianwali District," BOR 601/1/23/28. For the early history and records, 1862-1896, of these canals, see "Shahpur Canals—Private and Provincial," BOR H/251/5.

[54] See Griffin and Massy, *Chiefs of the Punjab*, Vol. II, pp. 191-210 and 217-35 for the Nun-Tiwana family history. They received a number of landed gentry, stud farm, and other colony grants, apart from the extensive leaseholds acquired at concessionary rates. In just one branch of the family, Umar Hayat, Khizr's father, left at his death a landed estate of some 24,500 acres, as well as valuable urban property in ten different towns, and private ownership of two canals. See "Kalra Impartible Estate Bill," BOR 613/6/19/3.

[55] The state was empowered to acquire privately owned canals under the Punjab Minor Canals Act (III of 1905): see Report of Select Committee, extracts from Punjab Legislative Council Proceedings, and text of bill; in PRAP(I), April 1905, Nos. 10-16.

[56] For information on the long and involved negotiations, correspondence, and investigations on the acquisition of the private canals and their proposed substitution by the Shahpur Branch, see BOR H/251/266, 251/32/19/2, 251/32/19/3, and 251/35/19/10.

reached over the amount of compensation to be paid, and the administration was unprepared to make any arbitrary resumptions.

With the outbreak of World War I, the services of the Nuns and Tiwanas proved to be of special value, for the supply of recruits and other contributions to the war effort. In repayment for this loyalty, the canal owners received an assurance from the lieutenant-governor in 1916 that they would not be deprived of their private canals, and this undertaking was reconfirmed in 1923 and 1930. The scheme for the construction of the Shahpur Branch was delayed and ultimately dropped, and the rights and wrongs of private ownership of canals in Shahpur District were not questioned thereafter. In order to placate politically loyal and important groups, the state was willing to tolerate an outmoded irrigation system and the semi-feudal social relations that accompanied it. The Nuns and Tiwanas certainly provided the loyal services that were expected of them, but they saw to it that the canal colonies would not threaten their vested interests, and would be exploited instead to strengthen their economic position.

Whereas the Nuns and Tiwanas exercised social authority in the northwestern parts of the canal colonies, there appeared diagonally opposite them, in the southeastern region, an equally influential family of landholders, the Daultanas. This family too had possession of a private canal, the Daulatwah, which irrigated lands leased from the state and then purchased at preferential rates. The channel was amalgamated into the Sutlej Valley Project in the mid-1920s, and as compensation for their loss of water rights the Daultanas received handsome compensation in the form of further grants of canal colony land.[57] The Daultanas figured as a major force in Punjab politics both under the British and after 1947. Indeed, Muslim landlord politics, as represented by the Punjab National Unionist party, was split by the factional struggle between the Daultanas and Nun-Tiwanas.

Another important family in politics was that of the Mamdots from Ferozepur District: they owned the largest private landed estate in the Punjab. They purchased seventy-six rectangles in Montgomery and twenty-two squares in Lyallpur, a total area of 2,500 acres. The Mamdots also irrigated their proprietary lands in Ferozepur, and sold water to other cultivators from their own private canals.[58] Waterlordship gave to these families an eminence even greater than that obtained from mere landlordship.

The larger grantees in the canal colonies had little to contribute to agricultural development. It was generally found that they were not self-cultivators, nor did most of them manage their grants directly and farm through

[57] For information on the Daultana landholdings in Multan District, see PRAP(G): June 1895, Nos. 42-53; and April 1896, Nos. 67-70. See also BOR: 301/4/27/27, 301/4/C9/33, and 601/1/27/165.

[58] For the Mamdot family history, see Griffin and Massy, *Chiefs of the Punjab*, Vol. I, pp. 229-33.

agricultural labourers. They most commonly rented their lands to subtenants, normally on half *batai* rates (half the produce in kind as rent). In this way they failed to act as agricultural capitalists, for they neither brought to the land entrepreneurial ability nor the investment of capital. They functioned, instead, in the noncapitalist economic role of rentiers, and were by and large parasitical absentee landlords. They could hardly be compared to the improving farmers of England, whose contribution had been so important for the agricultural revolution in that country during the eighteenth and nineteenth centuries. Initially, in the case of the capitalist grants of Chenab Colony, officials had hoped that the land would be properly developed through the investment of capital and entrepreneurial skills. Such expectations were quickly belied, for the grantees looked upon colony land as little more than a source of unearned income from rent. Thereafter, the only motive for making grants to landlords remained the political one, and this was done in order to ensure the stability of British rule in the Punjab.

Apart from the more specific failures of the landlord grantees in becoming improving farmers, their consolidation in the canal colonies had other adverse economic and political consequences. The class structure and social relations between the different classes needed to be changed rather than rigidified in order to achieve meaningful development. Growth that occurred within the confines of a social formation representative of a backward economy, as indeed the Punjab was in relation to the industrial economies, could have the involuting effect of leading to further stagnation. It was the misfortune of the Punjab that the social basis of agricultural colonisation assumed such a shape, but this was a cost that had to be paid in deference to the interests of those who dominated this process.

In bolstering landlordism through additional economic resources, the British helped to perpetuate a stratum that was receding in importance in other parts of South Asia during the twentieth century. This partnership found political expression in the Punjab National Unionist party, which continued to dominate the provincial legislature till the final months of British rule. Its repercussions continued to affect the political economy of the region after 1947, for the landlords remained a strong force in Pakistan. They have to date succeeded in preventing the implementation of an effective land reform. They have also helped to abort the functioning of a democratic political system, for fear that it might erode their privileged position. Moreover, they have found in military rule a useful substitute for the protective rulership provided by the British prior to 1947.

The Bourgeoisie

Apart from the landowning peasantry and gentry, there was a third class of people that obtained land in the canal colonies. These men were not agriculturists, but took up administrative service, or were traders, contractors, or other entrepreneurs. Some even came from the liberal professions, such as lawyers and doctors. They could be regarded as urban dwellers, though in a predominantly agrarian economy no clear dichotomy exists between town and country. They did not belong to the urban working class, a stratum that was not in the reckoning for colony land in the Punjab. In caste terms, these people formed a distinguishable group, for by and large they belonged, according to the classification imposed by the Land Alienation Act of 1900, to the "nonagricultural castes." Coming from the elite ranks of nonagriculturists, they belonged to such castes as Khatris, Aroras, Khojas, Banias, and Shaikhs. In some districts these castes held land, and hence had an "agricultural" status, while in others they were truly "nonagricultural." Caste derivation cannot, therefore, be upheld too rigidly for the identification of this class, though it can provide a useful frame of reference. This was primarily an occupational rather than a caste category, and the term "bourgeoisie" is the most appropriate for this section of the population. In the Punjab it had two major components: the "professional," which included government servants, and the "commercial," which comprised both manufacturing and nonmanufacturing entrepreneurs, and was largely non-Muslim in composition.

The professional bourgeoisie obtained colony land mostly in the form of land grants to retired public servants. Provision was made in most colonisation projects for such grants, which went only to Punjabis; the British officials never partook in such allotments. In Chunian Colony, most of the civil grantees were retired officials, selected from three districts in proximity to the colony: Lahore, Amritsar, and Gurdaspur.[59] In Chenab Colony, allotment to retired officials was made from the capitalist category, which they shared with landlords and entrepreneurs. In Jhelum Colony, officials again received the civil grants; though only about half of the 44,000 acres allocated could be allotted there owing to shortage of land, the rest being transferred to the Chenab Colony extensions.[60] In Lower Bari Doab Colony, while no specific allocation was made for government officials, they did obtain reward grants for recruitment and other services related to World War I. They were also given preferential treatment for purchase of land reserved for auctions. Known as sale by "private treaty," this allowed them to buy land direct from the government without having to endure the

[59] See "Civil grants of land in Chunian Colony," BOR J/301/794; and "Statement . . . of *nazarana*-paying tenants in Chunian Colony," in PRAP(I), March 1917, No. 247.

[60] See "Allotment of land on Jhelum Canal to Heads of Departments," BOR J/301/701; "Grants of land on Jhelum Canal to Public Works Department," BOR J/301/764; and for grants to officials of the North-West Frontier Province who also participated in this allotment, BOR J/301/724.

tribulations of bidding at auctions. In Nili Bar Colony, a further 20,000 acres were earmarked for grants to ex-officials.[61]

Thus a wide range of administrative services had an opportunity to reward their members with the valuable resource of colony land. Allocations were made to most government departments, and those retiring or retired officials were selected whose services were regarded as the most loyal and deserving. This remained the foremost consideration in the choice of a grantee. The selection was left to the head of the candidate's department, rather than to officials familiar with colonisation, who could have placed more emphasis on his suitability as a colonist.

Jhelum Colony provided an example of the breakdown of grants by provincial departments. The 1,790 squares allocated were divided among 25 departments. The Financial Commissioners' office received 180 squares, and the Punjab Government Secretariat discretion to dispose of 260 squares. Of the Divisional Commissioners' offices, those of Ambala, Jullundur, and Lahore received 100 squares each, that of Multan 70 and of Rawalpindi 200. The Police Department received 180, the Public Works Department 80, and the High Court 50. A non-Punjabi allocation was also made of 200 squares for the Chief Commissioner, North-West Frontier Province. The remainder was distributed in shares of 30 squares or less to the departments of the Accountant General, Agriculture, Civil Hospitals, Excise-Income Tax, Forests, Legal Remembrancer, Meteorology (GOI), North-Western Railways, Postmaster General, Prisons, Public Instructions, Sanitary Commissioner, and Settlement Commissioner.[62]

In addition to such official allocations, members of the native bureaucracy also gained hold of colony land through nefarious means. These subordinates misused their position in the colony administration to appropriate land, either in their own names or in those of near relatives. The extent of this form of illegal gratification will never be known, but it remained an open secret with British officials. The practice was only one of several forms of corruption endemic in the native bureaucracy, a problem that will be addressed in a later chapter. The British had not the administrative resources to eradicate these habits, nor did they impose, for reasons presumably of political convenience, stiff penalties on those exposed. In Lower Bari Doab Colony, where it was admitted that a large number of officials were involved in obtaining land illegally, the government merely required the officials in the cases brought to light to retire from service or relinquish

[61] See "Colonies—Reward grants—Allotment of land to officials in Lower Bari Doab Colony," BOR 301/3/24/1 A-H. See also "Nili Bar Colony—Grants of land to serving and retired civil officials—Policy," BOR 301/9/C9/1(d); and "Grants of land in Nili Bar Colony to serving and retired civil officials," BOR 301/9/C9/170.

[62] See BOR J/301/701, p. 153.

their grants. In that colony alone, it was officially conceded that over
10,000 acres had passed to native officials illegally, and in reality the area
must have been considerably more.[63] A truer measure was the caution made
by a senior official in 1924 against a repetition of the same process in the
forthcoming Nili Bar Colony:

> Barring the Colonisation Officer himself, there does not appear to have
> been a single man connected with the Montgomery Colony who had not
> obtained a grant, and I would strongly protest against such men having
> any connection whatever with the new colony where they are likely to
> repeat the old game.[64]

The amount of land obtained by the professional class was not significant
compared to the area allotted to the landholding peasantry, and not as great
as that allotted to landlords. Only a minority of professional people in the
Punjab actually obtained land, while in any colonisation project only a fraction of allotable area was reserved for such people. Nevertheless, they had
little cause to be dissatisfied, for they did obtain a share in the new agricultural resources, even though they came from nonagricultural occupations,
and their right to do so was clearly recognised by the state. Not only were
the services of the Punjabi bureaucracy appreciated and duly rewarded, but
its misdemeanours were condoned. No effective measures were taken to
curb corruption, for that might have bred discontent among this class.

The professional bourgeoisie also benefitted from the increased employment opportunities brought about by economic expansion.[65] In order to administer the canal colonies, an enlargement was required in various government departments such as public works, irrigation, revenue, agriculture,
and veterinary services. Thus at many levels this class was being productively absorbed in the economy. There seemed to be little economic basis
for any resentment it might have had against British rule. Certainly the
expanded employment opportunities that it enjoyed were not available to
any such degree to its counterparts in other provinces.

Land grants to the professional class could have had little value for agricultural development: this type of allotment was motivated instead by political considerations. The retired officials who obtained land made very

[63] Answer to Question No. 3033 (1926); in "Legislative Council Questions and Resolutions
regarding grants of land," BOR 301/18/00/1 F, pp. 45-46.

[64] Commissioner, Multan, to FC(D), 15 November 1924; in BOR 301/3/24/1 C, p. 159.
This file, which runs into eight parts, contains over 2,000 pages of correspondence relating to
officials who had acquired land illegally.

[65] This was true, for instance, of Prakash Tandon's father, who served in the canal colonies
as an official of the Irrigation Department: P. Tandon, *Punjabi Century* (Berkeley and Los
Angeles: University of California Press, 1968).

unsuitable colonists. Well past the prime of their lives, they had been used to the relative comfort and security of a bureaucratic career, and were little equipped to tackle the rigours and adversities of a pioneering life. At an age when they might have been expected to retire quietly to suburban obscurity, they were called upon to break virgin ground and develop agricultural skills in a remote and inhospitable environment. Since most came from nonagricultural backgrounds, they had little or no experience of practical agriculture, and lacked the service ties with labouring "menials" that were usually necessary for successful farming.

As it transpired, the great majority of these men were not equal to the task. They either farmed through paid servants or agents, or more usually let out their land to subtenants. The wisdom of the state in choosing this manner of rewarding its servants may be questioned, for they either sold off their grants or allowed them to pass into subtenancies and became absentee rentiers. The manner in which they were characterised in 1904 by a colonisation officer could not have been entirely unfair:

> It is clear that the majority have every intention of evading the residential condition as far as possible, and even they themselves must recognise that they are an unwelcome addition to the Colony. . . . One by one they appear, full of forlorn memories of Anarkali or the Chandni Chowk, and beg plaintively for land near a Railway Station. The best land in the Colony for them is that from which they can get away soonest.[66]

As with compensatory grants for agrarian landholders, the government utilised colony land to try and dissipate any discontent among professionals arising from economic dislocations. An example of this lay in the land grants allotted to unemployed graduates during the 1930s. With the economic depression, opportunities for employment deteriorated. Faced with revenue losses from remissions necessitated by low agricultural prices, the government curtailed administrative recruitment, and even had to implement retrenchment in certain services. To counteract the effects of a threatened oversupply of educated men, it undertook the experiment of allotting grants to graduates of Punjab University and to retrenched officials of the Agricultural Department.[67] Between 1932 and 1937, six villages in four colonies were allotted to such men, in units of two squares each. In addition, a number of graduates from the Agricultural College, Lyallpur, were

---

[66] *PCR*, 1904, p. 20. Anarkali and Chandni Chowk are attractive shopping areas in Lahore and Delhi, respectively.

[67] See "Grant of land to retrenched Agricultural Assistants in canal colonies," BOR 301/3/00/285; "Colonies—Grants of land to graduates in," BOR 301/29/00/1; and "Colonies—Literate grantees," BOR 301/29/00/38.

scattered in pairs in colony villages, in the hope that they would influence cultivators to adopt more scientific methods of farming.[68]

The grants to graduates were not significant in scale, but they did divert a number of men from seeking employment in a tight market for jobs.[69] British officials expressed the hope that such grants might herald a move to the land by educated men. If nationalist opposition to imperialism was to come from the indigenous bourgeoisie, then these grants no doubt symbol- ised British hopes that in the Punjab rural expansion would constrain the size and strength of an unwanted class.

Like its professional counterpart, the commercial bourgeoisie also ben- efitted from the canal colonies in various ways. It was never excluded from access to colony land, though in the earlier colonies the opportunities for this were limited. Men of means could obtain capitalist grants in Chenab Colony, and partake in the occasional auctions that were held. The auc- tioned area greatly increased in extent with Lower Bari Doab and Nili Bar colonies, providing more openings for nonagriculturists. Figures for auc- tion sales in Nili Bar Colony show that nonagriculturists bought substantial amounts of land. Their share of the land purchased was especially high after the depression of the 1930s, indicating that they suffered less from the crisis than agriculturists.

Auctions were also held of residential and shop sites in the market towns of the canal colonies, and these were usually purchased by entrepreneurs for purposes of investment and rental income.[70] The increasing population of colony towns, and the growth of commercial activity, also brought greater values in urban property. In time the income generated from urban investments was important enough to attract state extraction. By the late 1920s separate assessment reports were being framed for colony towns, through which different usages for urban property were identified and taxed. Thus there were sites for houses, shops, godowns, and factories, all taxed down to the minute unit of the *marla*, or almost half of one percent of an acre.

Agricultural expansion created new opportunities for entrepreneurial ac- tivity. There occurred a great increase in trade, for surplus agricultural pro- duce was exported overseas and to other parts of the country. Market

[68] See "Grant of land on temporary cultivation terms to successful candidates of Punjab Agricultural College, Lyallpur," BOR 301/11/24/164; and PRAP(R), December 1927, Nos. 12-18.

[69] For the progress of these grants during the 1930s, see "Colonies—Grants of land to graduates—Reports on progress of scheme," BOR 301/29/00/8; and *PCR*: 1933, p. 8; 1935, p. 6; 1936, pp. 1-3; 1939, pp. 4-5; and 1940, p. 4.

[70] Reports on auction of urban sites in Chenab Colony appear in PRAP(G), 1895-96; and reports on conditions in colony towns continued over the years in the annual *PCRs*.

towns, situated at convenient distances along railway lines or on main
roads, provided collection and distribution points for these commodities.
Whether the agriculturist sold the produce in the village to the itinerant
trader or marketed it in the *mandi* to the *arthi*, it had to pass through the
hands of the trading class, which derived its own profits from these transactions. The conviction that it is the middlemen who really profit from agriculture is to this day a pervasive one in the Punjab, and it is no doubt
grounded in the years of adverse treatment that the agriculturist has received at the hands of the merchant. Many names crop up in records of
firms of traders, such as, for Chenab Colony, Ganpat Lal-Diwan Chand
and Trikha Ram-Mutasaddi Ram in Lyallpur, Bali Ram-Balwant Ram and
Honde Ram-Tandoo Ram in Gojra, and Thakur Das-Gharu Mal in Toba
Tek Singh.[71] These traders, belonging to the Hindu mercantile castes, continued their hereditary occupations in the canal colonies. Economic growth
was not to lead to any major transition in social roles: caste delineations
accommodated themselves thoroughly to changing conditions.

Production for the market also created a great demand for credit facilities, and commercial and trading groups came to fulfil an important moneylending function. This role had traditionally invited the hostility of British
officials, for it was seen to have led to heavy indebtedness among cultivators. Malcolm Darling's classic work, *The Punjab Peasant in Prosperity
and Debt*, though it stressed the seemingly pernicious role of the moneylender, also brought out the importance of credit as a source of capital in
Punjabi agriculture. Not only the peasantry but even the largest landowners
became heavily indebted to commercial groups, especially during the
1930s when returns from agricultural rents were drastically reduced. The
credit role of the entrepreneurial class was another manifestation of the
strength it derived from agricultural growth in the Punjab.

There were, on the one hand, the large creditors, with whom families of
the rural gentry had incurred substantial debts. To give but a few examples,
among the debts of the Shah Jiwana estate of Jhang District were Rs 12,166
owed to Tara Chand-Mehndi Ratta and Rs 10,321 to Mansa Ram-Ram
Chand. A member of the Faqir family of Lahore District owed Rs 27,490
to Lala Ramji Das and Rs 22,729 to Shib Das-Ram Nath. Gurbakhsh Singh
Bedi of Montgomery owed Rs 19,244 to Karm Chand and Rs 41,000 to
Ram Rakha Mal; while the Jahanian Shah estate of Shahpur was indebted
to Narsing Das for Rs 14,737 and Parakh Diyal-Lakhmi Chand for Rs
24,400.[72] At a more modest level, market town moneylenders, and those

[71] PRAP(R), January 1925, Nos. 84-106.
[72] See the following Court of Wards records in BOR: 601/1/26/44, 601/1/12/70, 601/1/21/
112, and 601/1/29/93.

based in villages, had extended to agriculturists great amounts of credit by the 1940s. This heavy indebtedness to Hindu moneylenders became one of the major mainsprings of Muslim communal nationalism, for these debts could be revoked if the creditors were evicted, as they eventually were, from the western Punjab.

Another sphere of enterprise for the commercial bourgeoisie lay in the processing and semi-manufacturing plants that were established in the canal colonies. Ginning factories for cotton and flour mills for wheat were the most common type of plants, and these were owned predominantly by members of Hindu and Sikh commercial groups.[73] In the larger canal colony towns, sites of eight to ten acres were set apart and sold to entrepreneurs for the establishment of such factories. A few examples were the cotton ginning and pressing factories belonging in Okara to Kirpa Ram-Brij Lal, in Chuharkana to Bhagwan Singh, in Dipalpur to Harcharan Das Puri, in Mian Channu to Ujjal Singh, in Sargodha to Kartar Singh, and in Lyallpur to Dhanpat Mal-Diwan Chand.[74] Muslim ownership seems to have failed to emerge among such concerns, and there was little evidence of landlords establishing industrial works. The entrepreneurial sections of the Punjabi bourgeoisie, therefore, very largely monopolised the commercial opportunities opened up by the canal colonies. The factory owners could be seen as proto-industrial entrepreneurs; but despite such beginnings, the absence of full-blown industrial plants was yet another instance of the retention of the agrarian nature of Punjabi society under British rule. The cotton textile industry of western Punjab emerged only after 1947, before which this region remained primarily a supplier of raw agricultural produce.

On economic grounds, there was little reason for the Punjabi bourgeoisie to be alienated from British rule. Though it might have entertained nationalist pretensions, and at times expressed resentment against the British in verbal terms, the bourgeoisie in the Punjab did not resort to active opposition against imperialism. Proof of this lay in the ineffectiveness of nationalist organisation, as shown by the results of the elections of 1937, in which pro-British agrarian landlords swept to power. Such was the weakness of dissent that even in the 1940s there was not a single nationalist politician of all-India stature from the Punjab.[75] The landowning classes did obtain

[73] See "Establishment of cotton factories on Lower Bari Doab Canal," BOR J/301/1337 A-G; and PRAP(G), October 1919, Nos. 111-17.

[74] PRAP(R), January 1925, Nos. 84-106.

[75] Lala Lajpat Rai may be singled out as a prominent politician from the Punjab, but he was effective only before 1910, in the early stages of nationalism. This begs the question of why the Punjab did not produce a nationalist leader of eminence as South Asia moved closer to independence. Perhaps one outcome of agricultural colonisation was that a strong regional

far more resources than the bourgeoisie, and the retardation of nationalism could be ascribed to this factor. Nevertheless, the economic gains of the bourgeoisie were in themselves considerable, and were sufficient to prevent any deep dissatisfaction with British rule. The acquisition of resources averted tensions within this class, a situation that its compatriots in other provinces were unable to avoid (two examples being the Muslim service elite in the United Provinces and the *bhadralok* of Bengal).[76]

Here again, political adjustments advantageous for imperialism might have been in conflict with longer-term economic needs. The bourgeoisie in the Punjab, through its experience in the canal colonies, became closely tied to the agrarian structure. It could be hypothesised that the fruits of agrarian growth were too substantial to impel this stratum to diversify its economic activity. Did it become thereby less capable of spearheading a capitalist revolution, which could have initiated an industrialisation process? Certainly a "ruralisation" of the bourgeoisie occurred in the Punjab; and this, along with the strengthening of the landowning classes, furthered the entrenchment of the existing social structure that became the anomalous consequence of agricultural colonisation. Yet the formative phases of a bourgeois ethos were also clearly visible in the canal colonies. The stimulus depended essentially on non-Muslim elements, and it withered when they had to depart for India in 1947. This retarded further the historical challenge to established society by a class that could have brought in new notions of man and work.

The Rural Poor

In the canal colonies, landholding status and commercial benefits were confined to the classes discussed above: the landed peasantry and gentry, and the bourgeoisie. The landless rural population of the Punjab did not receive land grants, nor did it possess the resources to purchase land at the competitive prices bid at auctions. With each colony, the government decided against allotments to this class, with one exception that will be discussed presently. Landless workers, whether agricultural labourers, subtenants, or caste servitors, did migrate to the canal colonies to meet the new demands for labour. But they still fulfilled roles similar to ones they had been confined to in their home villages. With the availability of new lands, many took on subtenancies where they had previously been simple labourers. A favourable land/labour ratio also promised improved wages for

---

base, on which the credibility of many nationalist leaders depended, was not forthcoming in the Punjab.

[76] Francis Robinson, *Separatism amongst Indian Muslims* (London: Cambridge University Press, 1974); and John Broomfield, *Elite Conflict in a Plural Society* (Berkeley and Los Angeles: University of California Press, 1968).

them, and some relief from the harsher forms of exploitation they might have previously endured. In status, however, they were still *kamins* or "menials," the term officially used for them. They remained as the lowest stratum of Punjabi society. Though vital to the economy owing to their labour power, they were looked down upon by both the "agricultural" castes and the British rulers.

Despite the new agrarian environment of the canal colonies, traditional roles were generally preserved. The potency of caste values worked in combination with state policy in maintaining major socioeconomic continuities and in compromising prospects of mobility. In contrast to the careful selection by officials of the grantees of land, a laissez-faire attitude prevailed toward the intake of village "menials." These groups often moved into colony villages with the grantees from their home districts, thus continuing older *sepidari* relationships. Others formed new associations, the determining factor being labour demand and supply. Beyond allocating some residential space for the purpose, the state did not become directly involved in the intake of the "menials." These matters were kept for the social classes concerned to work out. Here again state intervention remained confined to dealings with upper social layers. Social relations were consequently left relatively undisturbed by state policy. The recreation of hierarchical caste patterns was strongly in evidence in colony villages, as was illustrated in two village studies conducted by the Punjab Board of Economic Inquiry in the late 1920s.

The first study was of a village called Kala Gaddi Thamman in Chenab Colony.[77] Land there had originally been allotted as peasant grants to Sikh Jats from Gurdaspur District. Thirty years later, these Jats continued in their dominant position as self-cultivating owners of land, while the other castes in the village provided labour and artisanal and petty commercial services. Among members of the nonagricultural castes there was some diversification in occupational activity, including subtenancy. But most stayed within their hereditary roles, and none had succeeded in acquiring land. The castes of barbers, carpenters, sweepers, weavers, and such remained the underclass of society, despite economic expansion.

In the second village surveyed, Abbaspur, in Lower Bari Doab Colony, a similar picture emerged of the dominance of the proprietary caste and the continued lowly status of nonagricultural groups.[78] The village land had

---

[77] Randhir Singh, *An Economic Survey of Kala Gaddi Thamman (Chak 73, G.B.), A Village in the Lyallpur District* (Punjab Village Survey No. 4, Punjab Board of Economic Inquiry, 1932), pp. 8-9.

[78] N. M. Khan, *An Economic Survey of Abbaspur (Chak No. 2/10L), A Village in the Montgomery District* (Publication No. 129, Punjab Board of Economic Inquiry, Reprint 1963), pp. 16-18.

been allotted in 1915 to Syed agriculturists from Jhelum District, and other castes had migrated into the village from different areas. The village was predominantly Muslim in composition, but this did nothing to alter its caste and hierarchical structure. The Syeds, who claimed honour through descent from the prophet Muhammad, enjoyed a sole proprietary status over land, and the service and labouring groups settled into the regimen of their traditionally servile roles. Most continued to perform the functions denoted by their caste nomenclatures, and any alterations in occupational patterns were confined to horizontal shifts. The caste system, based on birth-ascribed inequalities, was too entrenched to suffer any fundamental shocks from agricultural colonisation. Both identity and economic role continued to be circumscribed by it.

Physical representations of the hierarchical ordering of society were impressed upon the subaltern classes as comprehensively in the canal colonies as they had been in former habitations. In the layout of colony village sites (or *abadis*), the differences of rank were reinforced through the more spacious residential homesteads of the proprietors and their physical segregation from the meaner allotments made to their inferiors. Although such sites were free for the grantees of land, the others had to pay a ground rent for the privilege of living in colony villages. This exaction was levied for reasons bluntly asserted in a settlement report in 1915:

> Its object was to secure a return to Government from the vagrant hordes, who administered to the needs of the agricultural classes, shopkeepers, dealers, brokers, menials, artisans and the like—the flotsam and jetsam of the colony population. The right of Government to tax persons, who exploited the prosperity of the newly settled tracts for their private advantage, will hardly be disputed. Without some organised scheme of allotment, moreover, these persons would have swarmed promiscuously round every *abadi*, reproducing the squalor and congestion of the old homes, which it was the ambition of the Colony officers to avoid.[79]

The fact that the rural underclass did not experience social and economic mobility stemmed from its exclusion from the distribution of land. To complement their disadvantageous socioeconomic position, the landless poor were also deprived of political rights. They never obtained the power to vote under British rule, even after 1935 when the franchise was at its widest. The clearest expression of their political impotence lay in the fact that they could be kept away from landed resources so completely. Indeed, in a press communique issued in 1914, the government expressed its intention to do so in unambiguous terms:

[79] *Chenab Colony SR* (1915), para. 153.

It appears however to Government a sound principle that in making selections of grants of Government waste, tenants, labourers and other
landless men should not as a rule be chosen, as their selection involves
the aggravation of the difficulty, already acutely felt, of obtaining agricultural labour, and it is obviously undesirable that Government should
use its position as the proprietor of large tracts in such a way as to upset
the existing social and economic order. Tenants and landless men will
derive advantage from colonisation proceedings by the diminution of
pressure in their home districts, and by the opening given to them as
labourers and subtenants in the newly opened tracts.[80]

To this general exclusion of the landless population there was one exception; but it seemed, rather, to prove the rule. In Lower Bari Doab Colony,
grants were allotted to the "depressed classes." Well before the colonisation of the Lower Bari Doab, Christian missionary organisations had been
petitioning the government for land grants for their followers.[81] These converts generally belonged to the lowest castes, who held no land but were a
source of agricultural labour.[82] British officials were not sympathetic to
these applications. They believed that the allotment of land to this class
would be an injustice to landlords, as it would tend to make agricultural
labour less plentiful. It was felt that this would constitute an interference
with agrarian conditions, and by disturbing landlord-tenant relations might
even result in losses of revenue. One lieutenant-governor even complained
that the allotment of land to Christian "menials" would open the government to the charge of encouraging proselytisation.[83]

A limited area of less than 7,000 acres was allotted in Lower Bari Doab
Colony to the adherents of various missions. An area of 2,500 acres, comprising 200 grants, was distributed among converts of the following Protestant denominations (with the number of grants in parentheses): American

[80] "Press Communique," Punjab Government, 8 December 1914; in "Grant of land to the
depressed classes in Lower Bari Doab Colony," BOR J/301/1179 A, pp. 193-95.

[81] During the early 1900s, applications by missions for land in Jhelum Colony were rejected
by the government: "Grant of land on Jhelum Canal to Native Christians," BOR J/301/710.
Between 1905 and 1915 applications and enquiries for land in Lower Bari Doab Colony continued from several missions: BOR J/301/1179: A, pp. 79-273, and B, pp. 1-83.

[82] Land had been purchased in earlier years by some missions for their adherents: four
villages in Chenab and one in Chunian Colony had been purchased by the Church Missionary
Society, Roman Catholics, and American and Scottish Presbyterians. See "Grants of Colony
land to Native Christians," BOR J/301/792; "Catholic grant in Francisabad, Chak 500, Jhang
District," BOR J/301/1630; and PRAP(G): October 1893, Nos. 29-32; August 1895, Nos. 4-
18; and April 1898, Nos. 5-19.

[83] Notes by FC, 5 March 1913 and 26 February and 11 April 1914; and by LG, n.d.: in
"Agricultural settlements for criminal tribes," BOR J/301/987, pp. 71-74, 95-98, and 109-
18.

Presbyterian (26), American United Presbyterian (80), Methodist (14), Church of Scotland (30), and Church Missionary Society (50).[84] These missions were asked to become the grantees themselves, but they declined to do so, and so the grants were allotted to their nominees. The government allowed this because the individuals selected were considered to be suitable colonists, as they did not belong to the lowest castes.[85]

The rest of the area for the "depressed classes" grants was allotted directly to religious organisations rather than to their nominees. The recipients of this area were the Salvation Army (2,500 acres), the Roman Catholic Bishop of Lahore (500 acres), and the Arya Megh Udhar Sabha (1,250 acres). The nominees of these bodies belonged to the very lowest social groups, whom the government was unwilling to trust as grantees, for "there was no assurance as to the origin, type or status of the individuals who will be selected."[86] In their case, the government insisted on an intermediary who would bear the financial risk and the managerial burden. The refusal of the British to speculate with the productive capacities of the lower classes was one reason why colony land was never entrusted to them, and was throughout confined to men of landed and established status. Another factor was the unwillingness of the state to provide direct recognition to the lower orders as holders of land, a concession that landowning groups might not have appreciated.

Even for the small area allotted to the "depressed classes" the government made it patently clear that no concession whatsoever was intended. The size of the grants was kept down to 12.5 acres for each family. This was sufficient only for subsistence needs, or at best a small surplus, a large proportion of which when marketed would be needed to pay the revenue demand. Subdivision of these grants, which was inevitable, meant that they could hardly survive even as units of subsistence. In the 1930s many of these grantees had to seek employment as labourers in order to make ends meet. With grants of unviable size, these grantees fell ever more heavily into debt.[87] An important reason for their economic difficulties was the

---

[84] This was a proportionate distribution based on the number of converts of each mission around 1915, which was, in the same order: 15,000, 60,000, 14,000, 15,000, and 25,000; BOR J/301/1179 B, pp. 119 and 127-33.

[85] Officials had required that "with such large constituencies to select from the presumption is that the person selected would be of a superior class." See FC to RS, 10 May 1915; in PRAP(G), June 1915, No. 18.

[86] *PCM*, p. 112. The Salvation Army was initially unwilling to accept the role of grantee, and wanted this to devolve directly on its nominees. It was persuaded to agree when the government threatened to allot it not 2,500 acres but 375 acres, on the proportionate principle adopted for other missions: see letters of FC and Booth Tucker, Commissioner of the Salvation Army, in BOR J/301/1179: A, p. 212; B, pp. 189-90 and 199-201; and C, pp. 37-45.

[87] An example was the village of Bethlehem, allotted to nominees of the Church Missionary

price at which they had to purchase their land. The government insisted that this should be at the full prevailing market price, in order to emphasise that these grants were not meant as largesse to landless groups, but owed their existence to expectations aroused by missionary bodies. The actual purchase rates fixed by officials varied in most cases between Rs 200 and 300 per acre, to be paid in instalments over thirty years.[88] By contrast, the peasant grantees from the "agricultural castes" could purchase their land in the colony at Rs 40-100 per acre (depending on the time taken to pay the total). Established agriculturists usually had some stock and capital, whereas the "depressed class" grantees were much poorer, which made the high purchase prices set for them doubly iniquitous.

Most of these grantees were unable to keep up with their instalment payments, especially during the 1930s. The Arya Megh Udhar Sabha, a Hindu organisation, was unable to make any payments after 1924, and in 1939, after successive moratoriums, the government confiscated the entire grant.[89] Thus the Sabha's project ended in dismal failure, and its tenants, after twenty years of effort, were forced off the land, as they in their own right had no occupancy claim on it. The Roman Catholic Bishop, too, decided to vacate his grant because he was unable to collect rent in order to pay the instalments on the purchase price.[90] This area was then purchased by an Ahmadiya organisation, to which was left the responsibility of evicting the Christian settlers, who again did not possess any occupancy rights in the land, as the formal grantee had been the Catholic mission. The Salvation Army also defaulted in its instalment payments, but managed to survive the economic vicissitudes of the 1930s and completed its land purchase in 1946.[91] In the case of the adherents of the Protestant missions who were direct grantees of the government, most fell heavily into arrears with their payments and sank deeply into debt. Since they had little hope of ever

Society. These grantees were unable to make any instalment payments toward purchase after 1925. By 1937 they had an outstanding balance of Rs 169,846, with only ten years left to complete purchase, as well as an accumulated debt of Rs 50,647. With near-subsistence grants of 12.5 acres per family, they were helpless either to pay off the debt or to purchase the land. See "Grant of land in Chak 2 G.D., Bethlehem, Tahsil Montgomery, to Christians," BOR 301/7/24/159; and PRAP(R), January 1924, Nos. 4-8.

[88] PRAP(G): June 1916, Nos. 8-13; November 1916, Nos. 1-2; December 1916, Nos. 26-27; May 1918, Nos. 141-44; and November 1918, Nos. 132-33.

[89] "Grant of land to Arya Megh Udhar Sabha, Sialkot District, in Chak 70/10R, Tahsil Khanewal," BOR 301/7/27/160.

[90] "Resumption of land held by Roman Catholic Bishop of Lahore in Chak 6/4L, Tahsil Okara," BOR 301/7/24/56; and "Montgomery District—Sale of land to Ahmadiya Anjuman-i-Ishaat-i-Islam in Chak 6/4L, Tahsil Okara," BOR 301/7/24/181.

[91] "Grant of land to Salvation Army in Chak 72/10R—Shantinagar—near Khanewal, Multan District," BOR 301/7/27/160.

completing the purchase of their grants, their tenures were finally converted into ordinary peasant tenancies, for which the purchase price was much lower. The ''depressed classes'' grants revealed the obstacles that lay in the way of the landless poor in acquiring colony land. The state was hostile to this because it might have upset existing social roles, while they themselves lacked the political and economic resources to back their claims to land.

The stratification that existed in Punjabi society, along lines of larger and smaller landholders, of a bourgeois element and of a class of landless rural poor, was maintained in the canal colonies. Economic growth, in raising the demand for labour, might well have created some improvement for the landless in their terms of trade with landholders. Wages tended to be higher in the new canal tracts than in the older settled districts, and groups hitherto deprived of all but the most lowly functions could even take on subtenancies. But the many ''inferior'' castes that migrated to the canal colonies found little relief from traditional hierarchical adversities, for by and large they retained their traditional roles. To name but a few, the chamars, chuhras, musallis, and changars among the field labourers, and the artisanal castes of tarkhan, lohar, mochi, teli, dhobi, and nai all discovered that new economic opportunities held no guarantee for social change.

This is not to suggest that the rural poor passively accepted their lot, or were deferentially inclined toward their exploiters. The antagonistic contradictions in their relations with the latter were a fundamental feature of rural life, and these did not always remain inert. The popular outbreaks in 1919 in places like Gujranwala, where district offices and records were burned, the subtenants' agitation in the Nili Bar in the mid-1930s against the excesses of rack-renting, and finally the accession of the masses to the idea of a communal division of territories with decolonisation, were only a few examples of the autonomous contribution of the common people to the course of events. Their role has not received due attention or credit in historical research, a reflection not of their unimportance but of the elitist bias of prevailing historiography. With this qualification, it must nevertheless be stressed that the agrarian developments in the canal colonies made it more rather than less difficult for the underprivileged to change economy and society so as to fulfil their need for social justice.

THE RULE OF ''ORDER''

Apart from the impact of agricultural colonisation on the social structure of the Punjab, there also existed several specific examples of the use of colony land for purposes of political expediency and social control. The state utilised its ownership over landed resources to reward those who came to its aid; and the power of land in an agrarian economy was such that it could be used not only for ensuring deference but also for various corrective functions. Thus in the canal colonies loyalty clauses were being written into tenurial statements, punitive confiscations of grants were carried out for those convicted of crime, people who had rendered a variety of services to the ruling authority were rewarded with land, reformatory settlements were introduced and convict labour farmed out, and grants were even made to religious shrines for their maintenance. Such measures helped to create an obedience to authority that was reflected in the weak nationalist stimulus in this province, as compared to other parts of the British Indian empire. This section will discuss some of the uses made of colony land to propitiate this rule of "order."

As the value of a land grant increased, and it came to be seen more and more as a boon and concession, the government felt it desirable to impose a more deliberate connection between loyalty and land. In 1919 it decided to add a loyalty clause to all future grants of land. Under the clause, loyal behaviour was expected from the grantees, and active support for the government during any time of trouble or disorder.[92] In all such cases, the Punjab Government was the final authority in deciding whether the condition had been violated, and for imposing any penalty, such as the temporary or permanent resumption of grants. The loyalty clause could only be applicable to government tenants, and it lapsed when the grantee acquired proprietary rights. Since it was not till several years after allotment that grantees completed purchase of their land, this clause was applicable to most post-1919 grantees for the remaining period of British rule. However, it did not seem to discourage applications for colony land, indicating that the landholders did not perceive in it any conflict of allegiances.

In another example, a clause was included in the statement of conditions in Lower Bari Doab and Nili Bar colonies to try and deter grantees from indulging in crime. The clause enabled the government to resume the lands of any person who had committed an offence that resulted in a prison sentence of one year or more.[93] Since it encompassed crimes of all sorts, in-

---

[92] The loyalty clause ran as follows: "The tenant shall be bound to be and shall remain at all times of loyal behaviour, and to render active support to the Government and its officers in any time of trouble or disorder. The decision of the Local Government whether this condition has been violated by the tenant shall be final, and if the Local Government is of opinion that the tenant has committed a breach of this condition it may resume the tenancy or any portion thereof, either temporarily or permanently, and such resumption shall not affect any other penalty to which the tenant may be liable under these conditions or otherwise": Gazette Notification No. 5080, 21 February 1919; in PRAP(G), March 1919, No. 231.

[93] See the comprehensive "Confiscations of holdings in Lower Bari Doab Colony," BOR 301/2/24/7 A-I; "Confiscations of Colony grants," BOR 301/14/00/2; and PRAP(I): October 1913, No. 1; and December 1913, No. 31. A number of confiscations were for political activities: for association with either the Akali movement or the Congress party.

cluding political ones, the clause placed the government in a strong position for enforcing rural law and order. The cases of those imprisoned for one year or more were sent to the financial commissioner, who was responsible for sanctioning the confiscation of the grants. In Lower Bari Doab Colony alone, between 1915 and 1930, 168 grants were confiscated, and were reallotted to other persons or to co-sharers. The total number of confiscations was far greater, for increasingly during the 1920s the decision to confiscate holdings was made by lower officials, although this was not strictly legal. With only a few exceptions, the 168 grantees who suffered confiscation held less than twenty-five acres of land. Many possessed only five acres or so, which meant that they were either dwarf holders or co-sharers of grants. Since there were very few cases of men imprisoned for crime who held over twenty-five acres, a very clear link existed between economic position and criminal proclivities. Apparently, those with normal peasant-sized holdings, as well as the larger grantees, were not disposed toward unlawful activity, whether criminal or political.

In addition to acting as a deterrent to crime, land grants were also used more overtly for the maintenance of law and order. Although a law-abiding and deferential disposition was a general prerequisite for qualification to land, areas of 4,000 acres in Upper Jhelum Colony and 5,000 acres in Nili Bar Colony were reserved specifically for those who had helped with criminal administration. These grants were made to people who had resisted or apprehended criminals and dacoits, or had helped the police in other ways in its efforts against crime. [94] The first claim was of those men (or their dependents) who had risked or lost their lives in encounters with criminals, and then of those whose property had been destroyed or those who had incurred dangerous enmities for services against crime. The grants varied in size from one-half to two squares, and were allotted either to ordinary people on the strength of individual exploits, or to those who regularly helped with criminal administration, such as *zaildars* and *lambardars*.[95] The government publicised these grants widely; and this proved useful, for it was the prospect of a land grant, rather than the actual area finally allotted, that impelled people to assist the administration. It was reported that

[94] "Grant of land on Upper Jhelum Canal for services rendered to Criminal Administration," BOR J/301/1154; and "Reservation of 200 squares in Nili Bar Colony for Reward grants for services to Criminal Administration," BOR 301/14/C9/27.

[95] Help against crime was not interpreted in the limited sense, but was extended to political services as well, as in the case of one M. Faizul Hassan: "He is an accomplished Arabic scholar and is now translating a book written in Urdu by Kazi Siraj-ud-Din of Rawalpindi, the object of which is to disprove the claims of Turkey to the Caliphate and generally to inculcate loyalty to the British Raj." See Commissioner, Rawalpindi, to FC, 13 July 1916; in BOR J/301/1154 B, p. 21.

people had lost their apathy, and were more willing to resist criminals and dacoits, in the hope of obtaining land. This was confirmed in 1918 by the inspector-general of police:

> There can be no question to my thinking that the hands of the Executive would be enormously strengthened if the people know that land is ready and available for assistance rendered to the Police. There is no lure like it and it is the greatest inducement Government can offer the public in order to secure real co-operation in dealing with violent crime in particular.[96]

The canal colonies also provided opportunities for the reformation of convicts and the utilisation of their labour. A Reclamation Department was established in 1926 to supervise corrective work among prisoners on probation. In Lower Bari Doab and Nili Bar colonies, selected prisoners were regularly placed as labourers on both private and state farms, and with contractors on construction work. In Nili Bar Colony, two reformatory farms were established, one of 2,625 acres for adult probationers and the other of 1,225 acres for adolescents.[97] For the first few years the convict labourers on these farms were payed fixed wages. In 1931 the wage system was replaced with subtenancies, which were in more general usage in the canal colonies. The re-creation with tied labour of the prevailing preference for subtenancies reflected the strength of noncapitalistic forms of production in the canal colonies. This alternative proved both popular with the probationers and profitable for the administration: "It has not only resulted in a considerable financial gain to Government at over Rs 36,000 in the year of its introduction, but affords also an incentive to hard work which was previously lacking.[98]

The reformatory farms employed 350 to 400 probationers, while a further 1,500 to 2,000 were employed on private farms. There was a high demand for convict labour from the latter, for its probationary, semibonded status made it more reliable and docile than free labour. The government saved a great deal of money from the use of probationers as labourers in the canal colonies by dispensing with the need to maintain large penal and reformatory institutions. In addition, it derived rentier's profits from the two reclamation farms in the Nili Bar.

Colony land was utilised for the reclamation not only of convicts but of

[96] Note by Inspector-General of Police, 4 January 1918; ibid., pp. 119-21.

[97] *Annual Report on Reclamation Department* (Punjab Civil Secretariat Library, E75), 1927, p. 16. This department was established under the Good Conduct Prisoners' Probational Release Act and the Punjab Borstal Act (1926).

[98] Ibid.: 1931, Review; and also 1933, p. 3 and Appendix A; 1934, p. 2; and "Borstal and adults release farms in Nili Bar Colony," BOR 301/5/25/2.

"hereditary criminals" as well. Reformatory settlements were established in Lower Bari Doab and Nili Bar colonies for members of groups that were officially notified as "criminal and wandering tribes."[99] Such groups formed the underworld of Punjabi society, and had for generations practised crime of various types as their traditional occupation.[100] These tribes, of whom the Harnis, Sansis, and Baurias were the largest, were regarded as low-caste or outcaste; and there existed a mutual abhorrence between them and other sections of society. Several years of effort to reclaim these people had produced few results.[101] During the twentieth century, crime in the Punjab increased steadily, much of it due to the activity of these wandering tribes. The construction of a railway network gave them greater mobility, and the spread of settlement westward enlarged their operational area. Efforts by the police to control these groups had proved inadequate, for their methods did not properly encompass preventive or reclamatory work.

The government finally decided to utilise colony land to try and reduce the depredations of these people. From 1917 a scheme was introduced for the reclamation of the criminal and wandering tribes through the establishment of settlements for penal work. A threefold classification was introduced. The worst characters were removed to reformatory gaols, such as the one at Amritsar. The less desirable people were transferred to industrial settlements, as at Kala Shah Kaku near Lahore (which, interestingly, became a large industrial site after 1947). The best-behaved members were placed on agricultural settlements in Lower Bari Doab Colony (10,000 acres) and Nili Bar Colony (5,000 acres). This division of tribal members revealed a distinctive but predictable set of priorities: those who were most compliant and reformed were sent for agricultural work.

Although the settlements did not prove to be an unqualified success, they

[99] For information on these groups, see V.P.T. Vivian, *A Handbook of the Criminal Tribes of the Punjab* (1912) (British Library, I.S. PU 7/2); H. K. Kaul and L. L. Tomkins, *Report on Questions relating to the Administration of Criminal and Wandering Tribes in the Punjab* (Lahore: Government Publication Office, 1914); and *The Criminal Tribes Administration Manual* (Lahore: Government Publication Office, 1919).

[100] Social groups were officially designated as "criminal tribes" under the Criminal Tribes Act (XXII of 1871). This was superceded by the Criminal Tribes Act (III of 1911), which allowed for stricter enforcement of punitive measures and empowered the administration to restrict members of these tribes to villages under police supervision. From 1917 a Deputy Commissioner of Criminal Tribes was appointed to administer the designated groups.

[101] Reformatory settlements, called *kots*, had been established since 1871; but it had proved very difficult to keep their inmates in residence. The Salvation Army had managed some *kots*, as at Rakh Adhian. See "Lease of Rakh Adhian in Sialkot District for 32nd Lancers as a horse run," BOR J/301/1004; "Agricultural settlements for Criminal Tribes," BOR J/301/987; and "Criminal Tribes settlements in Sialkot, Sheikhupura and Karnal Districts," BOR 301/5/4-17-11/1(b).

did lead to some measure of reform among the inmates.[102] Supervision and management remained a problem. For several years, the settlements were run by missionary and philanthropic organisations, and efforts were made to bring these people within one or other of the major religious traditions. Muslim, Hindu, Sikh, and Christian organisations were involved, but all faced the persistent problem of finding men suitably committed and selfless to look after the settlements. Another handicap was that the missions seemed more interested in the spiritual rather than the economic welfare of their wards, though with people of such hardened convictions it was the latter alone that might have brought redemption. Finally by 1936, after several years of savings on administrative costs and obligations, the government assumed control of the settlements, and they were thereafter run by Probation and Criminal Tribes Officers.[103]

The settlements did well in the years of agricultural prosperity. The inmates worked on a subtenancy basis, which seemed to give them more incentive to work peaceably and productively than wage labour. During the 1920s, the settlements were regarded as the most successful method of weaning these criminal tribes from their ingrained habits. Absorption in agriculture, combined with the religious and moral instruction imparted by the missions, was reported to have gainfully advanced the reformation of people who had proved so consistently recalcitrant in the past. Since all members of the criminal and wandering tribes of the province could not be absorbed in such settlements, the solution was only a partial one. Total crime in the Punjab did not abate significantly, but fluctuated under the exogenous influence of economic and political conditions.[104] During the 1930s, much that had been achieved was undermined by the economic depression. As profits from agriculture disappeared, it became increasingly difficult to restrain these people from reverting to crime. Even so, the inmates of the agricultural settlements reportedly showed less proclivity toward crime than their compatriots elsewhere, for the former at least had the means of subsistence at their disposal. Once again, access to colony land was successfully used by the rulers to impose order on the population.

That colony land was being used for overt political ends was manifest in

[102] For information on the progress of these settlements, see *Annual Report on Administration of Criminal Tribes in the Punjab*, 1917-1940.

[103] The religious missions involved were the Salvation Army, Canadian Mission, Anjuman-i-Islam, Ahmadiya Anjuman-i-Ishaat-i-Islam, Qadian Society, Arya Samaj, Hindu Sabha, Sanathan Dharm Sabha, Dev Samaj, and Chief Khalsa Diwan: "Religious places of worship in Criminal Tribes agricultural settlements," BOR 301/5/00/1(a).

[104] For fluctuations in the crime rate and their purported relationship to food prices and political unrest during the sample years 1915-1922, see *Annual Report on Police Administration in the Punjab*: 1915, p. 2; 1916, p. 1; 1919, p. 2; 1921, pp. 2-3, 8, and 18-19; and 1922, pp. 2, 8, and 18.

the grants made to individuals who had rendered exceptional services to the state. Such grants were allotted in several colonies, either under a distinct category called "reward grants" or on an ad hoc basis. They were allotted for a variety of reasons, depending on the needs of the time.[105] Thus a large proportion of the reward grants in Lower Bari Doab Colony were allotted for help in the recruitment of soldiers and for other services related to World War I. The recipients were usually local notables or government officials. The type of men considered for the reward grants was described as follows in 1917 by the provincial to the central government:

> In every district there are men of this stamp who have for years given loyal support and assistance to the officers of Government, whilst since the commencement of the War many instances have come to . . . notice of excellent work in connection with recruitment to the army, the maintenance of public order, and the suppression of the revolutionary movement. . . . [T]he bestowal of grants of land in a limited number of particularly deserving cases will . . . be widely appreciated and will encourage and stimulate the growing ideal of civic duty throughout the province.[106]

That the government used colony land to combat political agitations was evident in the example of the Akali movement, which in the 1920s showed markedly violent tendencies. The Akalis formed *jathas*, or armed bands, which tried to seize *gurudawara*s and holy sites. The British, perturbed by these developments because of the importance of the Sikhs in the military and the canal colonies, allotted colony grants to those who worked against the movement. This undoubtedly made collaboration a more attractive proposition and strengthened the economic status of collaborators. About a hundred people obtained these grants, in sizes varying from half to four squares. The grants were made to informers, police and civil officials, and men of local influence. Grants were also made to the families of those killed or severely wounded by the Akalis.[107]

Clearly, the gratification of loyalty through land had become deeply embedded in the consciousness of Punjabis. The importance of this was acknowledged by the governor in 1925, while justifying the reservation of 37,500 acres for reward grants in Nili Bar Colony:

[105] For a voluminous record of reward grantees, with eight parts and thirty KWs, see "Reward grants in Extensions of Lower Chenab Canal and Nili Bar to non-officials," BOR 301/3/25-24/188 A-H; and also "Grants of land specially sanctioned on the new canals," BOR J/301/1124.

[106] RS to RAS, GOI, 5 March 1917; in PRAP(I), May 1917, No. 51.

[107] For land grants allotted to counter the Akali agitation, see BOR: 301/3/25/5, 301/3/25/22, 301/3/C9/215, 301/14/00/1, and 301/14/00/21.

The Punjab has been accustomed for many years to see rewards of this nature granted, and I fear that a definite decision to bring to an end what has now become an established system will have consequences that will be really harmful to the Administration. There are times of stress when we are actively dependent for the preservation of law and order on the efforts of men who have influence in their neighbourhood and community. . . . The system of rewards has sunk too deeply into the life of the province. Moreover, it is traditional to the East that a Government should reward its friends, and I am afraid that any Government, which denies itself the power of securing support by these means, is likely in the long run to add to the number of its enemies. In the last few years we have had to meet the shock of non-cooperation, the Khilafat movement, and the Sikh agitation, and I think that those who have loyally assisted us during this difficult period, have a stronger claim to consideration than many of those who have been our beneficiaries in the past, and there would be some reaction of feeling against us if they learnt that we had deliberately decided to deprive ourselves of the means of rewarding them.[108]

Social stability could be maintained not only through political control and law and order, but also by strengthening the forces of religion. The subject of religion and social control is quite outside the realm of this study, but it may be noted that in history, established religious institutions have remained vibrant as much through their control over economic resources as by the fervour and devotion of their adherents. While in the canal colonies the state did not in any concerted manner use land for religious purposes, there were several individual instances of this type. Cases have been mentioned above of grants to the "depressed classes" and the "criminal tribes," in which sectarian missions, both Christian and non-Christian, were appointed to supervisory roles. Control over land could only have given these religious bodies further opportunity for increasing their influence and gaining more adherents.

In a very different context, grants were made to holy shrines, as a contribution toward their upkeep and economic welfare. Personal grants were given to the custodians of the more eminent shrines, and some of these shrinekeepers, by obtaining landed gentry grants, were even placed on a par with the larger landlords.[109] These shrines commanded vast influence

---

[108] Note by Sir Malcolm Hailey, Governor Punjab, 21 August 1925, para. 14; in "Colonisation of Nili Bar," BOR 301/1/C9/3 B KW, p. 55.

[109] For a discussion of the political role of shrine keepers, or *sajjada nashins*, in the region, see David Gilmartin, "Religious Leadership and the Pakistan Movement in the Punjab," *Modern Asian Studies*, XIII, 3 (1979), 485-517; and A. C. Mayer, "Pir and *Murshid*: An

among the people, and the acceptance of land grants indicated that their influence would not be exerted against imperialist rule. Indeed, in many cases their custodians stood out for their loyal services to the British, whether in the field of recruitment, local administration, or provincial politics. One example was that of a powerful shrine in Attock District, whose Pir was given a personal landed gentry grant of ten rectangles in 1916, along with the lease of 15,000 acres of *rakh* land in his home district. Such being the rewards for war recruitment, the Pir was thanked by the lieutenant-governor for his services "in the sure knowledge that you will not relax your efforts as long as the army needs men."[110]

Though no comprehensive list exists of allotments to shrines, it is clear that the recipients were largely confined to the western Punjab and were predominantly Muslim.[111] In addition to the specific grants made to shrines and to their keepers, there were also numerous grantees whose social importance stemmed from their religious sanctity. The Syeds and Qureshis among Muslims were two such castes well represented in canal colony allotments. The aforementioned Baba Sir Khem Singh Bedi obtained his large grant of 7,800 acres because he was the leader of the Sejhdari Sikhs and the head of a family directly descended from Guru Nanak. Rather than sink into obscurity, this family like many others found that its religious significance enabled its fortunes to be greatly strengthened by the actions of an amenable rulership. If in many parts of the world the struggle against European imperialism drew upon religious consciousness for its inspiration, then the Punjab was but a barren ground for such enterprise. Its religious luminaries were actively collaborating with imperialist rule, and were being rewarded for their services with landed resources.

Agricultural colonisation also had a more general impact on the political environment of the Punjab. This was not a region that stood out for sustained, or even active, opposition to imperialism. Revolutionary tendencies, such as the Ghadr conspiracy, did at times flicker momentarily; and certain religio-political movements, such as the Akalis, were also extant.

Aspect of Religious Leadership in West Pakistan," *Middle Eastern Studies*, III, 2 (1967), 160-69.

[110] LG to Pir of Makhad, 20 February 1916; in "Proposal to make a grant of land to shrine of Pir Nuri Shah Padishah at Makhad and Pir Ghulam Abbas of Makhad," BOR 301/3/00/164 A, p. 83.

[111] For a list of some major shrines that obtained land grants in Lower Bari Doab Colony, see Imran Ali, "The Punjab Canal Colonies," Table 3.5. Some of these grants to shrines (with acreages in parentheses) were: from Delhi District, Nizamuddin Auliya (125); from Jhang District, Sultan Bahu (125), and Uchh Gul Imam Shah (125); from Montgomery District, Shergarh (175), and Pakpattan Sharif (175); from Multan District, Shah Gardez (193), Shaikh Kabir Qureshi (275), and Musa Pak Shahid (262); and from Muzaffargarh District, Dera Din Panah (200).

By and large, though, this province maintained its acquiescence to the alien power. Even in the final years of British rule, there was little in its politics to suggest that South Asia had moved close to independence. The nationalist movement in the Punjab always remained weak, even in the period after 1935, when nationalism had gained substantial ground elsewhere in India.[112] The measure of this lay in the results of the elections of 1936, which gave the Indian National Congress control of at least half a dozen provincial legislatures.[113]

In the Punjab, the 1936 elections gave an overwhelming victory to the Punjab National Unionist party (PNUP), whose members belonged to the rural elite and were firmly loyal to British rule. The PNUP comprised a cross-communal caucus in the Punjab Legislative Assembly, and it represented the interests of the Muslim, Sikh, and Hindu landholding classes. The success of the PNUP was an indicator of the retardation of nationalism in the Punjab, and of the continued strength of imperialist rule. The agrarian magnates who composed the power base of the PNUP, the likes of the Nuns, Tiwanas, Daultanas, and Mamdots, were to a man heavily involved with the canal colonies. This undoubtedly resuscitated the influence and authority that they used to ward off the incursions of nationalist organisations, such as the Congress and the Muslim League, and to hold the landowning stratum in continued alliance with British rule. When overt imperialism's days seemed numbered, and the Muslim agrarian leadership saw a parting of the ways, an important segment branched out to gain control of the Muslim League, thereby to continue landlord dominance of politics in the successor state of Pakistan.[114]

Accommodation with the alien power at the apex of society was founded on a pyramid of loyalties that stretched from the village upward. The *lambardar*s, or village headmen, were government appointees who aided local

---

[112] For an assessment of politics in the Punjab during the final years of British rule, see Imran Ali: *Punjab Politics in the Decade before Partition* (Lahore: South Asian Institute, 1975); and "Relations between the Muslim League and Punjab National Unionist Party, 1935-47," *South Asia*, 6 (1976), 51-65.

[113] For analyses of the gains of nationalist organisation in other parts of British India, especially the Hindu-majority provinces, see D. A. Low (ed.), *The Congress and the Raj* (Columbia, Missouri: South Asia Books, 1977).

[114] Political conditions in twentieth-century Punjab under British rule are discussed in Ayesha Jalal and Anil Seal, "Alternative to Partition: Muslim Politics Between the Wars," *Modern Asian Studies*, XV, 3 (1981), 415-54; I. A. Talbot, "The Growth of the Muslim League in the Punjab," *Journal of Commonwealth and Comparative Politics*, XX, 1 (1982), 5-24; and David Page, *Prelude to Partition. The Indian Muslims and the Imperial System of Control, 1920-1932* (Delhi: Oxford University Press, 1982). See also G. A. Heeger, "The Growth of the Congress Movement in the Punjab, 1920-1940," *Journal of Asian Studies*, XXXI, 1 (1972), 39-51; and S. Oren, "The Sikhs, Congress, and the Unionists in British Punjab, 1937-1945," *Modern Asian Studies*, VIII, 3 (1974), 397-418.

administration, and in the canal colonies received an extra grant to encourage devotion to duty. The next level of rural control were the *zaildari* circles, which brought together a number of villages of kindred proprietary castes under the leadership of persons of eminence appointed as *zaildars* by the administration. Combinations of kindred *zails* then formed the electoral circles for the District Boards, which brought rural leaders into closer liaison with the nethermost levels of British bureaucracy.[115] Finally, provincial elections sent to the legislature men who represented the chief landed interests of their districts, and these men associated with each other through the pro-British caucus of the Unionist party. The fact that this chain held together, that the enfranchised peasantry did not turn to nationalist politicians but continued to vote for its landlord nominees, reflected the lack of any serious disaffection of rural landholders with British rule. This outcome stemmed undoubtedly from the benefits of agricultural colonisation, a process so designed as to placate the influential elements of society. These interests were appeased not with words or honorific titles but by the grant of valuable economic resources. Had nationalist struggles and international geopolitics not intervened, the foundations for a perpetual raj were well on their way to being established in the minds of fomentors and abbetors alike.

[115] For information on the drawing up of *zaildari* circles and electoral circles for District Boards, see Imran Ali, ''The Punjab Canal Colonies,'' p. 176.

CHAPTER FOUR

Militarisation

THE MILITARY figured prominently as a recipient of land in the canal colonies, and, indeed, the absorption of landed resources for military purposes is a process that stretches back to remote antiquity. Perhaps no factor has been more constant in human history than the efforts made by governing authorities to ensure a viable military organisation. In feudal society, for example, the nexus between the military and the land was a central institutional feature. In industrial society, and especially in the twentieth century, the expenditure of society's resources on the military has reached unprecedented levels. The results for society have not always been negative: the demands of modern warfare have led to innovations in both technology and industrial organisation, to the advantage of society as a whole. But though the military was closely involved with the industrialisation process in such areas as Europe, North America, and Japan, did it play a similar role in British India? Can the participation of the military in the Punjab canal colonies be seen in the context of modernisation, or would it be more appropriate to draw parallels with feudalism?

An assessment of the role of the military in the western Punjab involves a number of questions with broader historical implications. The methods adopted in associating the military with development of the canal colonies were unique, and their impact on agrarian conditions was unreplicated elsewhere. That these measures were imposed by the British gave them a significance beyond their importance for the Punjab. They furnish a case study, on a quite extensive scale, of the kinds of interventions practised by colonialism in its subject economies. Involving as it did a substantial strengthening of the military, this process had important political consequences, after the transfer of power in 1947, for the nation state of Pakistan. The impact of the militarisation of colony land on economic development was a further dimension, raising the question of whether this phenomenon represented a diversion of resources from more productive uses, a shift of priorities from agricultural development to the strategic and political imperatives of the state. Assessments of the military tend to concentrate on its organisational structure, on its exploits in war and counterinsurgency, and on its enjoyment of political power. Much less is known of how the military was also penetrating, in this homeland of the "martial races'' of South Asia, into the seminal source of societal authority, the control and possession of agricultural land.

MILITARY MAN AND ANIMAL

Soldier Settlement

One major form of military involvement in the canal colonies was the allotment of large areas of land to ex-soldiers. The majority of such grants were of the peasant or *abadkar* type, varying from twenty-five to fifty-five acres in size. A number of larger grants were also allotted to Punjabi commissioned and noncommissioned officers. The scale of the allocation for soldier settlement was such that men from the Punjab came to expect, and obtain, colony land as their rightful due for service in the military. As new canal colonies were established, the share of ex-soldiers in land distribution increased, a reflection of the growing importance of the military in agricultural colonisation. A career in the army (which was the service that monopolised these grants) became an important means through which Punjabis could achieve upward mobility. If they already enjoyed an elevated status, military service probably provided individuals and social groups a more assured means of maintaining their social position than any other career. The economic resources dispensed to military personnel through canal colonisation enhanced the attractions of military service for Punjabis, and provided a basis for the continued over-representation of the province in the British Indian army. As a result, the strength of the military in Punjabi society grew ever greater. Such processes would strongly indicate that the historical preconditions for the political authority of the military in Pakistan after 1947 were founded on the developments of the previous era.

Land grants were being made to military men in India long before the canal colonies came into existence. Under the Mughals and the Sikhs, military strength and political power were indivisible, and the appropriation of economic resources by the military was an essential aspect of sovereignty and hegemony. From this tradition of feudal liens for the provision of military and administrative services, the British appeared to be bringing a transition, as part of the introduction of a ''modern'' state. They endeavoured to institute military and civil functions in the shape of distinct and professionalised services. But the society in which the colonial state was implanted retained its traditional mores, which could not easily be reconciled with either the vision or the practice of modernism imported from another continent. Essential to these ingrained values was the association of land with status. The endowment of land was seen to be a fitting reward for the valuable supportive role that military service provided to the governing authority. A career in the military was not regarded simply as a career in its own right. Such "professionalism" had not clarified itself in the consciousness of the Punjabis, just as the division of labour from which such specialisations arose had not established itself historically in the economy of the region. Instead, military service was regarded as a vehicle for establishing one's status, as an individual but more importantly as part of a social group; and the acquisition of land was essential to the consolidation of status.

Even the colonial rulers, despite their claims to modernism, did not seriously question these values, as can be seen by the scale at which military men were transplanted in the canal colonies. In a sector of the economy that was visibly innovative, with its engineering and hydraulic achievements, its commercial agriculture, and its transport and marketing systems, there occurred also an overpowering confirmation of preexisting values. This was the paradox that agrarian growth held for the Punjab, and it provided a sufficient contradiction for questioning seriously the assumption that social change follows easily from economic change.

Three aspects need to be considered in discussing the allotment of land to military grantees. The first is the sequence of soldier settlement: the extent of land allotted for this purpose as each major canal colony was established. The second aspect concerns the type of men who obtained such grants, in terms both of their social and regional origins and of their place in the military structure. Finally, the kind of grantees that the ex-soldiers made, their problems, and their relative success as colonists can be discussed, to cast light on their role in the agrarian economy.

Even prior to the development of the canal colonies, the British had made land grants and leases of waste land to those who had provided them with military services. Such grants and leases, which were convertible to proprietary rights at later dates, were made to men who had served them in their military campaigns, notably the struggle of 1857 and the Afghan wars.[1] Thus the tradition of assisting the alien invader against one's countrymen, and being rewarded for it, was already well established in the Punjab, though its dimensions were to be greatly extended with the canal colonies. Many of these earlier grants and leaseholds in the western Punjab came under canal irrigation, and thus increased considerably in value.

A few "reward" grants, so named because the purchase price was waived, had also been awarded each year to selected military officers. In the 1880s the usual size of such grants was around 500 acres.[2] After 1890

---

[1] For lists of such grantees, see PRAP(G): January 1894, No. 19; and August 1898, No. 28.

[2] There are several BOR files in the series J/301/1-1500, 301/3/-/1- and 301/14/-/1- on individual military reward grantees. A comprehensive file on major policy changes for such grants also incorporates individual cases: "Reward grants in Punjab to Native Officers," BOR J/301/182 A-H.

most of these grants were located in the canal colonies, where their size was smaller but rental earnings were equivalent to the larger waste land grants.[3] Development costs on the latter, which had to be incurred by the recipient, significantly adulterated the element of reward. Canal colony land carried few such costs, thus greatly enhancing the powers of the state to recompense its beneficiaries. The official vernacular designation for these allotments was *"jagir* grants," a term that reflected the responsiveness of the colonial state to indigenous norms of status and hierarchy. A trickle of annual *jagir* grants to military officers continued until the 1940s; this ran within, but yet was distinct from, the torrent of soldier settlement as it beset the canal colonies.

Another example of the way in which military servicemen could obtain land outside the mainstream of military grants was the three villages allotted in Chenab Colony to Mazhbi Sikhs. The Mazhbis were a low-caste group whose inferior social position relative to the landholding Jats gave the lie to claims of egalitarianism among Sikhs. They were allotted colony land because they provided manpower for three infantry battalions (the 23rd, 32nd, and 34th Pioneer Regiments).[4] As nonagriculturists, the Mazhbis would not otherwise have qualified for land. They had the reputation of being undisciplined in their social habits and highly prone to crime. British officials hoped that land grants would enable the recipients to settle down and continue to provide recruits to the army. Land would also give them an opportunity to raise their social status, which it was felt they deserved owing to their readiness for military service. In 1911, on the strength of their landholdings in Chenab Colony, the hitherto lowly Mazhbis were accorded the official status of an "agricultural caste" in Gujranwala and Lyallpur districts.[5] The route to higher social status through military service held up a mirror to those Mazhbis, still civilian and unruly, who had rejected the conformism of their soldier brethren.

It was in the four larger canal colonies that the bulk of military grantees were settled: Chenab, Jhelum, Lower Bari Doab, and Nili Bar. The smaller colonies also received military grantees, in the event of shortfalls in land in other colonies, or if they were situated closer to the grantees' homes.

[3] PRAP(R): February 1927, No. 1; and November 1927, No. 1.

[4] For information on the Mazhbi allotment in Chenab Colony, see "Mazhbi Settlement," BOR J/301/3 A-G; "Application for a grant of land to form a colony of Mazhbi and Ramdasia Sikhs," BOR J/301/1587; and "Description of Mazhbi Sikhs in revenue records in colony villages," BOR 301/2/00/205. See also PRAP(I): July 1902, Nos. 11-33; August 1902, Nos. 32-34. See also PRAP(A): May 1907, Nos. 1-12; October 1911, Nos. 17-25. See also PRAP(G): September 1912, Nos. 17-19; July 1913, Nos. 33-34; January 1914, Nos. 29-36; September 1914, Nos. 43-53.

[5] Punjab Government Gazette Notifications 128-129, 26 September 1911; in PRAP(A), October 1911, Nos. 23-24.

Though such grants were being allotted from the early 1890s, the beginnings of military settlement were tentative and almost unnoticeable. It was not originally envisaged that such considerations would form a significant part of any colonisation scheme. Military participation grew in importance as new colonies were developed, and as the British realised that it would be wise to make concessions to political realities. About 2,000 acres were reserved for this purpose in Chunian Colony. In Chenab Colony, on the first of the three major canal branches, the Rakh, an area of 6,000 acres was allotted; and a further 9,000 acres on the second, the Jhang. The recipients were to be military pensioners who had completed twenty-one years of service. It was on the third branch, the Gugera, that the first substantial allotment to military grantees took place: that of 70,000 acres, or roughly 10 percent of allotable area on this branch.[6] Even so, Chenab Colony remained primarily civilian in character, unlike subsequent projects.

In Jhelum Colony, the military interest was much more obtrusive. The dominant factor in colonisation here was the horse-breeding scheme. Military grantees, who were once again pensioners, were also prominent, obtaining about 18 percent of the total allotted land.[7] Initially, an area of 44,000 acres was allocated for them, but this was raised to 80,000 acres with the adoption of horse breeding. The increase went largely to cavalrymen, who were expected to do well as horse breeders. They alone obtained 44,000 acres in service grants, at a minimum of two squares (55 acres) each. The remaining 36,000 acres were allotted to men from other branches, on nonhorse-breeding tenures at one square apiece. The cavalry grantees also received better quality land, while the others were settled only after land had been found for all horse-breeding grantees, whether civil or military. Thus another military requirement, that of horse breeding, had attained such priority in colonisation policy that it was seen to act inequitably even within the ranks of the military grantees, who as a whole were accorded a more privileged position than civilian colonists.

Military grants became even more important in colonisation with the next project, Lower Bari Doab Colony, with an area of 103,000 acres initially reserved for them. On the outbreak of World War I, an additional 75,000 acres were added in a bid to stimulate recruitment.[8] To enhance the

---

[6] See "Reservation of land on Chenab Canal for Yeoman grants to native soldiers," BOR J/301/431; *PCM*, p. 104; and PRAP(I), January 1893, Nos. 7-13. See also PRAP(G): August 1895, Nos. 33-39; February 1896, Nos. 38-40; and June 1896, Nos. 39-43.

[7] Copious correspondence in the PRAP series on military grants in Jhelum Colony is included in the comprehensive file "Military grants on Jhelum Canal," BOR J/301/689 A-E.

[8] The offer of the additional 75,000 acres was made by the Punjab Government and gratefully accepted by the Government of India. See RS to RAS, GOI, 15 October 1914; RAS, GOI, to RS, 28 November 1914; and "Press Communique," PG, 9 December 1914: in

prospects of reward for war service, the 180,000-odd acres were reserved for war veterans rather than pensioners. But the latter were not neglected, for confidential orders were passed that they be found land from the allocation for civilian grantees.[9] The land reserved for war veterans alone comprised around 20 percent of the total allotted area in the colony. The large areas of inferior soil that were encountered there necessitated contractions under virtually all heads of allotment, except that of military grantees. Indeed, wherever suitable land became available in the years following 1918, the priority lay in reserving it for war veterans.

The timely availability of so much new land was highly significant for the war effort. The superiority of land grants over other forms of reward, such as cash subsidies and special pensions, further increased the willingness of Punjabis to offer themselves for war service. Such prospects of gratification were a major reason for the inordinately high proportion of Punjabis in the army, for other provinces had no comparable resources to offer as reward. Nevertheless, the basis of selection was none too benevolent. The proportion of land reserved for each regiment or unit was determined chiefly by the number of casualties sustained by that unit during the war.[10]

In the case of the last major colonisation project, Nili Bar Colony, military grantees again received a sizeable proportion of land. The grants reverted to military pensioners, the needs of war veterans having already been catered for. An area of 75,000 acres was allocated, and in addition at least another 25,000 acres were allotted to ex-soldiers from the civilian allotment.[11] In contrast, peasant grants for civilians in the perennially irrigated area of this colony amounted to only 225,000 acres. Thus military grantees received almost half as much land as that reserved for the entire civilian peasantry of the Punjab.[12] In the canal colonies as a whole, the total

---

"Grants of land on Lower Bari Doab Canal to military pensioners," BOR J/301/1178, pp. 168-73.

[9] RS to FC, 20 October 1914, Confidential; ibid., pp. 77-79. See also RS to FC, 11 January 1915, in PRAP(I), January 1915; No. 2.

[10] Secretary, Indian Soldiers Board, to Director of Staff Duties, 27 November 1920; in "Grants of land to Indian soldiers for distinguished services during the War," BOR J/301/1371, pp. 83-89. The contributions of the Punjab on the British side in World War I are described in M. S. Leigh, *The Punjab and the War* (Lahore: Government Printing Press, 1922).

[11] FC to Home Secretary, 12 November 1929; in "Grants of land to ex-soldiers and their families in Nili Bar Colony," BOR 301/3/C9/251, pp. 103-104.

[12] Military considerations were present even for the remaining civilian allotment. The Awan tribe of Jhelum and Shahpur districts obtained a large allotment in the colony as compensation for postwar army retrenchments, which were creating employment problems for this highly military-oriented tribe. The Awans certainly felt that their military services gave them a claim to colony land, and they made this clear during a visit by the deputy commissioner of Jhelum

amount of land allotted to military grantees was not much short of half a million acres. This constituted a major case of entrenchment of one of the chief coercive institutions of the state. The justification originally forwarded by the government for having military grants was that soldiers, owing to their absence from home, would miss the opportunities for selection enjoyed by civilians. While this was undoubtedly true, there were also other dimensions to these grants.

Perhaps the most important factor was the political capital that accrued to both state and soldiery from such substantial rewards for military service. This resulted in the strengthening not only of the military itself, but also of those classes that dominated military service. The primacy of the political rather than the agrarian consideration was manifest in the selection procedure for such men. The grantees were chosen not by civilian district officers but by the military authorities, on the recommendations of regimental commanders. The decisive factor in selection was a man's record as a soldier rather than his dependability as an agriculturist. Moreover, the ex-soldiers, except for war veterans, were eligible for grants only after completing twenty-one years of service.[13] This was certainly an inducement for a prolonged military career, but it worked against the interests of agriculture. The pensioners were beyond the optimum age for colonists, and were often incapable of undertaking the physical labour required for cultivating virgin soils.

Political considerations were also foremost in the decision to exclude those Punjabis who followed military careers in parts of the British empire not under the jurisdiction of the Government of India. Many Punjabis served in military units in a number of territories such as Hong Kong, Malaya, and Mauritius. The absence of such men from their homes placed them under disadvantages similar to those ostensibly suffered by soldiers of the British Indian army for selection as colonists. Yet they were held ineligible for the military allotment, for grants to them brought no special benefits to the Government of India. By contrast, it allowed Punjabis in certain units under its jurisdiction, but not strictly part of the army, to share in the military allotment. This happened in the case of the police forces of Quetta, Port Blair, and Burma.[14] Within British India, a share was appor-

in 1928: "I found . . . that demobilised soldiers, reservists, pensioners, and relations of those who had been killed during the Great War in action were coming forward as claimants in hundreds." See DC, Jhelum, to Commissioner, Rawalpindi, 1 December 1928; in "Selection of Peasant grantees in Nili Bar Colony," BOR 301/2/C9/188 C, pp. 9-11.

[13] Note by FC, 6 July 1892; in BOR J/301/431, pp. 8-9. See also Adjutant-General in India to RS, 1 October 1901; in PRAP(G), November 1901, No. 67. See also *PCM*, pp. 103-104.

[14] See PRAP(G): October 1901, Nos. 37-38; June 1903, Nos. 34-42; August 1903, Nos. 74-80; November 1903, No. 57; March 1904, Nos. 109-10.

tioned for purposes of allotment to each of the five military commands, centred in the Punjab, Bengal, Bombay, Burma, and Madras. Further subdivisions occurred within each command among the regiments and units that contained Punjabis, leading to the final nomination of grantees by regimental commanders.[15]

The social origins of the military grantees, briefly discussed earlier, were another important aspect of their settlement in the canal colonies. In Chenab and Jhelum colonies, these grantees had to belong, like other landholders, to the "agricultural castes."[16] Such groups not only supplied the great bulk of military recruits, but it was felt that ex-soldiers with agricultural backgrounds stood a better chance of achieving success as colonists than those without such traditions. These grantees were also chosen generally from the areas that provided civilian colonists, such as parts of central and northwestern Punjab. This was done in order to have the military grantees approximate as closely as possible their civilian counterparts, in the interests of agricultural efficiency.

With Lower Bari Doab and Nili Bar colonies, major changes were introduced for eligibility to military grants. In the former, eligibility in the case of combatant war veterans was extended to nonagriculturists, whereas noncombatants still had to come from the agricultural castes.[17] This measure was designed to stimulate war recruitment for combatant roles over a wider social base. But it did not end the exclusion of the professional and educated groups who held clerical and other noncombatant positions, unless they happened to belong to the agricultural castes. In Nili Bar Colony, even these distinctions were removed and caste origins no longer determined eligibility for military grants.

This liberalisation of the social basis of selection was accompanied by a relaxation of regional barriers. In both colonies, men from all over the Punjab were granted eligibility, and for the war veterans of Lower Bari Doab Colony, this was extended even to those from the Punjab princely states, Kashmir, and the North-West Frontier Province.[18] Thus colony land was

---

[15] See Imran Ali, "The Punjab Canal Colonies," p. 40 and Table 4.1 for a breakdown of land by military commands for Chenab and Jhelum colonies, respectively; and Table 4.2 for land distribution by regiments and units in Jhelum Colony, a more detailed picture that reveals the wide dispersal of Punjabis throughout the military organisation of British India.

[16] Assistant Military Secretary, Punjab Command, to All General Officers Commanding, Punjab Command, 9 February 1904; in PRAP(G), July 1904, No. 39. British officers were aided in their efforts to recruit from the agricultural castes by handbooks describing the different caste characteristics and configurations in the province. See, for example, J. M. Wikeley, *Punjabi Mussalmans* (Calcutta: Government Printing Press, 1915).

[17] For official correspondence on this issue, see BOR J/301/1178, pp. 13-122 and 231-51. See also PRAP(I): January 1915, Nos. 20-43; and September 1915, Nos. 14-51.

[18] Despite cautions from officials with experience of colonisation that such men would not

opened up to ex-soldiers from submontane, hilly, and distant regions, and to those with few or no agricultural traditions: types that were held to be unsuitable material for colonists in the case of civilians. Such concessions were motivated yet again by the political benefits that accrued from military settlement. They violated a basic administrative precept for agricultural colonisation, that peasant grants should only be allotted to people with sound agricultural traditions. Principles rigidly upheld elsewhere were superseded by military considerations.

Though large areas were reserved for military allotment, the fact remained that all aspirants could not be satisfied. Colony land was not unlimited, and competition for grants among soldiers left many unrewarded. The problem of supply of land became especially severe after World War I.[19] War veterans now pressed for the rewards they had come to expect from military service, and those who had seen combat duty regarded their own claims as second to none.[20] Men tried strenuously, through an inundation of applications, to secure land grants, and there was even a prospect that the political benefits from soldier settlement would be neutralised by the sense of grievance among the large host that remained ungratified. This led to demands from the army to reserve as much as 50 percent of the land in future canal colonies for military grantees. The Punjab Government was unable to accept such claims, though in practice it was as heavily committed as practicable to soldier settlement.[21] If the army was still not satisfied, it was because it had acquired an inordinate appetite for colony land.

The contribution of the ex-soldiers to economy and society in the canal colonies did little to vindicate such extensive allocations of land. These grantees were certainly orderly in their conduct, respectful of the law, and loyal to the state. They could be depended upon not to join the forces of dissension, and indeed to aid the administration in the imposition of its authority. But beyond providing a stabilising element among the body of

make proper settlers, concern about the political effects of withholding land from groups important for military recruitment had won the day. The government found unnerving such warnings as those from submontane Dogras of Gurdaspur District, made to an official on tour: "If you are so fond of your Arains and Sainis you had better get them to go fight for you." See Note by Senior Secretary to FC, 28 December 1914; in BOR J/301/1178, pp. 121-22.

[19] "The Punjab sent many thousands of soldiers to the war and I fear that it is only too true that for every man who has drawn a prize in the form of a land grant there are dozens, I might say even hundreds, who think they should also have participated in the allotment." See Secretary, Indian Soldiers Board, to Director of Staff Duties, 27 November 1920; in BOR J/301/1371, pp. 83-89.

[20] The Punjab Government in 1919 had to issue a press communique in an effort to dissuade soldiers from applying in large numbers to civil officials for land grants; they were asked to apply through the military authorities. See Tribune, 21 January 1919, p. 5.

[21] For this correspondence, see PRAP(I), September 1919, Nos. 161-64.

colonists, the military grantees did not stand out either for their role as agriculturists or for a civic consciousness elevated above that of their civilian counterparts. On the contrary, they often proved on both counts to be lacking in comparison with civilian colonists, even though the latter had not had the benefit of a life of discipline and regularity in the armed forces.

For one thing, the military grantees were a good deal more vociferous than civilians in making complaints. This was not because their condition was any worse, but because they realised that they had a better chance of having their grievances met. They had the ear of the military authorities, and it was through them that they channelled their protestations.[22] The civil administration was more sensitive and responsive to these complaints than to civilian ones, and was more prepared to undertake remedies than for civilians. The grievances of the latter usually had much less chance of reaching the higher officials, in any case, since civilian petitioners were generally unable to surmount the relations of power at the lower levels of bureaucratic authority. The effectiveness of their protests was in itself a measure of the more privileged position of the military allottees.

The first major problem for a soldier grantee was his settlement on a viable plot of land. Unlike the civilian colonist, who would have to be content with what he got, and in starting a new life accept stoically all the troubles associated with breaking virgin soil, the ex-soldier came to the land with greater expectations. Having served in the army for two decades or more, he regarded the grant as his due compensation, and in his maturer years had little tolerance for any hardships that might threaten his well-being. He felt it imperative that his grant be on soil of good quality, with irrigation arrangements that were efficient, if not faultless. If these conditions were not met, he expected to be given an exchange to better land. In Chenab Colony, land of good quality was found for the ex-soldiers.[23] In Jhelum Colony, the quality of land varied, and many obtained grants on inferior soil.[24] In later years they complained bitterly about this.

In Lower Bari Doab Colony, problems of inferior land appeared on a larger scale, and applications for exchanges from ex-soldiers were reported

---

[22] For example, a number of letters were sent to the Punjab Colonies Committee by commanding officers of various regiments, spelling out the complaints made to them by military grantees in Chenab and Jhelum colonies. See ''Running File on instructions to and proceedings of Colonies Committee, Punjab,'' BOR H/251/416, pp. 49-54.

[23] When land was first allotted to military grantees in Chenab Colony, many refused to take up land they considered inferior, though civilian colonists later accepted it readily. Thereafter care was taken to locate ex-soldiers on land of above-average quality. See PRAP(G): August 1895, Nos. 33-39; February 1896, Nos. 38-40; May 1897, Nos. 14-16.

[24] PCR: 1905, p. 32; 1906, p. 31.

to have assumed ''formidable proportions.''[25] Differences in the quality of land were inevitable, but so persistent were the ex-soldiers in wanting exchanges that ''every excuse is produced, every artifice is employed and every influence (from General Officers downwards) is enlisted in order to achieve the desired object. *Tabadla* [exchange] has become a universal game, and a knowledge of the different gambits is considered essential for a successful colonist.''[26] Because of these complaints and the procession of exchanges that resulted from them, the period of settlement for military grantees was extended over several years, with attendant disruptions. Even by 1930, well over a decade after soldier settlement had commenced in the colony, numerous applications for *tabadla* were still outstanding. This diverted colony staff from their normal duties, for ''the investigation (or even the summary refusal) of countless unwarranted petitions gives a great deal of unnecessary trouble.''[27] Thus the ex-soldiers were by no means a disciplined or acquiescent group of colonists when it came to protecting their own interests. Indeed, they displayed an assertiveness and a willingness to complain that stood in marked contrast to the more resigned attitude of their civilian counterparts.

Military grantees were also given special privileges over the matter of breaches in the conditions of tenure. Such breaches were common among all colonists, especially in the first few years of settlement; but the ex-soldiers were vociferous in their resentment against the lower officials responsible for reporting them. Once again, this was not such a problem in the earlier colonies, but the weight of protestations in Lower Bari Doab Colony induced the government to action. It tried to eliminate this source of vexation by bypassing its own functionaries and appointing in their place local committees of native military officers. The latter, themselves grantees, were given the responsibility of reporting breaches of tenure, thus saving the military colonists from the graft and petty tyrannies that civilians had to suffer at the hands of the subordinate bureaucracy.[28]

It was hoped that the seniority and apparent wisdom of the military officers would enable them to supervise the features of agricultural improvement written into the conditions of tenure. In this role, however, these officers reneged. They proved of little or no use in reporting breaches, nor did they display any interest in supervising tenurial stipulations. The committees simply became a means of obtaining status, the consideration that seemed uppermost for these officers: ''appointment to them is regarded as

[25] Ibid., 1922, p. 24. See also ''Applications from military grantees for exchange of land,'' BOR 301/12/00/51 A-G.

[26] *PCR*: 1922, p. 25; and see also 1920, p. 29; and 1925, pp. 51-52.

[27] Ibid., 1923, p. 44; and see also 1930, p. 80.

[28] Ibid., 1920, Governor's and FC's Reviews.

an additional mark of honour and there the matter is generally allowed to rest.''[29] Significantly, the administration was not unduly perturbed by such indifference. It neither penalised the wayward officers nor did it reconstitute the local committees. This failure to respond positively was governed by considerations of political expediency, but it reflected also the much lower priority given by this time to agricultural improvement and to the creation of a more well-ordered society in the canal colonies.

Whereas military officers were unable to provide leadership in matters that might have aided agricultural improvement, they displayed little apathy in the quest for personal advancement. They zealously pursued appointments to official positions, such as those of *lambardar* and *zaildar*. The latter were few and far between, and therefore open only to the most important men. It was for the *lambardari* posts, so it was reported from Lower Bari Doab Colony, that these officers contested most keenly. A *lambardari* carried with it an extra rectangle, a near certainty of obtaining another rectangle on horse-breeding terms, and authority and status in the village. Military grantees refused to accept a civilian as a *lambardar* over them, but agreed to have the seniormost officer in the village fulfil this role.[30] But there appeared invariably a large number of candidates, each with his own notion of seniority. So greatly was their instinct for status out of balance with their cooperative spirit that in the ensuing conflict large sums were said to be spent on legal costs. As the following report on competition for *lambardaris* brings out, the consciousness that the military grantees brought to the canal colonies was *not one benefitting from military order and discipline*, but one that smacked of the tangled rationality of the caste system:

> Competition in these villages has continued to be exceedingly keen; the grantees invariably profess themselves willing to accept military seniority as the criterion for the appointment, but when it comes to the application of this principle it is generally found that, by elaborate sub-division and cross-division of the grantees in the *chak*, several Indian Officers and non-Commissioned Officers claim the post on the grounds of seniority in their particular arm, regiment, district or caste. There are always various heterodox interpretations of the term seniority. It is, however, impossible from the point of view of colonisation and civil administration, to accept the principle of seniority without reservation, and this causes further difficulty and heart-burning.[31]

[29] Ibid., 1923, p. 48; and see also 1924, Governor's Review and p. 51; and 1926, p. 47.
[30] Ibid., 1924, p. 58.
[31] Ibid., 1922, p. 30.

It was over the vexatious question of residence that the military grantee appeared at his worst as a colonist. Residence near the grant was essential for success as an agricultural producer. Absentee landlords did not normally invest capital in the land, which merely became a source of unearned income cultivated through subtenants, a practice very disadvantageous for agricultural improvement. In Chenab and Jhelum colonies, absenteeism among military grantees was not a problem, for they belonged to agricultural tribes and were prepared to settle on the land. But the less restricted basis of selection adopted for Lower Bari Doab and Nili Bar colonies brought in as colonists men from nonagricultural castes and untried areas.[32] There were constant applications and petitions for exemption from residence, showing how unhappy many of them were in the canal colonies.

The response of the government was once again dictated by political expediency; the rules for supervising residence and the bases for granting exemptions were liberalised.[33] The government's attitude was especially conciliatory in Lower Bari Doab Colony, where war reward grantees were settled. Unauthorised absence from grants, as well, usually escaped the attention of the higher officials, for the military officers' committees failed to report breaches, and it was an easy matter to bribe petty officials.[34] Among military officers especially, absenteeism was said to be widespread. The administration abetted in this by freely granting exemption from residence if the officers were of landed gentry status, or served as loyal functionaries in their home districts in such capacities as honorary magistrate, *zaildar*, or member of a district board.[35] Yet absenteeism was acknowledged as a great curse, with little to recommend it on agrarian or social grounds.

Caste and area of origin were important factors in the willingness of the ex-soldiers to reside in colony villages. Sikh and Muslim Jats from the traditional areas for colonists, Lahore and Jullundur divisions, settled readily on the land and made good use of their grants. Men from submontane and distant tracts adapted least well. Dogras from Kashmir, Hindu Jats from Ambala Division, and Muslim Rajputs from the northern parts of Rawalpindi Division found it difficult to adjust to the remoteness and the harsh

[32] It had been argued that the hazards involved in this would be overcome by enforcing the compulsory condition of residence (the very issue over which the government showed such liberality later). See RS to AS, GOI, 2 September 1915; in BOR J/301/1178, pp. 47-51.

[33] The issue of exemption from personal residence of military grantees is dealt with for Lower Bari Doab Colony in BOR J/301/1593 and BOR 301/3/24/242; and for Nili Bar Colony in BOR 301/3/C9/177, BOR 301/14/C9/20, and *PCR*, 1928, pp. 90-91.

[34] *PCR*, 1926, p. 47.

[35] Ibid.: 1923, pp. 44-45; and 1930, p. 118. See also PRAP(I), January 1921, Nos. 11-12.

physical conditions of colony tracts.[36] It was reported from Nili Bar Colony that "unfortunately a high proportion of the grantees selected are not in the least of the class who are likely to make peasant farmers."[37] They put up "a ceaseless clamour for the relaxation of the [residence] clause." Though exemption was not granted where it was not justified, "evasion of this condition is I believe widespread but particular cases are learnt about with difficulty as knowledge of them depends in the last resort on reports from a patwari on very low pay."[38]

Tenurial conditions such as residence were a formal requirement only while the grantees were state tenants. Once they had acquired proprietary rights there was no hold on them, and they were free to become absentees or alienate their land. Indeed, many sold off their grants and moved back to their old homes.[39] This was already happening in Lower Bari Doab Colony by the early 1930s, while in Nili Bar Colony the government accelerated this process by giving another major concession to the military grantees. After continued protests from them, it agreed to reduce their purchase price of land by half: from Rs 200 to Rs 100 per acre.[40] Even in the straitened circumstances of the 1930s, the price of Rs 200 was well below market rates. A reduction to half this level was tantamount to leaving significant economic resources in the hands of one group at the cost of the rest of the community.

Military grants in the canal colonies reflected the desire of the colonial state to consolidate its position in a society in which it was an alien transplant. To establish lines of support, the British turned to placate those who had come forward as willing collaborators with their rule. The granting of land as a reward for military service had a long history prior to the British intervention in India, but the dimensions of soldier settlement as it occurred in the western Punjab were probably unprecedented. The fact that it was

[36] *Montgomery Tahsil AR* (1934), Section 9; *Okara Tahsil AR* (1934), Section 13; and *Lower Bari Doab Colony SR* (1936), para. 7. See also *PCR*, 1932, p. 6.

[37] *PCR*, 1929, p. 85.

[38] Ibid., 1928, p. 90.

[39] Ibid., 1932, p. 24.

[40] Military grantees seemed especially unhappy in Nili Bar Colony with its harsh environment, remoteness, and irrigation problems (for by this time the Punjab's water resources had been stretched to their limits). The economic depression of the 1930s wiped away the ex-soldiers' profits and left them struggling for survival, adding fuel to the many grievances they communicated to the military authorities. Investigations and information on these issues are contained in "Report of a tour by Major J. F. Peart of 10/2 Punjab Regiment—Consequential action thereon," BOR 301/2/00/438; "Military Officers—District tours—Grievances of military colonists of Nili Bar Colony," BOR 301/2/C9/461; and "Representation to HMR by military grantees of Nili Bar Colony regarding their troubles and grievances," BOR 301/3/ C9/210.

promulgated under the aegis of an external imperialism added distinctive implications to this process. With such landed resources at its command, the authority of the army and of those who served in it was further enhanced in Punjabi society. This was to have a major impact on the political fortunes of the nation state that inherited the canal colonies after 1947. Behind military rule in Pakistan lay both a long-established greed for economic resources and a strong and continued association with imperialism, which the outward apparitions of independent nationhood could only superficially conceal.[41]

The soldier recipients of land grants belonged in the great majority of cases to the landholding castes of the Punjab. This was the stratum that virtually monopolised peasant colonisation, and thus both civilian and military land settlement strengthened the dominant elements of rural society. Military service offered such rewards that its attractions increased for the "martial races," either in terms of maintaining existing status or achieving upward mobility. When the large host of Punjabi officers obtained land grants, the bonds between military service and the rural elite were further strengthened. In cases where soldiers from nonagricultural castes were allowed land grants, and such eligibility existed much more extensively for them than for civilians, a military career became an important means of improving social position. The fact that one type of profession, to a significantly greater extent than any other, was being compensated so liberally was bound to enhance its stature in society.

Camel Grants

The participation of the military in the canal colonies extended not only to land grants for military personnel but also to extensive settlement schemes involving the breeding and maintenance of animals for military use. The first scheme so devised was in Chenab Colony and concerned the camel. The Rechna Doab had among its indigenous peoples a camel-owning tribe known as the Biloch. Though large and important, this tribe was hierarchically inferior to the cattle-owning tribes of the *doab*.[42] Like the latter, the Bilochis qualified for colony grants as Janglis. However, unlike their brethren they were not to obtain ordinary grants, for in the camel they possessed an animal of much importance to military transport. The Bilochis had previously provided camels as transport animals for military expeditions to the northwest frontier and beyond. Their services were drafted by the army

---

[41] For an assessment of the role of the military and ruling elites in Pakistan, see Tariq Ali, *Pakistan: Military Rule or People's Power?* (New York: William Morrow, 1970); and H. N. Gardezi, "Neocolonial Alliances and the Crisis of Pakistan," in Gough and Sharma (eds.), *Imperialism and Revolution in South Asia*, pp. 130-45.

[42] RPCC, p. 103.

when campaigns were in the offing, though a certain degree of voluntari-
ness remained, which created an element of insecurity for logistical plan-
ning. With the canal colonies, the Bilochis entered into a new relationship
with the state, one that was designed not only to hold them to their traditional occupation but to make it obligatory for them to supply camels for
military service.

The arid and sparsely populated tracts of the western Punjab had provided ideal grazing grounds for the camel, but the spread of canal irrigation
began progressively to reduce these pasturages. Throughout this region in
the opening decades of the twentieth century, the camel retreated as irrigation spread. A great deal of administrative effort, attested to by voluminous government records, was diverted to the task of finding new grazing
areas and for relocating in them the transport camels maintained in this
region, known as the Silladari Camel Corps.[43] The problem appeared in-
soluble, for irrigation, wherever it could be introduced, took precedence
over pasturage. The matter was eventually resolved by the eclipse of the
camel itself as a military animal, with the mechanisation of army transport.

At the turn of the century, however, the British were faced with the immediate problem of rapid displacement of the Bilochis' camel pasturages
by canal irrigation. With the land grants to which they qualified as Janglis,
it was feared that the Bilochis would lose the incentive to maintain their
animals. They also stood to lose the means to do so with the smallholdings
of half a square per family that fell to the Janglis' lot. While such a fate
was allowed to overtake the strong cattle herds of the Janglis without any
restitution from the state, the military importance of the camel rendered a
similar outcome for it unacceptable. To avert this crisis the British resorted,
in this new agrarian frontier, to the imposition of feudalistic relations between state and individual. The Bilochis were not allowed to obtain ordinary grants, like other Janglis, but were allotted land solely on condition
that they continue to maintain their camels and provide them for military
duty. They were obligated to do so under formal tenurial contract, and they
stood to lose all claim to land if they did not accept such terms.[44]

Colony land was now being granted for the provision of military needs

[43] A large amount of official correspondence exists on the subject of grazing areas for the
Silladar Camel Corps in the Punjab. See, for example, for the period 1900-1905, PRAP(G):
October 1901, Nos. 15-20; April 1902, Nos. 23-32; June 1902, Nos. 3-8; November 1902,
Nos. 40-85, December 1902, Nos. 5-15; March 1903, Nos. 54-67, 75-95; August 1903, Nos.
68-73; February 1904, Nos. 121-41; and August 1905, Nos. 24-32.

[44] Note by CO, Chenab Colony, 20 September 1899; in PRAP(G), March 1900, No. 18.
The acceptance of service obligations was not entirely involuntary, for several leading Bilo-
chis did convey their support of the camel scheme through meetings and petitions: PRAP(I),
February 1899, Nos. 5-6.

in what came to be known as "service" grants.[45] From these Biloch beginnings, such tenures were to achieve great importance in the canal colonies. An area of 93,000 acres was thus allotted to the Bilochis, with grants on twenty-year leases, to expire in 1921. Four "camel corps," the 59th to 62nd Service Camel Corps, were supported on these grants, with a total complement of around 4,300 camels.[46] The establishment, to use the words of one official, of a "feudal service" and a "local advantageous feudal relation"[47] occurred at a time of seemingly rapid change, which in economic terms might well be called "modernisation." The paradox of agricultural colonisation lay in the fact that such feudal forms were emerging within a framework of economic growth—and were fostered in their most vivid form for the fulfilment of military functions. The British thus ensured, in the case of the Bilochis, tied suppliers for a vital transport animal that was often not voluntarily forthcoming.

The camel grants, representing as they did a more overt intrusion of military concerns on the society of the Rechna Doab, did not leave unaffected the hierarchy of the indigenous tribes. In order to make the maintenance of camels economically practicable, the Bilochis were allotted land at the rate of one square per camel, well above the half square per family allotted to cattle-owning Janglis. This violated the notions of hierarchical superiority that the cattle owners entertained toward the Bilochis. Many Janglis did not receive any land at all, despite their fervent lamentations, thus accentuating feelings of inequity and discrimination. Moreover, the state made no provisions for the upkeep of the cattle herds, in contrast to the elaborate arrangements made to retain the camels. Cattle-breeding grants would have been of greater agrarian benefit than camel grants, but the cattle were allowed to suffer inexorable decline as the environmental basis for their existence was steadily undermined.[48] The cattle owners could feel justifiably envious of their former inferiors: official reports spoke of the "considerable

[45] The camel scheme was first proposed to a transport committee by Chaudhry Aurangzeb Khan, the assistant colonisation officer, Chenab Colony. It was warmly supported by the financial commissioner and the committee as a means of obtaining "fit camels and fit *sarwan* attendants for employment in any trans-frontier emergency." But it was opposed by the lieutenant-governor for placing an unfair burden, which would in time appear increasingly onerous, on one section of colonists. The Government of India overruled this objection, and decided to implement the scheme. See *PCM*, p. 124.

[46] See PRAP(G), October 1919, No. 38; and *PCR*, 1905, p. 2; and 1908, p. 1. For proposals and correspondence leading to these tenures, see PRAP(G): March 1900, Nos. 1-26; October 1900, Nos. 1-12; and November 1900, Nos. 33-37.

[47] These were terms used for the camel scheme by G. F. de Montmorency, Settlement Officer, Lyallpur: see Note, 17 February 1911; in PRAP(G), December 1911, No. 21.

[48] The decline in the economic value of Jangli cattle is discussed in *AR Lower Chenab Colony of Jhang District* (1923), para. 19; and *Jhang District SR* (1928), pp. 18-19.

jealousy" that the larger camel grants aroused among them.[49] The state, normally so solicitous of hierarchical sensitivities, was prepared to intercede in the social structure when military considerations were involved. It was far less willing to take such initiatives in the pursuit of developmental goals.

Inequalities within the Biloch tribe were not reduced as a result of the service tenures, but reappeared and were consolidated through differentials in land distribution. Larger grants were allotted to the Bilochi tribal leaders, called *chaudhries*.[50] These luminaries were also given important supervisory roles, such as those of conveying government orders, ensuring the supply of camels and attendants, and reporting casualties and defaults. By such means they maintained their social eminence and the hold on their tribal followers that they had enjoyed in precolony days.[51] The ordinary Biloch camel owners obtained grants of one square per camel. But so much land had been allocated for this purpose that the supply of these "true" or "first class" Bilochis ran out, a sad contrast to the plight of other Janglis. The remaining land was allotted to Bilochis of lower rank, who came to be called "second class" Bilochis, at the rate of half a square per camel.[52] The low land-to-camel ratio kept these lower-order Bilochis indigent and economically depressed: canal irrigation was not to prove a source of upward mobility for such people.

Still further down the social scale were the retainers and servants, and they remained in that capacity despite the transition in economic conditions. They were the ones furnished as attendants, or *sarwan*s, to accompany the camels on military service. To discourage desertions they were bonded to this task by being brought under the Indian Articles of War when on active duty.[53] That this form of labour proved distasteful was shown by the growing difficulties faced by the Bilochis in retaining their *sarwan*s. With expanding employment opportunities in the canal colonies, these traditional "menials" preferred to offer their services elsewhere. Yet they only moved laterally, and remained at the bottom of the social structure,

---

[49] RPCC, p. 103.

[50] BOR H/251/416, p. 133; and *PCM*, p. 125.

[51] The state also catered generously to their needs. One example was the additional fifty-four squares allotted to leading Bilochis after they had petitioned that their military services had not been adequately rewarded. See "Reservation of certain areas of land in Pir Mahal and Buralla Extensions of Lower Chenab Canal for Bilochis of Lyallpur District," BOR 301/3/25/133, pp. 1-36.

[52] See PRAP(G), March 1900, Nos. 20-25; and *PCM*, pp. 126-27.

[53] See PRAP(G): December 1900, Nos. 1-5; and July 1901, No. 1. In 1902 a minimum period of two years was stipulated for the *sarwan*s, as they were being changed too frequently, thus providing few returns for the training they received: PRAP(G), November 1902, Nos. 1-2.

for the increased demand for labour did not lead to a relaxation in social inequalities. Their preference for other forms of work did create severe labour problems for the Bilochis, which were accentuated after 1914 with added pressure on labour supplies from new colonisation schemes and the outbreak of war. The grantees were forced to go outside the canal colonies to procure *sarwan*s, from whom they were faced with such demands as cash advances of Rs 200-300.[54] They had no option but to comply, for they faced heavy penalties for failing to fulfil their contract with the state.

Apart from labour shortages, there were several other problems that the Bilochis faced in meeting their service obligations. For one, the diminution and eventual disappearance of grazing areas proved an intractable problem for the camel scheme. These animals were almost wholly dependent on external grazing, for they were not assigned any grain rations while within the colony, and the Bilochi grants were not large enough to provide for both human and animal subsistence. Grazing areas were reserved for the Camel Corps, but with expanding irrigation these were situated progressively further away from the camel grants. The contraction in grazing grounds was an irreversible process, and with it was eroded the ecological balance for tied camel tenures in the Rechna Doab.[55] Another problem that bedevilled the Bilochi camelmen was faulty irrigation facilities. Their grants had been placed at the extremes of Chenab Colony, in its southeastern corner, in order to be close to grazing areas. But this also placed them at the ends of canal distributaries, areas that were the most susceptible to water shortages.[56] Many ordinary grantees also experienced similar difficulties, but they were not faced with the added obligation, accompanied by the threat of instant retribution, of maintaining and providing animals for military duty.

High camel mortality further strained the Bilochis' resources. The camel thrived in arid conditions, but moisture from irrigation brought fatal diseases such as the dreaded *surra*. Disease, the physical strain of increasing remoteness of grazing tracts, and finally the accelerated mortality from World War I created severe replacement problems for the Bilochis.[57] The

[54] DC, Lyallpur, to Commissioner, Multan, 5 July 1919; in PRAP(G), October 1919, Enclosure No. 2 to No. 38.

[55] Grazing reserves were established on vacant lands, but in time these came under canal irrigation, necessitating the location of such pasturages progressively further away from the camel grants. See PRAP(G): September 1901, Nos. 15-20; April 1902, Nos. 16-22; June 1902, Nos. 1-2; July 1902, Nos. 30-34; October 1902, Nos. 80-87; November 1902, Nos. 14-22; October 1906, Nos. 7-17; June 1909, Nos. 44-53; and April 1910, Nos. 55-57.

[56] For information on conditions prevailing in the Biloch camel grants, see *AR Gugera Branch II* (1912), para. 25; and *AR Gugera Branch I-II* (1923), paras. 13-16.

[57] See PRAP(I), December 1901, No. 3; *PCR*, 1906, p. 1; and H. E. Cross, *A Note on*

local supply of camels soon began to run out, and these grantees began to scour other parts of the Punjab for replacements. With the special demands placed by the war, the camel supply throughout the Punjab was exhausted, and the Bilochis had to resort to areas as far away as Sind for animals.[58] This defeated the very purpose of the camel scheme, which was to preserve the Rechna Doab as a camel-breeding region.

As a consequence of the many problems they encountered in meeting their service requirements, the Bilochis were placed under severe financial strain. High labour and replacement costs, canal failures, and lack of feed led to widespread indebtedness among these grantees. Especially affected were the "second class" Bilochis with their smaller grants.[59] Government efforts at stemming insolvency through a system of loans, known as *taccavi*, proved unworkable. Guarantors to underwrite such advances were not to be found, indicating that the service tenures were not fostering a communal spirit among these tribesmen.[60] Government attempts to organise cooperative societies also met with failure, so there was no pooling of resources that might have led to an improvement in their economic position.[61] Yet the Bilochis were reported to be heavily indebted, and even to have lost control of their grants to creditors: "The Biloch gets someone else's camel branded in his own name, and instals the real owner on his squares *sine die*. The latter takes the whole or nearly all the produce, the real Biloch grantee occupying the position of the servant or mortgagor."[62] The camel grantees were caught in a web of feudal obligation and economic servitude from which they were unable to extricate themselves.

The grievances the Bilochis expressed about their lot led to governmental reexamination of the scheme within a decade of its inception, through a Colonies Committee appointed after the 1907 agitation. Using an inverted logic, it warned that the abolition of the scheme, while desirable in itself, would incur the hostility of the Jangli cattle owners, for it would leave the Bilochis with larger grants untrammelled by service obligations.[63] Even so,

---

Surra in Camels for Commandants of Camel Corps (Lahore: Government Printing Press, 1914).

[58] DC, Lyallpur, to Commissioner, Multan, 5 July 1919; in PRAP(G), October 1919, Enclosure No. 2 to No. 38.

[59] "Note on half square grants on Camel Service conditions on Chenab Canal," by DC, Lyallpur, 18 October 1907; in BOR H/251/416, pp. 401-403.

[60] See PRAP(I): December 1901, Nos. 1-5; February 1902, No. 69; and June 1906, Nos. 22-24.

[61] "Attempts are being made to instil some idea of Co-operative Credit Societies into the Biloch; but one who was for years the obedient servant of the large Bar grazier incubates the sense of co-operative initiative slowly": *PCR*, 1906, p. 2.

[62] Ibid.

[63] RPCC, pp. 98-106: "It would undoubtedly be a source of great discontent on the part of

these tenures had produced such imbalances that the Colonies Committee recommended that they be terminated. A later enquiry by the Camel Browsing Committee of 1911-1912 made similar suggestions.[64] The abolition of the camel service scheme was finally sanctioned in 1913, well before the year of expiration of the leases (1921).[65] But World War I broke out before the decision could be implemented, and the four camel corps were retained for war service. They were sent into operation in Egypt and Iran and on the northwest frontier, and proved of value in these areas.[66] After the war, it was obvious that few returns could be expected from these grants. The scheme was finally abolished when the leases expired in 1921, with the incumbents retaining their land in the form of ordinary peasant tenures.[67]

The camel grants provided another example of the ways in which imperialism intervened in agrarian society to meet its military requirements. The effort to retain traditional roles; the onerous obligations placed on peasant holders, with compulsion exercised under threat of fines or confiscation; and the feudalistic bonding of land with service—such were the attributes of this particular involvement of the military in the economy of the Punjab. The impracticability of these demands, and the strains they placed on the smallholding economy of the Bilochis and on their tribal structure, were soon realised. Yet a generation or two of grantees were saddled with these obligations before they were lifted, and this included the trauma for man and animal of war service. The Biloch camel grants were the earliest, but not the only, instance of the propagation of military animals in the canal colonies. They were juxtaposed with service tenures of much greater magnitude, related to the breeding of cavalry horses.

Cavalry Horse Runs

The horse-breeding schemes that were so extensively introduced in the canal colonies, to be discussed presently, were designed to provide horses

---

the ordinary Janglis if those whom they were accustomed to look down upon as their inferiors were immediately raised by the action of Government to a material position considerably superior to their own'' (p. 103).

[64] "Report of the Camel Browsing Committee" (1911); in PRAP(G), December 1911, No. 18 (see also Nos. 20-23).

[65] RAS, GOI, to RS, 24 February 1913; in PRAP(G), May 1913, No. 8.

[66] FC to RS, 1 July 1918; in PRAP(G), August 1918, No. 95. See also "Portion of Lyallpur District War History regarding Camel Corps," n.d.; in PRAP(G), October 1919, Enclosure to No. 38.

[67] For proposals and correspondence regarding the abolition of the camel scheme, see PRAP(G): October 1919, Nos. 37-38; June 1921, Nos. 43-47; and July 1923, Nos. 7-9. For the final terms of commutation of the camel grants to ordinary peasant tenancies, see *PCM*, pp. 126-30.

for cavalry regiments of the British army stationed in India. For these the Army Remount Department acted as the purchasing agent. The remount requirements of cavalry regiments of the Indian army were organised along different lines. Until 1921, these regiments were based on the *silladari* system, a structure that had been inherited from the Mughal and Maratha cavalry. Under this form of organisation, "the regiment was a type of joint-stock company in which the trooper paid for his horse and equipment when he joined and sold them back when he left."[68] The regiments were required to be financially self-supporting, and their expenses, including the purchase of horses, were supposed to be met from a subscription fund known as *chanda*. By the turn of the century, the rising market price of cavalry remounts was seriously taxing the finances of these regiments and threatening to erode their "self-sufficiency."

Rather than make any additional subventions from the military budget to help these units out of their financial difficulties, the British decided to use land in the canal colonies to prop up this regimental structure. First a few and then gradually all the Indian cavalry regiments were allotted grants, known as horse runs, so that they could produce their own horses and would not need to purchase them in the market.[69] There were manifold advantages in this for the British. Indian cavalrymen could continue to pay their way through their service, while the government would not have to make budgetary allocations for their regiments. This facade of self-sufficiency would in reality be propped up by large land grants to the Indian cavalry in the canal colonies.

Allotted between 1900 and 1920, the horse runs were situated, with a couple of exceptions, in three different colonies: Chenab, Jhelum, and Lower Bari Doab. In 1921, the *silladari* system was abolished, and the Indian cavalry was reorganised along more modern lines, with the task of horse procurement delegated to the Army Remount Department.[70] With this the horse runs too were abolished, though this measure failed to terminate the army's occupancy of the land, which it insisted on continuing to utilise for other purposes. Though as a form of tenure they were short-lived, the regimental horse runs were highly significant in that they reflected the growing assertiveness of the military.

[68] P. Mason, *A Matter of Honour* (London: Jonathan Cape, 1974), p. 26 (see also pp. 376-77).

[69] The cavalry regiments were put in indefinite possession of their grants, and though the land remained public property, it passed completely under the control of the military: see Note by FC, 8 January 1909; in "Policy in regard to colony horse runs," BOR J/301/1020 A, p. 21. See also AS, GOI, to Secretary, PG, 7 May 1908; in PRAP(G), August 1908, No. 61.

[70] AS, GOI, to RS, 30 April-2 May 1921; in "Disposal of lands at present utilised as horse runs in canal colonies by certain regiments of Silladar Cavalry," BOR 301/6/00/3 A, p. 235.

The government had not originally intended to allot grants of the scale that finally eventuated. In the 1890s, applications were made by some regimental commanders for horse runs in Chenab Colony. These requests were at first withdrawn, when the government refused to allow the revenue concessions that the regiments demanded as a condition for taking up the land. In time the administration capitulated to the army's terms, leading to the allotment of horse runs to four regiments in Chenab Colony.[71] A further ten runs were allotted in Jhelum Colony, again after applications were received from regimental commanders.[72] Then in 1907 the army authorities prevailed upon the government to allot horse runs to all cavalry regiments of the British Indian army. It was argued that these allotments were necessary if the joint-stock basis of the Indian cavalry was to be saved from insolvency.[73] The internal funding system of the regiments was proving increasingly inadequate for purchasing horses and mules at market rates. These concerns led, by 1920, to the allotment of a total of twenty-five horse runs in the canal colonies, covering an area of 45,200 acres.[74] A few cavalry regiments remained without runs, because the land reserved for them on an extension of Chenab Colony was too high for flow irrigation. By 1921, when all horse runs were abolished, these regiments had still not obtained possession because government plans to irrigate this area through a hydroelectric scheme had failed to materialise.[75]

Once they had been settled on the land, territorial aggrandisement marked out the horse runs from all other types of tenure in the colonies. Regimental commanders incessantly applied for possession of vacant areas near their runs, for exchanges to land of better quality, or for improved irrigation facilities. At a higher level, the army continued to press the government for an increase in the overall size of the runs, until finally they were doubled and even trebled in area. Whereas originally areas of 750 to 1,000 acres were assigned to each run, the army succeeded in having this raised to a base area of 1,500 acres, and in some cases the size of holdings was extended to over 2,000 acres. In Jhelum Colony, the government wanted to keep their size down to 750 acres, since it had already allotted two large young-stock runs of 10,000 acres each to the Army Remount

---

[71] See "Applications for grants of land for horse runs on Chenab Canal," BOR J/301/365 A-B.

[72] See "Grants of land for horse runs on Jhelum Canal," BOR J/301/698 A-E.

[73] Deputy AS, GOI, to Secretary, PG, 16 May 1907; in PRAP(G), July 1907, No. 24.

[74] For a list of these horse runs, see Imran Ali, "The Punjab Canal Colonies," Table 4.10.

[75] The proposed lift irrigation facilities are discussed in the chapter on production. See also PRAP(G), November 1914, Nos. 1-15; "Lift area grants—Chenab Canal," BOR J/301/839; and "Lift area grants on Lower Chenab Canal," BOR 301/11/25/10.

Department. But here too the army had its way, and the horse runs were extended to a minimum of 1,500 acres each.[76]

The cavalry regiments also succeeded in securing for themselves the most lenient revenue terms to be found in the canal colonies. They refused to accept the grants unless a wide range of cesses and rates were waived, which was an anomaly since these *silladari* units were supposed to be self-supporting. State taxes such as *nazarana, malikana*, land revenue, and all minor cesses were waived entirely. One of these cesses was the "local rate," which was credited to District Boards for expenditure on local development such as the construction and maintenance of roads. The horse runs enjoyed such amenities without having to pay for them. The only charge levied on the horse runs was for irrigation water, and even for that they obtained a special low rate for grass paddocks.[77] No other grantees in the canal colonies obtained land on such concessionary terms. By contrast, all the colony land that could make a positive contribution to agricultural development, such as seed and cattle farms, was made to bear the full burden of government extraction.

These revenue concessions caused substantial losses in state income. It was calculated that in the three years ending 1909-1910, the loss of revenue on the Chenab and Jhelum Colony horse runs amounted to Rs 40,000 per annum. By 1912, with revenue reassessments, this had increased to Rs 64,000 per annum.[78] This amount almost doubled with the allotment of further horse runs in Lower Bari Doab Colony. In addition, the public exchequer was deprived of the large capital returns that the sale of these lands would have brought, for while they were under military usage they had to be withheld from sale. The government also had to forego the interest earnings that would have accrued from the capitalised value of the land. The annual loss to the province in interest earnings alone was estimated in 1921

[76] The extension of the Jhelum Colony horse runs involved the displacement of about 120 grantees, comprising the entire landholding body of eleven villages. After protracted negotiations, these men agreed to move to Upper Jhelum Colony. Since the army did not want to lose them as horse breeders, and there was no provision for such tenures in the new colony, the government went to the extent of altering the territorial limits of the two projects so that the area of resettlement became part of Jhelum Colony. See BOR J/301/698; "Conditions applicable to horse-breeding tenants transferred from Lower Jhelum Canal to Upper Jhelum Canal Colony," BOR J/301/1364; and Imran Ali, "The Punjab Canal Colonies," pp. 269-70.

[77] See letters of RS; Deputy AS, GOI; and Secretary, PWD, GOI: in BOR J/301/365 B, pp. 443-44, 569(a-g), and 753, respectively. See also PRAP(G): February 1900, Nos. 1-9; April 1903, Nos. 12-17; and May 1903, Nos. 28-29.

[78] RS to AS, GOI, 27 March 1911; in PRAP(G), March 1911, No. 32. See also FC to RS, 13 February 1912; in PRAP(G), March 1912, No. 12.

to be Rs 1.5 million.[79] With current interest rates at 6 percent, the value of land tied up in the horse runs stood at no less than Rs 25 million. These amounts represented losses borne by the ordinary citizens of the Punjab, for the large investments made in canal construction and colonisation were ill served by the appropriation of these tracts by the military, and that too on such gratuitous terms.

An even more egregious aspect of the horse runs lay in the flagrant deviation from the original purpose behind their allotment. The Indian cavalry had been provided these grants so that it could become self-sufficient in its horse supply. It was soon discovered, however, that the regiments were using the grants for commercial agriculture. Sizeable profits could be made from commercial undertakings on such large holdings, especially since care had been taken to locate them in areas with good soil, efficient irrigation, and proximity to railway stations.[80] As a result of the decision of 1907 to allot runs to all cavalry regiments, even those stationed over 2,000 miles away in southern India obtained these grants. Such far-flung units were patently unable to perform, or even properly supervise, the complex operations involved in horse breeding.[81] The Punjab authorities realised that the real intention of the army was to use this land for purposes of commercial profit. In 1909 they queried the central government, but ineffectually, on "whether the run would be anything more than a disguised subvention to regimental funds at the cost of general revenues."[82] To try and ensure that it really was used for rearing horses, the Punjab Government requested that the maintenance of a minimum number of animals be fixed for each run. The army rejected such a provision, though similar stipulations were applied to all other service grants in the canal colonies, whether military or developmental in function.[83]

The misuse of the horse runs became an open secret. It was reported in 1912 that "these so-called 'horse-runs' have ceased to be entitled to that

---

[79] FC to RS, 8 September 1921; and RS to AS, GOI, 30 September 1921; in BOR 301/6/00/3 A, pp. 237-40. See also PRAP(G), December 1921, Nos. 26-27.

[80] The need to locate the cavalry horse runs on good-quality land, with proper irrigation and transport facilities, had been laid down from the start by the government: see Note by Commanding Officer, 2nd Punjab Cavalry, 8 June 1901; in BOR J/301/698 A, pp. 4(e-f).

[81] The army authorities were evasive on this point when queried by the provincial government in 1910, simply replying that regiments based in South India would have to take the cost of transporting remounts into consideration when assessing whether their runs were profitable or not. See Secretary, PG, to AS, GOI, 18 February 1910; in PRAP(G), March 1910, No. 5. See also AS, GOI, to Secretary, PG, 24 August 1910; in PRAP(G), January 1911, No. 24.

[82] Secretary, PG, to AS, GOI, 26 September 1909; in PRAP(G), October 1909, No. 12.

[83] Secretary, PG, to AS, GOI, 5 October 1909; ibid., No. 17. See also AS, GOI, to Secretary, PG, 17 January 1910; in PRAP(G), March 1910, No. 4.

description and have become mere tillage farms.'"[84] In Jhelum Colony over 80 percent and in Chenab Colony over 90 percent of the allotted area was being sown with commercial crops, and was thus not being utilised either for fodder crops or for grass pasturage. Matters were no different in Lower Bari Doab Colony, where no more than 10 to 15 percent of the cultivated area was being devoted to fodder crops. Much more common on these horse runs were cash crops such as wheat, cotton, and oilseeds, with the land being farmed out to subtenants and contractors. Even the standard of cultivation left much to be desired, so that, as a chief engineer ruminated in 1918, the contribution of these grants to agricultural improvement remained minimal:

> Military farms, controlled, as they are, by British officers who have facilities for studying agricultural science, ought to be models to the privately owned estates in their vicinity; but they are, in fact, worse cultivated as a rule than the holdings of the average peasant occupiers in our canal colonies. The military farm tenant is, as a rule, ignorant and unskilled in agriculture; but he has sufficient intelligence to utilise the influence of his landlords for the purpose of obtaining most favoured treatment from the Canal Department.[85]

The runs merely amounted to grants-in-aid to the cavalry regiments, which did not appear in the military budget and were not subject to any regular financial audit. The Punjab Government continued to make the occasional protest about the misuse of this large area of land, but little redemption could be expected from the army, and none was offered. The cavalry runs made no positive contributions to horse breeding, let alone to agricultural progress. Indeed, profits from the runs were used to purchase imported remounts in the market. When the horse runs were finally abolished, Punjab officials could only bemoan the years of lost opportunity:

> It was never contemplated that the conditions of these grants would be broken, that instead of growing fodder crops, commanding officers would show a remarkable commercial instinct, and that instead of improving the indigenous breed of horses to mount their regiments well they would attain this object by purchasing foreign animals.[86]

The issue of the further utilisation of the area under the horse runs arose when they were abolished in 1921. The Punjab Government argued strongly that the land should revert to its own control. It wanted to use the

---

[84] FC to RS, 13 December 1912; in PRAP(G), March 1912, No. 12.

[85] Chief Engineer, Irrigation Works, to RS, 30 March 1918; in PRAP(I), June 1918, Enclosure to No. 35.

[86] FC to RS, 8 September 1921; in BOR 301/6/00/3 A, p. 239.

area for allotment to war veterans, for seed farms (for which there was a desperate need in Chenab and Jhelum colonies), and for compensatory grants to sufferers from waterlogging.[87] However, the army resolutely and successfully defended its right to retain the land for its own use, and to dispose of it as it wished. It argued that the ending of one form of military tenure did not end its lien on the land. It did make over fifteen of the twenty-five horse runs to the Punjab Government, but this was exclusively for allotment to war veterans. The rest of the area was reallotted in the form of large mule-breeding and filly-rearing farms, the recipients being three British ex-army officers and some Punjabi men of substance.[88] It proved to be virtually impossible to free land from the army once it had passed under its control. The requests of the Agricultural Department for seed farms were completely rejected, though officials were well aware of the great deficiency of such farms in the canal colonies.[89] Mule breeding and grants to ex-soldiers had greater priority for the state.

THE BEHEMOTH OF HORSE BREEDING

With the emergence of horse breeding, tenures entailing service obligations to the military as a condition for the granting of land became a widespread phenomenon in the canal colonies. Horse-breeding operations dominated two large colonisation projects, Jhelum and Lower Bari Doab. Their purpose was to provide remounts for cavalry regiments, initially of the British army stationed in India but later also of the British Indian army. The aim was to make India a self-sufficient producer of cavalry horses. In a period when the horse was being rapidly displaced as a military animal by technological change, the British in South Asia began diverting extensive agricultural resources for its production and upkeep.

Horse breeding was established on quite different lines and experienced varying fortunes in the two colonies where it existed, and they are best discussed separately.

Compulsion and Jhelum Colony

In Jhelum Colony, horse-breeding grants covered an allotted area of over 250,000 acres, on which about 4,000 mares were maintained.[90] About 80

[87] RS to AS, GOI, 30 September 1921; ibid., p. 240. See also AS, GOI, to RS, 26 May 1922; in BOR 301/6/00/3 B, pp. 11-17.

[88] For the conversion of certain horse runs to mule-breeding farms, and for information on the mule-breeding grantees, see BOR: 301/2/18-19/341, 301/6/19/8, 301/6/19/25/9, 301/6/19/25/12, 301/6/19/14, 301/6/24/18, 301/6/25/4, and 301/16/19/24/5.

[89] DA to FC, 30 June 1921; in BOR 301/6/00/3 A, pp. 65-71.

[90] *PCR*: 1908, p. 26; 1922, pp. 11-12.

percent of this area was distributed in the form of peasant (or *abadkar*) grants of two squares (55 acres) apiece. On each grant a brood mare had to be maintained for producing young stock, which if of acceptable quality were then purchased by the Army Remount Department. There were also the larger yeoman (or *sufedposh*) grants, for the maintenance of five to fifteen mares at the rate of 1.5 squares per mare. Also allotted were eight "stud farm" grants of substantial size, with a requirement of up to fifty mares. All the above grants were made to individual Punjabis, but there were in addition two large young-stock "depots" of 10,000 acres each with the Army Remount Department, plus several horse runs for cavalry regiments. Jhelum Colony was wholly given over to horse breeding, the only nonservice grants being those to indigenous Janglis, noncavalry military allottees, and "civil" grantees.

Horse breeding in Jhelum Colony marked a major break from earlier principles of land allotment. The original colonisation scheme did not envisage horse breeding, but was based on agrarian and demographic considerations similar to those that had governed land distribution in earlier colonies. This was replaced by a scheme that had service tenures as its chief aspect, a transition stemming from the proposals of the Horse and Mule-breeding Commission that colony land be used to breed and maintain military animals.[91] The pleas of the Punjab Government to apply the service condition only to a certain proportion of grants, and then only to added areas of land rather than to the principal holdings of the grantees, were rejected by the central government. The latter insisted that the scheme stood a better chance of success if the service tenure were made integral to each grant, and if it were applied universally rather than selectively over the colony.

This resulted in the imposition of a set of obligations from which the grantee had few means of escape short of disposing of his land, uprooting himself and his family, and leaving the colony. Since such a drastic alternative was not open to many, it created a pool of near-captive servitors who came increasingly to resent their predicament. Through contractual obligation, the very means of subsistence of the grantee became tied to the performance of horse-breeding functions. Any inadequacy or default in the latter threatened to incur the retribution of the supervising authority, the Army Remount Department. And apart from the ever-present prospect of coercion and punishment, even graver disabilities entered into the lives of the horse-breeding grantees. In order to retain them as viable units for horse

[91] Report of the Horse and Mule-breeding Commission, 1900-1901. See also President, Horse and Mule-breeding Commission, to AS, GOI, 7 January 1901; in PRAP(G), July 1901, No. 26.

production, the government had to impose a degree of regulation on these grants that was not required for ordinary tenures. Where such regulation violated the traditional practices and deeply held convictions of the grantees, it marred the harmony of their lives in the colony and brought them into a state of conflict with the administration. Horse breeding came to be regarded by the colonists as "a most deplorable and exceedingly unfortunate accident," through which "fear and misery prevail and the sufferings . . . have . . . become too terrible to describe and too numerous to enumerate."[92]

Modification in the rules of inheritance caused perhaps the most anxiety and resentment. The customary laws of succession that prevailed in the rest of the province applied also, after the passing of the Colonisation Act of 1912, to ordinary colony tenures. These could not be retained for horse-breeding tenures. Subdivision, inevitable with customary succession, would have destroyed the capability of the grants for horse breeding.[93] Allocating responsibility for the service function to any one heir would have been impracticable, whereas vesting a joint obligation on all the heirs was equally untenable. The government thus decided upon primogeniture for these grants. This denied succession to any sons except the eldest. It also prevented collateral relatives from inheriting the land of grantees without sons, the grant being escheated to the government in the absence of a direct heir.[94] Such a form of succession caused widespread discontent, being totally alien to Punjabi agriculturists; and it conflicted with the customary right of equal succession by all male heirs. It created in Jhelum Colony a large group of dispossessed and disaffected men: the younger sons, and after a generation the younger brothers, of the horse breeders.

The grantees continued throughout to oppose primogeniture because of the severe strain it placed on their family structure. The government held firm and refused to amend this rule, for to do so would have jeopardised the horse-breeding scheme. To impose military requirements it took upon

[92] Petition to Lieutenant-Governor from Captain Mangal Singh, etc., September 1922; in "Petitions from horse-breeding grantees of Jhelum Canal Colony regarding abolition of rule of primogeniture and other modifications of horse-breeding conditions," BOR J/301/1504 KW A, p. 114.
[93] Discussion took place among officials in 1917-1918 over proprietary rights for horse-breeding grantees. Though both the FC and Commissioner, Rawalpindi, recommended this, the Army Remount Department successfully opposed it, arguing that it would seriously imperil the horse-breeding scheme. See "Grant of proprietary rights in Lower Jhelum Colony," BOR 301/2/19/31 A, pp. 1-7, 12(a-b), 15-19, 47-48.
[94] After years of protest and under threat of further agitation, the government in 1936 finally relented on this rule and allowed succession by relatives of the last holder. See "Lower Jhelum Canal Colony—Shahpur District—Succession to horse-breeding tenancies—Policy," BOR 301/16/19/1(a); the case of a Ghulam Jilani in BOR 301/3/19/368; and *PCR*, 1936, p. 3.

itself a heavy, and invidious, administrative burden for in practice it was not easy to enforce primogeniture. Even by the early 1910s, no more than a decade after settlement, it was reported that evasion of this clause had become the rule rather than the exception.[95] Some villages denied all social intercourse to eldest sons if they deprived their younger brothers of a share in the proceeds of the grant. Many fathers in their lifetime induced their eldest sons to execute agreements acknowledging the rights of their younger brothers. In many cases, grantees sold off their land and returned home in order to escape the succession laws.

Despite such expedients, the great majority of younger sons were in fact disinherited, and as a result suffered various disadvantages. Deprived of a share in landholding, they could seek employment in agriculture as subtenants or labourers, but this entailed a loss in status. Many were unable to contract satisfactory marriages, an issue that was close to the heart of rural Punjabis. Efforts made to help the younger sons did not come to much. In 1914, about 10,000 acres were reserved for them in Lower Bari Doab Colony, but the size of grants was kept down to 12.5 acres. Virtually all the men selected threw up their land and returned to Jhelum Colony. Little was ever achieved for them. By the 1940s, assistance had proceeded no further than vague proposals for endowments to help with education and land purchase, but these made no headway.[96] Even after horse breeding in the colony was abolished (this took place in 1940), younger brothers failed to gain access to land, for proprietary rights were obtained by the incumbents in possession of the grants.[97] Private ownership by the latter, in fact, further weakened the claims of other heirs to land.

The deep divisions that primogeniture created within the families of horse breeders led to outbreaks of litigation, fratricidal crime, and political agitation. The disinherited younger sons, known as *lawaris* (without guardians), became one of the most politicised groups in the canal colonies. They provided sustained opposition to the government during and even after the period of the horse-breeding scheme. Several conferences and protest

---

[95] *PCR*, 1911, p. 17. The report noted: "The legality of such agreements is doubtful . . . but it is impossible not to feel sympathy with the frequent petitions and deputations of fathers asking to be allowed to ensure in some way that their younger sons shall not be turned out of home and lands as soon as they themselves die."

[96] See "Horse-breeding scheme for Lower Bari Doab Colony," BOR J/301/1101 A, pp. 157-59 and 219-21, and B, p. 67; and "Lower Jhelum Canal Colony—Horse-breeding grantees—Provision for younger sons and widows of those who hold land upon conditions involving primogeniture—Policy," BOR 301/16/19/1(c).

[97] For the *lawaris* issue and succession to grants subject for years to primogeniture, see BOR files 301/16/19/30 and 301/16/19/44, both titled: "Lower Jhelum Colony—Shahpur District—Abrogation of horse-breeding conditions—Question of cancellation of primogeniture condition with retrospective effect."

meetings, some addressed by major politicians, were held in their support, and organisations were founded to represent their interests.[98] Resentment against primogeniture provided the mainspring for a number of agitations against horse breeding that periodically shook Jhelum Colony in the four decades after 1900. In the frequent petitions presented by the service grantees bewailing their lot, the most violent sentiments were reserved for the laws of succession. Primogeniture was said to have "given rise to a flood of discontent and disaffection among other sons." This often led to fratricidal crime: it "is having a terrible effect upon the domestic and social lives of . . . petitioners. It is contrary to the wishes of all of us. . . . It is against all our traditions and social rules."[99] So great were its social costs that even eldest sons, who stood to be sole inheritors, pleaded for an end to primogeniture. A petition in 1922 from 219 eldest sons of grantees made some telling comments on social conditions in the colony:

> They venture to believe, that it is only in the fitness of things that the grants be shared by all the sons of the original grantees. . . . That the stress and strains of the horse-breeding conditions has become past all bearing, and the rule of Primogeniture has given occasions to family feuds amounting in many cases to bloodshed, and we the eldest sons would rather have our fair and just share of our fathers' estates than live under such stress and strain which in many cases is more than flesh and blood can endure.[100]

These men must indeed have suffered extreme antagonism and alienation, if they could plead so fervently to be allowed to give up land. And that too in a society such as the Punjab's, where landed property was regarded with such reverence. Yet the government refused to relax the stringent succession laws, for to do so would have spelt disaster for tied horse-breeding.

Service tenures also caused complications in other forms of succession, such as those of widows and minor sons. Widows could be willed grants for their lifetimes by heirless grantees, and even with male heirs they were allowed maintenance from the proceeds of half a square of land. If they remarried they stood to forfeit all claims to their husband's grants. The prospect of losing a sizeable income through further matrimony induced many to seek nonmarital liaisons, usually with the *sarbarah* (warden) who

[98] *PCR*, 1936, p. 3; 1937, p. 4; 1938, p. 5. Some of the organisations involved were the Lawaris Kisan Committee, the Lawaris Ghoripal Association and the Naujawan Bharat Sabha: see "Horse-breeding agitation in Lower Jhelum Colony," BOR 301/2/19/229.

[99] "Petition to LG from *ghoripal abadkars* of Lower Jhelum Colony," n.d. (1921); in J/ 301/1504 KW A, Enclosure to p. 30.

[100] "Petition from eldest sons of horse-breeding military grantees on Lower Jhelum Canal," February 1922; ibid., KW A, p. 59.

managed horse breeding and cultivation. It was found that widows were frequently changing *sarbarahs*, and this almost invariably meant that they had changed lovers.[101] The competition for the favours of widows, both pecuniary and romantic, became a source of dissension among villagers: "The results are most detrimental to horse-breeding and many *chaks* which were formerly good horse-breeding *chaks*, have gone to pieces after the mutation of a grant in favour of a widow."[102] The government recognised these practices as incentives to immorality and more seriously for its own interests, as detrimental for horse breeding. During the 1920s it considered taking remedial measures, but finally decided against any steps to reform these ills.[103] So unpopular had horse breeding become that the government feared that any action on its part, however "moral" in intent, would provoke a further outbreak of political agitation.

Grants inherited by minor sons also fell foul of the law, chiefly because of the misdemeanours of their *sarbarahs*. Such grants proved notoriously inefficient for horse breeding, and incurred frequent penalties. Officials conceded that it was unfair to punish a minor, for the fault really lay with the *sarbarah*. The latter, who was usually a relative or a paramour of the grantee's mother, was beyond the reach of executive punishment, for he was not bound by any formal obligations to the state. Such men often appropriated all the profits of a grant, and at the end of the minority absconded with substantial sums of money.[104] They left the minors destitute and at odds with the administration, because of the poor condition of mares and young stock. By the mid-1910s there were three to four hundred minor grantees, making this a problem of some importance for the state of horse breeding in the colony.

The government decided in 1916 that, in cases of continued default in breeding obligations, half a minor's grant should be temporarily resumed. These resumed halves carried with them the service requirement, and were leased out to the highest bidders on condition that such persons were adept

---

[101] *PCR*, 1909, FC's Review; and 1912, LG's Review. It was estimated in 1928 that widows who received maintenance from half a square earned a rental income of Rs 300 a year, or Rs 25 a month. Widows with two square grants were even more attractive, for they stood to earn four times as much. See DC, Shahpur, to Commissioner, Rawalpindi, 16 March 1928; in "Succession of tenancies allotted to or inherited by families of horse-breeders," BOR 301/2/00/300, pp. 3-6.

[102] District Remount Officer, Shahpur, to Director of Remounts, Army Headquarters, 14 September 1927; ibid., pp. 7-8.

[103] DC, Shahpur, to Commissioner, Rawalpindi, 16 March 1928; Commissioner, Rawalpindi, to DC, Shahpur, 10 May 1928; and DC, Shahpur, to FC, 25 June 1930: ibid., pp. 3-6, 13, and 17-18, respectively.

[104] DC of Shahpur's letter, 16 March 1928; ibid., pp. 3-6. See also *PCR*, 1916, FC's Review.

horse breeders. The lease money was to be banked at compound interest until the minor grantees came of age. Even this measure did not end their tribulations. In 1930 heavy arrears were discovered in the payment of the lease money into the minors' accounts. Recovery from lessees was hampered by the severe liquidity problems caused by the prevailing economic depression. Consequently, minors with half resumed grants suffered heavily from these transactions.[105] On the other hand, the government did not interfere at all with guardians who exploited their wards but continued to meet horse-breeding obligations. The state's options of intercession or inaction were dictated by its self-interest regarding the fulfilment of military needs, and not by a concern for the minor's welfare.

An examination of the lease and sale markets in land in Jhelum Colony reveals further complications caused by horse breeding in agrarian conditions. The expedient of lease or sale was of much importance for grantees, for it provided a means of escaping, temporarily or permanently, from the colony. Even as state occupancy tenants they were allowed by law to lease or alienate their grants, whereas as proprietors there could be no bar on them from doing so.[106] Ordinary grantees in the canal colonies faced few obstacles in availing themselves of this opportunity. In the case of the service grantees, though this right was not withheld by the government, market forces were nevertheless considerably impaired. Grants could only be leased or sold along with the service obligation: the government would not allow such transactions to lead to a reduction in the horse-breeding area.

This resulted in contrary trends for leases and sales, induced in both cases by the influence of the service tenure on the market for land. The area of horse-breeding land under lease tended to be depressed, and the rates of lease money higher, in comparison to nonhorse-breeding land in Jhelum Colony. In the case of sales, more horse-breeding land tended to be alienated than ordinary land, but it fetched lower prices.[107] Although several factors were responsible for determining the rental and capital value of agricultural land, there is little doubt that service tenures played a major role in creating such price differentials in Jhelum Colony.

In the case of leases, there was a decided preference for nonservice as opposed to service grants. For the latter, the constraints on leased area occurred because the presence of horse-breeding complicated the relations between lessee and lessor; and this increased transaction costs. Even though he might have taken over such operations, the lessee was not for-

[105] *PCR*, 1916, LG's and FC's Reviews; 1917, LG's Review; and 1930, p. 30.

[106] FC to RS, 20 March 1914; in "Power of service grantees to sublet their holdings," BOR J/301/1188, p. 39.

[107] For figures and a more detailed analysis of leasing and alienation of land in Jhelum Colony, see Imran Ali, "The Punjab Canal Colonies," pp. 235-42 and Tables 4.3-4.6.

mally liable for the breeding obligation. Any default on his part could result
in penalties for the grantee, and these could extend for the most serious
offences to the permanent confiscation of the grant.[108] Such considerations
also led officials to discourage the leasing of breeding grants; they preferred
to avoid any duality between the legal and the actual servitor. At times
when the administration tried to enforce breeding rules more rigorously,
grantees were less prepared to increase the risk of penalties by entrusting
their land to others. Service grantees were also less likely than ordinary
holders to obtain exemption from residence, and this further constricted the
likelihood of leasing their grants. All these factors combined to discourage
the leasing of horse-breeding land.[109]

Although a smaller area of horse-breeding than ordinary land tended to
be leased, horse-breeding grants consistently fetched higher lease money
than ordinary grants. One reason for this could have been the better quality
of horse-breeding land, for nonservice grants were the last to be allotted in
the colony. The capital stock of a breeding grantee was larger than that of
an ordinary grantee, and this, along with the possibility of profits from
horse breeding, could also have raised rental values. But one further reason
was the peculiar connection between debt and horse breeding in Jhelum
Colony. By law (and here there was a further concession to the military),
civil courts could not attach a service grantee's land, produce, or horses for
indebtedness; nor could his debts be applicable to his heirs, except for
moveable property. Consequently, moneylenders encountered considerable difficulty in recovering their dues. One solution for them was to try and
redeem these loans by offering very favourable terms for the leases of their
debtors' grants.[110] This tended to raise rental levels for horse-breeding
land, and reflected not the economic buoyancy of such grants but instead
the negative influence of horse breeding on an optimal economic utilisation
of colony land.

[108] To avoid all such complications, the Punjab Revenue Department recommended in 1914
that the power of alienation be withheld from service grantees. The government refused to
accept this, as it was not prepared to risk the protest and discontent that such discrimination
between ordinary and horse-breeding tenures would have caused. See FC to RS, 20 March
1914; and RS to FC, 4 May 1914: in BOR J/301/1188, pp. 39-40.

[109] The breeding tenure was not, of course, the only influence on leases: the effects of
market forces cannot be discounted. Price movements of crops could cause fluctuations in
leased area by varying the attraction of leases. Higher prices could lead to debt and mortgage
redemption, and thus reduce the rented area, as many leases were in reality disguised mortgages. Nevertheless, horse-breeding grants were generally situated on better land, and if one
assumes that this was more likely to be leased than poorer land, then the service tenure assumes even greater importance as a factor of constraint. See PCR, 1914, p. 26, 1915, p. 17;
1916, p. 1; 1918, p. 1; 1919, p. 1; 1924, p. 31.

[110] Ibid., 1927, p. 34.

Sales were a more permanent form of estrangement from the colony. These comprised, strictly speaking, the alienation of occupancy rights, for proprietary rights were not allowed by the government in Jhelum Colony. Sales of horse-breeding land normally exceeded those of ordinary land, indicating that service grantees were more ready to divest themselves of their colony possessions than other holders. The service tenure had to be retained on the land sold, and the administration allowed sales only if the purchaser was an acceptable horse breeder. This narrowing in the field of buyers was compensated for by the fact that officials actually encouraged such sales as a way of ridding the colony of unsatisfactory horse breeders. They also looked favourably upon the subdivision of the larger grants through land alienation, for the smaller holdings were proving to be less inefficient for horse breeding than the yeoman grants. In both supply and demand, service considerations influenced the sale of land. Many grantees sold out in order to escape from the problems associated with horse breeding, among them being regulated succession and greater official interference. Conversely, there were always service grantees who wanted to acquire more land in order to provide for their younger sons and brothers. The purchasers were predominantly residents of the colony who were already in possession of one or more service grants.[111]

Though there was a distinct readiness by horse-breeders to alienate their grants, the presence of the breeding tenure tended to depress the price of such land. Despite the fact that it was situated on the better quality soils and in the more central parts of the colony, horse-breeding land more often than not fetched lower prices than ordinary land. The price of both types of land rose over the years, showing that both remained fully responsive to market trends. Yet the differential also continued. In 1926 it was calculated that there existed a 7 percent price difference, or around Rs 25, between the two types of land; and there was official admission as to its causes: "this represents the depreciation of the value of land caused by the infliction of conditions of horse-breeding and primogeniture."[112]

One of the greatest distortions that horse breeding produced was the debarring of the Jhelum Colony grantees from obtaining proprietary rights. After the agitation of 1907, and with the passing of the Colonisation Act of 1912, the state conceded the right of landownership even to peasant grantees. Since very concessionary rates of purchase were fixed, the new status of proprietor came as a windfall to thousands of landholders, who when taking up their grants had contracted to remain merely as state occupancy

[111] Ibid.: 1917, p. 1; 1921, p. 1; 1928, p. 33. See also "Alienations of horse-breeding grants on Lower Jhelum Canal," BOR J/301/1081.

[112] *PCR*, 1926, p. 32.

tenants. This right of ownership was withheld from Jhelum Colony, for it would have been impossible to impose horse-breeding obligations unless the grantees were retained as state tenants. In order not to exacerbate feelings of inequity, even nonservice grantees in Jhelum Colony were disallowed from obtaining proprietary rights.

The Jhelum colonists continued to suffer the twin irritants of closer state intervention and deprivation of a proprietorial status. Over the years there appeared little prospect of relief from the injustices that they perceived. This contrasted adversely with the situation of grantees in other colonies, who settled into a more placid routine as political and agrarian conditions stabilised in their favour. The fundamental disjunction from their customary succession laws and the continued demand for young stock from remount officials remained the lot of the Jhelum colonists. Feelings against horse breeding were deep-seated and pervasive, and they increased in intensity with time. The successors of the original generation of grantees showed growing impatience with the continued enforcement of service obligations. They could not see why such hardships should be prolonged, and as one petition put it, "the condition of services is always limited to some time and cannot be imagined to be eternal."[113]

These antagonistic feelings against the administration involved the Jhelum grantees in a level of political protest and agitation that was absent in other colonies. Not only did they participate actively in the events of 1907, but the colony experienced several major outbreaks of political opposition in later years, as in 1921, 1928-1930, and 1936-1938.[114] These movements were marked by political meetings, conferences, and petitions, all expressing the hope that the horse-breeding scheme would be abolished and the grantees freed from their tenurial disabilities. Activism was maintained at village level through political workers belonging both to extra-colony organisations, such as the Indian National Congress, and to associations oriented specifically toward colony conditions, such as the Zamindara Ghoripal Committee.[115]

The political activity in which the colonists engaged was generally peaceful. There was little call even in these straitened circumstances for sanguinary opposition; and the tide of agitation tended to wane when any hopes of an end to horse breeding were dashed by government proclama-

---

[113] Petition from *ghoripal abadkars* (1921); in BOR J/301/1504 KW A, Enclosure to p. 30.

[114] For the political movement during 1928-1930, see Imran Ali, "The Punjab Canal Colonies," pp. 225-27; "Canal Closures in Lower Jhelum Colony," BOR 301/2/19/227; and BOR 301/2/19/229. See also *PCR*: 1928, pp. 30-31; 1929, pp. 30-31; and 1930, p. 32.

[115] Some others were the Zamindara Association, the Colony Association, and the *lawaris'* organisations. Officials reported that, apart from the Congress, the Bolsheviks were also active in the agitations.

tions to the contrary. Unrest in the colony was undoubtedly influenced by political developments in other parts of India: activism among Muslim and Sikh grantees was greatest at times, respectively, of Khilafat and Akali activity.[116] An agitation in 1928 could well have had its political inspiration elsewhere: "The events of Bardoli, boomed in the Vernacular Press, were telling on the minds of the *abadkars*."[117] Nevertheless, the primary stimulus for protest was the hostility toward horse breeding itself. The grievances that the grantees justifiably held over such matters as fines and punishments for defaults, the problem of disinherited heirs, and the bar against ownership, simmered in Jhelum Colony throughout the currency of the horse-breeding scheme, and frequently broke through into active political opposition.

Despite the agitations, the government refused to abandon tied horse breeding. The need of the military for an internal supply of cavalry horses was considered of "paramount importance," and was allowed to override the dangers of political dissension.[118] With time, however, the pressure of continued strife with the grantees did begin to tell on official attitudes. Criticisms of the scheme, made at first by lower officials, came in later years from men further up in the official hierarchy, until eventually the Punjab Government itself stood out against it. This transition toward an adverse official attitude was itself a comment on the degree of success of horse breeding in Jhelum Colony. Yet the final decision regarding its termination lay with the Government of India, where the influence of the army prevented for several years any relaxation in policy.

Early criticisms of the scheme had come from none other than W. M. Hailey, colonisation officer of Jhelum Colony and the person deputed to select grantees and to supervise the scheme in its early years. Hailey, who was later to become an eminent colonial administrator, wrote as early as 1905 of the unpopularity of the service contract, and especially of primogeniture: "everything tends to show how repugnant this rule is to native feeling. . . . [the service obligations] have the further effect of heightening the demoralisation occasioned by that dependence of the grantee on the state which is an unfortunate though inevitable feature of the present irrigation system."[119] Such adverse assessments proved ineffective, because the more senior Punjab officials were not prepared to give in to pessimism;

[116] See reports by DC, Shahpur, in BOR 301/2/19/227 and BOR 301/2/19/229.

[117] *PCR*, 1928, p. 30.

[118] The argument used was once again that of developing an indigenous supply so as to render India independent of foreign sources for cavalry horses, which in time of war or a frontier emergency might not be forthcoming: AS, GOI, to FC(D), 23 October 1922; in PRAP(R), December 1922, No. 2.

[119] *PCR*, 1905, p. 30.

and they cautioned against emphasising the demerits of the scheme in view of the wider strategic interests involved.[120]

The Punjab Colonies Committee of 1907-1908 was also not prepared to recommend the abolition of "the very promising horse-breeding scheme," but its proposals about service tenures were dramatically different from those made by the Horse and Mule-breeding Commission less than a decade earlier. Whereas the latter had wanted all future colony grants to be subject to service conditions, the Colonies Committee advised that "except with a view to meeting requirements of State, so urgent as to override all other considerations, the tenure of land should not, on any large scale, be made conditional on the rendering of service."[121]

By 1911, H. J. Maynard, the commissioner of Rawalpindi Division, added his authoritative voice against the scheme. Directing his criticisms especially against primogeniture, he remarked "on the impossibility of permanently maintaining a condition which is so out of harmony with social sentiment and economic facts. . . . Primogeniture is for countries where the sources of subsistence are numerous and varied."[122] The Punjab Government rejected the idea of abolishing the scheme, and cautioned officials that any indications of pessimism would only encourage further agitation. During the years of World War I, there could be no basis for a reevaluation of horse breeding. However, it was not long after the end of the war that feelings against it permeated to the highest levels of the Punjab administration.

In 1922, following upon another political agitation, the attitude of the Punjab Government swung dramatically against horse breeding. It requested the Government of India to consider abolishing the compulsory nature of the service tenure in Jhelum Colony. It argued that the scheme was not only highly unpopular with the grantees, but had also caused substantial losses of public revenue, owing to the lack of capitalisation resulting from the withholding of property rights. To compensate for any loss in horse supply suffered by the military, the Punjab Government offered to share with the centre the proceeds from the sale of land to the grantees. The Government of India was unmoved by these arguments. It refused to abandon the scheme, and insisted that autarky in Indian horse production was a major military goal.[123] The two governments retained their rigidly contrasting attitudes for a further two decades. The centre continued to reject the idea either of abolishing the scheme, or of compensating the province for

---

[120] FC to Chief Secretary, 8 February 1905; ibid., 1905.

[121] RPCC, p. 118 (see also pp. 108 and 118-20).

[122] *PCR*, 1911, p. 17 (see also LG's Review).

[123] Ibid., 1922, Governor's Review. See also letters of FC(D) and AS, GOI, 10 February and 23 October 1922; in PRAP(R), December 1922, Nos. 1-2.

the inequitable burden placed on it for the defence interests of the entire country.[124] The last was a matter that was plaintively put in 1924:

> The Punjab Government appreciates the importance attached by the Government of India to the provision of horses as an essential military requirement, but the necessity for such a provision is an all India matter and the Local Government may be excused for failing to understand why the financial loss incurred in making this provision should fall on the Punjab alone. It is not aware that other Local Governments are called upon to make similar sacrifices in supplementing Imperial requirements, either civil or military.[125]

Horse-breeding in Jhelum Colony was finally abolished in 1940, by order of the Government of India. The primogeniture rule was abrogated, and the grantees were allowed to purchase their land.[126] It might have seemed that the prayers of the colonists over the years had finally been answered. But it is unlikely that humanitarian considerations had much to do with the abandonment of the scheme, though political ones must certainly have weighed in the decision. The real reason was technological change. The army no longer required such a large area under horse-breeding operations, owing to the increased mechanisation of cavalry units.[127] Tied horse breeding in Lower Bari Doab Colony was continued, and this was deemed sufficient for the new level of demand for horses. The abandonment of the scheme in Jhelum Colony, nevertheless, was the final admission of the extent to which it had been beset by serious shortcomings and injustices.

In terms of efficiency and productivity, the horse-breeding scheme in Jhelum Colony left much to be desired. Certainly, this colony became the

---

[124] For further correspondence during the 1920s between the Punjab Government and the Government of India on the abolition of horse breeding and compensation to the former, see "Question of reducing or adjusting the amount of agricultural land held on horse or mule-breeding conditions in Lower Jhelum and Lower Chenab Canal Colonies," BOR 301/2/00/33.

[125] FC(D) to AS, GOI, 26 July 1924; in BOR 301/2/19/31 B, pp. 1-7. It was calculated at this time that the value of the horse-breeding grants was Rs 30 million. The Punjab Government asked for the credit of a sum equivalent to its foregone interest earnings on this amount; but the Government of India refused to accept that there were any grounds, legal or moral, for such compensation.

[126] See the following files for Lower Jhelum Colony and Shahpur District: "Abrogation of horse-breeding conditions in," BOR 301/16/19/1(d); "Abrogation of horse-breeding conditions—Purchase of proprietary rights," BOR 301/16/19/29; and "Purchase of proprietary rights by old military grantees in their grants," BOR 301/21/19/93. The purchase price was set on a sliding scale, from Rs 40-100 per acre, depending on the period taken to acquire ownership.

[127] The issue of modernisation and mechanisation of Indian army units is discussed in P. Mason, *A Matter of Honour*, pp. 466-70.

most concentrated region of horse breeding in India, to be matched only by Lower Bari Doab Colony after 1920. The cavalry obtained a steady supply of remounts, which it would otherwise have had to import. Yet the two schemes, supplying around 8,000 mares, failed to provide sufficient young stock of acceptable quality for the cavalry: even in the 1930s India had failed to achieve self-sufficiency in this area.

Horse sales in Jhelum Colony remained depressed throughout. In relation to the total number of mares, there remained a very low rate of acquisition of young stock by the purchasing agency, the Army Remount Department.[128] From the figures available, it appears that the proportion of foals purchased to number of mares in the colony remained below 20 percent in all years, and in some years it was closer to 10 percent. This unsatisfactory performance resulted from a narrowing in the prospects of eventual purchase at each stage of production. The proportion of mares not covered varied in different years from 12 to 25 percent. The number of foals born was only 40 to 55 percent of the mares covered. Never more than half, and at times as few as 10 to 15 percent, of the foals born were actually purchased by the army. In most years, the number of foals thus acquired remained under 500, which was less than one-eighth of the mare capacity of over 4,000 in the colony.[129]

Several factors contributed to this low productivity in horse breeding. The incentive to produce more and better animals was constrained by low demand levels. The army was the chief, if not the only, purchaser of young stock; and before 1920 this was further confined to British cavalry regiments, for the Indian cavalry obtained its own horse runs. The horses had only a minimal linkage into the agrarian economy, for there was little demand for them in agriculture, apart from occasional purchases for mare replacements from within the colony.[130] The horse breeders were saddled with a commodity that was virtually unmarketable apart from its use for the

[128] See Imran Ali, "The Punjab Canal Colonies," pp. 243-45 and Tables 4.7-4.8.

[129] For information on the general progress of the horse-breeding scheme over the years, see *PCR*: 1904, FC's Review and p. 24; 1905, pp. 25 and 34; 1906, p. 36; 1907, pp. 35-37 and 39; 1908, pp. 24, 27, and 29; 1913, p. 8; 1916, pp. 1-2; 1919, p. 1; 1921, Governor's Review and p. 3; 1923, p. 32; 1929, p. 32; 1930, pp. 28-29; 1931, pp. 5-6; 1932, pp. 7-8; 1934, p. 8; and 1936, p. 3.

[130] The limitations on the marketability of young stock affected the standard of their maintenance. It was reported in 1913 that the number of horses ruined annually by starvation ran into hundreds. Cattle, being more important for agriculture, were better cared for, and land was set apart for fodder crops for them. Not more than 10 percent of the colonists did so for mares, many of which had to survive by grazing along canal banks and water courses. See Superintendent, Army Remount Department, Jhelum Canal Colony Circle, to DC, Shahpur, 25 October 1913; in "Proposed resumption of part of the horse-breeding grants in Shahpur District for the neglect of conditions of grants," BOR 301/2/19/87 A, p. 99.

military, though some hacks could have found their way pulling urban transport vehicles. In the absence of greater demand, there was little incentive for grantees to increase production or improve breeding standards.[131]

It could be argued that the army would have increased its procurement had the quality of horses been better. However, horse breeding was never organised along scientific lines in the colony, nor was it practicable to introduce improved production methods among a mass of small-scale producers. A high degree of apathy toward horse breeding was reported among the grantees, and a large number were found to be almost completely inept as breeders.[132] This situation did not improve over the years: by 1940 only a quarter of the grantees were said to take any interest in horse breeding, with over a half being utterly unproductive.[133] Individualisation among grantees accentuated the problems of small-scale breeding. Each grant functioned as a distinct operation, making it impossible to achieve either economies of scale or more efficient production through cooperative methods. It was indicative of horse-breeding standards that mares and young stock were kept in stables, since individual grantees did not have enough land for paddocks. Efforts to introduce a paddock scheme met with complete failure.[134] Without any place for regular exercise, deficiencies in the quality of the animals were inevitable, as one report in 1924 brought out:

> At the present the common practice is either to tie up the mares and young stock or else to shackle their forefeet and allow them to go out and graze. As a result brood mares very often prove infertile either from over-feeding and lack of exercise or from starvation. If a foal is pro-

[131] Nevertheless, grantees did look to supplementing their incomes through the sale of young stock, especially during the hard times of the 1930s. One report noted that "the rejection of a colt or filly for which a breeder had hoped to obtain a good cash price amounted in many cases to a domestic calamity": *PCR*, 1931, p. 5.

[132] It was reported in the mid-1920s that "there are many men who take no interest in horses, and who, although perforce bound to keep a mare, have either never sold a horse to Government or have only sold one during the last 20 years." See "Report on horse-breeding in India" by Lieut.-Colonels J. Bruce and G. W. Ross, n.d., para. 83; in BOR 301/2/00/33, p. 15.

[133] "Proceedings of meeting in FC(D)'s office," 4 June 1939; in BOR 301/16/19/1(d) A, p. 1. As early as 1912, one report stated that the horse breeders "will not learn to look after their mares and foals properly and they persist in neglecting the most elementary principles of horse-breeding. Not only are they apathetic about getting their mares into foal, but in many instances they starve and neglect the foals which are born, and there is therefore considerable wastage." See Superintendent, Army Remount Department, to Quartermaster-General in India, February 1912; in PRAP(G), June 1914, No. 3.

[134] For information on the paddock scheme and its outcome, see PRAP(R), January 1925, Nos. 14-23; and "Allotment of land to Army Remount Department for paddocks in horse-breeding *chaks* in Lower Jhelum Colony," BOR 301/6/19/2. See also *PCR*, 1925, p. 31; 1926, p. 29; 1927, p. 32; 1928, p. 29; and 1939, p. 4.

duced, it does not obtain sufficient food in many cases and in practically all cases it fails to obtain sufficient exercise. It, therefore, grows up undersized and crooked limbed. It is hobbled by the forefeet, its pasterns are permanently ruined.[135]

Whatever disabilities and inadequacies the smallholding grantees displayed, these paled in comparison to the patent failure of the larger *sufedposh* and stud farm grantees. The families of rural magnates were unable, by and large, to transfer successfully to the colony environment the equine skills for which they had been selected.[136] They did not take to horse breeding with any professionalism, but merely tolerated it for the sake of the economic and social benefits that their colony grants brought them. The state itself abetted their inefficiency by granting them exemption from residence in the colony, because of the usefulness of their political and administrative services in their home districts. Primogeniture further prevented proper investment on the grants, for the resources of these families were often under joint control.[137] The *sufedposh* grantees inevitably incurred penalties for failing to fulfil their service obligations. These usually took the form of fines, but the more serious offences led to the resumption of half the grant, which was then leased out to an acknowledged horse breeder. Total confiscations were rare, but officials did encourage the *sufedposh*es to sell out to other breeders, preferably in subdivided lots of under five squares.[138] Compared to these middling grantees, the peasant holdings were regarded as quite a success. The performance of the stud farms was equally disappointing. Officials consistently expressed dissatisfaction at the state of the seven studs allotted to large landlords, five of whom came from the Nun-Tiwana clan of Shahpur District.[139] Only the eighth, obtained by the professional horse dealer Agha Wusat Khan and later managed by his son Wazir Khan, was run along efficient lines.[140]

[135] DC, Shahpur, *to Commissioner, Rawalpindi, 12 June 1924; in* PRAP(R), January 1925, Enclosure No. 1 to No. 14.

[136] Lists of candidates and recommendations for *sufedposh* grants, along with offices held and caste origins, is contained in "Allotment in Jhelum Canal Colony of land to selected Peasants and Yeomen for maintenance of brood mares," BOR J/301/684 A-D + KW 1-3.

[137] See *PCR*: 1909, p. 25; 1917, p. 1; 1918, p. 1; 1929, p. 32. See also DC, Shahpur, to Commissioner, Rawalpindi, 31 March 1910; in PRAP(G), May 1910, No. 38.

[138] See BOR files on the resumption and confiscation of horse-breeding grants, J/301/1395 and 301/2/19/87; and PRAP(G): May 1910, Nos. 36-41; December 1910, Nos. 34-37; February 1911, No. 47. See also PRAP(R), September 1910, Nos. 35-36; and *PCR*: 1920, p. 2; 1921, p. 3; 1927, p. 33; 1928, p. 32; 1929, p. 32.

[139] There was one Nun, Hakim Khan, and four Tiwana grantees: Khuda Bakhsh, Mubariz Khan, Muzaffar Khan, and Umar Hayat Khan. The remaining two were Hafiz Abdullah Khan of Dera Ismail Khan and Painda Khan of Jhelum.

[140] For information on these stud farm grants, see *PCR*: 1905, FC's Review and p. 31; 1906,

It cannot be said, therefore, that the horse-breeding scheme in Jhelum Colony was a success. From the start, it had been the cause of suffering and deprivation. The complete change from the original scheme of colonisation had resulted in the disqualification of a large number of men, already selected, from obtaining grants. For many others, the rush for mares had led to financial stringencies. With the years, colonists became more and more intolerant of what they perceived as the injustices of the scheme. Several political agitations occurred in the colony, the greatest cause of discontent being the laws of succession that were so alien to Punjabi agriculturists. Horse breeding had, moreover, a distorting effect on agrarian conditions. It complicated leasing arrangements, and thereby acted as a constraint on leases. It encouraged alienations, but reduced the value of the land. Horse breeding as it was practised had in addition a low level of productivity and efficiency; and both supply and demand factors were responsible for this. The grantees were either incapable of doing better, or were indifferent to this activity in view of the low levels of demand from the cavalry. The larger grantees, on whom high expectations had been placed, proved to be the most disappointing breeders and colonists. The scheme had throughout found critics among British officials, and from the early 1920s the Punjab Government was firmly committed to its abolition. But arguments of defence and strategic interest were upheld by the Government of India to reject such a step. Finally, it too gave in, and tied horse breeding in Jhelum Colony ceased in 1940. It had been one of the most unhappy experiences of colonisation.

Competition and Lower Bari Doab Colony

The problems and deficiencies encountered with horse-breeding in Jhelum Colony induced the government to introduce a modified scheme in Lower Bari Doab Colony. The principle of competition was substituted for that of compulsion.[141] Instead of the service tenure being integral to each holding, ordinary grants were allotted. The grantees could compete for additional leaseholds of twenty-five acres each, which carried with them the horse-breeding obligation. The period of the leases was fixed at ten years, after which a new lessee could be selected if the incumbent proved unsatisfactory. This encouraged competitiveness among grantees, for horse breeding now became a means of obtaining additional landed resources. The grantee could obtain proprietary rights on his personal holding, which was situated in the same village, and which still provided him with a means of survival

p. 30; 1907, p. 36; 1920, p. 2; 1921, p. 3; 1922, FC's Review and p. 10; 1923, Governor's Review; 1927, p. 33; 1928, p. 32; and 1929, p. 32.

[141] See Report of the Remount Department Committee (1912) in "Horse-breeding for Lower Bari Doab Colony," BOR J/301/1101 A, pp. 7-18.

if he lost or failed to obtain a breeding leasehold. The *sufedposh* grantees, whose performance in Jhelum Colony had been so disappointing, were also excluded; and the competition for breeding grants took place only among the peasant, or *abadkar*, grantees. As noted in the chapter on colonisation, the competitive aspect was soundly criticised by some Punjab officials for the divisiveness and conflict it would create in village society.[142] Such sentiments did not have the weight to prevent the army from having its way. The Punjab Government sought no longer to question the rationale of such major interventions by the military in agrarian society, but endeavoured instead to adopt the most convenient methods for their implementation.

Depending on the ratio between ordinary grants and leaseholds in the village, between two to five grantees competed for each breeding tenure. The scheme covered an allotted area of 500,000 acres, and within this about 3,500 leases were situated. Originally as many as 7,000 leaseholds were planned, but contractions were necessary when large areas of inferior land were encountered during settlement proceedings. The initiation of the scheme was delayed by over five years, owing to the outbreak of World War I. Not only were officials of the Army Remount Department away on war duty, but horse-breeding land could not be fully allotted until the war veterans were settled. The actual selection of horse-breeding lessees did not begin until 1921; the selected men either already possessed suitable mares or were required to obtain them within a specified period. Officials allowed and indeed preferred the system whereby the grantees of a village themselves selected the lessees, but lots had to be drawn where too many men came forward as candidates.[143]

One major modification was made to the breeding scheme that had been originally sanctioned for this colony. Mule breeding was to take up two-sevenths of the area under service tenures. It was a less costly operation than horse breeding, and the government was undecided whether to place it in areas with soils too poor to support the latter, or to locate it on rectangles given to *lambardar*s for their official duties (a practice followed in Chenab Colony). However, in 1917 the government decided to do away with mule breeding altogether.[144] One reason for this was shortage of land, the abolition of mule breeding being preferred to a reduction in horse breeding. A more important factor was the official apprehension that grantees

[142] See especially Note by Personal Assistant to Chief Commissioner, Delhi, 13 December 1912; and DC, Montgomery, to FC, 23 December 1912: ibid., pp. 145-46 and 149-51.

[143] For the initial period of the scheme, see ibid.; and "Horse-breeding scheme for Lower Bari Doab Colony," BOR 301/2/24/61. See also *PCR*: 1921, pp. 32-33; 1922, pp. 21, 26, and 32; and 1924, p. 5 of Governor's Review.

[144] See "Mule-breeding—Lower Bari Doab," BOR J/301/1206. See also PRAP(I): February 1917, Nos. 135-36; and June 1917, No. 95.

might find mule breeding too attractive, which would work to the detriment of horse production. Mules as transport animals had a linkage into the agrarian economy, and as such they were remunerative and had a ready market. In Chenab Colony, voluntary horse breeding had been markedly reduced by the popular adoption of mule breeding. Officials feared that if both systems existed in Lower Bari Doab Colony, horse breeding, which for the imperial requirement was more important, would be looked upon with disfavour and a sense of grievance by those on whom it was imposed. The decision to forego mule breeding epitomised the nature of military involvement in the canal colonies.

The horse-breeding scheme in this colony was largely free of the political conflicts that beleagured its counterpart in Jhelum Colony. The introduction of the competitive basis appeared to have had the desired effect, for there were no protest movements or agitations against horse breeding. The lessees could not afford to protest unduly against any iniquities by remount or civil officials, for they realised that there were many others to take their place. Fines in this colony for nonfulfilment of breeding obligations equalled and at times even exceeded those in Jhelum Colony, and a sizeable area of leased land was resumed each year. Yet it was a measure of the greater acquiescence of these grantees that such punitive actions did not provoke the responses that they did in Jhelum Colony. The lessees were more willing to make amends, with the state now enjoying primacy.[145]

Official records claimed the horse-breeding scheme in the colony as an undoubted success. Perhaps this was so only because of the relative absence of the problems and tensions that the administration faced in Jhelum Colony. There were no marked differences between the two schemes in terms of efficiency and productivity. The purchase of young stock by the cavalry from Lower Bari Doab Colony remained at an average of around 500 animals per year. Even after purchases for replacements, a significant majority of lessees either failed to breed young stock or were unable to dispose of them. Despite the extensive areas reserved for this purpose, the two schemes were between them unable to make India self-sufficient in cavalry horses.[146]

Colonists involved with the service tenures acquired the material re-

[145] For a comparison of horse breeding in the two colonies, see "Note on horse-breeding conditions in Shahpur and Montgomery Districts," by ex-DC, Shahpur, 26 February 1929; in BOR 301/2/19/229 A, pp. 52-55. See also *PCR*, 1923, p. 42; and Imran Ali, "The Punjab Canal Colonies," Table 4.9.

[146] *PCR*: 1926, p. 42; 1930, p. 59. See also Imran Ali, "The Punjab Canal Colonies," Table 4.8. It was reported in 1932 that the army was compelled to purchase over 1,000 cavalry horses from Australia annually: AS, GOI, to Chief Secretary, 27 July 1932; in BOR 301/2/24/61 B, pp. 7-11.

sources to establish themselves as the village elite. The lessees, with at least fifty acres under their control, became firmly ensconced as rich peasants. They became the largest landholders in the *abadkar* villages, a stratification that emerged from services to the military.[147] This differentiation was further sustained by the high degree of continuity in the leaseholds. At the expiry of the ten-year lease periods, renewals not in favour of the incumbent were very much the exception. Undoubtedly, grantees with breeding leases had consolidated their dominant position in the village, and thence secured renewals through mutually beneficial links with the subordinate bureaucracy. Government emphasis on reserving breeding leases for *lambardar*s further concentrated resources with the upper echelons of village society. The system was not entirely rigid, however, and there was a slight but perceptible turnover of lessees. Efficiency in horse breeding remained an important consideration, and officials endeavoured to weed out unsatisfactory breeders both at the time of renewals and with the occasional cancellation of leases.[148]

Indeed, the need to replace lessees created in many villages the problem of availability of suitable candidates. That there was actually appearing a shortage of prospective lessees within villages was in itself a sign of the impracticability of imposing horse-breeding services on peasant holders. The manner in which this issue was resolved revealed further the extent to which military considerations had come to determine state policy. It was a basic rule of the horse-breeding scheme in this colony that only grantees from within the village qualified for leaseholds. This was part of the general belief for all colonies that social friction would ensue if outsiders were allowed access to land in peasant villages. As more and more cases occurred where the supply of suitable horse breeders from within the village dried up, the army authorities began to press the Punjab Government to allow outsiders to obtain leases. The alternative was a diminution in the horse-breeding area, and this the army was not prepared to tolerate. In 1932, under strong pressure, the government finally yielded to the army, and outsiders were given access to such leases.[149] The forcefulness of military demands was such that the state was prepared to risk social friction and forego

---

[147] One example of the added resources that the horse breeders received was the governmental *taccavi* loans for the replacement of mares. Such loans came out of civil revenues, yet they were utilised for a military function. In the three years 1926-1928, Rs 160,000 were sanctioned for this purpose. See *PCR*: 1926, p. 42; 1927, p. 47; and 1928, pp. 50-51.

[148] For the renewal of leases, see ibid.. 1927, p. 47; 1929, p. 49; 1930, pp. 58 and 78; 1933, pp. 5-6; and 1934, p. 8.

[149] See ibid.: 1931, p. 7; and 1932, pp. 8-9. See also BOR 301/2/24/61: A, pp. 51-56; and B, pp. 13-14.

its own established principles to meet military requirements. It was never prepared to do so for developmental goals.

Lower Bari Doab Colony also contained two large horse-breeding grants, of "latifundia" proportions. These were allotted to two British ex-cavalry officers, Major D. H. Vanrenen and Colonel(later Sir) E. H. Cole. Vanrenen had been a member of the Remount Committee that had formulated the horse-breeding scheme in this colony, and the initiative for these two grants came from him as well. He justified these grants with arguments similar to those used by the Government of India: concern over declining external sources and the need to generate an internal supply of cavalry horses. Cole used more earthy reasons for wanting the grant: adverse prospects of promotion in the cavalry, and a preference to farm "in a country that I know rather than one I do not know."[150] Each grant was about 7,500 acres in size, with an obligation to maintain around 180 mares. This gave a very favourable ratio of horses to land, around forty acres per mare, as compared to the peasant grants, which even at the optimal rate of two ordinary grants for each breeding leasehold provided only one mare for every seventy-five acres.[151]

The Vanrenen and Cole estates proved to be among the most efficient horse-breeding enterprises in the canal colonies. They were certainly much more successful than the *sufedposh* and stud farm grants in Jhelum Colony. Through entrepreneurial skill, proper capital investment, and personal care, both grantees were able to develop horse breeding along scientific lines. Horses from these two farms won several prizes at horse shows, and were well known on racecourses throughout India. The estates continued after 1947, and they were managed by private companies owned by the Vanrenen and Cole families.[152]

In the late 1930s, however, Colonel Cole expressed great unhappiness at the continued obligation to breed horses for the army. He argued that with mechanisation fewer cavalry remounts were required, and that there was practically no other market for horses. He claimed to be losing Rs 25,000-

[150] See Lieut.-Colonel E. H. Cole, 11th Lancers, to Director-General, Army Remount Department, 3 September 1913, Confidential; and also Captain D. H. Vanrenen, Superintendent, Army Remount Department, to Quartermaster-General in India, February 1912: in PRAP(G), June 1914, Nos. 31 and 3, respectively.

[151] Over the years some minor adjustments occurred in both grants in areas of land and numbers of animals required. Vanrenen and Cole also received further areas on temporary leases, thereby increasing the profits they derived from the canal colonies. See "Application from Major James and Captain Vanrenen for grants of land to improve horse-breeding in the Punjab," BOR J/301/1053; and PRAP(G): February 1919, Nos. 136-37; and June 1920, Nos. 24-25.

[152] The BOR files relating to the management of the Cole and Vanrenen estates are 301/2/24/28, 301/11/24/258, 301/11/24/274, and 301/11/24/276.

30,000 per annum on his horse-breeding operations, and felt that he had amply demonstrated, after very considerable expenditure, that it was not practicable to breed horses fit for the army from indigenous stock in India.[153] Cole requested that his tenurial terms be changed to ones providing for the needs of agriculture rather than those of the military. He suggested seed farming or the breeding of rams for the improvement of wool production as possible alternatives. The government firmly rejected these proposals, declaring that it had no intention of curtailing horse breeding in the colony (one reason being that abolition of the scheme in Jhelum Colony was under contemplation). Coming as it did from a European and an ex-military officer, Cole's criticisms were a great indictment of horse-breeding in the canal colonies.

The input of such a large amount of land and labour on horse breeding raises the question of the cost of this undertaking. One kind of cost was the financial loss sustained by government revenues, and indirectly by the people of the Punjab, because of these schemes. Proprietary rights had to be withheld from land on service tenures, so that the province was deprived of capital returns from land and of interest earnings on these amounts. Calculations made in 1930 revealed another form of economic burden.[154] This was the high unit cost of production of horses, estimated in this case for Lower Bari Doab Colony. It was shown that if the total annual income from the horse-breeding grants (from both agriculture and horses) was divided by the number of young stock purchased, the average cost per animal stood at Rs 1,612. If to this was added the cost of remount and veterinary staff, of buildings, stallions, and other incidentals, the unit cost rose to Rs 3,000, with the animal in a completely raw and untrained condition. This cost was significantly higher than the price of imported young stock, and it called into question the entire rationale of horse breeding conducted under compulsion. Perhaps production costs would have been lower if horse breeding had been confined to large stud farms managed by public or private agencies—and the Vanrenen and Cole estates demonstrated that these could be viable. It would, however, have been politically unwise to withhold such extensive areas from colonisation by the peasant population. Horse breeding as it existed was a costly compromise between military and political needs. The horse-breeding scheme in Lower Bari Doab Colony was retained at the time that its counterpart in Jhelum Colony was abolished. The scheme even survived well into the post-1947 period. In 1940, half the

[153] Sir Edward Cole to FC(D), 18 April 1938; and Sir Edward Cole to DC, Montgomery, 3 December 1938: in "Lower Bari Doab Colony—Horse-breeding conditions—Colonel Sir E. H. Cole's application for their relaxation," BOR 301/16/24/15 A, pp. 1 and 5-6.
[154] *PCR*, 1930, pp. 59-61.

breeding capacity was transferred to the production of mules.[155] These animals retained for some time longer their importance for military transport, whereas by 1940 the horse had been eclipsed as a military animal. It still had a role in police work, especially during riots and for the control of crowds and mobs; and one can speculate that it was for this purpose that the animals from the canal colonies were being increasingly utilised.

Though horse-mounted cavalry had become technologically outmoded as a form of warfare, substantial landed and human resources were devoted to it in the canal colonies. Such an enterprise did not have the capability of acting as a vehicle of progress. Horse breeding had no long-term contribution to make to the agricultural sector on which it was based, and even less did it provide any kind of stimulus for industrialisation. It was indeed based on classical feudal lines, entailing a contribution to the military structure in return for the grant of land. Such service tenures in the canal colonies were a retrogressive phenomenon, yet they consumed for half a century vast inputs of land, capital, labour, and managerial effort.

[155] AS, GOI, to Development Secretary, 20 September 1940; in "Turning over a portion of 'bound' horse-breeding operations in Montgomery area into Mountain Artillery mule-breeding," BOR 301/16/24/1(e).

CHAPTER FIVE

Extraction

THE INCOME generated by agrarian growth in the western Punjab was distributed among a number of claimants. This income arose from the efforts of the agricultural labourers, the subtenants, the *jajmani* servitors, and the self-cultivating peasant grantees. Though proprietorial, supervisory, and distributive functions were appropriated by other classes, the new wealth generated through canal colonisation emerged squarely from the efforts of the rural work force. Yet those physically responsible for the task of production invariably found themselves at the lower end of the social spectrum. These groups were placed at the bottom of a pyramidical structure of extraction that seemed to exist mainly from its capacity to expropriate the surplus of the productive class. Punjabi hierarchy was heavily influenced by agrarian inequalities because agriculture remained the dominant sector of the economy. Industrial growth during the colonial period was negligible, while commerce existed as an appendage to agrarian activity.

Agricultural growth in the canal colonies brought about significant increases in the income both of the state and of those classes that owned the means of production. The increase in state revenues came largely from imposts on expanded cultivation and from capital returns on the sale of land. To the holders of colony land, a whole layer of intermediaries ranging from the more substantial peasant grantees to middle and large landlords, the profits of agricultural production accrued not from their own labour but from subtenancy and rental income. In addition, the subordinate bureaucracy, Punjabi in composition, obtained substantial though often illegal benefits from the canal colonies. Government salaries were only one source of income for this class: another was the graft and corruption in which it was so intimately involved. The extractive system, as this process may be collectively termed, was a pervasive influence on social relations in the canal colonies, not only in the relations of the state with the colonists but among the settlers as well.

Various aspects of the extractive structure in this region will be examined in this chapter. A discussion of public revenues reveals that the canal colonies were undoubtedly profitable for the state. Yet the revenue system itself, both in the nature and method of assessment, contained some basic faults and inefficiencies that the government, despite repeated efforts, was unable to eradicate. This lack of success stemmed largely from the entrenched position of the landholders and the lower bureaucracy, who were able to resist any major reform of the revenue system.

The reduced effectiveness that such failures signified was part of a more general loss of control by the state over its own bureaucratic apparatus. Investigations revealed that malappropriations were widespread and the circumvention of proper official procedures endemic. Again it was the combination of subordinate officials and landholders that compromised governmental efficiency and public income.

This concatenation of forces could have produced a dynamic transition toward capitalistic agriculture. Since socialised production was not a tenable alternative, given the state structure and political economy of the time, it was the development of capitalistic forms that provided, albeit with their disruptive and amoral sides, a more realistic indicator of economic "progress." The final part of this chapter will be concerned, through a discussion of cultivating occupancy, with the extent to which capitalistic relations of production had emerged in the canal colonies.

STATE EXTRACTION

The Profitability of the Canal Colonies

Assurance regarding the profitability of a canal project was a prerequisite for its sanction by the government. For each of these public works, careful project estimates were drawn up beforehand, and canal construction was only commenced after the proposals were shown to be financially viable. For this the project not only had to be self-supporting but also had to provide a suitable rate of profit for the state. The distinguishing feature of the perennial canals of the western Punjab was that they were classed as "productive" works, which made them into commercial propositions, as distinguished from the "unproductive" or "protective" works that were occasionally taken in hand, and which usually ran in deficit.

Great care was taken by the state to ensure that the canal colonies proved profitable for it. Before the actual settlement of colonists, the available area was carefully surveyed. This provided a grid of markers within which cultivable land and village sites were situated. This was followed by a demarcation of "squares" (and in the later colonies "rectangles"), which made up the units—in terms of wholes, multiples, or fractions thereof—that became the grants of land. The operation of square-laying provided for orderly settlement; through it the chaos that might have ensued had the grantees been allowed to carve out their own holdings was avoided. The regular composition of the grants also made them easier to assess for purposes of state revenue. A further subdivision through the delineation of field boundaries created even more well-defined units of assessment, measuring approximately one acre each. By such means, the state was able to identify, through its assessing staff, every local incidence of cultivation, on which it could then impose its own extractive requirements.[1]

The assessment and recovery of revenue occurred under several heads of taxation. The heaviest impost was that of water rates, also called occupiers' rates, or *abiana*.[2] This was the payment made by the cultivator for the use of irrigation water, and it was levied on the area sown (in the earlier years on the area matured). Different rates of taxation existed for different crops, with the more remunerative ones incurring heavier dues. Some degree of flexibility was introduced through variation in rates between the stronger and poorer soils, so that the demands of the state could be harmonised with the productive capacity of the land.

A further levy was the land revenue, the traditional source of state income on the soil and its produce. This was usually less exacting than the water rates, and was computed as a proportion of the net assets that remained with the landholder after meeting the costs of production. These dues functioned along the system of fluctuating assessment, comprising a field-to-field appraisement of crops at each harvest. This differed from revenue practice in the rest of the province, which was based on fixed assessment—an issue to be discussed presently.

In addition to water rates and land revenue, a number of cesses were also levied. One was the *malikana*, paid by grantees until such time as proprietary rights were acquired by them. This was a kind of ''seignorage'' that acknowledged the ownership rights of the state over crown waste. Other imposts were the rents payable on village and town shop sites, and the ''local rates'' credited to District Boards for local development. Another charge, imposed consequent to settlement, took care of much infrastructural expense. This was the ''acreage rate,'' intended to recover from colonists the costs of survey and demarcation and of village road and watercourse construction. This effectively passed some of the capital costs on to the colonists. In a period when state fiscal policy was dominated by the concept of the balanced budget, agricultural colonisation was very much a self-financed affair by the Punjabis rather than the product of heavy public developmental expenditure. Though loath to invest unduly in the process of agrarian settlement, the state had nevertheless much to gain from its fruits. The major expense was the outlay on canal construction, and this was not long in providing significant returns of public revenue.

---

[1] For a discussion of survey and demarcation procedures for Chenab Colony, see *Chenab Colony SR* (1915), paras. 208-11; and *PCM*, pp. 35-47. For Lower Bari Doab Colony, see *PCR*: 1913, p. 33; and 1914, pp. 43-44.

[2] The revenue assessment system of the canal colonies is described in *PCM*, ch. 8; and *Chenab Colony SR* (1915), paras. 156-92.

One source for estimating the profitability of the canal colonies for the state are the statistical records of the Irrigation Department (or more accurately, the Public Works Department, Irrigation Branch).[3] These records show the annual revenues and profits derived from each project, as well as capital outlay, working expenses, and interest charges. From figures of areas irrigated and revenue receipts, it is also possible to calculate the income of the state per acre cultivated for each canal. With such data it is certainly possible to make an elaborate quantitative analysis of the annual performance of each canal works. Here a more simplified assessment is presented in Tables 5.1-5.5, comprising selections and extrapolations derived from figures for every tenth year between 1915-1916 and 1945-1946.

The figures are based on the main canal of each system as the unit. For this reason the only colony not represented is Chunian, for it was part of the Upper Bari Doab Canal and disaggregated figures for the Chunian Colony section of this canal were not provided. Sohag Para Colony was represented in the records by the Upper Sutlej Canals, which after 1925-1926 were incorporated into the Sutlej Valley Project. In Tables 5.1-5.5, the former are tabulated for the years 1915-1916 and 1925-1926, and the Sutlej Valley Project (which included Nili Bar Colony) for the years 1935-1936 and 1945-1946, under the composite heading of "Sutlej Canals/Project." In all other cases, the colonies were coterminous with the canals of the same name.

One measure of profitability was the ratio between working expenses and gross receipts. The lower the proportion of working expenses to gross receipts, the higher was the profit derived by the state. Table 5.1 shows working expenses as percentages of gross receipts for each canal for the selected years.

On most canals, working expenses were under 30 percent, and in many cases under 20 percent, of gross annual receipts. Thus, the highest figure for working expenses for the Lower Chenab Canal in any of the selected years was 20.5 percent (in 1915-1916), and for the Lower Bari Doab Canal 17.7 percent (in 1925-1926).[4] Two canals, the Upper Chenab and Upper Jhelum, showed a consistently high rate of working expenses. This could

[3] *Punjab—Public Works Department—Irrigation Branch: Annual Administration Report with Statistical Statements and Accounts* (New South Wales State Library: NQ 631.706/12). This is also the source, in the present section of this chapter, for figures of actual revenue receipts, given in rupees. These figures have also been compiled in Imran Ali, "The Punjab Canal Colonies," Appendix III.

[4] The exception for the Lower Bari Doab Canal was in 1915-1916, when the canal had just opened and working expenses exceeded receipts (Table 5.1). The Upper Chenab and Upper Jhelum canals also showed high working expenses in 1915-1916 because of their recent construction.

TABLE 5.1. ANNUAL WORKING EXPENSES AS A PERCENTAGE OF GROSS
ANNUAL RECEIPTS

Name of Work	1915-16	1925-26	1935-36	1945-46
Sidhnai Canal	17.5	10.6	17.8	—
Lower Chenab Canal	20.5	14.2	18.7	16.1
Lower Jhelum Canal	19.8	23.7	26.8	23.4
Lower Bari Doab Canal	117.6	17.7	17.2	13.7
Upper Chenab Canal	82.0	38.7	46.6	45.4
Upper Jhelum Canal	5,488.5	43.9	70.2	65.4
Sutlej Canals/Project	54.9	72.5	28.0	29.9

SOURCE: Statement IIC in *Punjab—Public Works Department—Irrigation Branch: Annual Administration Report with Statistical Statements and Accounts* (New South Wales Library: NQ 631.706/12).

have been caused by the fact that they cut across natural lines of drainage in the *doab*s, thus requiring several training works, syphons, and overhead passages. These canals also caused much waterlogging, which by the 1930s required costly remedial expenditure—though it is unlikely that such costs were included in working expenses. The Upper Sutlej Canals, figuring under "Sutlej Canals/Project" for 1915-1916 and 1925-1926, were inundation rather than perennial works, and they too had very high working expenses. On the larger canals, the low proportion of working expenses to gross receipts indicated that these projects were very productive as revenue earners. Their maintenance costs were never high enough to impair their remunerativeness.

Apart from working expenses, a further charge on the canal system was the annual interest payments. Interest was paid on the loans originally raised from the central government to finance canal construction, the rate of interest being 3.48 percent until the early 1920s, when it was raised to 4 percent. The annual interest charges for the Lower Bari Doab Canal remained between Rs 700,000 and 900,000 over the years; those for the Lower Jhelum Canal were roughly similar; while those for the Lower Chenab Canal, Upper Chenab Canal, and Upper Jhelum Canal varied between Rs 1 million and 1.8 million each. The earlier and much cheaper Sidhnai and Upper Sutlej canals paid interest of between Rs 40,000 and 60,000. The Sutlej Valley Project was the latest work to be constructed and proved a good deal more expensive. It also bore higher interest rates, with the result that annual interest payments on it were in the region of Rs 3.5 million.

Figures for returns from the canal colonies, in terms of both gross receipts and net incomes, are given in Table 5.2. The table shows that, by the time working expenses and interest charges were deducted, final revenues from the canals, shown as net profits, could be substantially reduced. Such deductions on gross receipts amounted in the Sutlej Valley Project to almost 70 percent in 1935-1936 and over 50 percent in 1945-1946. Net profits on the Upper Chenab Canal also remained only a fraction of gross receipts, while the Upper Jhelum Canal, the least successful venture financially, actually returned a deficit after maintenance and interest charges had been met.

At the other end of the scale, the Lower Chenab Canal proved to be the most remunerative project, and it was also the largest one. This work in the 1910s, 1920s, and 1930s continued to provide net annual profits of between

TABLE 5.2. GROSS RECEIPTS, NET REVENUES (EXCLUDING INTEREST) AND NET PROFITS OR LOSSES (−) (INCLUDING INTEREST) (RS 000)

Name of Work		1915-16	1925-26	1935-36	1945-46
Sidhnai	Gross receipts	833	971	837	—
Canal	Net revenues	686	868	688	—
	Net profit/loss	641	825	645	—
Lower Chenab	Gross receipts	15,922	22,133	19,590	30,295
Canal	Net revenues	12,650	18,999	15,934	25,420
	Net profit/loss	11,574	17,805	14,355	23,603
Lower Jhelum	Gross receipts	4,122	6,041	5,149	6,445
Canal	Net revenues	3,304	4,610	3,767	4,934
	Net profit/loss	2,763	3,927	3,059	4,018
Lower Bari	Gross receipts	553	9,117	9,314	14,000
Doab Canal	Net revenues	− 97	7,506	7,716	12,084
	Net profit/loss	− 800	6,793	6,927	11,211
Upper Chenab	Gross receipts	1,017	4,352	2,987	5,066
Canal	Net revenues	184	2,669	1,594	2,768
	Net profit/loss	− 963	1,431	374	1,163
Upper Jhelum	Gross receipts	6	2,347	1,680	2,033
Canal	Net revenues	− 336	1,317	500	704
	Net profit/loss	− 1,747	− 129	− 982	− 1,044
Sutlej Canals/	Gross receipts	746	915	9,307	16,951
Project	Net revenues	336	252	6,700	11,744
	Net profit/loss	277	194	2,932	8,293

SOURCE: Same as Table 5.1.

Rs 10 and 20 million, whereas in 1945-1946 it returned Rs 23.6 million. The Lower Bari Doab Canal was also very profitable, reaching a level of net profits in excess of Rs 11 million by the mid-1940s. The income from this canal more than compensated for the lower returns from the Upper Chenab and Upper Jhelum canals, which had been constructed to service it. Overall, and despite variations in financial performance between works, the state obtained a substantial level of profits from the canal colonies, and this continued to increase with time in all cases.

Profit differentials between the canals and the very great profitability of certain works also become apparent when their annual incomes are compared to their total costs. Such calculations are produced in Table 5.3, which estimates annual net revenues (before interest) and net profits (after interest) as percentages of total capital outlay. The table shows that the Sidhnai Canal, with low construction costs and working expenses, returned the highest rate of profit, paying for itself roughly every two years. The Lower Chenab Canal can be regarded as the most successful work, for despite its large size it returned between 30 and 50 percent in net revenues and profits each year. Even after meeting all working and interest charges,

TABLE 5.3. ANNUAL NET REVENUES (EXCLUDING INTEREST) AND NET PROFITS (INCLUDING INTEREST) AS A PERCENTAGE OF TOTAL CAPITAL OUTLAY

Name of Work		1915-16	1925-26	1935-36	1945-46
Sidhnai	Net revenues	51.55	65.35	51.45	—
Canal	Net profit	48.18	62.13	48.24	—
Lower Chenab	Net revenues	39.78	54.04	35.95	50.67
Canal	Net profit	36.40	50.64	32.38	46.74
Lower Jhelum	Net revenues	20.07	24.36	18.60	18.46
Canal	Net profit	17.37	20.75	15.10	15.03
Lower Bari	Net revenues	0.46	34.10	33.09	50.43
Doab Canal	Net profit	-3.79	30.86	29.70	46.80
Upper Chenab	Net revenues	0.53	7.15	4.22	6.39
Canal	Net profit	-2.79	3.83	0.99	1.69
Upper Jhelum	Net revenues	0.79	2.97	1.11	1.49
Canal	Net profit	-4.12	-2.90	-2.18	-2.21
Sutlej Canals/	Net revenues	18.50	13.83	7.27	13.23
Project	Net profit	15.23	10.69	3.18	9.34

SOURCE: Same as Table 5.1.

this lucrative canal repaid its entire capital outlay every 24 to 36 months. The Lower Bari Doab Canal was almost equally remunerative, with annual net returns of 30 percent or more.

The performance of other works was less spectacular. The combined profits of the Triple Canal Project were somewhat reduced by the very low returns from the Upper Chenab and Upper Jhelum canals: net profits from the former remained under 5 percent, while the latter actually showed losses rather than profits. These two canals had been expensive to construct, thus entailing high interest payments, and they were also expensive to maintain. Profitability of the Sutlej Valley Project too was significantly reduced by its high capital cost, as well as by higher interest rates. The economic depression of the 1930s retarded the development of Nili Bar Colony, and this kept down revenue returns. During its first decade of operation, the Sutlej Valley Project registered net annual losses on capital outlay, in the mid-1930s net profits were under 5 percent, and even by the mid-1940s these remained below 10 percent.

Physical and economic factors thus induced variations in capital costs, and in interest and maintenance charges. These were, in turn, responsible for the sizeable profit differentials between different canal projects. The more remunerative ones showed very high annual returns, of up to 50 percent, on capital outlay, whereas others were less successful financially. In the aggregate, the state continued to obtain a large and steady flow of revenue from the canal colonies.[5]

Another measure of profitability for the canal colonies was the ratio between revenue returns and irrigated area. This is shown for each canal in Table 5.4, in the form of gross receipts and net profits per acre irrigated. This indicator, too, reveals that substantial differences in the rate of profits existed between the canals. The differences were not so great for gross receipts per acre as for net profits, indicating that working and interest charges heightened differentials. Variations of 100 percent in gross receipts per acre between different works were rare, but they were common for net profits per acre. Especially on the Upper Chenab and Upper Jhelum canals, high working expenses and interest charges were responsible for heavy reductions in revenue. This was also true of the Sutlej Valley Project. For the Sidhnai and Upper Sutlej canals even gross receipts were very low, suggesting that these earlier inundation and seasonal works, while cheap in

---

[5] Thus the financial commissioner noted in 1913 that the area irrigated by the Rakh Branch in Chenab Colony, though no larger than an average *tahsil*, provided higher revenue than any *district* of the Punjab, other than its parent district, Lyallpur. The revenue demand proposed for Rakh Branch in 1913 was Rs 2,382,501 per annum, whereas the highest revenue from any Punjab district other than Lyallpur was Gurdaspur, and this stood at Rs 1,855,346 per annum. See FC's Review of *AR Rakh Branch* (1913), para. 1; in PRAP(R), April 1913, No. 44.

TABLE 5.4. GROSS RECEIPTS AND NET PROFITS ON AREA IRRIGATED
(RS PER ACRE)

Name of Work		1915-16	1925-26	1935-36	1945-46
Sidhnai	Gross receipts	3.08	3.10	2.66	—
Canal	Net profit	2.37	2.64	2.05	—
Lower Chenab	Gross receipts	6.97	8.81	8.29	10.37
Canal	Net profit	5.07	7.09	6.07	8.08
Lower Jhelum	Gross receipts	4.94	6.72	5.95	6.42
Canal	Net profit	3.31	4.37	3.53	4.00
Lower Bari	Gross receipts	1.95	7.47	7.54	9.09
Doab Canal	Net profit	− 2.82	5.56	5.61	7.28
Upper Chenab	Gross receipts	3.13	7.39	5.55	6.10
Canal	Net profit	− 2.96	2.43	0.69	1.40
Upper Jhelum	Gross receipts	—	6.73	5.84	5.36
Canal	Net profit	—	− 0.37	− 3.41	− 2.75
Sutlej Canals/	Gross receipts	2.74	3.31	6.90	7.58
Project	Net profit	1.02	0.70	2.17	3.71

SOURCE: Same as Table 5.1.

terms of construction and interest expenses, lacked the intensity of canal
water application that perennial irrigation possessed, thus reducing the
level of state extraction. The fact that a large area in the Sutlej Valley Project was confined to seasonal irrigation also explains its relatively modest
performance in all the financial indicators discussed here. By contrast, the
Lower Chenab and Lower Bari Doab canals yielded the highest remunera-
tion for each acre irrigated, in terms of both gross receipts and net profits.
Also, with time, they registered sizeable increases in extraction per acre
under crop. The figures in Table 5.4 reveal, in general, that the state was
making a profit that in many cases reached as high as Rs 8-10 on every acre
of land irrigated in the canal colonies.

Finally, the cumulative financial performance of each canal project over
time can be assessed. This has been done in Table 5.5, in terms of accumulated surplus revenues or accumulated arrears, as well as the multiples
of total capital outlay that such amounts represented. It will be seen that the
Lower Chenab Canal had by far the greatest accumulated surplus, amounting by 1945-1946 to Rs 587,806,000. This work had paid for itself almost
twelve times over in roughly half a century of operation: it proved on any
terms a highly profitable venture. Similar conclusions could be reached

TABLE 5.5. ACCUMULATED SURPLUS REVENUES OR ACCUMULATED ARREARS OF INTEREST (−)

Name of Work		1915-16	1925-26	1935-36	1945-46
Sidhnai	Amount (Rs 000)	5,934	11,039	17,245	—
Canal	% of T.C.O.	446	831	1,290	—
Lower Chenab	Amount (Rs 000)	114,061	257,722	418,819	587,806
Canal	% of T.C.O.	359	733	945	1,172
Lower Jhelum	Amount (Rs 000)	13,877	44,559	71,669	110,835
Canal	% of T.C.O.	87	235	354	415
Lower Bari	Amount (Rs 000)	− 3,181	25,639	92,509	181,847
Doab Canal	% of T.C.O.	− 15	116	397	759
Upper Chenab	Amount (Rs 000)	− 6,804	1,589	− 1,393	16,140
Canal	% of T.C.O.	− 20	4	− 4	37
Upper Jhelum	Amount (Rs 000)	− 7,465	− 19,506	− 28,467	− 34,790
Canal	% of T.C.O.	− 18	− 44	− 63	− 74
Sutlej Canals/	Amount (Rs 000)	3,029	5,498	21,436	28,469
Project	% of T.C.O.	167	302	23	32

SOURCE: Same as Table 5.1.
    T.C.O. = Total Capital Outlay.

about the Lower Bari Doab Canal, which had an accumulated surplus of Rs 181,847,000 by 1945-1946, which represented a return of 759 percent on total capital outlay from 30 years of operation. The multiple for the Sidhnai Canal was the highest, reaching 1,290 percent by 1935-1936. However, Table 5.4 suggests that in terms of the intensity of cultivation, the Sidhnai was not a very productive work. Among the other projects, both the Upper Chenab Canal and the Sutlej Valley Project actually ran in arrears for several years, but began to produce revenue surpluses in the 1940s. The Upper Jhelum Canal remained in arrears throughout this period, for reasons already mentioned. The lower productivity and deficits, if any, of these works paled in comparison with the spectacular gains from major revenue earners like the Lower Chenab and Lower Bari Doab canals.

The Lower Jhelum Canal remained an anomaly. It produced lower revenue returns than could be expected from a work that suffered neither from the hydraulic demands placed upon the Upper Chenab and Upper Jhelum canals nor the interest charges borne by the Sutlej Valley Project. It was comparable to the more straightforward hydraulic systems of the Lower Chenab and Lower Bari Doab canals. Yet it remained at a low level of profitability. In terms of each of the indicators of financial performance, the Lower Jhelum Canal seemed to lack efficiency. Although its working expenses were no more than average (Table 5.1), its gross receipts, net revenues, and net profits were unexceptional (Table 5.2). Its annual revenue and profit rates, relative to capital outlay, were well below those of the Lower Chenab and Lower Bari Doab canals (Table 5.3), while the returns per acre irrigated were also much lower (Table 5.4). By 1945-1946, its accumulated surplus revenue was only 415 percent of total capital outlay (Table 5.5), showing retarded incremental earnings.

The only plausible explanation for such low overall performance must lie in the domination of Jhelum Colony by military interests. State income was reduced by the lower intensity of cultivation resulting from the allotment of peasant horse-breeding grants of a minimum of 55 acres. Revenue reductions were also caused by the lower pitch of government revenue demand, made in order to compensate horse-breeding grantees for accepting service tenures. Further losses stemmed from the sizeable areas devoted to private, regimental, and Remount Department horse runs, all of which were poor revenue payers.[6] Jhelum Colony served as an unambiguous statement of the diversion of economic resources away from the public weal, undertaken to fulfil military needs. This resulted throughout in the lowering of profits from this colony.

Total state revenue from the canal colonies, after all working and interest charges had been met, and taking only the indices considered here, was close to Rs 1,000 million. The canal colonies provided the state with a valuable source of income, which further increased its authority in the Punjab. These enhanced earnings could have been reinvested for the betterment of society. However, colonial rule failed to utilise this surplus for developmental purposes. Greater financial resources enabled it to increase the size of its bureaucracy as well as its police and military forces. The revenue surpluses from the canal colonies also averted the need to make excessive extractive demands on the possessors of resources in the Punjab as a whole. The sharing of an enhanced surplus between the state and the owners of the means of production allowed for the continued adherence of the latter to their alien masters.

The linkages between extraction and political economy were important because the state was by no means the only, or even the greatest, claimant to the agricultural surplus produced in the canal colonies. The holders of land were allowed to absorb a major part of the surplus, and even the native

[6] That Jhelum Colony was more sparsely peopled than other colony regions was also reflected in figures of population growth, in Table 2.8. These show that Shahpur did not expand as rapidly as Lyallpur, Montgomery, Multan, or Sheikhupura.

bureaucracy extracted its share. Quantitative analysis provides an incomplete picture of the extractive structure. Behind the indubitable fact of the profitability of the canal colonies for the state lay a number of factors that rendered the system inefficient, and at times even ineffective.

An Intransigent System of Assessment

The revenue system in the canal colonies was based on the practice of fluctuating harvest-by-harvest assessment, a system not in harmony with revenue arrangements in the rest of the Punjab. The latter were based on fixed assessment, with land revenue rates held constant over a stipulated period, which usually varied between ten and thirty years. Fluctuating assessment was highly inconvenient for the government, for it required the surveillance of every harvest by an assessing staff. This not only entailed a great deal of extra work but also greatly increased the opportunities for graft and corruption by the subordinate bureaucracy. A double staff of *patwaris* had to be maintained, one belonging to the Revenue and the other to the Irrigation Department. The responsibility for the assessment of water rates and land revenue lay with the latter, and through it with canal *patwaris*. The Revenue Department, and hence the revenue *patwaris*, held responsibility for the maintenance of land records and accounts in such matters as the acquisition of occupancy and proprietary rights on agricultural land and in village and town sites.[7] This situation led to bureaucratic complexities of which the financial commissioner wrote in 1909 that "a determined effort should be made to free ourselves from the maddening complications of accounts. At present every *patwari* has to work out several different rates on each holding, with, in some cases, complicated fractions, and the result is a tangle of figures which the cultivator cannot possibly understand and the superior officers find very difficult to check."[8]

The government realised that it was losing substantial amounts of money from fluctuating assessment, and wished to convert to fixed demand at the earliest opportunity in each colony. The former had been adopted in the early years of colonisation, for it suited tracts with unsettled economic and demographic conditions. It was expected that as conditions became more stable a few years after settlement revenue practice would be changed from fluctuating to fixed assessment. Officials felt that it was in the interest of colonists to convert to the fixed, as it would reduce the exactions of the

---

[7] See *PCM*, chs. 8 and 14.

[8] FC's Review of *AR Upper Jhang Branch* (1909), para. 31; in PRAP(R), October 1909, No. 77. The Colonies Committee investigated the problem of a double staff of revenue and irrigation officials at some length: see RPCC, ch. 9. In the 1910s, efforts to amalgamate the two staffs of *patwaris* proved unsuccessful: see PRAP(I), April 1911, Nos. 54-63; and PRAP(R), March 1919, Nos. 318-20.

subordinate bureaucracy and remove feelings of uncertainty and instability caused by variations in the scale of government demand with each harvest.[9] With this object in mind, the government tried to introduce fixed assessment at the first major opportunity, with the revenue resettlement of Chenab Colony in the early 1910s. The outcome of this and later efforts was to be quite contrary, however, to the hopes and expectations of the administration.

In 1909, G. F. de Montmorency, settlement officer of Lyallpur District, was directed by the Punjab Government to report on the possibility of replacing fluctuating with fixed assessment in Chenab Colony.[10] In his report in 1910, based on investigations he conducted in the colony, Montmorency established that agrarian and hydraulic conditions were favourable for a conversion to fixed assessment. If the fluctuating system was to be confined to areas with unsettled conditions, where the soil was too poor or the water supply too unreliable, then Montmorency estimated that fixed assessment ought to be applied to 65 to 95 percent of the land in the areas he was currently assessing.[11]

Montmorency reported, however, that there was much opposition among colonists to a change in the existing system; over the years similar arguments continued to confound official efforts to reform the revenue structure. Colonists objected that fixed demand was workable only if the water supply could be maintained at equalised and standardised levels over lengthy periods of time, and they felt little confidence in the ability of canal officials to provide water distribution on an equitable basis for sustained periods.[12] Rather than ensure a reliable supply of water, the Irrigation Department was believed to be constantly altering outlets and reducing supply in order to divert it for use elsewhere. Grantees feared that with fixed assessment, canal officials would lose the incentive to maintain efficiency of irrigation, while the commitment to pay a fixed amount of revenue could spell disaster if the water supply were reduced. Under the fluctuating system, the Irrigation Department had a direct interest in providing optimum irrigation facilities, for this ensured a higher matured area and consequently higher revenue returns. A further objection was that owners and tenants had become accustomed to the fluctuating system, and its abolition would

---

[9] FC's Review of *AR Rakh Branch* (1913), paras. 10-13; in PRAP(R), April 1913, No. 44.

[10] Chief Secretary to FC, 5 October 1909; in PRAP(R), October 1909, No. 119.

[11] Note by SO, Lyallpur, n.d.; in PRAP(R), June 1910, No. 44.

[12] Two decades later, in 1933, the settlement officer of Lower Bari Doab Colony was faced with similar objections to fixed assessment: "Once a fixed abiana demand is introduced a canal officer loses his direct interest in maintaining as high a standard of irrigation efficiency as possible." See Note by SO, Montgomery, 18 May 1933; in PRAP(R), August 1933, Enclosure No. 1 to No. 121.

have disrupted existing tenurial relations. Another important consideration for the grantees of land was that any major change in revenue practice threatened to disturb their ties with the subordinate bureaucracy. The fluctuating method provided ample opportunities for lowering the revenue burden through bribery and corruption. State losses would have been reduced with the fixed system, which left fewer openings for illegal gratification.

Grantees also complained that with fixed assessment the revenue contract would be based on the village (or *chak*) instead of the individual holding. Any suspensions or remissions of revenue would have to be given to the village as a whole.[13] This, the grantees feared, would not allow for failures of crops or water supply in the case of individual irrigators, or of those on a particular water course or outlet. Under fixed assessment, such people could get no relief if the village as a whole continued to do well. The grantees preferred the fluctuating system both because it was based on individual rather than collective assessment and because it emphasised the water channel rather than the village as the focal point of revenue extraction. Such preferences reflected the weakness of social cohesion in colony villages. This lack of communal ties was partly an outcome of the settlement within single estates of people who came from different areas. The importance of market production in this region could also have led to greater individualism, and perhaps even a dominance of economic over social relations in these villages.

Further difficulties in the conversion to fixed assessment lay in synchronising the revenue demand with the proportion of land cultivated in each village. In Chenab Colony, 70 percent of the grantees' holdings was regarded as the *haq*, or permissible area to be sown.[14] In reality, many villages were normally maturing over 100 percent, and some even up to 115 percent, of allotted area (this was possible through double cropping). On the other hand, in several villages with poor soil or inadequate irrigation, the proportion of matured crops fell below 70 percent of allotted area.[15] The Irrigation Department promised to equalise water distribution by bringing all villages to the utopian level of 70 percent *haq*.

This undertaking was difficult to put into practice, for problems existed

---

[13] Note by SO, Lyallpur, n.d.; in PRAP(R), June 1910, No. 44.

[14] The term *haq abpashi*, though popularly used, did not represent an official commitment for a minimum area to be irrigated, but rather an acceptable standard to strive for, which in Chenab Colony was 70 percent of each holding. See *PCM*, pp. 226-27; *Chenab Colony SR* (1915), para. 47; and RPCC, p. 126.

[15] Assessment reports contain information on differentiation in matured areas between villages. For Chenab Colony, see: *AR Upper Jhang Branch* (1909), ch. 3, para. 3; *AR Gugera Branch I* (1911), para. 5; *AR Gugera Branch II* (1912), para. 7; and *AR Rakh Branch* (1913), para. 7.

with both upward and downward adjustments in water supply. A fixed demand based on above-average irrigation levels would become untenable where irrigation was later reduced to the 70 percent level. Where the supply was below average at the time of assessment, the government would incur financial losses if it was later raised to around 70 percent from the lower level.[16] Clearly, fixed assessment depended on an effective standardisation in water distribution over long periods of time. The landholders maintained that the hydraulic regime lacked such evenness, but was subject to constant variations and inconsistencies. These arguments won the day. For Chenab Colony in the early 1910s, Montmorency recommended that fluctuating assessment be retained, and that the situation be reviewed at a later date. The Punjab Government accepted this proposal, but it restated its belief that the fixed method was the most desirable, and called for further efforts to facilitate its adoption in the canal colonies.[17]

In 1915, an important experiment was conducted to investigate the possibility of converting to the fixed system. The scheme involved the conversion of villages on the Shahkot Distributary of the Rakh Branch, in Chenab Colony, to fixed assessment for a period of five years.[18] All the colonists concerned had agreed to the project, and the fixed demand had been kept at a liberal level so as not to jeopardise its success. The government itself entertained the hope that the experiment would lead to the extension of the fixed system to other colony tracts, thus ''removing the many opportunities that exist under the fluctuating system for the canal subordinates to enrich themselves at the expense of the 'zamindar.' ''[19]

The results proved disastrous, for the entire experiment broke down during its very first season (*rabi* 1915). The problem lay with a maldistribution of water in the distributary, caused by silting. This led to a proportionately greater supply to the upper villages on the channel, which created a shortage in the lower villages.[20] Irrigators in the latter suffered a heavy reduction in their cropped areas, which fell well below the averages assumed for the fixed assessment. Faced with bitter complaints, irrigation officers closed off water outlets to the upper villages in an effort to normalise supply. This in turn led grantees in the upper reaches to complain of a violation of the conditions of fixed assessment. The government decided to revert immediately to the fluctuating method, and in this ignominious fashion the ex-

---

[16] Note by SO, Lyallpur, n.d.; in PRAP(R), June 1910, No. 44.

[17] Chief Secretary to FC, 14 October 1910; ibid., No. 45.

[18] See PRAP(R): October 1913, No. 34; January 1914, No 78; and January 1915, Nos. 36-45.

[19] RS to RAS, GOI, 25 October 1913; in PRAP(R), October 1913, No. 35.

[20] Note by FC, n.d.; in PRAP(R), May 1916, No. 34. See also *PCM*, pp. 197-98.

periment came to an end.[21] Though failure was imputed to the faulty design of the distributary, the episode dissuaded colonists even further from accepting fixed assessment. The government never again went to the extent of introducing fixed demand in colony areas, even for purposes of experiment.[22] Yet at every opportunity that presented itself (and this occurred with the reassessment of different tracts), officials continued to explore fully the possibility of converting to the fixed system, for they remained convinced of its superiority over fluctuating assessment.

Investigations were conducted in 1922 into the possibility of introducing fixed revenue on the Gugera Branch of Chenab Colony. Colonists were once again completely opposed to the scheme, largely because they did not believe that irrigation officials would continue to maintain a reliable water supply. Realising that its imposition would cause great discontent, the government yet again postponed a conversion to fixed rates. The chief obstacle was not any technical problem with the new measure, but the inability of colonists to achieve the harmony and cooperation that it demanded, as the chief irrigation engineer pointed out in 1922:

> Fixed assessment on outlet capacity lies within the range of practical politics if irrigators on the outlet become sufficiently advanced to form themselves into a cooperative body and elect representatives who would be responsible for the just distribution of water from the outlet and the collection of revenue. At the present time I fear this is also a theoretic ideal.[23]

In the 1930s, when Lower Bari Doab Colony was reassessed, fresh efforts to replace fluctuating with fixed assessment once again met with failure. In 1933, the settlement officer of Montgomery District, reporting on the prospects of converting to the new system, stated that single villages with different classes of soil or uneven irrigation facilities would pose difficulties for fixed rates if the landholders failed to harmonise the internal distribution of the revenue demand.[24] Such problems did not seem to arise in noncolony villages, where social homogeneity enabled the revenue demand to be accepted for the estate as a whole. This level of cohesion had

[21] See ''Precis of history of Shahkot experiment,'' n.d.; and Note by Revenue Member, 29 November 1922: in PRAP(R), January 1923, Nos. 18-19.

[22] One disincentive was the expense involved. The Shahkot experiment had proved to be an expensive failure: Rs 80,000 at prewar prices were spent on adjustments to outlet modules alone. See Note by Inspector-General of Irrigation, 28 July 1917; in ''Economy in use of canal water by a system of volumetric supply and payment,'' BOR H/251/563 KW, p. 5.

[23] Note by Chief Engineer, Irrigation Works, 7 April 1922; in PRAP(R), January 1923, No. 20 (see also No. 20a: Report by FC, 4 December 1922).

[24] Note by SO, Montgomery, 18 May 1933; in PRAP(R), August 1933, Enclosure No. 1 to No. 121.

not emerged in Lower Bari Doab Colony, where proprietary bodies appeared unlikely to be able to reapportion a fixed revenue demand amicably. Officials hoped that in time harmonious ties would develop in colony villages, though even by the 1930s this had failed to occur in the older colonies, which continued to have a fluctuating system.[25] The British, in fact, never succeeded in reforming the revenue structure of the canal colonies, despite over forty years of effort.

Much disappointment was caused among Punjab officials by the failure to introduce fixed assessment, and by the realisation that an unsatisfactory revenue system had to be retained. For instance, F. L. Brayne, a leading official expert on the rural Punjab, was unambiguous in his criticisms of fluctuating assessment. He wrote in 1933 that a practice that had been introduced as a temporary measure had with time come to be regarded as normal, and its evil results as inevitable. Brayne remarked that ''one has only to tour in these areas to realise the demoralising influence of the fluctuating assessment. The complaints, the bitterness, the jealousies, the uneasiness and the lack of any corporate sense in the villages are very striking.''[26] He held that agrarian conditions under canal irrigation were more stable than in *barani* tracts, so that there was no practical need to retain fluctuating assessment. From the early days of British rule, the fixed system had been gradually introduced into estates until it had become the accepted norm. Yet the administration was unable to achieve this in any part of the canal colonies.

Despite several efforts, the state was forced to continue with a revenue system in the canal colonies that was not in keeping with the revenue traditions of the rest of the province, and that had been introduced merely as a transitional measure. The fixed method could not be imposed largely because of the opposition of the grantees. One major reason for this was the lack of social harmony within landholding groups in colony villages. The individual basis of tenurial rights, the disincentive for cooperation induced by market production, and the lack of previous ties in many villages militated against the adoption of fixed assessment. Even so, the revenue system could have been reformed, but at certain political cost. Instead, the government continued with a procedure that caused it financial loss, required a great deal of administrative effort, and encouraged corruption in the subordinate bureaucracy. This indicated that the balance of forces between the state and the grantees was by no means weighted decisively in favour of

[25] Deputy Secretary, Development, to Commissioner, Multan, 27 July 1933; ibid., No. 123.

[26] Note by Commissioner, Multan, 23 May 1933; ibid., Enclosure No. 2 to No. 121. F. L. Brayne wrote on village uplift: see his *Better Villages* (Bombay: Oxford University Press, 1937).

the former. In the face of the vested interests of the intermediaries to whom it had alienated colony land, the state seemed to exert a weak and ineffectual impulse for change in agrarian affairs. This was borne out by other aspects of the extractive structure in which reform was attempted.

The Search for the Economic Value of Water

One important aspect in which the state tried to make its extractive arrangements more efficient was in the economic distribution of water. As irrigation spread over wider areas, water became an increasingly scarce resource. It was of primary importance that water should not be wasted by cultivators, or even that undue amounts were not utilised for crops. The most effective way of ensuring this was through the revenue system; if water could be taxed by volume, then it could be saved from unnecessary or excessive use. Unfortunately, this was not the practice adopted in the canal colonies, but it became the ambition of the government to try to introduce it, in order to conserve a resource that was even more valuable than the colony land on which it was applied.

Assessment of irrigated land in the canal colonies was based not on the amount of water used but on the area of land sown (in the earlier years on the area matured). This was known as the acreage system, and the tax was known as the *abiana* or water rate (or often as the occupiers' rate). Cultivators were free to employ, subject to rotational usage, as much water as they could obtain. They did not need to worry about costs as long as they took into consideration the area under cultivation.[27] There was little inducement to save water, and in fact the emphasis on assessment by acreage encouraged them to overirrigate the area sown. Such practices had been introduced in the early years of colonisation as an incentive for breaking new ground.[28] But with the passage of time the government became increasingly concerned about the absence of a proper method of water measurement, for it was failing to obtain equitable returns on the economic value of water. The acreage system was also detrimental to the colonists as a whole, for it allowed carelessness in water utilisation.

The sharing of water by cultivators was generally done on the basis of *warabandi*, or access to outlets by turn. Each cultivator was allowed a certain period of time in which to irrigate his fields.[29] During his period there was no limit to or measurement of the quantity of water he could use or the number of waterings he received. He paid tax on the area he cultivated, regardless of whether the land had obtained one or several waterings. This

---

[27] FC's Review of *AR Upper Jhang Branch* (1909), para. 4; in PRAP(R), October 1909, No. 77.

[28] Note by Chief Engineer, Irrigation Works, 20 August 1921; in BOR H/251/563, p. 125.

[29] For a description of the *warabandi* system, see *PCM*, p. 229.

type of rotational running became necessary with the expansion of wheat cultivation, which placed great demands on the water supply during the *rabi* season, when it was at its lowest. The only check on wasteful consumption was the time allowance for each irrigator, but this was insufficient to ensure an economic utilisation of water. Indeed, more water was reportedly applied by cultivators in the canal colonies per unit of area irrigated, and waterings were more frequent during the life of crops, than was necessary for successful cultivation.[30]

Irrigation officials worked constantly at introducing a system of assessment based on the sale of water by volume. It became the ambition of every irrigation officer of note to realise this ideal.[31] Experiments for a ''volumetric'' assessment had been conducted in northern India during the nineteenth century, and they were continued in the canal colonies.[32] The problem had technical, economic, and social dimensions. A viable method of water measurement depended on the design of an accurate ''module,'' and several efforts were made in the canal colonies to evolve a satisfactory gauge. With the rise in prices of steel and cement, however, the costs involved in fitting a suitable module throughout the canal network acted as an economic bar on an innovation that might have been within the reach of existing technology. Purely masonry outlets proved to be feeble water dispensers that required constant attention, involving much expense. The cultivators had to be trusted not to tamper with outlets and to resist making illegal openings that would bypass the measuring device. It was found that individuals could not generally be relied upon to shut off or reduce the rate of flow, even though overwatering threatened to harm their crops. A module lost its effectiveness, and its reputation, after ways were discovered to tamper with it successfully, and the search for another design had to begin anew.[33] Thus a number of factors were arrayed against the government's ambition to procure an economic value for irrigation water. The lack of dependability among the ranks of its own bureaucracy made the need for a water outlet that could not be interfered with all the more urgent:

[30] See Notes by Chief Engineer, Irrigation Works, 6 July 1920, and by Inspector-General of Irrigation, 28 July 1917; in BOR H/251/563, p. 113 and KW p. 5.

[31] For two discussions of the technical aspects and advantages of volumetric assessment, see: ''On the distribution of water by measurement'' and ''The sale of water for irrigation at volumetric rates,'' Punjab Irrigation Paper Nos. 12 and 24 (both IOR: [7]4617/1).

[32] For a short account of such experiments during the nineteenth century, see Note by Inspector-General of Irrigation, 28 July 1917; in BOR H/251/563 KW, pp. 5-6.

[33] The two modules in most common use in the canal colonies were the Gibb and Kennedy gauge modules. For their performance in Chenab Colony/Lyallpur District, see: *AR Gugera Branch II* (1912), para. 9; *AR Rakh Branch* (1913), para 9; *AR Jhang Branch* (1921), para. 11; *AR Gugera Branch I-II* (1923), para. 12; and *AR Jaranwala Tahsil* (1936), para. 6.

There is probably no branch of colony management which provides more openings for extortion and illicit gratification to subordinates than the regulation of water-course outlets . . . alarm would be felt by the lower ranks of officials at any measures which would introduce the fixity of supply which above all things the cultivator prays for.[34]

Several proposals and schemes for introducing water measurement were examined and initiated over the years. In 1913, F. W. Schonnemann, an irrigation officer, reported on the irrigation system prevailing around the town of Lorca in southeastern Spain. Water there was sold to farmers at bulk rates, at auction sales held daily by a syndicate representing both the irrigators and the proprietors of the water supply. Schonnemann noted that the Lorca method appeared to be free of friction, disputes, and complaints; and he recommended that its best features be introduced to the Punjab. In 1915 the government decided to undertake such an experiment, but this was not possible during the war years owing to the shortage of British irrigation officers.[35]

After the war, in 1920, an effort was made at the initiative of the government to form "cooperative irrigation societies" in Montgomery and Ly-allpur districts. It was agreed that a committee, elected by member irrigators of each society, would control the distribution of water, and assessing officials such as canal *patwari*s and *zilladar*s, would be withdrawn. The experiment was proposed for one year in a few villages in Chenab and Lower Bari Doab colonies, though it was realised that volumetric arrangements on an extensive scale would only be possible with syndicates representing colonists over large areas. Such agreements, a prerequisite for reform in the revenue system, were dependent upon harmony among the cultivators. But this proved to be sadly lacking. In 1921, within a year of its initiation, the government conceded that the experiment with cooperative irrigation syndicates had not only failed but was virtually unworkable in the Punjab; and the project was abandoned.[36] It appeared impossible to avoid conflicting demands for water at the same time, or at different places, on a distributary. The venture was never introduced on ordinary estates of peasant grantees, in the absence of sufficient cooperation over internal distribution among smallholders in the canal colonies. For its part, the state had neither the means nor the will to implement such reforms in the face of opposition from colonists.

When it became clear that there were too many obstacles to a direct in-

---

[34] FC's Review of *AR Rakh Branch* (1913), para. 15; in PRAP(R), April 1913, No. 44.

[35] For Schonnemann's proposals and their subsequent implementation, see Note by Chief Engineer, Irrigation Works, 6 July 1920; in BOR H/251/563, pp. 113-21.

[36] See ibid., pp. 121-26.

troduction of volumetric assessment in villages of small grantees, experiments were conducted with a few large landholders in the hope of obtaining insights on the working of the volumetric system. Some contracts and leases were entered into for this purpose in Lower Bari Doab Colony in the early 1920s. They were designed to test whether the volumetric method would result in an economy of water distribution and in greater financial returns to the state.[37] These larger grantees turned out to be hardly less prodigal than their smaller counterparts.

One of the colonists involved in the project was Major D. H. Vanrenen, the "latifundia" horse-breeding grantee. Officials discovered that, though Vanrenen undertook and proceeded to pay revenue on the volumetric basis, he kept his arrangements with his subtenants on the acreage basis, as in the rest of the colony.[38] As far as the actual cultivators were concerned, no efforts were made nor were any incentives provided to economise on water or to cope with the demands of cultivation under a volumetric system. Vanrenen simply acted as an intermediary who accepted an innovation in assessment from the government, but did not pass this on to his subtenants. In so doing he made a substantial profit for himself, for the volumetric rates were pitched lower than the acreage rates.

Another grantee on the volumetric system was Sardar Jogindra Singh, on his estate of Iqbalnagar in the same colony. Jogindra did not employ subtenants but used a steam plough, which required wide furrows to avoid frequent turnings. Although the mechanical ploughing method resulted in a great saving of labour, no care was taken to combine this with the conservation of water, and in consequence much wastage took place.[39] These experiments failed to produce results that could be recommended for other estates: with both tenant and mechanised farming, the volumetric trials proved to be discouraging.

In a third case, in Chenab Colony in the early 1920s, a lease of the sizeable area of 2,300 acres was given specifically on conditions of volumetric assessment. Officials placed much hope on this experiment, for they believed that the sale of water by measurement on such a considerable scale would serve as an important precedent for a more general extension of the volumetric system in the canal colonies. Conditions for the lessee were

[37] See "Further notes on the sale of irrigation water at volumetric rates," Punjab Irrigation Paper No. 27; in "Canal administration—Volumetric system—Sale of water at volumetric rates," BOR 251/48/00/1 A, p. 11.

[38] "Report on volumetric contracts in Bulloki Division, Lower Bari Doab Colony, during the years 1920-21 and 1921-22," by E. S. Crump, Executive Engineer, 18 December 1922; ibid., p. 26.

[39] "Report on volumetric supply at Iqbalnagar," by W. D. Dench, 25 November 1922; ibid., p. 31.

favourable: the land itself was extremely rich and rents in the neighbourhood were high (Rs 20-30 per acre, with the tenant bearing the revenue
burden). However, the prospects of success were diminished when the
choice of lessee fell on a political appointee rather than a genuine entrepre-
neur. A lease of three years was made in 1921 to Syed Mehdi Shah, a
resident of Chenab Colony who had rendered meritorious services to the
administration, especially in war recruitment.[40] When the lease expired in
1924, Mehdi's application for an extension was rejected, the volumetric
experiment was discontinued, and the land was put up for auction.

The main object of Mehdi Shah's lease had been to encourage the economy of water, but in fact the lessee was found to be notorious for the heavy
watering of his land. He was reported to be least bothered about the prodigal use of water, and always asked for his maximum supply. He used, acre
for acre, much more water than ordinary colonists, and in the process
reaped handsome profits for himself.[41] As an experiment in water economy, the negative results of the lease to Mehdi Shah further emphasised
the difficulties faced by the government in obtaining equitable returns on
irrigation water.

Nevertheless, so important was the issue that renewed efforts were made
between 1925 and 1940 to evolve a workable system of water measurement. By 1930, modifications in the criteria for volumetric assessment
were introduced, ones considered better suited to conditions in the canal
colonies. A new method called the "contract system" was adopted.[42] This
entailed water supplied at fixed rates for each harvest, from a modular outlet designed to discharge authorised amounts calculated on the area dependent on the outlet. A "contract rate" was derived from a formula based on
the average revenue rates and water discharges of an irrigation division,
which consisted of several villages. The contract system was first introduced in 1930, and was readily accepted by a few large owners, mostly
sole proprietors of areas covered by a single water outlet. These landholders were shrewd enough to ensure that charges under the new arrangement
would be lower than those under the acreage system, and indeed this became a precondition for all those who accepted the contract rates. Once

[40] The financial commissioner "is almost daily solicited to use Crown land as a means of
supplementing the resources of men who have deserved well of Government, and he thinks
this opportunity should be taken of recognising good service or assisting the representative of
a distinguished family in difficulties." See FC's letter, 9 January 1920; in "Proposed leases
in Buchiana Reservoir on terms of volumetric payment of canal charges," BOR J/301/1411
A, pp. 87-88. The file also contains correspondence on the terms and conditions of Shah's
lease, and his testimonial of services.

[41] See "Sale by auction of Chakku land in Lyallpur District," BOR 301/8/25/16.

[42] See "Ch. 10 of Canal Act Committee Report—Sale of water by volumetric or contract
system," BOR 251/43/00/20.

again, little success was achieved with small cultivators, owing to the lack of cooperation over the internal distribution of the revenue demand among a large number of co-sharers on a single outlet. By 1936 there were fifty outlets taking water by contract, consisting mostly of large owners in Lower Bari Doab Colony, though even among this class the contract process failed to achieve wide popularity.

Officials soon realised that the government was suffering a heavy financial loss on contracts made under the divisional average formula. To make it more responsive to local variations, the formula was altered in several cases to the mean of divisional and outlet averages. Even this modification entailed revenue losses, for cultivators only accepted a new measure if it was financially more favourable than the previous one. The contract method failed to spread in the canal colonies: between 1936 and 1940 only ten new outlets were added. By 1940 both the volumetric and contract systems were still in an experimental stage, despite almost thirty years of effort in the canal colonies, and indeed over a century of trial and error in northern India.

The colonists who agreed to experiment with the volumetric and contract alternatives did so for purposes of financial gain. They would not have accepted the new terms of revenue payment if the rates had not been kept lower than acreage rates, and they were not prepared to continue with the new system if the two rates were brought on a par.[43] Even water rates on the acreage system were regarded by officials as lower than desirable; and it was not considered politically feasible to upgrade them substantially.[44] Cultivators, on the other hand, could not be induced to accept volumetric payment as long as the existing water rates were so moderate. This "scissors" effect defeated the government's dual intention of achieving an economy of water and equitable revenue returns. A similar impasse had been reached in the quest for fixed assessment. The financial commissioner in 1922 represented this dilemma, and its political ramifications, as follows:

> In its desire not to charge more than what was reasonable, the Government has undoubtedly charged rates which were far below the rates which it could have charged theoretically and even below those which it could have charged if it was to do justice to people in the Punjab, who had not benefitted by canal irrigation. . . . These low rates have been maintained for a long series of years and one may say that the owner of land has gained some sort of vested interest in the surplus profit which Government has left to him and which Government might and (in part)

[43] Note by Chief Engineer, Irrigation Works, 20 March 1925; in BOR 251/48/00/1 A, p. 79.

[44] Note by F. J. Waller, Executive Engineer, 29 January 1923; ibid., p. 17.

ought to have taken. . . . These are considerations which are not in any sense economic. A very large area in the Punjab is now canal irrigated, and the owners and occupiers of these canal irrigated tracts are among the wealthiest and best educated of the inhabitants of rural areas. They wield a very great influence and any attempt to raise the rates is bound to meet a strenuous opposition from them. It is true that there are other areas that have not benefitted from canals, but the inhabitants of those areas are comparatively poor and insignificant. The fact that injustice is being done to them is likely to be obscured. . . . Having regard to all these considerations I do not think that we can possibly raise the rate on existing canals to anything like what can be justifiably demanded on theoretical grounds.[45]

The adoption of a reformed system, with volumetric assessment, involved other complications that were difficult to overcome. The notion that cultivators would be relieved of harassment and interference by the assessing staff was questionable. It was feared that, though the *patwari* might be removed, the gauge reader would appear, and cultivators would be subject to the same exactions from him.[46] The maintenance of an efficient irrigation network required a large staff for duties such as the supervision of fields and watercourses and for the collection of statistics (on which later remodellings and alterations would have to be based). It was unlikely that a new system would lead to any substantial reduction in the numbers of the subordinate bureaucracy, or in the weight of its perquisites from agriculturists.

Problems of a technical nature were also difficult to solve. Measuring instruments were expensive and not immune to damage resulting from the inexperience or deliberate action of cultivators and petty officials. The water supply was assessed on readings made by low-paid officials, on whom complete confidence could not be placed. Assessment by volume of water was itself a complicated task, for it depended on variable factors such as river supplies, crops, and seasons. Officials had no method of arriving at fixed rates that would give satisfaction to all cultivators, or be understood by them. Whereas an extensive canal network required a uniformity of flow for its successful operation, the individual irrigator under volumetric rates expected and demanded that his private supply be regulated according to his requirements. These factors forced upon the government a degree of caution in working toward volumetric assessment. Such efforts as were

---

[45] Note by FC, 17 August 1922; in "Enhancement of occupiers' rates on all canals," BOR H/251/599 KW 1, p. 25.

[46] These difficulties in the implementation of the volumetric system were brought out in the comprehensive Note by the Chief Engineer, Irrigation Works, 20 March 1925; in BOR 251/48/00/1 A, pp. 79-119.

made were not reciprocated by the colonists, with the result that not a single workable solution entailing the measurement of water could be propagated in the canal colonies. The only measure of this scarce resource remained the sown area, and this took little cognisance of the volume of water expended.

The abortive search for a volumetric basis of assessment revealed the limitations suffered by the state in bringing about reforms in agrarian conditions. The position of the grantees of land and the subordinate bureaucracy was too entrenched to allow the implementation of any major changes in existing practices. Although the state had exercised a decisive role in the choice and settlement of grantees, it failed to retain much power of regulation in the period subsequent to colonisation. The weakening of its administrative effectiveness was reflected in several other aspects of agrarian and tenurial conditions. Indeed, the lapse in efficiency was so advanced as to cast grave doubts on the degree of bureaucratic and social orderliness in the canal colonies.

SOCIAL EXTRACTION

A Disordered Society

Several types of irregularities and illegal practices existed among colonists and petty officials in the canal colonies. Some of these were, throughout, well known to British officials, whereas others were uncovered during inspections and audits of colony offices in the 1930s. These investigations revealed a wide range of misdemeanours on the part of colonists, as well as the low level of honesty and efficiency to which the administration of the canal colonies had fallen. British officials ascribed many of the shortcomings to corruption within the subordinate bureaucracy, which controlled the administration at the local level at which the irregularities existed. Corruption was, undoubtedly, rife among native officials. There was widespread collusion between petty officials and grantees, which seemed to work against the interests of both state and society. Such collusion, and the irregularities that stemmed from it, permeated the relations between private men and public servants. Some major types of misdemeanours unearthed in the canal colonies will be discussed here.

Infringements in the distribution of water, called *warashikni*s, became a common occurrence under canal irrigation.[47] Since cultivation depended so

[47] There was official concern by the 1900s at the incidence of unauthorised irrigation and deliberate breaches of channels, and as late as the 1940s such crimes were still widespread. See "Procedure in investigations under Sections 33 and 34 of Canal Act," BOR H/251/423; and "Ch. 3 Section B of Canal Act Committee Report—on *warashiknis*," BOR 251/43/00/13.

heavily upon it, canal water was always in great demand, and complaints by irrigators of its scarcity were endemic.[48] Water also had its price, for water rates formed the major proportion of the revenue burden, and they were an important part of the costs of cultivation. There was consequently much incentive for irrigators to obtain water illegally, or in greater quantities than their due share.

The distribution of water to cultivators was itself an intricate process. Known as *warabandi*, it involved the taking of water by turn from an outlet. Such systems of rotational access had been authorised by the Irrigation Department for a large number of villages. For almost as many villages, however, there was no such authorised *warabandi*, and no official records were maintained on mutual arrangements among irrigators for the sharing of water. Even where it was officially authorised, *warabandi* was not legally binding but was dependent on the good will of the irrigators. There existed, therefore, both opportunity and inducement for infringements in water distribution in the canal colonies, and that these were availed of in good measure was shown by the series of complaints reaching officials on this issue.

By disrupting the supply of water, *warashikni*s caused much disturbance in agrarian affairs.[49] The cutting of a large distributary could cause a great deal of damage: thirty or forty villages below the cut could be affected, and the entire channel would have to be closed off for repairs. It was estimated in 1929 that an ordinary cut on an important distributary could mean a loss to the cultivators affected of about Rs 100,000, and to the government of about Rs 10,000.[50] With an annual average of ten to fifteen cuts, which most large distributaries suffered, the cultivators stood to lose at least one million rupees a year, and the government one-tenth of that amount. Cuts were most common during the sowing period, when the demand for water was keenest, and the failure to obtain water could ruin crops. Disputes over water frequently caused violent encounters, and spawned a number of

[48] At times discontent over water supply spilled over into political agitation. For reports on political meetings during 1939 and 1940, demanding improved irrigation facilities, see: "Resolutions passed by Kisan Committee on 28 February 1940 complaining of shortage of water in Nili and Ganji Bar Canals," BOR 251/4/24/37; and "Moga agitation—Demands of Nahri Committee, Dipalpur," BOR 251/4/24/39.

[49] *Warashikni* (taking water out of turn), which includes here unauthorised irrigation (*najaiz abpashi*) and waste of water (*ab-zaia*), included such actions as opening and cutting canal banks, enlarging and breaking outlets, diverting canal supply, and using water outside sanctioned boundaries and periods. See "Ch. 3 Section A of Canal Act Committee Report—Unauthorised irrigation and waste of water," BOR 251/43/00/12.

[50] Note by DC, Shahpur, 5 July 1929; in "Procedure to be adopted in cases relating to cutting of canal banks," BOR 251/31/00/1, pp. 35-37. For the deleterious effects of *warashiknis*, see also *AR Lower Chenab Colony of Jhang District* (1923), para. 11.

crimes, including murder. *Warashikni*s were also induced by the profit motive: they reportedly increased at times when agricultural prices were high, as in the immediate post-World War I years and the mid-1920s.[51]

The administration was unable to exercise much control over *warashiknis*. All *warabandi* schemes depended eventually upon common agreement among irrigators, rather than any official sanction or legal recognition of the schedule of claims. Breaches were difficult to punish, since they were either beyond the pale of the law or were committed at night, making it difficult to apprehend the culprits. A large number of cases were never reported, for there was little hope of obtaining redress from the guilty party through executive action. The only recourse was to civil courts; but the disposal of such cases took several months. Moreover, only an insignificant number of cases resulted in convictions; a survey in 1940 placed this at 3.8 percent of the cases tried.[52] The government lacked a clear legal right to tackle *warashiknis* effectively: the existing legislation, the North India Canal and Drainage Act (VIII of 1873), was found to be inadequate for this purpose. Consequently, the police took no particular trouble to control this crime, and magistrates were reluctant to convict people for it.[53]

Officials were aware that *warashiknis* constituted a failure of justice on a considerable scale, but the suppression of such activities seemed not have been politically feasible. For *warashiknis* were an infringement by the strong against the rights of the weak. Such acts could only have been arranged by individuals or groups who possessed the resources to bribe the lower officials, and to enforce a silent if unwilling compliance on their weaker neighbours. Though no group of irrigators could have been without water for sustained periods of time, for this would have created virtual anarchy, there was at the same time no established and accepted system of water distribution at the local level to ensure a secure and regular supply to irrigators. The state was unable to ensure that *warabandis* were reliable and equitable.[54] The frequent occurrence of *warashiknis* would suggest that ac-

[51] See Answer to Question No. 1032 (1929) of Dr S. M. Alam; in "Council Questions regarding the number of murders on account of *warashiknis*," BOR 251/53/00/14, p. 1. See also "Policy for criminal offences connected with unauthorised irrigation," BOR 251/31/00/1(a).

[52] BOR 251/43/00/13, pp. 31-32.

[53] Note by Commissioner, Rawalpindi, 17 July 1929; and "Precis of question of cutting of canal banks," n.d.: in BOR 251/31/00/1, pp. 41 and 67.

[54] Investigations by the Canal Act Committee showed that even by the 1940s *warabandi* practices were not standardised. Authorisation by the Irrigation Department extended to only a portion of such schemes, compensation for damages suffered required recourse to civil law, the disposal of cases was slow, and village *panchayats* had not been given responsibility for *warabandi*s. See BOR 251/43/00/13, pp. 32-34.

cess to water provided a basis on which inequalities within the body of cultivators were maintained, and even enhanced.

Another problem common in the canal colonies was illicit cultivation. This consisted of the cultivation of areas which were not included in any tenancy, or the use of which was not otherwise authorised by the government. The offence was punishable by fines, confiscations of crops, or the levy of punitive rates of rent (usually from four to eight times the land revenue).[55] Illicit cultivation was reported to cover large areas; but records of it were very improperly maintained in colony offices. Registers and files were either completely missing or covered only a fraction of the cases. A large number of instances were discovered in which no punitive measures had been imposed, or where great leniency was shown over fines levied (many being even less than the land revenue assessable). Little coordination existed between the Revenue and Irrigation departments, which were jointly responsible for the disposal of such cases. All this resulted in financial losses to the government, while the illegal use of colony land went unchecked—a situation made possible by the connivance of the subordinate bureaucracy.[56]

A further source of corruption occurred with the transfers of state land to colonists. Since land was highly coveted, such transfers comprised a valuable exchange of resources, and opened up further opportunities for corruption. Despite their economic importance, they were not being effected by formal and standardised procedures; and little was done to curtail malpractices. Even as late as 1937, the Legal Remambrancer of the Punjab complained of incorrect procedures in numerous cases.[57] Deeds for the sale and transfer of land contained many defects. They needed to be examined and approved by law officers, but this did not take place. Possession of land was not supposed to be given until such deeds were executed and registered, but in this too a large number of infringements were discovered. Though standard forms had been introduced, the Legal Remambrancer argued in his complaint in 1937 that the attention of law officers was needed

[55] *PCM*, p. 233.

[56] Audit and inspection reports of government offices in the 1930s uncovered several malpractices, and the serious discrepancies in official records that they revealed made it ever more difficult to ascertain the extent of such problems. For cases of illicit cultivation, see (these are abbreviated titles for the BOR files containing the audit reports): "Monograph of Inspection and Audit of Demands and Recoveries of Government dues in canal colonies" (1934), BOR 301/14/00/144, pp. 57-59; "Lower Chenab Canal Extensions—Lyallpur—Audit" (1938), BOR 301/31/25/5, pp. 181-201; "Lower Jhelum Colony—Shahpur—Audit" (1938), BOR 301/31/19/7, p. 151; "Chunian Colony—Lahore—Audit" (1938), BOR 301/31/12/40, p. 51; "Nili Bar Colony—Pakpattan—Audit" (1938), BOR 301/31/C9/36 A, pp. 377-409.

[57] Note by Legal Remembrancer, 2 July 1937; in "Colonies—Policy—Procedure for executing transfers of Government land," BOR 301/14/00/113, Notes, pp. 1-3.

to look into the special requirements of each case. Deeds for hundreds of sales, mutations, and leases were executed in each colony district every year. Although processing by specialists of each individual case might have involved an intolerable administrative burden, there was clearly a need for a trained legal staff to supervise such work. In reality, control over the transfer of the state's landed assets was in the hands of a revenue staff that had no acquaintance with the laws pertaining to the transfer of property, and had little time to devote to such matters.[58]

In the absence of proper management of land transfers, administrative procedures failed to work smoothly. A great deal of litigation occurred as a result of the mistakes that were constantly being made over the selling and letting of state land. The revenue staff not only lacked a knowledge of the relevant laws, but it did not possess even the rudimentary level of commercial training that a private proprietor might have expected from his estate agent. The Legal Remambrancer provided some examples of errors in bureaucratic management, but he added that the list could be extended indefinitely.[59] Grants of land were sanctioned on scraps of paper of no legal value and of uncertain meaning. Land was often granted, leased, or auctioned on terms that made irrigation compulsory, though it was known that the land was unirrigable. The same plot of land was granted twice over to different people: no registers were kept that might have averted such mistakes.

Several other types of distortion in land transfers were reported by the Legal Remambrancer. Persons were put in possession of land without the execution of any document that could enable the government to enforce the terms of the grant. Standardised forms were in use, but they frequently contained meaningless or inconsistent alterations. Persons with short-term tenancies were left to carry on, sometimes for as long as ten or twenty years, without the renewal of their tenancies and with no recognisable legal status. Even persons who had never received grants of any kind were allowed to occupy land such as village and town sites, and were treated as if they were established state tenants.[60] Despite these obvious shortcomings, the government failed to act upon the pleas for reform made by the Legal Remambrancer in the late 1930s. Misdemeanours and irregularities in official procedures were so deep-rooted in the canal colonies that the im-

---

[58] For an evaluation of these problems by the financial commissioner's office, see Notes by Superintendent, Colonies III, 7 July 1937; and Junior Secretary, FC(D), 29 July 1937: ibid., pp. 3-6 and 16-18.

[59] Note by Legal Remembrancer, 5 October 1937; ibid., pp 19-22.

[60] The financial commissioner's office acknowledged that though rules existed for standardised procedures there was wide discrepancy between theory and practice, and a large volume of mistakes and misdemeanours continued to occur. See Notes by Superintendent, Colonies II, 8 July 1937 and 19 October 1937; ibid., pp. 6-11 and 27-31.

provement of specific aspects seemed pointless. On the other hand, overall reform of the system, involving a fundamental restructuring of administrative functions, was a task that imperialist rule in its final years was unwilling or unable to undertake.[61]

The government also experienced much trouble over residential and shop sites in villages. Although residential plots for the grantees of land were free, entrepreneurs (such as shopkeepers) had to purchase such sites as well as pay rent on work sites. Since this increased the costs of commercial enterprise, it caused much friction between the villagers and the government, but the latter continued to insist on the stipulation.[62] Despite the official position, it was discovered that in a large number of cases these obligations were not being fulfilled in practice. In Chenab Colony, demands and payments for shop sites were never scrutinised by any gazetted officer, nor did the Colony Office possess any information on arrears of rent. It was estimated that in Chenab Colony alone such arrears came to over Rs 200,000, and that hundreds of shopkeepers occupied village sites without paying rents.[63] This practice was further encouraged by the fact that no penalties were levied on rent defaulters.

Discrepancies also existed in the sale of village sites. No register existed in the Chenab Colony Office showing such sales. Rough lists existed for sales in each village, but several entries were either improper or were omitted altogether. None of the entries had been initialled by a gazetted officer, all the work having been left to low-paid clerks. Nor were recoveries watched by any officer, and shopkeepers were left to make payments at random.[64] Shop sites were often sold at prices that were half or even one-third of those fixed by the government. All these irregularities caused heavy financial losses to the state, the shortfall remaining with petty officials and with those villagers who could afford to pay bribes.[65]

[61] The audit reports scratched only the surface of such malpractices, and concentrated largely on procedures to be followed in colony headquarters. They did not discuss the actual methods of misappropriation by officials, nor could they estimate total public revenues lost, though they did so for individual accounts. Even in what they revealed, it was apparent that by the 1930s bureaucratic management in the canal colonies had reached a low ebb.

[62] Discontent among shopkeepers over the financial burden of having to rent and purchase village sites led to concerted agitation against these conditions in the 1930s. This is comprehensively covered in "Future treatment of village sites in Chenab Colony," BOR 301/2/00/9 A-I.

[63] "Lower Chenab Colony—Lyallpur—Audit" (1938), BOR 301/31/25/4, pp. 63-65 and 71; BOR 301/14/00/144, pp. 63-69; and *PCR*, 1936, p. 12.

[64] Similar discrepancies were discovered for village sites in other colonies: see "Sidhnai Colony—Multan—Audit," BOR 301/31/27/39, p. 15; BOR 301/31/19/7, p. 125; BOR 301/14/00/144, p. 75; and (at length on the irregularities uncovered) BOR 301/31/C9/36 A, pp. 279-331.

[65] Surveillance over town sites too was allowed to lapse, with municipal committees and

The actual sale of agricultural land composed by far the most valuable transfer of resources between the state and the colonists. Under the Colonisation Act of 1912, peasant grantees were allowed to acquire proprietary rights, and this greatly increased the scale of alienation of state land. The volume of such transactions provided much opportunity for corruption and the misappropriation of public revenues. Numerous cases were recorded in the audit and inspection reports of the 1930s concerning illegal practices, and in reality such cases must have been legion.[66] In Lower Bari Doab Colony, for instance, there was the remarkable situation that only fourteen deeds of conveyance had ever been executed or registered. The grantees had saved themselves from this expense with the collusion of the lower officialdom, but the valuable rights of the state in land had been transferred unconditionally. In Lyallpur, Jhang, and Sheikhupura districts, single registers were not maintained to show the purchase of proprietary rights by government tenants. There existed, instead, a separate register for each village, which created considerable problems of referencing and accountability. In these districts, too, as well as in Chunian Colony, no deeds of conveyance had been stamped, executed, or registered. Indeed, in Chunian Colony there was no record to show any accounts of sale proceeds from the acquisition of proprietary rights. Information on this had to be gleaned from assessment records, a painstaking process.

It was also found that supervisory tasks subsequent to sales were not followed up. In the Colony Office of Lyallpur District, no reports had been received or records kept to show that the conditions of sale had been observed. Responsibility had not been assigned to any official to supervise breaches of such stipulations. In numerous cases, no efforts were made to enforce the condition of residence, a vital aspect of colonisation. As a result, it was reported that absenteeism had become a normal feature. Violations of residence requirements were also common in the case of shared grants, where only one co-sharer would reside on the grant, with the others remaining as absentees.

Perhaps the most troublesome aspect of administrative supervision was "temporary cultivation." This was a system of temporary leases of state land, an expedient resorted to where land was lying vacant, pending permanent allotment or sale. Temporary cultivation leases could be given for

---

district boards failing to ensure that buildings were completed according to sanctioned plans, or within the stipulated eighteen months. Supervision of such matters as land revenue assessed on town sites, or management of state land by local bodies, was also inadequate. See BOR 301/31/25/4, pp. 83-87; BOR 301/31/25/5, pp. 163-71; and *PCR*, 1938, p. 16.

[66] See, for example, BOR 301/14/00/144, pp. 83-87; BOR 301/31/25/4, p. 4; BOR 301/31/25/5, p. 217; BOR 301/31/12/40, pp. 11, 21, 25-27, and 59; and "Lower Bari Doab Colony—Khanewal—Audit" (1940), BOR 301/31/27/57, pp. 35-53.

one or two harvests only, or could extend for further periods. The areas of leases also varied; if small, they were usually given out to grantees within the village. In Nili Bar Colony in the 1930s, leases were given of large blocks of 2,000 to 5,000 acres from lands awaiting auction sales.[67] Temporary cultivation proved to be an alternative source of revenue for the state from land that might otherwise have remained fallow. The system of temporary leases was extensive enough to make the state by far the largest rentier in the Punjab.[68] It assumed special significance when auction sales planned for Nili Bar Colony in the 1930s had to be postponed, owing to the collapse of the land market brought about by the economic depression. In that and other colonies, major irregularities and misappropriations occurred with temporary cultivation leases. Such tenancies came to be regarded by the higher Punjab officials as a great evil, but a necessary one for the sake of public finances. The audit and inspection reports of the 1930s devoted much attention to this problem. They uncovered a large amount of evidence on official corruption, of which some instances will be mentioned here.

One major source of irregularity was the failure to observe the rental levels stipulated for temporary cultivation leases. Under government rules, rent was levied either on allotted or matured area. A common abuse of the latter method was the diversion of water, where possible, from the leased areas to the permanent plots of the grantees. Temporary cultivation in these cases became no more than a contrivance to obtain extra water "at infinitesimal cost."[69] On the other hand, rents levied on allotted area had to be kept low and flexible, for invariably only a certain proportion of the leasehold was actually cultivable. Rental levels under both systems were vulnerable to manipulation, with consequent reductions in public income. Certain remedial measures were adopted, such as the disposal of leases by tender, specification of minimum rents, or the fixing of rents as multiples of land revenue. Nevertheless, regardless of the formal measures adopted by the government, the actual running of the temporary cultivation system was in the hands of the subordinate bureaucracy. This provided ample opportunity for irregularities.

[67] The subject of temporary leases of state land in this colony is comprehensively covered in "Leases of temporary cultivation in Nili Bar Colony," BOR 301/11/C9/51 A-T.

[68] Temporary cultivation leases first began in the late 1890s in Chenab Colony, when about 40,000 acres were leased to the numerous indigenous inhabitants who had been dislodged from their old homes and not yet permanently resettled. They became a handy method of placating groups that had suffered dislocation (another example were the victims of waterlogging from the mid-1920s), and also enabled the state to reward individuals for services rendered with concessionary leases, though they did open "an unequalled field for corruption" (*PCM*, p. 177). See also PRAP(I), December 1900, Nos. 1-23.

[69] BOR 301/14/00/144, p. 15. See also *PCR*, 1936, Review and pp. 7 and 9.

It was found in 1934 that, except for Jhelum Colony, proper records for temporary cultivation were not maintained in any colony, and in most cases there was no trace of records for the period prior to 1930. It was impossible to estimate the extent of losses and irregularities when the records themselves were missing. Where records were available, several distortions were detected, such as incomplete or falsified entries in registers.[70] Arrears of rent, representing serious financial losses to the government, were a common phenomenon. Even in Jhelum Colony, no information was forthcoming in the Colony Office on arrears of rent in any particular year, so that no action could be taken against defaulters. There was no record to show who the actual defaulters were. Moreover, there was no evidence of any action taken against defaulters for the realisation of government dues. In most cases, demand statements in registers were given by villages, which was a serious lapse because it obscured any knowledge of payments by individuals.

The rules for tendering for temporary cultivation were mostly disregarded. In Chenab Colony, where a system of tenders prevailed in the 1930s, temporary cultivation was the source of a large number of irregularities. The audit reports revealed that records of tenders either did not exist or were seriously incomplete. The correct procedures for giving out tenders were hardly ever observed; this important matter was left to low-paid clerks. As a result, very little income reportedly accrued to the state, and arrears of rent were heavy. In Chunian Colony, temporary cultivation was subject to the tender system, but no records of tenders existed, and no lease deeds were executed, stamped, or registered, for which alone the government suffered a good deal of financial loss.[71]

In Lower Bari Doab Colony, too, a great many serious irregularities were uncovered by the audit reports. In contravention of government orders, underlings in the Irrigation Department rather than the collector continued to assess rent on temporary leases. Consequently, little attempt was made to provide a fair rent to the government. No records of temporary cultivation prior to 1931 were to be found in the Colony Office. In several cases, land was leased out in large blocks, but the sanction of higher officials that was required for this had not been obtained. As in Jhelum Colony, demand had been recorded by villages, making it impossible to trace defaulters. Temporary cultivation registers did not show recoveries of rent, nor had the demand figures entered in the registers even been initialled by a gazetted officer. Under government rules, the deputy commissioner

[70] A thorough investigation of the temporary cultivation system is contained in "Colonies— Temporary cultivation—Audit," BOR 301/31/00/18 A-E.

[71] See BOR 301/14/00/144, pp. 15-29 and 41-51; BOR 301/31/25/4, pp. 39-57; BOR 301/ 31/25/5, pp. 35-123; BOR 301/31/19/7, pp. 21 and 85; and BOR 301/31/12/40, p. 33.

should have checked these registers every month, but such checks had never been made, and as a result, various discrepancies existed in the records. Sizeable differences in demand levels between colony and *tahsil* offices were discovered, and local officials were unable to account for these.[72] It was noted in the audit that the leakage of government revenue must have been considerable, but accounts were so improperly maintained that it was impossible even to estimate the amount lost. Ample evidence was found of collusion between office clerks and lessees, such as the large number of cases where rent statements fixed by gazetted officers had subsequently been tampered with: alterations that did not bear the signatures or initials of any official.

These were some of the numerous instances of corruption and mismanagement uncovered in the canal colonies. It was clear that the state was unable to act as landlord, rentier, or supervisor without the incidence of major distortions, and without serious lapses in efficiency. Once landed resources were put on offer, they were best disposed of permanently to elements within the social structure rather than retained by the government itself. The necessity for this had been recognised in the expeditious concessions made under the Colonisation Act of 1912. Once these resources had passed to the grantees of land, however, little control could be exercised over the manner of their utilisation. But the state did not remain altogether bereft of benefits: although it lost its developmental impetus, it ensured to a more than adequate degree that its political, military, and extractive needs were preserved.

By the 1930s, the standards of bureaucratic management in the canal colonies had fallen to unsatisfactory levels.[73] The dynamism instilled by the colonisation process had been replaced by inefficiency and corruption, which seemed to have reached proportions beyond the capacity of the state

---

[72] BOR 301/14/00/144, pp. 35-41.

[73] Two individual examples of corruption in the subordinate bureaucracy were those of Khaliq Dad Khan and Vidhya Dhar in the 1930s. As assistant colonisation officers in the Chenab Colony extensions, they committed several irregularities in collaboration with local men of influence, such as unauthorised grants and leases and concessionary terms of rent and tenure. Official investigations were effectively obstructed by the veil of silence imposed on witnesses by the local notables, who included the *zaildars* of Magneja, Jhakkar, Kamalia, Koranga, and Bhusi. The commissioner, Multan, wrote in 1937 that "the whole procedure was an exhibition of patronage and power unrivalled in the administration. . . . The scandal did not come to light earlier, probably because there is hardly an important man in the area who was not among the favoured: or did not hope to be favoured sooner or later." See "Inspection of Office of Extra Assistant CO, Lyallpur, by Commissioner, Multan," BOR 301/19/25/24, p. 37 (and also pp. 5-89). See also "Lower Chenab Canal—Lyallpur District—*Sufedposhi* grants in—Policy," BOR 301/3/25/1(b); and "Colonies—Grants of land on well-sinking conditions—Policy," BOR 301/3/00/1(h).

to reform.[74] In addition, the state itself failed to pursue economic development as a policy objective, but gave priority to the other considerations
discussed in this work. At the local level, administrative supervision seems
to have virtually broken down, as indicated by the irregularities that
plagued the extractive system. The resultant reductions in its income were
partly responsible for the inability of the state to invest in the development
of either an appropriate infrastructure or secondary sector. The financial
constraints on the state were mainly induced by its own willingness to allow
resources to rest with the intermediary class to whom it had alienated the
means of production in the canal colonies. In this too the political motive
seems to have been the dominant consideration; but such a policy reduced
the prospects of far-reaching economic change.

Sustained economic progress would have depended more on developments within the social structure than any role the state might have pursued.
Here two different mechanisms had widely disparate momentums. Modern
hydraulic works could be introduced in much less time than it took to
change traditional social norms; the task of creating Englishmen, even
brown ones, could well prove more onerous than the achievement of ambitious hydraulic and agricultural goals. Yet, economic changes could in
turn have generated behavioural ones. The major historical transition from
noncapitalist relations of production to capitalistic agriculture could itself
have introduced profound changes in Punjabi economy and society. One
method of assessing the development of agricultural capitalism in the canal
colonies is through a discussion of cultivating occupancy, which is addressed in the next section.

Tillers and Rentiers

The extractive process was not confined to the revenues obtained by the
state, or to the efforts of the subordinate bureaucracy to divert some of this
income for its own ends. It was also deeply rooted within the social structure. Social and economic inequalities were based on the ability of a class
of nonproducers to extract and retain the surplus generated by the productive section of the population. This process of extraction stretched from the
landless labourer and the subtenant to the rentier landlords at the apex of
the Punjabi social hierarchy. This cross section, as earlier chapters have
shown, reemerged in the landholding structure of the canal colonies: it was

[74] The commissioner, Rawalpindi, remarked as follows about the lower bureaucracy in
1934: "As has been frequently pointed out in recent inspections it is in the interest of local
staff to keep everything in as much confusion as possible. If the work is done punctually and
correctly, there is but little opportunity for making illicit gains." See Commissioner, Rawalpindi, to FC, 29 August 1934; in "Draft Standing Order No. 67, Shahpur Colony Office,"
BOR 301/14/00/61(b)-1, p. 5.

brought on by the land distribution policies of the state. The major proportion of land was allotted as smallholdings of up to thirty acres, and the rest in the form of larger grants from a few dozen to several hundred acres. From this process arose the patterns of cultivating occupancy that revealed the lines along which production and extraction were organised.

Most of the land in the canal colonies was allotted as peasant grants, which were supposed to remain as self-cultivated units of production. In terms of peasant land occupancy in South Asia, these holdings were of substantial size. Although they were supposed to be operated on the basis of peasant family production, even holdings of twenty-five or thirty acres, the size of most peasant grants, could be in fact too large for a family farm. This left room for the use of either paid labourers or subtenants. On the larger grants, the choice also lay between self-cultivation and self-management through the employment of agricultural labour on the one hand, or the letting out of land to subtenants on the other. The former would have been indicative of the emergence of agricultural capitalism and rural entrepreneurship, with the grantees not merely residing on the land but also contributing to agricultural development through the investment of skill and capital. Conversely, resort to subtenancies implied that agricultural production was organised along noncapitalistic lines, with the owners of land acting in the extractive and essentially unproductive role of rentiers. These competing systems of cultivation reflected the degrees of transition to capitalistic agriculture and the extent to which noncapitalistic forms of production were retained in the canal colonies.

The discussion of tenancies and rents will be confined here largely to Chenab Colony.[75] For this period, the existing data do not allow a reliable analysis of different forms of occupancy for the canal colonies as a whole. There did not exist any single series of statistical abstracts or statements on tenancies and rents for the colonies, nor was there a continuous series for any single colony. The data utilised here were included in revenue assessment reports, and they provide information on cultivating occupancy in particular colony tracts. Chenab Colony furnishes the clearest insight on this subject. As one of the older colonies, it had three separate assessments, for each of which statistics on tenancies and rents were collected. These figures extend from the 1900s to the 1930s—though the qualification made above applies to them as well, for they do not relate to the colony as a whole but to different parts of the colony at different periods.

[75] The figures are drawn from Chenab Colony assessment reports quoted in Imran Ali, ''The Punjab Canal Colonies,'' Table 5.6 (see also the figures in Tables 5.6-5.13). The period of revenue settlement in the canal colonies was normally ten years (though for the first assessment on the Rakh Branch a period of twenty years was adopted). For a discussion of the term of settlement for Chenab Colony, see PRAP(R), January 1912, Nos. 1-11.

Assessment circles in Chenab Colony did not have regular boundaries during this period. In fact, the geographical basis of each circle changed completely during this time, from the canal branch (Rakh, Jhang, and Gugera) to the *tahsil* (such as Lyallpur, Samundri, Toba Tek Singh, and Jaranwala). The three major canal branches had to be adopted initially for assessment purposes, as colonisation on each branch occurred at different times.[76] The eventual conversion to *tahsil* boundaries was in keeping with assessment practice in the rest of the province. With such major changes in assessment circles, it is only possible to assess the tenurial and rental situation in particular areas and at specific times. Nevertheless, the figures are interrelated and comparable, since they refer to the proportions of land that were either self-cultivated or rented to subtenants, and to the proportionate share of the types of rents that prevailed on the rented area.

Moreover, the local region of the assessment circle provides a more accurate picture of tenancies and rents than either the single village, which could be subject to peculiar circumstances and need not be representative, or the colony as a whole, the aggregated statistics of which might bear little resemblance to actual conditions. The figures for assessment circles were based on the investigations and observations of the settlement officer, who needed accurate information in order to arrive at a realistic revenue assessment. These figures were, therefore, less susceptible to the distortions and inaccuracies that are commonly associated with statistics on Indian agrarian conditions.[77] The figures were, however, biased downward in one important respect. The extent of subtenancy tended to be understated by the grantees, both because they tried to conceal their true incomes and because the practice was often frowned upon by officials, especially in the case of peasant grantees, who were supposed to remain as self-cultivators. Particularly in the years before they acquired proprietary rights, grantees engaged in concealed forms of subtenancy in order to pass themselves off as self-cultivators. The area rented, therefore, was in reality greater than that conveyed in these statistics.

What, then, was the relative extent of self-cultivated and rented area? The figures reveal that in Chenab Colony the self-cultivated area varied from 50 to 67 percent, and the rented area from 33 to 50 percent. They also

[76] The delineation of assessment circles by canal branches "recognises too, more than any division by tahsils could do, the all importance of irrigation units in the every day life of the people, who commonly group together the chaks on a single distributary, and compare their several assessments with almost meticulous precision": *AR Jhang Branch* (1921), para. 3.

[77] The problem of inaccuracies and inconsistencies in Indian agrarian statistics is examined in C. Dewey, "*Patwari* and *Chaukidar*: Subordinate Officials and the Reliability of India's Agricultural Statistics," in C. Dewey and A. G. Hopkins (eds.), *The Imperial Impact: Studies in the Economic History of India and Africa* (London: Athlone Press, 1978), pp. 280-314.

show that at no time were less than 45 percent of the number of holdings rented to subtenants; in most cases, over 50 percent were rented. Given the tendency to understate the rented area, the figures show that self-cultivation in Chenab Colony covered only half the cultivated area, and took place on less than half the number of holdings. Since 80 percent of the land in the colony was allotted as peasant grants, clearly a large number of such grants, which were supposed to be self-cultivated, were in fact sublet to tenants. As for the larger, *nazarana*-paying grantees (capitalists and yeomen), subletting had become virtually a general rule. For instance, on the Upper and Lower Jhang branches, the *nazarana* grantees rented out 87 and 78 percent of the cultivated area, while even peasant grantees rented out 27 and 35 percent, respectively.[78] In the area devoted to subtenancies, the system of production could not be said to be capitalistic. The owners of land were content to draw from it the passive owners' share of output, with little or no productive contribution from themselves.

The government had expected the *nazarana* grantees to be enlightened farmers who, while not cultivating with their own hands, would spearhead agricultural progress and improvement in the canal colonies by providing inputs of capital, hired labour, and entrepreneurial ability. The figures on tenancies show that they failed to play this role, for instead of exercising personal supervision over their grants, they almost wholly let them out to subtenants. Qualitative evidence, too, suggests that they used their colony grants merely as a source of income, and were content to play the parasitic role of absentees and rentiers.[79] As absentees they were required by the government to appoint an agent in their stead. Such a person became yet another claimant to the produce, and often an unscrupulous one; in most cases he was none other than a large subtenant. Because of their absenteeism, the *nazarana* grantees had to be content with the worst type of subtenants. This affected the quality of agriculture, as one assessment report in 1909 noted: "Tenants in peasant villages are either relatives or of the same class as the grantees. In nazarana grantee villages they are heterogenous and changing collections from all districts, Sialkot sweepers predominating."[80] Even the yeoman grantees, who were chosen from social groups with sound agricultural traditions, failed to provide an impetus to productivity and agricultural improvement. The same assessment report commented:

---

[78] *AR Upper Jhang Branch* (1909), ch. 5; and *AR Lower Jhang Branch* (1909), ch. 5.

[79] This was borne out for Chenab Colony: "Not uncommonly the nazarana-paying grantee who is exempt from residence lets his entire holding to his agent and never approaches the village." See *AR Lower Jhang Branch II* (1909), para. 24. See also *AR Rakh Branch* (1913), para. 27; and *AR Gugera Branch I-II* (1923), para. 29.

[80] *AR Upper Jhang Branch* (1909), ch. 3, para. 2. The next quote is from the same source.

The Yeoman of the tract singularly fails to fulfil the role of the local aristocracy. Where he resides he spends his time in petty animosities with the other yeomen varied by oppression of his tenantry. The officer passes with a sigh of relief from his squalid abadi and carelessly tilled estate into the chaks of the peasant grantee.

The very high proportion of *nazarana* area devoted to subtenancy showed clearly that the larger grantees had failed to act as agrarian capitalists. As rentiers, their contribution to agricultural development remained minimal. On the other hand, the larger grants served to consolidate the position of the landlord class in Punjabi society, and this acted as a constraint on social change. Such an outcome was implicit in the land distribution policies of the British, whose efforts to preserve the existing class structure were not compatible with the emergence of capitalistic or progressive agriculture. The larger grantees relapsed into the extractive roles to which they were accustomed, and they were thereby unable to achieve a transition to capitalistic relations of production.[81]

The figures from assessment reports also reveal that subtenancy was not uncommon among peasant grantees. Three factors could have contributed to this situation. First, a peasant grant of twenty-five acres or so was probably too large for a family to cultivate, unless the holder was prepared to hire additional labour. With the existing level of technology, the most suitable size for a peasant family farm was around fifteen acres. This allowed grantees to rent out the remaining land, and the high level of subtenancy indicates that they preferred this practice to hiring labour and keeping the surplus land under their own management.[82] The average area for self-cultivated units varied between 12.6 and 18 acres, about the size of an average family farm. This was consistently larger than the average size of rented holdings, which varied between 8.1 and 12 acres (on total rented area; disaggregated rents will be discussed presently).

The peasant producer hesitated to extend self-cultivation and self-management over his entire holding. He seemed to conform to the Chayanovian view that he worked not toward profit maximisation within a capitalistic

---

[81] For discussion of the performance of the *nazarana* grantees in Chenab Colony, see: *AR Upper Jhang Branch* (1909), ch. 3, para. 1; *AR Gugera Branch I* (1911), para. 10; and *AR Gugera Branch II* (1912), para. 16.

[82] Even on the self-cultivated area, the labour employed by peasant grantees was often not paid in wages but represented instead graduated forms of subtenancy. In Chenab Colony, two types of helpers were common, the *sanji* and *arthri*. The former usually obtained one-eleventh to one-fifteenth of all produce, plus his food, and paid the revenue demand on his share. The *arthri* normally received his food and one-eighth to one-eleventh of all produce, except cotton and sugarcane, but paid no revenue on his share. See ibid. (1909), ch. 5, para. 1; and *AR Jhang Branch* (1921), para. 30.

context, but toward a "balance between subsistence needs and a subjective distaste for manual labour (dis-utility) for this determines the intensity of cultivation and the size of the net product."[83] The peasant grantee ceased to extend production after an equilibrium had been achieved between his consumer needs and the drudgery of his efforts. Production remained limited to the needs and capacities of the working family unit, and subtenancy was preferred to hired labour for the utilisation of surplus land. In this manner, as a petty rentier, the peasant grantee fell in with the prevailing extractive tradition to which his larger, *nazarana*-paying counterpart subscribed so universally.

Second, those peasant grantees whose total holdings were of inadequate size for subsistence needs would most probably have had to sublet their land. Such situations could readily develop in peasant agriculture through subdivision; and the legal sanctions for them had already been provided by the concessions on the partibility of holdings made in the Colonisation Act of 1912. Holdings below a certain size might not have been viable as independent units of production, making it uneconomic for the holders to practise self-cultivation. Such small-scale holders would then have sought alternative employment, most commonly as agricultural labourers, or they might simply have eked out an existence from rental earnings. The subtenants in such cases would have been men of greater substance, who possessed the instruments of production and had the capacity to take on additional land. This could well have been the way in which differentiation within the landholding body took place in colony villages, with the smaller holders being displaced by an emerging class of rich peasants. This must to some extent have led to a "rationalisation" of the landholding structure, by eliminating those least capable of agricultural efficiency. However, the benefits of this process for agricultural development were certainly reduced by the lingering legal and economic connection, in the form of petty rentiers, of the unproductive owners with the land.

Third, areas recorded in subtenancy figures could in reality have been disguised mortgages. Rural credit was a necessary source of capital for the smallholder, and he often had to offer his land as a collateral for loans. The problem of agricultural indebtedness reached serious proportions in the Punjab, and received much attention among British officials (two examples being the works of Thorburn and Darling).[84] The owner-cultivator could, by failing to redeem his mortgage, be reduced to the position of a mere tiller of his land, with the real control over land and produce passing to the

[83] D. Kerblay, "Chayanov and the Theory of Peasantry as a Specific Type of Economy," in T. Shanin (ed.), *Peasant Societies* (Middlesex: Penguin, 1971), p. 153.
[84] S. S. Thorburn, *Mussalmans and Moneylenders in the Punjab* (Edinburgh: W. Blackwood, 1886); and M. L. Darling, *The Punjab Peasant in Prosperity and Debt*.

moneylender. With legal rights over dispossession vested so securely in favour of the landowner, the only practical course open to the moneylender for the recovery of loans was to take the debtor's land on mortgage. Often this had to be done on lenient rates of rent, for the alternative was a complete lapse in repayments. In any event, whether the mortgagor remained as a coerced labourer or was ousted and replaced by a subtenant, the mortgagee's lien on the land was not conducive to agricultural efficiency, for he was less concerned with reinvestment and upkeep than even the most indifferent of rentier grantees.

Whichever factor motivated grantees to sublet their land, the outcome was not likely to be conducive to agricultural progress. The very fact that approximately half the produce of the entire rented area was being absorbed by men who played little or no part in producing it was an unhealthy phenomenon. If the grant was too large for the family's labour output, then the fact that it was rented out rather than farmed with hired labour indicated a weak capitalistic stimulus. Holdings that were rented out because they were too small to act as viable units of production were a serious reminder of the hazards of subdivision. They were an inevitable outcome of the state's policy of devoting the major proportion of land to smallholdings and not restricting partibility. And if the subtenancies happened to be hidden mortgages, this in itself pointed to the unsuitability of smallholdings for commercial agriculture. Thus, the tenancy systems in the canal colonies revealed that the extractive factor was an important aspect of cultivating occupancy, and it was not one that betokened any major improvement in the agrarian base.

One essential feature of the extractive system was the nature of the rental structure. Three broad categories of rents existed in the canal colonies: rents at revenue rates, produce rents, and cash rents. Again, the figures quoted here pertain to Chenab Colony, and are drawn from assessment reports.

The least common type of rents were those at revenue rates. These varied from 5 to 10 percent of the area rented, but since their area per holding was less than the average for total rented area, they accounted for between 7 and 13 percent of the number of holdings rented. Such tenancies were of a concessionary nature, under which the subtenants would normally pay no rent to the grantee over and above the payment of government revenue. They usually existed on land given out to close relatives or associates, who might have had a special claim on the grantee or might have helped to develop the grant through cost and labour-sharing.

Such generosity on the part of grantees in alienating rent was not a common feature. Indeed, they jealously guarded their right to sole enjoyment of the grant, and did their best to prevent relatives and helpers from obtaining any security of tenure.[85] On the Jhang Branch in the late 1900s, the acquisition of occupancy rights by grantees was actually accompanied by a decline in population. One reason for this phenomenon was "the unloading by peasant grantees of the tenants who had assisted them in pioneer days to level and clear their grants."[86] Because it removed labour from the land, this ousting of the erstwhile helpers and co-sharers often led to a less intensive level of agriculture. The grantees preferred to leave their holdings underutilised rather than allow others to obtain a lien on them.[87] The area under rents on revenue rates was held by those whose claims were too strong for the grantees to shake off. The area per holding for this category, between 5.3 and 8.2 acres, was also well below the figure for produce and cash rents, an indication of the smaller plots devoted to this type of subtenancy.

Produce, or kind, rents took up by far the greatest proportion of rented land. In terms of both the area rented and the number of holdings, produce rents accounted for under 70 percent of the total rented area in only three of eight sampled assessment circles of Chenab Colony. At times, over 80 percent of both rented area and rented holdings were under such tenancies. Since there was a tendency to understate the extent of subtenancy, rents in kind were even more prevalent than the figures show, and they were possibly more ubiquitous in the canal colonies than self-cultivation itself. This form of tenancy entailed sharecropping (*batai*), in which owner and subtenant shared the produce. The most common rate was a half-and-half division of the output. To this general rate many adjustments were possible, as with the proportionate sharing of inputs and government demand, or even variations in the share of the produce.[88]

Produce rents provided little incentive for agricultural improvement. The subtenants who cultivated the land did not enjoy any occupancy rights, and since they stood to lose half the output, they did not see the point of making

---

[85] See *Revised AR Upper Jhang Branch* (1911), para. 11; and *AR Gugera Branch I* (1911), para. 12.

[86] *AR Upper Jhang Branch* (1909), ch. 3, para. 1.

[87] The settlement commissioner remarked on this process in 1907 as follows: "But the colonists have, I think, in their desire to prevent the acquisition of any rights by tenants to whom they often made lavish promises, which subsequently they did not wish to fulfil, somewhat overreached themselves. . . . I am afraid that for many long years lack of tenants will be one of the most serious disabilities under which the colony will labour. . . . In fact it may be said that during the next generation we cannot expect anything in the nature of intensive cultivation in the Chenab Colony. The soil will yield very much less than could be won from it by really careful husbandry." See SC's Review of *AR Upper Jhang Branch* (1909); in PRAP(R), October 1909, No. 79.

[88] See *AR Upper Jhang Branch* (1909), ch. 5, para. 3; *AR Lower Jhang Branch II* (1909), para. 22; *AR Gugera Branch I-II* (1923), para. 27; and *AR Samundri Tahsil* (1935), para. 23.

extra efforts. As one proverb expressed it: "He who stays for a night at an inn does not go on to the roof to stop a leak; he shifts his bed."[89] The sharecropping subtenant felt little need to maintain the fertility of the soil, use superior seeds, plant trees, acquire improved implements, or cultivate the more valuable crops such as sugarcane. Although all these inputs entailed higher costs, any differentials in profits would have been wiped away because rents were in kind. The smaller areas per holding under produce rents, as compared to cash rents or self-cultivated land, also indicates that the sharecroppers were smallholders who could not benefit from any economies of scale. It is doubtful whether this type of tenancy could have made any meaningful contribution to agricultural development.

The rentiers' efforts to maximise rates of extraction served to further dissuade sharecroppers from making any substantial improvements. The following report, made by a settlement officer in 1909, describes how *nazarana* grantees in Chenab Colony contrived to obtain as much as they could from their subtenants:

> The nonresident *nazarana*-paying grantee is continually inventing methods to prevent himself being robbed in taking produce rents from his agents and tenants. While he aims at taking half batai and half rates in his grant, he often compounds with his tenants that his half share of a killa of makki shall be six maunds and that all the landlord's share of chari, senji, lucerne and pulses shall be sold back to the tenant at Rs 2 per kanal. He allows his tenant to grow cotton but instead of taking batai of cotton, he takes the whole of the produce of wheat for every killa of cotton sown. . . . The agents of the capitalist grantee often contrive to lend the tenants money and seed, when they first come and hold them in a perpetual serfage of debt ever afterwards.[90]

The third category was rents in cash. The incidence of cash rents showed a sharp increase from around 10 percent of rented area in the mid-1900s to a peak of over 40 percent in the early 1920s. The increase corresponded with a period of rising agricultural prices in the post-World War I years. The area under cash rents went down again to under 20 percent in the early 1930s, a period when prices were depressed and profits from agriculture seriously constrained.[91] Economic factors were similarly responsible for changes in the number of holdings under cash rents. These showed a rise from around 6 percent in the mid-1900s to about 30 percent of total rented

[89] H. Calvert, *The Wealth and Welfare of the Punjab*, p. 90.

[90] *AR Upper Jhang Branch* (1909), ch. 5, para. 3.

[91] *AR Jhang Branch Circles* (1921), para. 31; *AR Gugera Branch I-II* (1923), para. 29; *AR Lower Chenab Colony of Jhang District* (1923), para. 22; *AR Jaranwala Tahsil* (1936), para. 17; *AR Lyallpur Tahsil* (1936), paras. 14-15; and *AR Samundri Tahsil* (1935), paras. 13-15.

area in the early 1920s, and then a reduction to under 20 percent in the early 1930s. Cash rents throughout had a lower percentage of the number of holdings rented than of the area rented. This was because the area per holding under cash rents was in all cases larger than that for either the total rented area or the area under produce rents. Both the larger size of holdings and the form of payment indicated that cultivation in the cash-rented area was directed toward market production to a greater degree than in other types of cultivating occupancy.

The price of agricultural commodities formed the single most important influence on the level of cash rents. Not only did these rents go up during periods of high prices, but the cash rented area also increased. The average rate for cash rents rose steadily from Rs 5.1 per acre in 1900-1901 to a peak of Rs 31.8 per acre in 1926-1927, a rise of over 600 percent. During the economic depression, the fall in agricultural prices led to a fall in rents as well, to Rs 14.3 per acre by 1932-1933. These figures, representing as they do average values over large areas, concealed the wide diversity in cash rents caused at the local level by physical and economic differences. Nevertheless, they show dramatically the emergence of cash renting as a major form of cultivating occupancy in the canal colonies. That they increased to the detriment of produce rents during periods of high prices indicated their greater efficiency for extractive purposes.

Though price movements of agricultural commodities dictated the general pitch of cash rents, several specific factors were responsible for divergence in rental rates at the local level. The quality of the soil accounted for one source of differentiation in cash rents. Variations of up to 300 percent could exist within the same assessment circle between villages with good and poor quality soils.[92] Location was an important factor: cash rents tended to exist on lands where the more valuable crops could be cultivated. Such rents were concentrated in areas with stronger soils or with better marketing facilities. They were uncommon on poorer lands, though during years of high prices they did spread to such areas. Cash rents were often the consideration for a loan, and they could be affected by the relations between debtor and creditor. Such transactions were in effect quasi mortgages, with the rent written off against the balance due. The debtor usually continued to cultivate on behalf of the creditor, to whom the land was leased. The level of rents also depended on whether the grantee was resident or not. Many absentee *nazarana* grantees had to settle for unsatisfactory terms, for they were not prepared to frequent their grants often enough

---

[92] On this subject, one assessment report stated in 1909: "Nothing is more striking than the difference in the rate of rent between good and poor mauzas, or between the rate of rent taken on good and poor land within the same mauza." See *AR Upper Jhang Branch* (1909), ch. 5, para. 2, and also para. 4; and *AR Lower Jhang Branch II* (1909), para. 24.

to ensure suitable tenants and adequate rents. More competitive rents prevailed where the grantee was resident, or himself cultivated a part of the grant.[93]

Competition for land was a major influence on the level of rents. The pressure of population and the quality of subtenants available in each locality, as well as the degree to which grantees were selective about the social origins of their subtenants, could affect the pitch and incidence of cash rents. Grantees who were unable to obtain central Punjabi tenants had to fall back on the less efficient cultivators from the western districts, or on the floating population of indigenous inhabitants.[94] Extractive proficiency too varied among different types of grantees. Sikh Jats, who were regarded as the most efficient and market-oriented of agriculturists, were also the ones who sought the most profitable rates from their subtenants. A higher level of competition for land existed in their villages, and this induced a greater degree of commercialism among them. Their predilection for profit could even cut across the bonds of blood:

> In the Mid-Punjab chaks tenants who have developed a grant are usually turned out when a grant is fully cleared and levelled, and are eager to take up land on even more stringent terms. The Amritsar Jats take rents even from their fathers, brothers and sons where there are numerous in the family.[95]

On the other hand, many Muslim grantees, not so commercially inclined, often allowed noneconomic considerations such as kinship or customary ties to influence their dealings with their subtenants.[96] This provided for lower rents, as also did the unwillingness of certain proprietary groups to allow strangers to reside in their villages. Thus the degree of extraction varied in different localities and among different groups. The several forms that it took, and the various aspects of agrarian life on which it had a bearing, revealed that the extractive process was very much an integral part of social and economic relationships in the canal colonies.

---

[93] *AR Jhang Branch* (1921), para. 31; and *AR Gugera Branch II* (1912), para. 19. The indigenous Jangli and Biloch grantees were especially susceptible to such transactions: *AR Gugera Branch I-II* (1923), para. 29; and *AR Gugera Branch I* (1911), para. 20.

[94] *AR Rakh Branch* (1913), para. 27. An assessment report noted in 1912 that: "Real competition rents are, however, frequently found among *nazarana* grantees and pensioners. Much depends on the presence in the vicinity of Arain or Sikh villages. These castes are very populous, and there is always a superfluous element in their midst, anxious to obtain land and willing to pay liberally for it. Where lessors have to depend on Jangli tenants, prices rule much lower." See *AR Gugera Branch II* (1912), para. 19.

[95] *AR Gugera Branch I-II* (1923), para. 29; and *AR Upper Jhang Branch* (1909), ch. 5, para. 2.

[96] *AR Gugera Branch I-II* (1923), para. 29.

The structure of tenancies and rents discussed above prevailed in a colony that had a more egalitarian basis of land distribution than any of the other major canal colonies. Chenab Colony had a higher percentage of land distributed in the form of peasant grants (80 percent of total allotted area) than did Jhelum, Lower Bari Doab, or Nili Bar colonies. Though these smallholdings were meant to be self-cultivated, the large proportion of land in Chenab Colony rented to subtenants signified that even peasant grantees had become rentiers, and thus unproductive consumers of the agricultural surplus. In the other major colonies, grants of such small size composed a much lower proportion of total allotted area, and the incidence of extractive relations must thereby have been greater in them than in Chenab Colony.

In Jhelum Colony, the dominant form of tenure, the peasant horse-breeding grant, was 55 acres in size. This would have induced most grantees to sublet the greater proportion of their land, if 12 to 18 acres is to be taken as the average size of a family farm. The higher incidence of subtenancy in Jhelum Colony was confirmed during assessment investigations in the early 1910s. Of the assessment circles of the colony, the Bhera Bar circle had a self-cultivated area of 40 percent, the Sargodha Bar Utla circle of 32 percent, the Bhera-Chenab circle 31 percent, and the Bhera-Jhelum circle 42 percent.[97] Well over half the cultivated area in each of the assessment circles was rented to subtenants.

In Lower Bari Doab Colony, the proportion of peasant grants to total allotted area fell to about 65 percent, lower than in both Chenab and Jhelum colonies. The incidence of subtenancy increased, since a higher proportion of land was allotted in larger-sized holdings (such as the landed gentry grants). Moreover, a large number of twenty-five-acre tenancies consisted of "official" horse-breeding rectangles, which were leased to men who already held peasant grants. By assuming the horse-breeding tenure, these men obtained possession of at least fifty acres, and thus became substantial landholders who would have indulged in subtenancy. Figures were collected for cultivating occupancy in the early 1930s, for the eleven assessment circles in the three *tahsils* of Lower Bari Doab Colony.[98] They revealed a very high incidence of subtenancy. In no circle did the self-cultivated area exceed 55 percent, and in two circles it stood as low as 20 and 22 percent. Subtenancy was, therefore, widespread in this colony as well; it had become even more common than self-cultivation.

In Nili Bar Colony, peasant grants had shrunk to below 50 percent of the perennially irrigated land. Approximately half the perennial area in the col-

[97] *Revised AR Lower Jhelum Canal, Shahpur District* (1912), paras. 50, 54-55, and 58.
[98] The three colony *tahsils* were Montgomery, Okara, and Khanewal *tahsils*. See Imran Ali, "The Punjab Canal Colonies," Table 5.14.

ony was reserved for auction sales; but since auctions were disrupted by the economic depression, no clear picture of cultivating occupancy had emerged by the 1940s. The utilisation of the vacant land through temporary leases turned the state itself into the largest rentier in the province.[99] The system of temporary cultivation relied very largely on the subletting of land by lessees, for most of the land was leased in large holdings of hundreds of acres. This dramatic move toward temporary ''latifundias'' created a politically unstable situation, with the severe rental demands on subtenants by lessees leading to an agitation in the colony in the mid-1930s. As a consequence, the government began to place upper limits on rents charged by lessees, and also to devote more area to smaller-sized leases.[100] But the move away from regular peasant grants stood in marked contrast to the solid investment in smallholdings in the earlier colonies, providing even greater opportunity for rentier extraction.

Clearly, extractive processes were deeply entrenched in the social structure. The landholders, where they were not self-cultivators, were more inclined to rent out any surplus land than farm it themselves through hired labour. The failure to convert to capitalistic agriculture, and the reversion instead to the kind of rentier roles that existed traditionally, led to the neglect of reinvestment and improved techniques in farming. The grantees of land became intermediaries between the ruling and productive elements. They absorbed most of the surplus from agriculture, and the rate of extraction increased as market production intensified with the rise in prices (as shown by the incidence of cash rents). The extractive aspect was an essential economic ingredient in the consolidation of the existing class structure. Overall profits from agriculture formed the true economic measure of such consolidation; but the substantial proportion of land not self-cultivated meant that rental payments diverted a major part of the total surplus. Indeed, it could be said that the potential for agricultural development was largely vitiated by the extractive processes that beleaguered production.

It could be that purely economic factors can account for the proclivity toward subtenancy and rack-renting in the canal colonies. Perhaps this indicated the weakness of market demand, which might not have been sufficiently buoyant to induce such economistic behaviour as profit maximising self-cultivation, the optimal employment of factors of production, and the cut and thrust of marginal utility. Marketing might well have stemmed more from the need to pay rent and tax, from extractive considerations,

---

[99] By 1936 the area of state land under temporary cultivation leases in Nili Bar Colony alone amounted to 261,232 acres: BOR 301/11/C9/51 P, p. 27.

[100] In 1937 it was calculated that 63 percent of the area under temporary cultivation, which amounted to over 400,000 acres, was leased to 262 lessees. See *PCR*: 1937, pp. 13-14; 1938, Review and pp. 8-12; 1939, Review; and 1940, Review and p. 10.

than from any fundamental commercial orientation of producers. But if this was so, then it was not any more powerful than the other dynamic behind subtenancy, that of cultural and power relationships. The strong impulsion toward the dominance of man over man, which subtenancy allowed, was deeply rooted in traditional practice and consciousness, whose mainsprings lay in semi-feudal rather than capitalistic urges.

CHAPTER SIX

Production

THE EXTENSION of canal irrigation to the western Punjab provided a real opportunity for the economic development of this region. New resources were made available which, if utilised properly, could have led to sustained agricultural progress. That structures did not emerge to exploit this potential adequately is evident from the foregoing chapters.[1] The impact this had on agriculture in the canal colonies needs to be examined more closely, as does the notion that major constraints remained on agrarian development, though *not necessarily on agrarian change.* The discussion here will focus first on specific attempts at agricultural improvement, and second on more general aspects of agricultural practice and production. An examination of agricultural change in the canal colonies over several decades would justify a work on its own, and only a representative cross section of issues relevant to agricultural improvement, and to agriculture in general, will be discussed here. In the first part of the chapter, dealing with developmental aspects, the problems of seed provision, cattle breeding, arboreal development, land reclamation, and the application of higher technology to irrigation are examined; and in the second part, some of the salient features affecting cropping and cultivation.

IMPROVEMENT THROUGH PROXIES

Seed Supply

The provision of high-quality seed was important for agricultural improvement in the canal colonies. Improved crop varieties, especially with such major cash crops as wheat and cotton, were important for the commercialisation of agriculture. Traditional crop strains, apart from providing generally lower yields, were less competitive as marketable commodities. Long-staple cottons, for instance, commanded both a better price and a greater demand as an export commodity than indigenous strains. There was also a much lower demand for indigenous varieties of Punjabi wheat in the world market than for certain improved hybrids. Furthermore, to prevent

---

[1] For an assessment that emphasises that the Punjab, despite the greater commercialisation of its agrarian sector, suffered features of structural backwardness similar to those experienced by other regions of South Asia under colonial rule, see Mridula Mukherjee, ''Some Aspects of Agrarian Structure of Punjab, 1925-47,'' *Economic and Political Weekly*, XV, 26 (1980), pp. A-46 to A-58.

any deterioration in the quality of existing varieties, it was important to ensure that the cultivator had access to fresh seed.

The government's role could prove crucial for this input. Since the great majority of production units in the canal colonies, whether self-cultivated or subtenanted, were in the form of smallholdings, the cultivators could not be expected to rely entirely on their own resources for the provisioning of new seed. Nor could they be expected to have a grasp of the technical and scientific aspects of seed deterioration, or a knowledge of hybridisation that might have enabled them to produce better seed on their own. The need existed for governmental action to facilitate the development and diffusion of new seeds, and of maintaining the quality of existing varieties.[2] These aims could have been achieved through experimental agricultural stations and seed farms. The former could have acted as centres of research into new crops, while the latter would have supplied cultivators with good quality seeds in sufficient quantities.

In fact, seed farms and experimental stations, wherever they were established, were extremely limited in size.[3] In Chenab Colony, 500 acres were set aside in 1901 for an agricultural station. Of this only 150 acres were directly managed by the Department of Agriculture; and by 1907, even this was transferred to the newly established agricultural college at Lyallpur for its own work.[4] The remaining area was rented to subtenants, with the Agricultural Department obtaining seed either as rent or through purchase options. It rejected direct management of the land through a European official because of the high salary costs involved, while it feared that Punjabi officials would indulge in corruption and misappropriation. This left little alternative but to use groups of subtenants for supplying seed improvements to a colony of over two million acres.

Despite their limitations, similar practices were adopted in other colonies as well. In Jhelum Colony, a 600-acre seed farm, allocated in 1904, was reduced to 150 acres in 1910,[5] and this too remained mostly subtenanted.[6]

---

[2] Officials commonly acknowledged the need for seed farms, the colonisation officer of Jhelum Colony noting in 1904: "It is only by the cultivation of really large areas from good seed that any real impression can be made on the agriculture of the Colony." See *PCR*, 1904, p. 25.

[3] For more details on seed farms, see Imran Ali, "The Punjab Canal Colonies," pp. 360-68.

[4] See *RODA*: 1906, pp. 4-5; 1907, pp. 2-4; 1910, pp. iii-iv and 3; and 1923, p. li. See also RS to FC, 4 February 1901; in PRAP(G), April 1901, No. 15.

[5] The remaining 450 acres, which was also superior land, were allotted to Sir Harnam Singh Ahluwalia, a member of the ruling family of Kapurthala State. For information on the seed farm, see *PCR*, 1904, p. 25; and PRAP(A): October 1904, Nos. 3-8; and May 1905, No. 15. See also *PCR*, 1922, pp. 11-12; and *RODA*: 1914, p. 9; 1916, p. 6; and 1918, p. lxvi.

[6] A portion of the farm was under direct management, on which in 1910 the deputy commissioner, Shahpur, wrote that even regular inspections would not prevent the "wholesale

In a colony where over 65 percent of allotted land was reserved for military purposes, only 0.026 percent was used for seed farms.[7] In Lower Bari Doab Colony, too, state seed supply resources remained meagre. There were only two seed farms totalling 500 acres, and they were again predominantly subtenanted.[8]

Other methods were tried in Lower Bari Doab Colony for securing seed. The government contracted with some large grantees for supplying seed, and similar arrangements with smaller cultivators that proved less reliable.[9] In addition, two large farms had specific seed-supply conditions. These were allotted in 1919 to Sardar (later Sir) Jogindra Singh (2,000 acres) and Mr. H. T. Conville (3,000 acres). Portions of each farm were utilised for seed, but this reliance on intermediaries provided mixed results. Jogindra Singh's grant, whose other function was to test mechanised agricultural implements, was not run properly. In 1926 its management was handed over to the British Cotton Growing Association, which was involved with cotton production in the colony. The BCGA ran the grant till 1939, when Jogindra exercised his option of acquiring proprietary rights, thus ending his seed-supply obligations.[10] (This patchy performance did not impair his public career: he was knighted and in the 1940s served as minister of railways in the Government of India.)

Conville's grant proved more successful.[11] It continued to supply large

---

swindling or leakage of profits . . . on the seed farm, and it is not surprising that complaints against the manager by tenants etc. should be numerous and incessant.'' See DC, Shahpur, to Commissioner, Rawalpindi, 19 January 1910; in PRAP(A), April 1910, No. 33 (see also Nos. 31 and 39, letters of FC and Secretary, PG, for the grant of land to Ahluwalia).

[7] The director of agriculture estimated in 1921 that a requisite area for wheat and cotton seed for Chenab Colony should be 30,000 and 8,000 acres annually, and for Jhelum Colony 20,000 and 4,000 acres. Yet the total area under his control for the provision of seed was only 262 and 148 acres in the two colonies, respectively. His request for utilising some of the land released from cavalry horse runs for seed farming was rejected by the government, and it was diverted instead for mule breeding and grants to war veterans. See DA to FC, 30 June 1921; in "Disposal of . . . horse runs . . . ,'' BOR 301/6/00/3 A, pp. 65-71.

[8] There was a seed farm of 250 acres at Montgomery, and one of 260 acres at Shergarh. The Shergarh farm was originally sanctioned in 1923 as an agricultural research station of 2,550 acres. However, either the land proved unculturable or it was allotted to military war veterans, and only 260 acres were finally utilised for seed farming. See RODA: 1921, p. xxvi; and 1926, p. 31. See also "Agriculture farm—Shergarh,'' BOR 301/2/24/3; and PRAP(R): January 1925, Nos. 5-13; and March 1925, Nos. 1-2.

[9] RODA, 1922, p. xxxvi.

[10] See "Lease of land to Sardar Jogindra Singh for the demonstration of cultivation by steam power,'' BOR 301/11/24/18; and "Sir Jogindra Singh's seed growing farm at Iqbalnagar—Inspection Reports by Director of Agriculture,'' BOR 301/19/24/48. See also PCR: 1919, p. 17; and 1939, p. 5.

[11] The government only sanctioned the grant after assurance that no revenue sacrifice was entailed by the special tenurial conditions: see DA to FC, 5 June 1913; in PRAP(G), May

amounts of seed, with regular crop experiments and use of farm machinery. Even during the difficult years of the 1930s, official reports on Conville's estate were consistently favourable.[12] The few such grantees of European origin seemed to make a success of their ventures: not only Conville, but Vanrenen and Cole in horse breeding, and F. W. Mitchell in fruit farming. But for political reasons, Europeans could not be given much land. The state had to rely on Punjabi grantees as proxies for improvement, though they seemed more interested in the social and extractive benefits of colony land.

The circulation of new and hybridised seeds was of much importance to agricultural development, and the inadequate provisions made for the supply of seeds in the canal colonies must have acted as a retarding influence.

Cattle Breeding

The opening up of the canal colonies provided an ideal opportunity for the development of cattle breeding on systematic lines. This industry could have been spurred on by the greater demand for plough and dairy cattle with the extension in cultivated area. Though livestock from private suppliers would undoubtedly have remained the major source of procurement for colonists, the state could also have stimulated cattle breeding by allotting colony land on service tenures for this purpose, on the lines of the horse- and camel-breeding schemes. Indeed, in the pastoral society of the Janglis there already existed the animal and human resources for creating a large network of peasant grants based on the breeding of livestock. This could arguably have been of greater benefit to agriculture than the investments made on animals of military use. Alternatively, the government could have established sizeable cattle runs under its own management, or allotted large grants for cattle breeding, on the lines of the horse-breeding grants of Vanrenen and Cole.

The cattle of the Janglis in the western *doab*s of the Punjab, rather than flourishing under the transition to a hydraulic society, became one of its greatest victims. The traditional grazing areas of these breeds disappeared

---

1914, No. 9. Conville was an agent for the firms of Volkart Brothers and Wallace and Sons. He sold agricultural machinery, and also acted as a large buyer of cotton. He was required to devote for seeds up to 400 acres for cotton, 550 acres for wheat, and 100 acres for other crops. See "Grant of land on Lower Bari Doab Canal to H. T. Conville, Volkart Bros., for a seed farm, etc.," BOR J/301/1137; *PCM*, pp 150-51; and *PCR*, 1919, p. 17.

[12] See reports of the director of agriculture and deputy director of agriculture, 1927-1938, in "H. T. Conville—Seed growing at Convillepur, Montgomery District—Inspection Reports by Director of Agriculture," BOR 301/19/24/49. See also *PCR*: 1929, p. 51; 1934, Review; 1936, p. 7; 1937, p. 6, 1939, p. 6; and 1940, p. 2. H. T. Conville died in 1939, and the management of the farm continued under his son, L.H.G. Conville, whom he had made a co-grantee in 1915: PRAP(G), December 1915, Nos. 7-11; and *PCR*, 1939, p. 6.

under canal irrigation, and the only source of subsistence for the cattle remained the meagre Jangli grants of half to one square per family. From
these smallholdings the Janglis were hard put to provide for their own subsistence as well as meet the state's revenue demand. The retention of the
cattle herds no longer remained feasible, for their dependence on fodder
crops entailed a low economic utilisation of commercially valuable colony
land. The Janglis did continue to maintain more cattle than other grantees,
but these became increasingly an economic liability that prevented their
owners from growing the more profitable crops. The Janglis may well have
marketed dairy products, but official records are silent on this as an alternative source of income. The demand from towns for such products was
largely met by buffalo-keeping Gujars who lived on the urban fringes,
rather than by Janglis settled in outlying rural tracts. Colonists, too, normally maintained sufficient livestock for their own needs, further reducing
the potential market for the Janglis' cattle-based goods. Yet the Janglis had
enjoyed a thriving pastoral economy in precolony days, exporting dairy
products such as *ghee* to neighbouring regions, and their cattle herds were
strong and resilient. They could undoubtedly have improved on these assets
had their potential been tapped.

One reason why the state had failed to make proper tenurial provision for
Jangli cattle was the disorganised and confused process of settlement of
these pastoralists. The indigenous tribes were displaced from their original
habitats to make room for immigrant colonists. It was only later, when
there appeared to be no other means of their reabsorption, that land was
made available to them on the fringes of colonies. In the atmosphere of
mistrust and grievance produced by this upheaval, there appeared little
prospect of devising and successfully maintaining service tenures for the
upkeep of cattle. But the failure to utilise the livestock wealth of the Janglis
really originated only in part from the lateness of allotment to them. The
neglect stemmed also from the lack of military and revenue contributions
from these pastoralists in any way comparable to those of the agricultural
castes of central Punjab, whom the state in turn gratified with favoured
treatment as colonists.

Only in Lower Bari Doab Colony did a section of Janglis receive cow-
breeding grants, in a local area near Shergarh.[13] One rectangle per family
was allotted in the 1920s on cow-breeding terms, but supervisory functions
were assigned to a family of Syed Pirs, to whom as an additional favour
two ten-rectangle grants were allotted. These *pirs* enjoyed much influence

---

[13] For information on these grants, see "Janglis and Syeds on cattle-breeding conditions—
Lower Bari Doab Canal," BOR 301/26/24/2. See also *PCR*: 1927, p. 49, 1936, p. 4; 1937,
p. 7; 1938, p. 5; and 1939, p. 5.

over the local Janglis because of their control of the Shergarh shrine, and "agricultural development" now provided a further context for their dominance. The grantees themselves did not lack enthusiasm for the cow-breeding venture, but diseconomies of scale and the lack of expert supervision hindered its progress. The limited extent of the scheme prevented it from making any fruitful contribution to the cattle industry of the Punjab.

Another alternative was to establish cattle farms under government management. The need was clearly recognised, and several schemes were posited over the years. In the early 1900s, a bull-rearing and breeding run was planned for Jhelum Colony; in 1920-1921, a buffalo-breeding farm was proposed for Lower Bari Doab Colony and a dairy farm for Jhelum Colony; and in the late 1920s three cattle farms were planned for Nili Bar Colony.[14] All these were to be state-managed farms, to be run jointly by the Agricultural and Civil Veterinary departments. However, not one of these schemes was implemented. The land for the Jhelum Colony bull run was allotted to a local Punjabi landlord.[15] The buffalo and dairy farms proposed in the early 1920s were also rejected on the grounds that land was not available, though at this time large areas were being allotted to war veterans. In Nili Bar Colony, the original plan for 10,000 acres under three cattle farms was also not realised.[16] In short, not even a small amount of the vast area of state land in the canal colonies was utilised for cattle-breeding purposes.

To achieve progress in this area, the administration again resorted to indirect methods. Six large cattle-breeding grants were allotted to individuals in Lower Bari Doab Colony for cattle breeding and dairy farming.[17] A stipulated number of cows and bulls had to be maintained on each grant, with young stock and milk being sold privately. These grants achieved varying degrees of success in the years that followed. Their mixed performance reflected the insecurity inherent in the reliance on intermediaries for achieving agricultural goals, with the fortunes of each venture subject to the va-

[14] See PRAP(G), May 1904, Nos. 29-41; and "Buffalo-breeding, Lower Bari Doab Colony," BOR J/301/1462. See also *PCR*: 1904, p. 25; 1921, p. 16; and 1922, p. 12.

[15] For the bull-breeding proposals, see PRAP(G): December 1904, Nos. 4-17; September 1906, Nos. 1-2; and July 1909, No. 34. See also PRAP(A): January 1906, Nos. 39-55; April 1906, Nos. 1-5; and October 1907, Nos. 1-13.

[16] See "Nili Bar Colony—Application of S. Santokh Singh for lease of cattle farm lands for buffalo-breeding conditions in," BOR 301/11/C9/278.

[17] These farms were at Qadirabad, Allahdad Farm, Jehangirabad, Bahadurnagar, Kot Fazalabad, and Montgomery. For a closer examination of their performance, see Imran Ali, "The Punjab Canal Colonies," pp. 371-77. For information on these grants, see also "List of grants supervised by Director of Agriculture," BOR 301/2/00/8; "Lower Bari Doab Colony—Montgomery and Multan Districts—Cattle-breeding grants in—Policy," BOR 301/26/24/27/1; *PCM*, pp. 149-50; and PRAP(I), October 1915, Nos. 21-29. See also PRAP(G): September 1914, Nos. 37-42; and April 1915, Nos. 21-29.

garies of individual ability.[18] Although one farm was deemed successful by officials, two others proved abortive, with their leases not renewed at expiry after twenty years.

The method of resuscitating indigenous cattle breeds through grants to individuals had certain advantages, but it was not without its risks. The government saved itself the financial outlay and administrative burden involved in direct management. State-controlled farms might not have achieved even the limited results obtained by the private grantees, since little confidence could be placed on the subordinate bureaucracy to perform efficient and honest work. On the other hand, reliance on individuals presented little certainty of success. The cattle-breeding lessees were, not unnaturally, interested primarily in financial gain, and the extent of their contribution to cattle breeding was constrained by the need to ensure adequate profit margins, which could only be obtained by cultivating cash crops. Their preference for commercial agriculture incurred repeated warnings from officials, but violations of stipulated ratios for fodder and nonfodder crops could not be eradicated: "Modern methods of husbandry have been neglected and too much attention concentrated on the profits of agriculture."[19] The grantees did continue over the years to supply buyers with livestock and meet other tenurial requirements, but their degree of success varied, and their impact remained inconclusive.

The unwillingness of the government to operate self-managed farms had left no alternative but to use these proxies. That this option too was impracticable was emphasised by the decision not to continue with such grants in subsequent colonisation projects. Despite the extensive landed resources that became available in the canal colonies, neither the state through its administrative effort nor its intermediaries through their entrepreneurial abilities were able to make a significant contribution to the livestock industry of the region.

[18] The Board of Revenue files containing reports on the workings of these farms are BOR: 301/19/27/40-41, 301/19/24/42-43-44, and 301/11/24/199. See also BOR: 301/11/24/201 and 301/11/24/330.

[19] *PCR*, 1934, Review, p. 2. The report further states (pp. 8-9): "On the whole the system of leasing out large parcels of land on cattle breeding conditions has not proved very beneficial and in the light of experience it may be regarded as an expensive method of fostering the cattle breeding industry by Government. The disappointing results are very largely attributable to their want of practical knowledge and the lack of interest shown in modern methods of animal husbandry by the grantees, to whom the temptation of making quick profits of commercial crops at the expense of their cattle has proved too great for them. On one or more of these farms where grantees have followed departmental advice there has been a very reasonable measure of progress made in building up pedigree herds, the surplus male and female stock of which are readily purchased by breeders in the district."

Arboriculture

The maintenance of arboreal wealth is important for any agrarian society. In the canal colonies, this feature acquired special significance with the rapid and extensive conversion of existing wooded areas to cultivated land. Colonisation also caused a rise in the demand for wood for such diverse uses as housing material, implements, and fuel. The Forest Department of the Punjab Government met with little success in its efforts to preserve existing forest reserves in the western *doab*s, and depletion followed rapidly upon the spread of canal irrigation.[20] The failure to maintain adequate forested areas was especially marked in the earlier colonies; to this the irrigated plantation at Changa Manga near Chunian Colony was the only notable exception. The situation was to some extent rectified in the later colonies with the establishment of irrigated timber plantations on 7,200 acres in Upper Jhelum Colony and 30,000 acres each in Lower Bari Doab and Nili Bar colonies.[21]

Owing to the many demands on colony land, priority could not be placed on forestation. Nor could it be expected that the timber requirements of colony tracts would be met solely from reserved state forests. Much depended on the ability of the colonists themselves to develop and maintain arboreal resources at the local level. Rather than leave this to the voluntary initiative of the colonists, in which case little might have eventuated, the administration undertook to achieve such aims through tenurial regulation. In several instances, clauses for the maintenance of trees and copses were either included in the tenurial conditions of existing grants, or else separate grants were made for this purpose. These arboreal ventures reflected the extent to which colonists responded to an impetus toward the improvement of their agrarian environment. They also revealed the degree to which the state was successful in achieving such improvements through the implementation of tenurial requirements.

With the rapid clearance of timber to make way for cultivation, and the consequent shortage of wood, the government realised that in the case of the earlier colonies it had not made any formal provisions for the retention and maintenance of trees.[22] After 1900, an effort was made to rectify this situation. For Jhelum Colony and the later tenancies of Chenab, Chunian,

[20] For efforts by the Forest Department to conserve forest areas in the Rechna and Bari *doab*s in the face of expanding canal irrigation, see PRAP(I): July 1901, Nos. 1-3; December 1901, Nos. 30-35; January 1902, Nos. 13-22; June 1902, Nos. 23-26; and August 1902, Nos. 1-6.

[21] PRAP(I): December 1916, No. 14; May 1917, No. 64; and July 1927, No. 4.

[22] For a discussion of arboriculture in the canal colonies, see *PCM*, pp. 281-82; and RPCC, pp. 39-41. For a more detailed discussion of the issues examined here, see Imran Ali, ''The Punjab Canal Colonies,'' pp. 377-83.

and Sohag Para colonies, provisions were included that obligated grantees to plant and maintain two trees for every acre of their holdings. This promised to lead to an appreciable increase in arboriculture in the canal colonies, with at least fifty trees on every peasant grant of twenty-five acres, and scores of trees on the larger grants.

Unfortunately, the tenurial clauses pertaining to arboriculture proved highly unpopular. Along with several other measures of agricultural improvement included in tenurial conditions in this period, they created much friction between grantees and officials. Landholders resented interference in agrarian matters, and so effective was their resistance that the government was largely unsuccessful in enforcing compliance with the tree-planting obligations.[23] State-sponsored agriculture received further setbacks after the political agitation of 1907. The Punjab Colonies Committee deprecated the inclusion of tree-planting clauses in tenurial conditions, and these were subsequently removed as part of the concessions made to colony landholders. With this, the prospects of a concerted drive for arboricultural development in the canal colonies receded permanently.

In tree planting, too, the government tried the alternative of using intermediaries to achieve results. Nursery, or *zakhira*, grants of five to ten acres were allotted to village *lambardar*s and others in Chenab, Jhelum, and Lower Bari Doab colonies.[24] Though trees were planted, their maintenance remained a problem. In the search for proper management, control of the nurseries fluctuated between individuals, village communities, and district boards. Finally in the 1930s they were either auctioned off or converted to ordinary grants.

Another effort at arboreal development consisted in the tree-planting, or *darakhtpal*, grants, for the provision and maintenance of roadside trees.[25] These grants in Lower Bari Doab Colony were allotted on about 20,000 acres, and were normally 12.5 acres in size. By and large, the stipulated trees were successfully planted along avenues in the colony. The administration then insisted that the grantees were still obligated to maintain them. This created much discontent, because the grantees expected the district boards to take them over, but the latter lacked the resources to do so. The

---

[23] It was with hindsight of such resistance that the *PCM* stated that arboriculture should be left to the village community. It advised colony officials to be "seen and not heard," with an occasional visit or warning being more appropriate than "volumes of instructions which result in the harassment of the colonists by subordinates." See *PCM*, pp. 251-52.

[24] For these grants, see ibid., pp. 283-86; RPCC, pp. 42-43; and "Treatment of *zakhiradar* grants in Lower Jhelum Colony," BOR 301/2/19/12. See also *PCR*: 1930, p. 63; and 1932, p. 10.

[25] See "*Lambardari* and *darakhtpal* conditions," BOR J/301/992. The progress and outcome of these grants are also reported in *PCR*s, 1917-1926.

Public Works Department was delegated this task in Nili Bar Colony—an admission of the impracticability of obtaining trees through land grants and local bodies. Indeed, the efforts at arboriculture in the canal colonies served as an example of the difficulties faced by the state in generating improvements through indirect methods.

The Reclamation of Inferior Lands

The reclamation of lands with soils of inferior quality posed a major challenge to the existing state of agricultural organisation and technology in the canal colonies. In the course of colonisation, many areas were encountered that appeared unsuitable for settlement. Grantees either did not agree to accept such land, or after initial allotment they succeeded through the process of "exchanges" in transferring to better land. Inferior soils were often bypassed in the earlier stages of settlement of a colony. They either remained unutilised or were allotted after the better lands had been taken up, when the remaining candidates had no choice but to accept them. Such methods proved effective in colonies where marginal lands were either not significant in area or where they were below average in quality but were still cultivable.

This proved to be true for the earlier projects. In Chenab Colony, land was generally of good quality and in relatively abundant supply, so that grantees could move off the weaker soils through exchanges. The presence of soil variations was recognised by the government through differential revenue assessment rates, but such variations were not so excessive as to preclude either cultivation or state extraction. A larger proportion of inferior land was encountered in Jhelum Colony, but this too did not present any major inconvenience. It was disposed of by allotment to indigenous Janglis, for whom no other land remained after the better areas had been appropriated for military purposes. In these two colonies, inferior lands did not place any serious checks in the way of agricultural settlement, and this was true of the smaller colonies as well.

In Lower Bari Doab Colony, lands of inferior quality presented a more serious problem. During colonisation, sizeable areas were encountered with soils too harsh for cultivation by ordinary methods, and colonists were not prepared to settle permanently on such land. This resulted in a cutback in the official colonisation scheme from 1,192,000 acres to 883,000 acres, reducing the scale of settlement by a quarter.[26] Grantees were not prepared to invest money and labour where a high risk of failure was involved, and

[26] Under the category of inferior lands came alkaline and deflocculated soils known in the vernacular as *kalrathi, bari, maira, ghasra, kallar amez*, and, most notorious of all, *bara*: Report by CO, Montgomery, 10 July 1918, in PRAP(G), September 1918, Enclosure No. 3 to No. 41. See also *PCR*, 1921, p. 31; and for rules for land exchanges, *PCM*, pp. 172-76.

they would not accept inferior soils if there was a prospect of better land. Yet, given sufficient time, attention, and careful husbandry, much of this low-quality area was reclaimable, and from as early as 1914 the administration undertook reclamation work on it. Characteristically, the means adopted for such improvement lay not through direct, official management of reclamation projects, but through the indirect method of leases and grants to individuals for the purpose of soil improvement.[27] As the better areas were absorbed, it became easier to find candidates for the inferior lands. These came largely from the host of unsuccessful applicants for ordinary grants: clearly the reservation of extensive areas for military purposes and larger grantees was creating an excess demand for land within the civilian peasantry.

The "reclamation" grants grew from small and tentative beginnings to assume a substantial position in the colonisation of the Lower Bari Doab. Initiated in 1914 with only 1,000 acres, they expanded in the next decade to an allotted area of 150,000 acres. They comprised lease terms of one to five years on concessionary revenue rates.[28] Since better land also had to be given as an incentive, however, the lessees were found to concentrate on it at the cost of reclaiming the inferior soils. With time, a modified tenurial form took up most of the area under trial. These were leases on "half-resumable terms," with lessees allotted two rectangles each, one of which they could retain after reclamation, with the other passing to the state for further allotment as a normal grant.

Within a few years, it became clear that little soil improvement could be achieved.[29] Even the immediate aim of demonstrating that these soils could produce crops was difficult to fulfil. Reclamation was certainly possible: relevant options included use of fresh soils, effective cropping patterns, green manuring, and proper washing and drainage of land. But the lessees, being smallholders, were either disinclined or unable to make the patient investments in labour and capital required for soil rejuvenation. They continued to cultivate the better areas and neglect the inferior patches. Larger grantees might have proved more effective, and a few that were tried did perform well.[30] But these leases were, beyond the ostensible aim of recla-

[27] The government had one experimental station, for the reclamation of *bara* soil. Started in 1917, it continued during the 1920s, but was adjudged a failure and was closed in 1931. For reports on the station, see *PCR* and *RODA*: 1917-1932.

[28] See "Temporary leases of bad and inferior lands, Lower Bari Doab Canal, Montgomery District," BOR J/301/1396; and *PCR*: 1919, p. 22; and 1923, Review.

[29] The progress of these allotments is reported in *PCR*: 1916-1923 and 1930-1931. For more details, see Imran Ali, "The Punjab Canal Colonies," pp. 383-93.

[30] Two larger reclamation grants on inferior land proved more successful: see "Lease and sale to S. Ujjal Singh in Lower Bari Doab Canal Colony," BOR 301/11/24/7; and "Lease of

mation, a means of accommodating smallholders on a canal project where relatively greater areas had been allocated to the military and larger land-holders.

The unfavourable performance of these reclamatory leases forced the government to devise methods to terminate them.[31] By 1925, the soil improvement requirements had been dropped, and the holdings converted to ordinary tenures. The half-resumable leases were subdivided, if a co-sharer could be found: by 1930 over 40,000 acres were thus converted. Another recourse was sale by auction or tender. Between 1925 and 1927, 73,000 acres were sold at land values inflated by some years of high agricultural prices. Financial conditions changed dramatically after 1930, and with collapsing rents and prices the auction purchasers were unable to meet their instalment payments. The state first reacted through confiscations, but such draconian measures were politically unwise. As part of general fiscal remissions these holdings were commuted to peasant tenancies, with a uniform purchase price of Rs 100 per acre. Even this was difficult to meet during the depths of the depression. These auction purchasers seemed unlikely to achieve soil reclamation; they were reported to be highly unsatisfactory colonists, unwilling to reside on their holdings and able to attract only the worst of subtenants.

The administration had not long remained faithful to the original purpose of soil improvement. In the face of early failures to achieve the desired goals, it had shown little hesitation in either foregoing tenurial contracts or profiting from selling land at speculative rates. Within a decade of their initiation, the prospects of any contribution from these service tenures to agricultural development had been forsaken. The state showed much greater resilience in maintaining service schemes oriented toward military needs. The facility with which the service clauses in the inferior land leases were removed casts doubt whether soil improvement was their real motive. These allotments arose from the great demand for land from the peasantry.[32] The heavy concentration of smallholdings on these harsh lands was too impracticable a proposition to suggest any explanation other than the

bara land in Montgomery District to S. Bishen Singh and S. Satwant Singh," BOR 301/11/24/353.

[31] For the disposal of the inferior lands in Lower Bari Doab Colony, see: "Disposal of unallotted balance of inferior lands," BOR 301/8/24/2 A-H; "Sale by auction or tender of inferior lands in 1925 and 1927-28—Grant of concessions to purchasers in," BOR 301/8/24/27/2-G; and "Modification of Clause 17 of conditions of sale of inferior lands sold in the years 1925-28," BOR 301/14/24/43.

[32] A number of applications were made for larger grants by men who promised to invest capital on land reclamation. These the government decided to reject. See correspondence on these applications, BOR J/301/1196 B, pp. 87-121.

need to placate land hunger.[33] About half the lessees were hereditary agriculturists from the central Punjab, whose compatriots had received large
areas in other colonies. The rest were Janglis of the Bari Doab, who had
been dislodged from their old habitats and had no other means of subsistence. Within the ostensible framework of agricultural improvement, an
"underclass" of grantees was created in the canal colonies: men who suffered various vicissitudes and failures because colony land of better quality
was being redirected to meet the military and political imperatives of the
ruling authority.

Lift and Tubewell Irrigation

River water dispersed through a network of canals and distributaries was a
highly cost-efficient method of irrigating large tracts of land. Both the capital outlay and working costs of canal irrigation were low enough in relation
to net returns to render this undertaking profitable to state and cultivator
alike. The hydraulic system of the canal colonies depended almost wholly
on "flow irrigation," which brought under cultivation lands commandable
by the natural flow of water from the irrigation network. There also existed
some lands that could not be commanded by gravitational means, either
because of elevation or because the irrigation design made them inaccessible.

Supplementary forms of irrigation to bring such areas under cultivation
entailed more advanced irrigation technology than that of flow methods.
Tubewells run by electric power could have tapped the subterranean water
that existed in good measure in the Punjab, which received runoffs from
the greatest mountain chain in the world. Another method was the lifting
of canal water by mechanical means. Such alternatives could raise the intensity of cultivation through both an increased and a more flexible application of water. Both tubewell and lift systems depended on the generation
of electrical power, however, without which water could not be raised except in minute quantities.

A significant extension of such irrigation facilities was severely constrained in the Punjab during British rule by the absence of any large-scale
development of electrical energy. The one large plant that was established,
at Mandi in eastern Punjab, was too distant to provide electrical energy to
the canal colonies. As a consequence, there never was a basis for any major
investments in tubewell and lift irrigation. Alternatively, localised power
generation, through plants placed at gravitational falls on canals, could
have serviced nearby lift and tubewell networks. After 1900, some meas-

---

[33] "I have been deluged with applications for these grants and have every belief that they
will turn out to be very popular with a class which has very nearly given up hope of getting
more land": CO, Montgomery, to Commissioner, Multan, 16 December 1920; in BOR J/310/
1396 B, p. 5. See also *PCR*: 1921, p. 31; and 1922, p. 25.

ures were undertaken to utilise canal falls, but once again indirect methods were adopted. The state did not itself establish power stations and tube-wells, but instead utilised proxies for this purpose, requiring such services from individuals as a condition for obtaining colony land.

The foremost personality involved with lift irrigation methods was Rai Bahadur (later Sir) Ganga Ram, an ex-government engineer who took up large areas of land in the canal colonies. In 1902-1903 he was granted in Chenab Colony a high plot of 2,800 acres that was not commanded by flow. Ram provided lift irrigation to his land, known as the estate of Gangapur, by obtaining hydroelectric power from his own generating plant at a nearby canal falls.[34] He then extended his lift operations into neighbouring state land by obtaining on lease a high plot of about 12,000 acres at Buchiana. This was an area that the government had planned to irrigate by installing its own hydroelectric plant, and then to allot to cavalry regiments for horse runs. The official project never eventuated, and Ram's lease continued until 1921, when a remodelling of the canal system brought this area under flow irrigation. Ram's lease was thereupon terminated, and the land was allotted to military war veterans (regimental horse runs having been discontinued by then).[35]

Ganga Ram made further contributions to lift irrigation in Lower Bari Doab Colony. Between 1917 and 1919 he obtained 48,650 acres on lease, and irrigated this land through pumping plants driven by steam power.[36] The normal tenure of these leases was only three years, after which the state took possession of all land, pumping plants, and other installations free of cost. Despite such onerous terms, Ganga Ram was still able to make handsome profits, for revenue rates were pitched at half those for flow irrigation. For its part, the government obtained interim income from land that would otherwise have remained unutilised, and after repossession it received installations gratis and could then levy revenue at normal rates. So mutually advantageous were these tenures that they came to be known as "Ganga Ram terms," when applied to some other lessees who took up land on similar conditions.[37]

During the 1920s Ganga Ram made further advances in the cultivation

[34] See PRAP(R): December 1914, Nos. 18-29; and July 1923, Nos. 3-4. See also PRAP(G), January 1920, No. 82; and Punjab Financial Proceedings, October 1934, No. 64. For further details on lift and tubewell irrigation, see Imran Ali, "The Punjab Canal Colonies," pp. 393-405.

[35] See "Lift area grants—Chenab Canal," BOR J/301/839; and "Lease of lift lands on Lower Chenab Canal (Buchiana)," BOR 301/11/25/10. See also PRAP(G): November 1914, Nos.1-15; and July 1915, Nos. 16-22.

[36] See "Applications for lift land or for land on special experimental terms on Lower Bari Doab Canal (Sir Ganga Ram's lift grant)," BOR J/301/1340.

[37] For these lessees see "Lease of lift land on Lower Bari Doab Canal Colony," BOR 301/11/24/9; and for individual cases, BOR 301/11/24/299-304.

of elevated lands. After complicated negotiations stretching over four years, he obtained in 1923 a lease on a large area of around 70,000 acres near Renala in Lower Bari Doab Colony. The lease was of seven years' duration, during which time Ram undertook to build and maintain a full-scale hydroelectric power station to provide lift irrigation to the leased area. Once again, all land and installations were surrendered to the government at the expiry of the lease period in 1930.[38] While Ganga Ram obtained only transitory benefits from his enterprise, a family of Syed Pirs in the vicinity, who controlled the Shergarh shrine, enjoyed more permanent gains. Despite Ganga Ram's protests, they persuaded the government that he should share irrigation from his lift works with them. Their loyal involvement with local administration, army recruitment, and the Unionist party won them this handsome compensation.[39] Like the military grantees at Buchiana, their lien outlasted that of the man who had pioneered these innovations.

The state had shirked from the introduction of higher levels of irrigation technology from its own resources and on its own accord. In order to economise on capital and management costs, it had left these important initiatives to its proxies. Such an approach seemed to work well in the case of lift irrigation, owing primarily to the abilities of one man, Ganga Ram. But the reliance on intermediaries could also abort technological progress, as the case of tubewells illustrated.

Tubewell irrigation could achieve both greater intensity and flexibility of cropping, and also help to control the rising water table that by the late 1920s threatened large areas with waterlogging and salinity.[40] Yet the absence of a generally available source of energy constrained the spread of tubewell technology in the canal colonies. Tubewells remained confined to localised experiments that relied on small-scale energy generation. As with lift irrigation, the state did not involve itself directly with any major tubewell schemes, but instead tested their feasibility through grants to individuals. Such grants were limited in size and number: under the British, tubewell irrigation in the Punjab remained at an experimental stage.[41]

An opportunity to promote tubewell technology presented itself in Upper Chenab Colony, once again through the innovative Ganga Ram. In 1912,

[38] See "Colonies—Leases—Sir Ganga Ram's lift grants—Lower Bari Doab Canal," BOR 301/11/24/32; and "Disposal of land leased to the late Sir Ganga Ram in Clifton Lift Area," BOR 301/11/24/289.

[39] For testimonials for this family and a record of its services to the British, see "Colonies—General administration—Compensation to Sir Ganga Ram," BOR 301/2/24/139; and BOR 301/26/24/2.

[40] See "Waterlogging in Sheikhupura District," BOR 251/39/17/7.

[41] For a survey of tubewell irrigation in the Punjab, see "Report on factors affecting irrigation in the Punjab from tubewells," A.M.R. Montague, Executive Engineer, PWD, 1 July 1938, 127 pp. (Punjab Civil Secretariat Library, 0 52).

Ram proposed that a high plot of 5,000 acres (at Kuthiala) be leased to him, where he would develop a network of fifty tubewells to be run by power generated at a nearby canal falls.[42] By 1915, negotiations with the government had broken down, with disagreement over the eventual purchase price and interim irrigation facilities. The lieutenant-governor at the time, Sir Michael O'Dwyer, was not well disposed toward commercial enterprise and the middle classes, and he inspired the government's uncompromising stand.[43] Ganga Ram ceased further efforts with tubewell leases, and the entrepreneurial ability, financial resources, and technical expertise of this talented man went unutilised.

The opportunity for tubewells at Kuthiala was not allowed to lapse entirely. The terms that Ganga Ram had rejected were taken up by two members of the Punjabi aristocracy, Nawab Sir Zulfiqar Ali Khan and Raja Daljit Singh, from the ruling families of the princely states of Maler Kotla and Kapurthala, respectively.[44] The Kuthiala venture proved to be a complete failure. The tenurial conditions were too adverse, the lessees failed to manage the project personally, and the postwar financial stringencies increased costs. The lessees incurred serious losses, and could only construct three or four tubewells instead of the fifty promised by Ganga Ram.[45] Some other experiments with tubewells also proved discouraging. They too were conducted through lessees, and either had to be terminated or led to operational

[42] See "R. B. Ganga Ram's application for grant of land on Upper Chenab Canal," BOR J/301/1055. Sir John Maynard, the financial commissioner, was strongly in favour of Ganga Ram's proposals: "But by far the greatest advantage to Government lies in the potential demonstration, at the cost and risk of an enterprising private person, of a great possibility. . . . [U]tilising the canal falls for pumping from wells having once been demonstrated on a considerable scale, we may look forward to an immense development on the same lines over a large portion of the province, with the resultant economies of canal water and the solution of the ever more and more persistent problems of waterlogging. I feel strongly that it would be an unfortunate excess of caution to allow this opportunity to pass." See Note by FC, 12 February 1914; in BOR J/301/1055 A, p. 203. John Maynard was also the author of *Russia in Flux: Before October* (London: V. Gollancz, 1941), and *The Russian Peasant, and Other Studies* (London: V. Gollancz, 1942).

[43] O'Dwyer's autobiography provides a useful reflection of his attitudes toward the subcontinent: Sir Michael O'Dwyer, *India as I Knew It, 1885-1925* (London: Constable, 1925). The Jallianwala Bagh massacre took place while he was in office: see Robert Furneaux, *Massacre at Amritsar* (London: Allen and Unwin, 1963); and Helen Fein, *Imperial Crime and Punishment* (Honolulu: University of Hawaii Press, 1977).

[44] For the family histories of these two men, see Griffin and Massy, *Chiefs of the Punjab*, Vol. II, pp. 495-506 and 529-36.

[45] The experiment was terminated when the lease expired in 1925. The lessees were allowed to retain 750 acres in full proprietary right, but had to surrender the remaining 4,250 acres. See "Lease of land in Rakh Kuthiala, Gujranwala District, to Khan Zulfiqar Ali Khan and Sardar Daljit Singh," BOR 301/11/16/11; and *PCR*, 1926, p. 55.

losses.[46] Thus tubewell irrigation achieved only embryonic development in the canal colonies during British rule. As with the other efforts at planned improvement, the recourse to intermediaries failed to achieve sustained benefits for agriculture.

CROPPING AND CULTIVATION

The most telling aspect of the canal colonies was agricultural production itself. The extension of cultivation, rather than the sponsoring of commercial or industrial development, was the primary function of economic growth in the canal colonies. This area became one of the foremost regions of market-oriented agriculture in South Asia, and its landholding peasantry was reputedly one of the most prosperous in the entire continent. A well-developed trading network, stimulated largely by the emergence of rail-borne traffic, provided for the export of produce to other parts of the country and to overseas markets. Agricultural production would deserve a study on its own, and the brief discussion attempted here deals only with some of its salient features.[47]

Analysis of the "crop mix" provides one method for discussing cropping patterns in the canal colonies. This indicated the type and relative importance of the more commonly cultivated crops, as well as the proportionate share of each of the two harvests, *kharif* and *rabi*, in the total cropped area. Water was the critical variable. It was more plentiful for the *kharif*, or autumn crop, owing to monsoonal rains and to the increased run-off from the melting snows of the northern mountains. It was relatively scarce during the *rabi*, or spring crop, for this was the dry season. This difference in water availability might have been expected to produce a larger cropped area in *kharif* than in *rabi*.[48] The popularity of *kharif*, more-

[46] See BOR 301/2/00/8; "Lease of land in Mauza Kala Shah Kaku to S. Gurdit Singh, Rais of Shamgarh, Karnal District," BOR 301/11/17/4; "S. Gajindar Singh's tubewell grant—Chak 30 Upper Chenab Canal, Sheikhupura District—Inspection Reports by Director of Agriculture," BOR 301/19/17/50; "Application by R. B. Hari Kishen Kaul for lease of land in Rakhs Ladheke and Deo Syal, Lahore District," BOR 301/11/12/54; "Application from S. Habibullah Khan and others for lease of land in Chak 68, Chunian Colony," BOR 301/11/12/94; and PRAP(R), November 1914, Nos. 1-7

[47] Information in this section is drawn essentially from the *RODA* and from assessment reports and settlement reports of canal colony regions, for which see Bibliography.

[48] The impact of canal irrigation on agricultural production has been discussed in terms of specific economic effects in: Ian Stone, "Canal Irrigation and Agrarian Change: A Preliminary Investigation in the Ganges Canal Tract in the District of Muzaffarnagar, United Provinces, 1840-1900" (Indian Economic and Social History Conference paper, Cambridge, 1975); and M. M. Islam, "Irrigation and Punjab Agriculture, 1906-1945: Some Preliminary Notes," *South Asia*, New Series, I, 1 (1978), pp. 29-37.

over, should also have been enhanced by the fact that cotton, a major cash crop, was grown in that season.

In reality, *rabi* cropping far exceeded that of *kharif*. Figures from assessment reports reveal that the proportion of the two harvests in the total cropping pattern averaged two-thirds for *rabi* and one-third for *kharif*. These striking differences existed in all colonies, and they were maintained over time. Several assessment circles even had a 75-to-25 ratio for *kharif* and *rabi*. In Chenab Colony, figures from assessment reports, spanning a period of thirty years from 1901 to 1933, show a remarkable continuity in these proportions. Of twenty-seven observation years in different colony circles, the lowest *rabi*-to-*kharif* ratio was 65 to 35, and the highest 79 to 21.[49] The consolidated average for these ratios stood at 71 to 29. For Jhelum Colony in the years 1908 to 1911, the average for six assessment circles was 74 to 26. In Lower Bari Doab Colony, with figures from the 1920s, the proportion of *kharif* stood somewhat higher, the average for ten assessment circles being 59 to 41.[50] British officials expressed consternation at this imbalanced cropping pattern, for government revenues were affected by the fact that periods of high demand for water were not commensurate with its supply. Yet government efforts at reducing the popularity of *rabi*, by methods such as increased differentials in water rates between *rabi* and *kharif* crops, did not meet with any discernible success.[51]

Several factors were responsible for the higher incidence of cropping during *rabi*. It was found that even though less water was available, the *rabi* harvest had a greater degree of reliability than the *kharif*. A higher proportion of crops were successfully matured in *rabi* than in *kharif*. Figures from virtually all parts of the canal colonies confirmed that failed area, or *kharaba*, comprised a significantly lower percentage of cropped land in *rabi* than in *kharif*.

Physical conditions in the western Punjab also proved adverse for *kharif* crops. The sandy loam soil common to many colony tracts was well suited to the cultivation of *rabi* crops such as wheat, gram, and *toria* (oilseed). It was found that the major *kharif* crop, cotton, tended to exhaust the soil. After an initial burst of success on virgin land, cotton production started to fall as soil fertility declined. The extreme heat of the summer also made it difficult to mature *kharif* crops, for rapid evaporation caused the soil to burn

[49] These figures on the crop mix have been compiled from various assessment reports of Chenab Colony: see Imran Ali, "The Punjab Canal Colonies," Table 6.1.

[50] For figures on the crop mix in Jhelum and Lower Bari Doab colonies, see ibid., Tables 6.2 and 6.3.

[51] See "Rabi irrigation on Lower Jhelum Canal in view of Triple Canal Project," BOR H/251/425; and "Joint Reports on restriction of perennial irrigation and reduction of waterlogging on Lower Jhelum Canal," BOR H/251/480.

off under the plants. The hot, sand-laden summer winds caused further injury to *kharif* crops, especially cotton. It was found that the "duty" of water was higher in *rabi*: the same amount of water proved more efficient, and went further in bringing crops to fruition, in the winter than in the summer.

The major cause of the high *rabi* cropping was the great popularity of wheat in the canal colonies. This crop alone generally took up more area than all the *kharif* crops combined. Figures from Chenab, Jhelum, and Lower Bari Doab colonies show that wheat was over 30 percent of the total cultivated area in all tracts, in most it was over 40 percent, and at times it even stood in excess of 50 percent. These high levels denoted that as much wheat was grown as almost all other crops put together. The popularity of wheat rested on a coalescence of favourable factors. Soil conditions, the supportive winter weather, and the availability of canal water all facilitated the cultivation of this crop. The traditional familiarity of colonists with wheat was also important. It was the staple food of the Punjabis, and they retained their dietary habits in the canal colonies. Wheat also continued to command high prices, and the wide availability of marketing facilities that it enjoyed made it the chief cash crop of the colonies.[52] Thus both subsistence and commercial considerations combined to make it the most popular crop of this region: "It is the great Colony crop, and everyone tries to sow and mature as large a wheat area as he can. Other crops have their seasons of great profits, but none can compare with wheat in certainty of results and average profits."[53]

The prospects of higher profits, greater marketability, and improved harvests led to the adoption of new varieties of wheat in the canal colonies. The new strains were especially oriented toward export (though after 1920 exports fell away with the growth of internal demand). The traditional red bearded wheats of the Punjab gave way after 1900 to white wheat, which was better adapted to consumption needs for flour and bread in importing countries like Britain. In the 1910s an improved variety called "Punjab 11" became the predominant type cultivated; and after 1920 this was replaced by an even stronger strain, called "8-A." In the 1930s other varieties with a high commercial orientation gained popularity. Crop innovations were accompanied by the emergence of a sophisticated market mechanism for wheat in colony towns. In Lyallpur and Okara there was a thriving futures market in this commodity, and even in the smaller towns

---

[52] For a discussion of marketing facilities for wheat, see S. Kartar Singh, *Finance and Marketing of Cultivators' Wheat in the Punjab* (Lahore: Civil and Military Gazette Press, 1934); and I. D. Mahendru, *Some Factors Affecting the Price of Wheat in the Punjab* (Lahore. Civil and Military Gazette Press, 1937).

[53] *AR Upper Jhang Branch* (1909), ch. 4, para. 2.

the latest information was readily available on the prices of wheat prevailing not only in the major market and export centres in the country, but also those in the more important places of import overseas.

The other major cash crop was cotton. Though it was not cultivated as profusely as wheat, it had great economic value. A much higher proportion of the total crop was marketed than was the case with wheat, for parts of the latter had to be withheld for the subsistence needs of cultivators.[54] Cotton proved difficult to cultivate in the early years of colonisation, being subject to crop failure owing to such factors as insect attack and soil exhaustion. It tended to establish itself better after some years, when soil conditions became less harsh and the cultivators more adept at its cultivation. Between 1910 and 1940 in Chenab Colony, its proportionate share in total cultivated area increased by roughly 50 percent. A similar increase occurred in Jhelum Colony. Cotton cultivation became still more significant in Lower Bari Doab Colony, where at times it even equalled the area under wheat. The popularity of cotton was based chiefly on the high rates it fetched, though its price was subject to dramatic fluctuations as well. Its cultivation also gave a stimulus to indigenous commercial enterprise, with the establishment of several ginning and pressing factories that enabled raw cotton to be processed before deterioration began to occur.[55]

After 1915, a truly significant innovation took place in the cultivation of cotton in the canal colonies. This was the spread of American long-staple cotton, which was found to be well suited to the soil and climatic conditions of the region.[56] One initial obstacle to its acceptance among cultivators had been the absence of a secure market for American cotton. Before 1915 proper marketing facilities did not exist, since the staple was grown in small quantities, and ginning and spinning firms were unwilling to handle such

[54] "Cotton is the crop on which dependence is placed for cash profits. The small holder sells as much wheat as he must to meet his liabilities with the money lender or with Government. He and his dependents eat the rest. But the amount of cotton he keeps for spinning is very small. The rest means money with which to renew his credit with his Sahukar, or to purchase new bullocks, or to finance a wedding, or just to amuse himself." See *AR Okara Tahsil* (1934), Section 7.

[55] For information on ginning and pressing factories in the canal colonies, see "Establishment of cotton factories on Lower Bari Doab Canal," BOR J/301/1337 A-G; "Lease of Government land at Lyallpur to Delhi Cloth and General Mills Ltd. for cotton ginning factories etc.," BOR 301/11/25/180, K. T. Shah, *Industrialisation of the Punjab* (Lahore: Government Printing Press, 1941), p. 62; and Punjab Financial Proceedings (Development), October 1933, Nos. 7-10.

[56] During the latter half of the nineteenth century, numerous attempts were made to foster the cultivation of American and Egyptian varieties of cotton in the Punjab, but they proved unsuccessful. In the canal colonies American cotton adapted well to local conditions, though efforts to cultivate Egyptian cotton remained unfruitful. See *RODA*: 1908, p. 7; and 1918, Appendix III.

amounts. The problem was circular, for cultivators, unable to obtain a fair price for American cotton, were in turn dissuaded from increasing its cultivation. From 1915, successful auctions were organised by the Agricultural Department, in which cultivators were assured of a premium price.[57] With its marketability thus established, the cultivation of American cotton spread rapidly. From a few hundred acres in the Punjab in 1910, it reached 514,000 acres in 1920, 801,000 acres in 1930, and 1,432,000 acres in 1940.[58] The phenomenal rise in American varieties was accompanied by an equally significant increase in improved varieties of indigenous, or *desi*, cottons. By the mid-1930s over 700,000 acres of improved *desis* were under cultivation in the Punjab, where improved varieties after 1925 took up well over 50 percent, and in some years 80 percent, of total area under cotton.

The cultivation of improved cotton was aided by the better provision of seed, which could be obtained through the public and private seed farms discussed earlier. Another source was the grant of about 7,500 acres in Lower Bari Doab Colony to the British Cotton Growing Association. The primary function of this allotment was to grow improved cottons for export to the textile mills of Lancashire. In addition, the BCGA was bound by tenurial conditions to supply wheat and cotton seed to the Agricultural Department and to other cultivators in the canal colonies. The BCGA grant continued to perform both these functions over the years, though even on this grant, cultivation was given over to subtenants. The BCGA became, in fact, one of the largest rentiers in the Punjab, for after 1925 it leased large areas of state land on temporary cultivation terms in Lower Bari Doab and Nili Bar colonies. This area was estimated to be about 70,000 acres in 1929, and cultivation on it was entirely dependent on the subtenancy system.[59]

The crop mix in the canal colonies was subject to many influences, but

[57] Such government-sponsored auctions continued into the early 1920s, and they were a major factor in establishing a market for American cotton. The buyers at these auctions were firms of cotton agents, such as Tata, Forbes Campbell, Volkart, Ralli, and a host of smaller Punjabi brokers, the great majority of whom belonged to the Hindu commercial castes. See ibid.: 1919, p. 11; 1921, p. 17; 1922, Annexure IX; and 1923, p. 37.

[58] See the figures on cotton cultivation in the Punjab in Imran Ali, "The Punjab Canal Colonies," Table 6.5.

[59] For information on the BCGA landholdings, see "Proposed grant of land on Lower Bari Doab Canal for cultivation and treatment of cotton of standard type," BOR 301/11/24/14; "British Cotton Growing Association, Khanewal—Inspection Reports by Director of Agriculture," BOR 301/19/27/47; "Lease of agricultural land to British Cotton Growing Association—Waiving of condition relating to steam tackle," BOR 301/11/24/362; and "Proposal to dispose of large areas of 10R Distributary of Lower Bari Doab Canal, Montgomery District—Chak Shahana," BOR 301/8/24/19.

perhaps the most important of these was price: "the whole system of agriculture is essentially commercial, for the bulk of the produce being exportable everything depends on *Mandi* prices, and their fluctuations are watched with intense interest."[60] Much of the success of cultivators in producing for the market lay in their ability to regulate their crop mix in accordance with price trends. Officials reported that the more astute agriculturists from the central Punjab were the most responsive to price changes. The more backward cultivators, like the Janglis, maintained more inflexible cropping patterns, presumably more closely aligned to subsistence needs. The more commercialised cultivators concentrated on the more marketable cash crops, marking a move away from foodgrain production. The heavier emphasis on cash cropping led to a declining per capita output of foodgrains in the Punjab. This trend, despite the great extension in agriculture, became increasingly perceptible after 1921.[61]

One example of the influence of prices on crop mix was sugarcane. Though it was the sole source of sugar, its cultivation never rose above 4 percent of total cropped area, and in most colony tracts it stayed below 2 percent. A valuable crop, being a monoculture it was nevertheless unsuited to double rotation systems, such as a combination with either wheat or cotton. As long as high profits could be obtained from rotational cropping, there was a disincentive to cultivate sugarcane. (This also accounted for the neglect of other forms of monoculture, of which the most conspicuous by their absence were fruit orchards.) Nevertheless, a rise in the price of sugar after 1918 led to an increased area under sugarcane. The price of cotton also caused fluctuations in sugarcane cultivation. A fall in the price of cotton caused the area under sugarcane to rise by 11 percent in 1927 and 1928, and 11.5 percent in 1932.[62] Thereafter, the sugarcane area contracted in the face of a rise in cotton prices and a fall in the rate for *gur*, or unrefined sugar. And though price remained very important, other factors also influenced cropping decisions: sugarcane cultivation, for example, was constrained because "the crop suffers from diseases, severe cold, lack of rain, and temporary failings of canal supply."[63]

Individual crops retained their popularity as long as their prices remained competitive. This was illustrated by the contrasting fortunes of *toria* and maize. The oilseed crop of *toria* was delicate and prone to failure from insect attacks and excessive cold. Though its cultivation was a gamble, it remained popular because it commanded high prices in overseas markets,

[60] *Jhang and Gugera Branches SR* (1925), para. 16.

[61] See George Blyn, *Agricultural Trends in India, 1891-1947* (Philadelphia: University of Pennsylvania Press, 1966).

[62] *RODA*: 1928, p. 59; and 1932, p. 44.

[63] *AR Upper Jhang Branch* (1909), ch. 4, para. 5.

and in some colony tracts it took up at times as much as 15 percent of total cropped area. *Toria* completely overshadowed *sarshaf*, the great oilseed crop of central Punjab, and it can be regarded as an important crop innovation in the canal colonies. In contrast to *toria*, maize was grown primarily for subsistence needs. The low value of maize as a cash crop placed effective constraints on its cultivation, displaying again the diversion of land from foodgrain production. In Chenab Colony it varied from 3 to 7 percent of total cropped area prior to 1910, but by the early 1930s its cultivation did not exceed 3.5 percent. In other colonies, too, maize remained insignificant: in two of the three *tahsil*s of Lower Bari Doab Colony it did not figure at all as a percentile in the crop mix.

Apart from price, there were factors of state policy that also influenced the cultivators' choice of crops. Irrigation patterns were of considerable importance in determining the crop mix. Rotational systems were dependent on the timely availability of water. Successful husbandry depended on the cultivator's awareness of the periods in which he could obtain access to canal water, and on his ability to make precise calculations as to the best way of utilising the water allocated to him. The Irrigation Department was responsible for the supply of water to the cultivator, but beyond this he was free to deal with it as he pleased. He could concentrate the water on a small area, and hope to obtain reliable results. Alternatively, he could distribute it over a larger area, and try for a higher output through less intensive but more speculative cultivation.

The method of assessment adopted by the state also influenced the amount of area colonists wished to cultivate. The major levy, the water rate, varied with different crops, being higher for the more valuable ones. Cultivators had to decide whether differentials between revenue extraction and prevailing prices warranted the choice of a particular crop. Cultivation was also affected by the government's decision on whether to assess the gross (sown) or net (matured) area. Up to 1912, under the system of "holding-to-holding *kharaba*," assessment was only on the area matured, whereas areas of failed crops were not subjected to taxation. This encouraged excessive and careless cropping, and also allowed for graft and corruption by assessing officials. In 1912, the *kharaba* system was abolished, and assessment thereafter was on the sown area, which included failed crops.[64] This induced colonists to cultivate more carefully.

The quality of the soil also had an important bearing on the type of crops grown. In Lower Bari Doab Colony, large patches of inferior land proved impervious to conventional methods of cultivation. In Chenab Colony, soils were more uniform and generally of satisfactory quality. Neverthe-

[64] *PCM*, pp. 48-51; and RPCC, pp. 48-51.

less, there existed sufficient differences in soil and water supply to necessitate the division of villages into eight different classes for assessment purposes. In Jhelum Colony, one assessment circle, the Ara tract, had soils that were too harsh for any but the hardiest crops. Wheat was able to survive there, but cotton withered away on the hard clay soil, while rice cultivation was prevented by an insufficient supply of water. In fact, water constraints meant that rice was not extensively grown at all in the canal colonies. Its cultivation was confined either to low-lying lands or to soils of stiff and impervious quality. Rice was later to emerge, however, as a major cash crop in tracts prone to waterlogging, especially in the Sheikhupura area of the Rechna Doab. After 1947, this region provided the famed aromatic basmati rice for export and for upper-end market consumption.

A number of factors converged to promote the cultivation of gram. This crop enjoyed little popularity during the early years of a colony, for it fared poorly on virgin land, which proved too "warm" and hard for it. Gram cultivation increased in later years, when the soil became less friable and needed less moisture, conditions that suited this crop. The rise of gram was evident in the Chenab Colony crop mix. After 1920 it took up 7 percent or more of total cropped area. Gram held this place because it commanded prices sufficiently high to make it competitive with wheat, and this position it continued to enjoy over the years. Gram also required minimal amounts of irrigation water, and could often be sown and matured *barani* (with rain water). Moreover, it had a recuperative effect on the soil, required little attention, and occupied the ground for only a short period. These circumstances favoured the cultivation of grain and gave it a prominent role in cropping patterns.

Another set of determinants of agricultural activity were the strengths and weaknesses, and the caste and tribal characteristics, of different groups of colonists. The canal colonies were the repositories from most areas of the Punjab of peasant caste groups that had for generations practised agriculture as their traditional occupation. They had developed specialised agrarian skills best suited to their own ecosystems; and these were superimposed on the practices they had to adopt in the colony environment. According to official reports, the most expert cultivators were those from the central Punjab. Officials spoke highly of the agricultural skills of Sikh and Muslim Jats from central districts such as Amritsar, Jullundur, Gurdaspur, Ludhiana, Hoshiarpur, and Sialkot. The Arains were also highly efficient cultivators. They were especially adept with small pieces of land: they practised intensive cultivation and were the traditional market gardeners of the Punjab. Many of the Amritsar grantees had prior experience of canal irrigation, from the Upper Bari Doab Canal. The fewer adaptations they required contrasted with the challenge faced by groups from other regions,

who had to acquire an entirely new repertoire of skills for cultivating under
conditions of canal irrigation. The commercial orientation of the central
Punjabis was reflected in their unwillingness to increase costs beyond minimum levels. The amount of livestock they maintained was strictly regulated by its utility: cattle was usually confined to a plough team, which
doubled for carting produce to the market, and a cow or buffalo for dairy
products. The more competitive agriculturists were not content to sell their
produce to village or itinerant traders, but transported it to market towns in
order to obtain the best prices.

The juxtaposition of agriculturists from different parts of the Punjab
brought about a synthesis of agricultural techniques and practices. Men
learned from new-found neighbours in this melting pot of agrarian profi-
ciencies. This was a process already well advanced in Chenab Colony by
1920, a quarter of a century after colonisation:

> The grant of proprietary rights has now given them an additional interest
> in their holdings, and though different tribes retain many of their inher-
> ited predilections, the example of their neighbours has taught them to
> adopt improved methods and to discard practices likely to prove a hand-
> icap in the race for wealth. The original grantees are now giving place to
> a generation born or at any rate bred in the colony and even more recep-
> tive of new influences than themselves. The result has been not merely a
> levelling up of agricultural methods but an advance in the economic po-
> sition of the *zamindar*.[65]

Not all colonists were efficient, and many failed to be successful. The
larger landholders, such as the capitalist grantees of Chenab Colony, were
disappointing, and they failed to spearhead agricultural progress in the
canal colonies. They were in general unprepared to manage their land personally, or even to reside on it. Among the worst were the landed gentry
and other elite grantees, to whom land had been allotted as a political favour. Such men consolidated their economic position through their colony
grants, but showed little capability or enthusiasm for agricultural enterprise
or innovation.

Another group of grantees who proved more backward than the central
Punjabis were the indigenous inhabitants of the western *doab*s. The Janglis,
on whose grazing lands the canal colonies were established, had to face a
difficult transition from a pastoral life to a dependence on canal-irrigated
smallholdings. The paucity of hereditary agricultural skills among them
resulted in a low level of cultivation. Hostility toward outsiders, aided by
a love of cattle theft, deterred the more competent subtenants and labourers

[65] *AR Jhang Branch* (1921), para. 18.

from their holdings. For some Jangli groups the transition proved too trau-matic. Certain tribes unable to curtail cattle theft and other misdemeanours came to be notified officially as "criminal tribes" under the Criminal Tribes Act. These groups were placed under police surveillance, or con-fined to their villages, or in some cases they were moved to special reser-vations.

The landowners of the *hithars*, or riverain tracts, were the other indige-nous group in the canal colonies. They were allotted colony land as com-pensation for the adverse effects of the perennial canals on their agricultural systems. But the Hitharis preferred not to move to the colony areas, and continued to reside in their riverain homes, renting out their grants to sub-tenants. They failed to become enterprising landholders, and were reported to be among the worst of grantees. In short, there was wide variation in the quality of colonists with regard to agricultural performance. The social origins of cultivators had a differentiating effect on agricultural develop-ment, which was just as significant as those variations attributable to di-verse natural conditions.

Agricultural technology in the canal colonies did not undergo any signif-icant transition in the period of colonial rule. Most smallholdings were un-der twenty-five acres, and in these units traditional, labour-intensive meth-ods of cultivation were retained, and little or no development of mechanised farming occurred. The larger grants, being mostly rented out to subtenants, also remained tied to existing levels of technology. Occa-sionally, large self-managed farms did employ mechanical devices, but these were too few to have a major impact on agriculture in the region. The more sophisticated farm implements such as reaping machines, mechanised winnowers, and steam threshers failed to gain substantial usage in the canal colonies. Even those individuals who could afford to buy machinery were dissuaded by its high depreciation and running expenses. Initial capital costs were also substantial, relative to agricultural incomes.

In the absence of home production, agricultural machinery had to be imported, and this was done largely from Britain. After World War I the prices of these imports rose to prohibitive levels, checking what had earlier promised to be a steady growth in the use of such equipment.[66] The postwar years witnessed increasing inequalities between the prices of manufactured and agricultural goods, with the terms of trade moving distinctly in favour of the former. This made the prospect of introducing higher technology in

[66] In 1909 Volkart Brothers opened an agency for reaping machines, and in the next few years did a brisk trade in them: 49 were sold in 1909, 72 in 1910, and 30 in 1915. Up to 1915 their price stood at Rs 250 each, but rose to Rs 350 by 1917 and to Rs 440 by 1919. See *RODA*: 1909, p. v; 1910, p. 5; 1915, p. 9; 1917, p. 6; and 1919, p. x.

Punjabi agriculture increasingly remote.[67] As the cost of such technology increased, the use of labour-intensive methods became more attractive. With the steady rise in population after 1920, and in the absence of industrial growth, there was little alternative for an expanding labour force but to look for continued employment in agriculture. With a plentiful supply of labour, the need for mechanised farming receded still further. The absence of ancillary services, itself a product of low demand levels, proved an additional disincentive for investment in the larger machines.

Simpler agricultural implements were more widely diffused in the canal colonies. Many types of improved equipment were imported from Britain in the years before World War I, especially ploughs, harrows, and hoes, and to a lesser extent, drills, chaff cutters, and cane crushers. Such instruments were considered to have advantages over the local varieties, and ploughs such as the "Raja," "Meston," and "Jat" earned great repute. These simpler, cheaper implements were within the reach of the smaller cultivator. They did not require elaborate maintenance, and could usually be repaired locally. But after World War I even the price of these goods became inordinately high. Partly as a result, such implements increasingly came to be produced by indigenous manufacturers, most of whom were based in the town of Batala in Gurdaspur District. Within a decade, Indian-made implements began to outsell imported ones. In 1929, for example, 14,207 Indian and 7,120 imported implements were sold in the Punjab. By 1930, Batala had twenty-six iron foundries, with a total output of over 19,000 machines valued at Rs 537,000.[68] The use of only these smaller implements, although a promising sign, provided a contrast to the advances in agricultural technology that were taking place in the more industrialised parts of the world. Moreover, in the majority of cases cultivators in the canal colonies continued to use their traditional implements, and did not convert to the new improved ones.

No major changes occurred in cropping techniques in the canal colonies. Double cropping was practised where the water supply permitted, and a number of crop combinations were extant. The strength of a particular village in agriculture could be measured by the proportion of annually matured area to allotted area. A combination of good water supply and skilled agriculturists could result in the regular maturing of over 100 percent of allotted area. This was often achieved, though a matured area in excess of 110 percent was rare. Poorer villages matured 80-90 percent, and some as little as 70 percent. Several rotational systems were practised, each village

---

[67] The assessment reports of the 1930s confirmed that the use of improved implements was uncommon: see *AR Khanewal Tahsil* (1934), Section 23; *AR Okara Tahsil* (1934), Section 15; and *AR Montgomery Tahsil* (1934), Section 23.

[68] *RODA*: 1929, Annexure II; and 1930, p. 70.

and indeed each cultivator having its own ideosyncratic sequences. These were invariably arranged around the two staple crops of wheat and cotton. Crop rotations normally included regular periods of fallow, the usual pattern being a period of rest after every two crops. Tillage systems intensive enough to do away with the fallow were not in vogue, nor is there any evidence that such systems were being evolved over the years.

There were major lags in the diffusion of other improvements as well. Chemical fertilisers, though known, were used only in isolated cases. The two most common sources of fertiliser remained town sweepings and farm-yard manure, and the use of these did not mark a departure from traditional practice. The cultivators were well aware of the advantages of obtaining good seed, and did not hesitate to adopt new crop varieties wherever these promised to be more marketable or profitable.[69] In several other respects, however, cultivation continued to be carried out in a careless and slovenly manner. Grass and weeds were a common sight in fields, and these not only taxed the soil but also prevented the intercultivation of different crops. Even the more important cash crops, such as cotton and wheat, were sown broadcast rather than in lines or with drills. Such methods reduced output, yet they continued to persist over time.

The failure of the majority of cultivators to adopt improved techniques of farming was revealed in a survey conducted in Montgomery District in the mid-1930s. A settlement officer, working at the time on the reassessment of Lower Bari Doab Colony, drew up six points representing elementary requirements for an improved form of agriculture.[70] Some big farms did meet these standards, but enquiries revealed that their observance was sadly lacking among peasant cultivators. The villages surveyed were divided into three classes according to the proportion of the six stipulations that they fulfilled. It was found that of the 386 villages surveyed, only 7 were in the first class, 22 in the second, and 54 in the third. The rest of the villages, 303 in number, did not meet any of the six standards: they kept entirely to traditional ways of cultivation. Such methods could be quite

[69] One assessment report in 1909 noted: "Probably no part of the Punjab takes such an interest in seed selection as the Chenab Colony. The colonist selects his seed for ordinary crops carefully and in addition has the leisure, affluence and the acres on which to try experiments with exotics. American cotton and Australian wheat, Mauritius sugar-cane, western lucernes, occupy the attention of the colonist, and he is usually ready to reap anything which the agricultural department or private enterprise may bring to his ken." See *AR Upper Jhang Branch* (1909), ch. 4, para. 3.

[70] The six points were: 1. use only of pure seed; 2. conservation and experimental use of manures; 3. sowing of crops, especially cotton, in lines and not broadcast; 4. use of furrow-turning ploughs to break up and aerate the soil in the early stages of cultivation; 5. use of light harrows to keep the surface of the soil open and free from weeds after sowing; and 6. a carefully thought-out rotation of crops. See *AR Montgomery Tahsil* (1934), Section 23.

effective, but agricultural technology and techniques were bound to remain backward as long as they continued in their unreformed state.

There was no "leading" commodity in the canal colonies whose production might have led to a series of innovations in agriculture. Cotton could have been expected to fulfil this role, but on the contrary its cultivation amply demonstrated the constraints that were imposed on agricultural progress. Cotton vied with wheat as the chief cash crop of the canal colonies, and in certain areas it replaced wheat as the chief money earner for the cultivator. The spread of improved varieties of cotton linked the canal colonies to the world market, for long-staple cotton provided one of the basic raw materials for the textile industry. Yet the cultivation of cotton did not prove an unmixed blessing for the canal colonies. An inordinately large area under cotton did not make for balanced farming. Not only did cotton tend to exhaust the soil but it replaced the fodder crops which had a rejuvenating and replenishing effect on arable land. In devoting larger areas to cotton, cultivators were guided more by the attraction of immediate profits than by concern for the quality of the land in the long term. This was especially true of subtenants, who held a large area but had no permanency of tenure. In 1920, the colonisation officer described the situation in Lower Bari Doab Colony as follows:

> Good land is being overtaxed by continued croppings of cotton, and inferior land, which is capable of bearing good fodder crops, is being made weaker still by attempts to grow cotton on it. The zamindar is reducing his acreage of kharif fodder crops to a dangerous minimum and if the failure of cotton on inferior land together with a fall in the price results in a reduction of the area under cotton, it would be no bad thing for the general condition of farming in the Colony.[71]

Nor did the growth of cotton lead to any major innovations in cultivation techniques. It was not part of any improved rotational system, which might have increased productivity or dispensed with the fallow. The cotton seed was generally sown broadcast, and rather than develop a more intensive form of farming through interculture, cultivators generally allowed the crop to remain interspersed with weeds and grasses. The colonisation officer of Lower Bari Doab Colony reported in 1923 that:

> The standard of farming improves very very slowly. I do not know that the increased area under American cotton is a matter for high congratulation. A lot of the cotton is cultivated in a very slovenly manner and produces far too low an outturn. The main result is to impoverish the land and prevent the sowing of what may be called "recuperative"

[71] *PCR*, 1920, p. 32

crops. It is perhaps a pity in the interests of good farming and the maintenance of the Colony's reputation for high grade cotton that legislation to restrict the area under cotton is outside practical politics.[72]

The impact of the profit motive, too, was not altogether beneficial for agriculture. The profitability of the improved American cottons led to nefarious practices that could only harm the reputation of the canal colonies as a cotton-producing region. From the early 1920s, within a few years of its establishment as a profitable crop, American cotton was being adulterated with the indigenous *desi* varieties. The sale of such mixtures was motivated by considerations of short-term gain. The problem was almost impossible to eradicate, it being difficult to trace whether the impurities had been added by cultivator, middleman, or ginner. The practice was ultimately a self-defeating one, for a decline in the standard of the staple harmed the interests of all concerned.[73] Reputation and goodwill were all-important in the selling of cotton in the world market, since no accurate tests were made to assess its quality until it reached the spinning mill in the country of import. Adulteration in the canal colonies was sufficiently widespread to cause a slump in the premiums for American varieties in 1925, a reflection of the loss of confidence in the staple.

The evil continued unabated, however. While impurities of up to 5 percent with *desis* were virtually undetectable at spinning mills, it was found that adulteration went well beyond this level. American cottons leaving ginning factories reportedly contained *desi* mixtures of 25 percent, and at times even 30 to 40 percent. A Cotton Ginning and Pressing Factories Act was passed in 1925 to assist in checking this malpractice, but the mixing of cotton continued to increase. By the 1930s, seed quality had begun to suffer, and it became increasingly difficult, and expensive, to obtain pure American seed. Deterioration, once under way, was virtually impossible to counteract. After 1935, Agricultural Department reports ceased to give disaggregated figures for areas under improved seeds, as this had become impossible to determine.

With such constraints on agricultural progress, the reasons for the absence of an "agricultural revolution" become clearer. Though great economic growth occurred in the canal colonies, agriculture did not experience any major transition from traditional modes. Quantitative increase was not

[72] Ibid., 1923, pp. 46-47.
[73] The Agricultural Department report of 1924 commented on this aspect: "No honest dealer can compete in such conditions, and so everyone falls into the competition of who can make money fastest. But the reputation of Punjab cottons comes down, and the Punjab farmer is the loser, for the spinner is not going to get a higher quality than he gets, and the middleman is not going to pay the farmer more than he gets from the spinner." See *RODA*, 1924, p. 20.

accompanied by qualitative change. Some of the reasons for this have been outlined in this chapter, in the discussion of both the general aspect of agriculture and that of specific forms of agricultural improvement. One other feature responsible for this outcome has been alluded to earlier. This was the social organisation of agriculture, which remained tied to its traditional moorings. It did not experience any structural innovation which might have allowed it to effect major changes in agricultural production and technique. This was one important reason why agriculture itself remained unredeemed and unprogressive.

CHAPTER SEVEN

Growth and Underdevelopment

AGRICULTURAL colonisation produced significant economic growth in the Punjab. An assessment of agriculture in the canal colonies, measured with such indices as cultivated area, output, marketing, and trade, would indicate an impressive process of growth. In the space of fifty years, human settlement spread over the hitherto barren and sparsely populated *doab*s of the western Punjab. The process transformed this region into one of the most important areas of commercial farming in Asia. Agricultural produce was marketed not only in other parts of South Asia, but commodities such as cotton, wheat, and oilseeds were exported overseas. The rural population of the Punjab benefitted from the more favourable ratio between land and man, and many thousands migrated to the canal colonies in response to new labour opportunities.

The canal colonies represented the most extensive form of socio-economic and demographic engineering attempted by the British in South Asia. The gains that accrued from agricultural colonisation made the Punjab appear to be the success story for British rule in India. The British regarded the agricultural prosperity that they had brought to the Punjab as one of the crowning achievements of their participation in Indian history. While they looked with regret and concern at the nationalist-minded bourgeoisie that they themselves had fostered in the subcontinent, and at the development of an industrial capacity that might one day challenge that of the metropolis, they were in no doubt that the extension of the agrarian sector in the Punjab was a desirable phenomenon. Seen from this perspective, the canal colonies were an example of imperial benevolence, and a refutation of the arguments of those who held that imperialism had a destructive impact on the subject economies.

Closer examination reveals a very different picture. Canal colonisation released vast resources and provided a real opportunity for economic development in the Punjab. However, despite significant economic growth, the Punjab remained an underdeveloped region. Important reasons for this lay in the political and social context in which growth in the canal colonies occurred. One determinant of change was the colonisation policy of the state. The kind of goals that the state pursued and the use it made of colony land had a major influence on the economic outcome. Land distribution was governed by the need of the British to consolidate their political position, to fulfil military requirements, and to maintain an extractive system in order to finance their administration. The state failed to provide a determined developmental stimulus; the many opportunities for it in the canal colonies were not properly utilised. The role of the state as an agent of improvement was aborted by the agitation of 1907, after which it became politically expedient for it to withdraw from an intrusive supervision of agrarian affairs. The decision to concede proprietary rights to peasant grantees subjected the colonies to the same legal and organisational forces that had kept agriculture in a stagnant and backward state in the rest of the Punjab.

The pursuance of political goals had a rewarding outcome for the British. The nationalist movement in the Punjab did not, until the very eve of independence, gain enough strength to challenge the configuration of pro-British politicians that were brought together in the Punjab National Unionist party. Political benefits accrued to the state in the use of colony land, both at the level of placating social classes and of removing particular sources of tension. The major proportion of land was allotted to the "agricultural castes," with the result that the landholding peasantry of the Punjab had little economic basis for any grievance against British rule. Indeed, this class remained loyal to the Unionist party in the 1935 elections, at a time when its counterparts in most other provinces of British India opted for the Indian National Congress. The landlords were the other class that received a substantial allotment of land. The benefits that they obtained from the canal colonies provided a sound economic basis for their continued loyalty to the British. Even the incipient bourgeoisie of the province obtained sufficient material rewards to remain ineffective, though not always silent, advocates of nationalism. The one class that was excluded from access to land grants was that of the landless poor, who were not considered important enough to be eligible for such benefits. They did obtain employment opportunities in the canal colonies, but the British believed that their continued role as labourers and tenants-at-will was sufficient reward for them.

A range of other grants also proved of political value to the state. Land was given for help to the administration against political movements or against crime, for various individual services, and for compensation for sufferers from calamities such as waterlogging and river flooding. Land distribution made it possible to avoid or overcome tensions in agrarian society. Dislocation from physical and economic crises might have led agrarian groups in other provinces into opposition to the British, and eventually into the nationalist movement. In the Punjab, owing to the availability of new lands for settlement, the outlet for such tensions became the basis for consolidating the bonds between the state and the agrarian structure.

A very large amount of land in the canal colonies was reserved for the

fulfilment of military requirements. Not only was the Punjab a major supplier of recruits to the British Indian army but with agricultural colonisation
it became clear that the military would also participate prominently in the
utilisation of new economic resources. Land grants to ex-soldiers made
military service particularly attractive to the Punjabis: no other career held
the prospect of such material rewards on retirement. The substantial allotment to veterans of World War I was of special benefit to the British, for it
encouraged war recruitment; the large human contribution of the Punjab to
the war effort could be matched by a more remunerative scale of rewards
than any other province of British India could offer to its soldiers.

The other significant form of military involvement was the breeding of
animals by colony grantees for army use. This constituted a major diversion
of economic resources toward an activity that could be of little benefit to
agricultural development. Horse-breeding schemes were important enough
to dominate two large colonies, Jhelum and the Lower Bari Doab, though
their only function was to provide young stock for the cavalry. During the
twentieth century the cavalry horse ceased to have a military value, in terms
of conventional warfare, yet the schemes continued. Cavalry horses were
still useful for action against civilian mobs and for counterinsurgency operations, and it may be surmised that the British had such purposes in mind
in maintaining a horse supply for their army in India. Had the resources
devoted to military needs been utilised instead for purposes of agricultural
improvement, the economy of the Punjab might well have assumed a different shape by the mid-twentieth century.

The canal colonies proved to be financially profitable to the state. Extractive needs were one of the foremost considerations in government policy, and much of the administration was involved with revenue work. Annual net profits of as much as 40 percent on capital outlay were obtained
from the more remunerative canal works, and this was after all maintenance
and interest charges had been met. There is no evidence that developmental
expenditure played any significant part in the state's utilisation of this surplus. Part of the revenues from the canal colonies were sent to the centre,
where they were utilised for military expenditure and for the maintenance
of the imperialist political and administrative superstructure. The rest was
used for administrative expenses within the Punjab, largely on the irrigation, revenue, and police departments.

Though aggregate profits from the canal colonies seemed impressive, the
revenue system was in fact quite inefficient, and was riddled with corruption. Despite repeated efforts, the government did not succeed in reforming
revenue procedures. It was unable to introduce fixed assessment, which
was practised in the rest of the province, and it had to continue with the
highly inconvenient system of fluctuating assessment. Nor was the govern-

ment successful in adopting a method whereby water could be sold by measurement. Consequently, cultivators felt little need to economise on this scarce resource. These reforms could not be carried out because of opposition from colonists. Such measures would have been politically inexpedient, though they would have reduced revenue losses and inefficiencies in water usage.

The corruption of the lower, native bureaucracy also went largely unchecked. Here too the political costs of reform were allowed to outweigh the need for administrative efficiency. An effective and orderly bureaucracy would have been essential had the state wished to play an active role as an agent of transformation. The extent to which the subordinate staff was able to manipulate official procedures for its own pecuniary gain made it difficult for the state to involve itself productively in agrarian affairs. The agitation of 1907 was proof of the friction that corrupt subordinate officials could cause between the government and the colonists. On the other hand, collusion between the lower bureaucracy and landholders seemed to compromise numerous state initiatives. Such relationships diverted greater parts of the economic surplus toward the upper social layers, and with time they became more and more difficult to suppress. A state that coexisted with such malpractice risked having its capacity for reform seriously undermined, just as the nonbeneficiary social classes stood to be further deprived of rights and resources when the perquisites of their superiors went unregulated.

Compared to its political, military, and extractive motivations, the state devoted little attention to the improvement of agriculture. The establishment of a canal and rail network was certainly a major public investment, and on it rested the production and export of agricultural crops. But the state made few efforts to intervene directly in improving the quality of agriculture. To achieve results in features such as the provision of seed, cattle farming, arboreal development, land reclamation, and lift and tubewell irrigation, the government preferred to use indirect methods. These were based on service tenures, under which the fulfilment of specific agricultural goals was made a tenurial obligation. This proved by and large to be an awkward and ineffective method of achieving agricultural improvement, for a successful outcome depended on the willingness and ability of individual grantees to fulfil their conditions of tenure. In the case of the larger service grants, the prospects of success were further reduced, with the selection of many of the grantees not for their professional or entrepreneurial qualifications but as a reward for political services rendered to the government. Small-sized grants were allotted for objectives such as land reclamation and tree planting, although larger units might have been more effective for this purpose. The government declined to participate directly in the application of higher technology to irrigation in such matters as electrical energy, tubewells, and lift works. This prevented the adoption of more intensive forms of cultivation, and consequently agriculture remained at the levels permissible only under simple flow irrigation from canals.

The extent to which the Punjabis themselves were amenable to change had a vital influence on the prospects of development. Some colony land was obtained by men from the nonlanded elite of the Punjab, such as retired public servants. The rest was allotted to men who belonged to landholding groups. The fact that those who already held land were also the ones who acquired colony land was highly significant. Such men might have been the only ones capable of organising agricultural operations on the vast scale that was entailed in the canal colonies. Their actual achievement lay in bringing large areas of virgin soil under cultivation. Yet the grantees of land proved to be unprogressive farmers. The larger holders, belonging mostly to the landlord stratum, became absentees and rentiers. Their reliance on subtenants rather than on their own capital and entrepeneurial skill indicated that they had little interest in raising agricultural productivity. The tenants from whom they extracted rent were most often smallholders who lacked both means and incentive for improved farming.

The peasant grantees, drawn from the landholding peasantry of the Punjab, were more apt to cultivate the land themselves. They proved to be more enterprising than their larger counterparts, though in agricultural methods they too were of a conservative disposition. Rather than exploit the potential for improvement and innovation that was possible in the canal colonies, they preferred to revert to the agrarian and social conditions with which they were familiar in their old homes. With the Colonisation Act of 1912 they gained the rights of proprietorship over their grants, and with this it became impossible to avoid the shortcomings, such as subdivision, from which peasant agriculture suffered in the old districts. In the canal colonies, even peasant grantees preferred to become rentiers: extra land tended to be rented out rather than be brought under self-managed cultivation through paid labour. Capitalistic forms of agriculture, therefore, did not emerge on any significant scale.

The impact of agricultural colonisation on the social structure of the Punjab was of crucial importance in determining whether the backward economy of this region could be modernised. Colony land was allotted predominantly to landholding groups, and this had the effect of strengthening the position of the dominant classes in society. Those who were already landlords, and those who belonged to the landholding sections of the peasantry, acquired further economic resources in the canal colonies. This enabled them to maintain and consolidate the dominance that they already enjoyed, with the result that the social structure became more rigid. The landless poor obtained employment opportunities in the canal colonies, but they were denied access to land. Their position grew weaker as their superiors monopolised the new resources. Even the bourgeoisie, the class that in other regions had spearheaded the capitalist revolution, suffered a process of "ruralisation" in the Punjab. Agricultural expansion tied this class more closely to the values of agrarian society, thereby weakening the impetus to diversify its economic activity. Agricultural expansion did not produce a social base conducive to rapid change; indeed, the reinforcement of the existing class structure created, through the very process of economic growth, a situation that was hostile to an economic transformation.

The impact of the processes discussed in this work extended well beyond the termination of British rule. The state of Pakistan has experienced major continuities from the colonial period. One example lies in the impediments placed on political development. The retardation of nationalism was undeniably linked to agricultural colonisation, with the British retaining loyal legislatures till the very point of independence and partition. This meant that Pakistan did not inherit any widely based and well-entrenched political organisation along the lines of the Indian National Congress. One consequence has been the lack of success of legislative politics. Pakistan has been unable to sustain an electoral process based on adult franchise and competitive party politics. In India, on the other hand, legislative institutions have managed to survive since 1947. This is largely because political organisations like the Congress party have prevented authoritarian or undemocratic forces from subverting the electoral system.

The absence of such checks in Pakistan has afforded greater prominence to some other institutions that matured with agricultural colonisation. It would be all too obvious to suggest linkages between the political role of the military after 1947 and its growing claims to canal colony land under the British. The undeniable eminence that the military attained in colonial Punjab could well have facilitated its assumption of political power in the new nation. The bureaucracy too has enjoyed much arbitrary privilege in Pakistan. It could be argued that its position was strengthened to such an extent while managing the hydraulic society of the canal colonies that it came to wield unfair power in the postcolonial era. Finally, the landlords, without doubt strengthened economically through agricultural colonisation, have exercised continued eminence in Pakistani politics. They have strongly articulated their class interests through effective opposition to such redistributive policies as land reforms and an agricultural income tax. Can the lineages of authoritarianism in Pakistan be traced to a ruling triad of landlords, bureaucracy, and military; and are these so prominent because of their propitiation in the canal colonies? Such notions must remain intriguing hypotheses until further investigation and interpretation can differentiate cause from effect more clearly.

The present work has opened up a number of questions that might provide an agenda for further research. The intention has been to throw light on some of the more important themes in this study of significant economic growth under colonial rule. The broader perspective of the development of the canal colonies as a whole has precluded detailed discussion of particular processes, which will now require closer attention.

One example of this lies in the selection of grantees. It was assumed that the British were able to decipher the major sociological categories of the Punjab, and to replicate them in the canal colonies. More focussed investigation could show with what sociological theories they approached the problem of conservative replication; whether their methodology of selection entailed use of the census, or revenue records, or consultation with village officials or local leaders, or of conducting village tours. These questions can be addressed properly only in a separate exercise.

Similarly, further work can focus more thoroughly on the perspective of the people who settled in these tracts. Official records have provided the substance of the present study; others can utilise nonofficial sources, as well as locally based and more detailed official materials. There are various aspects of the canal colony population that require more research: the indigenous tribes, participants in the horse-breeding schemes, traders in the market towns, landowners and subtenants, and many others.

Another dimension that remains to be addressed is the comparative aspect. This work has concentrated on narrating and explicating themes specific to the Punjab and the canal colonies, the essential initial step in the historiography of this region. Now comparison with similar processes in other parts of India, or in other colonial economies, would provide a useful perspective on developments in the western Punjab. Among areas that might provide fruitful insights would be the corruption of the native bureaucracy and the inequitable results of the conduct of amoral actors in the water distribution system.

The issue of the British as "agents of change" also needs to be examined further. The Punjab can be an important case study of what the colonial state attempted to do. The question remains whether British rule can be excoriated for what it never set out to achieve, namely, the transformation of Punjabi society. Such goals were not normally part of the economic policy parameters of Victorian and Edwardian governments, and still less of any European colonial system. It could be argued, on the other hand, that questions of economic development are not only of central importance to economic history, but they provide valid criteria for assessing the performance of any state, even a colonial one. This would be especially appropriate for the colonial Punjab, where the state attempted and achieved change at multiple levels, from social engineering to new crop varieties. Moreover, by the late nineteenth century, governments did realise that state policy could play an important role in developmental thrusts: two of the more successful examples were Germany and Japan. The British in the Punjab themselves claimed that they were bringing about major change, leading to the prevailing assumption that the Punjab was a long-term beneficiary of colonial rule. In providing a corrective to that assumption, this work could open an important debate on the methods and criteria for assessing colonial rule in general, and British rule in South Asia in particular. Such a debate can become as significant as the older one on the "drain theory," and it will incorporate the new research on regional histories, much of which might need to be reexamined in the light of new and different questions.

GLOSSARY

abadi   village site
abadkar   colonist; peasant grantee
abiana   water rate; occupier's rate levied for irrigation water
abpashi   cultivation through irrigation
ab-zaia   waste of water
anjuman   society, organisation
arthi   commission agent
arthri   agricultural labourer, generally of low caste, receiving payment in kind
bania   Hindu shopkeeper and money lender
bar   tableland between two rivers
bara, bari   types of inferior soil
barani   watered by rainfall
batai   rent taken by division of crops
bhadralok   respectable people
chak   block of units of land grouped together for purposes of administration; a
        colony village
chanda   subscriptions
chaudhry   headman of camel service grantees in Chenab Colony
chos   river action
chuhra   low-caste sweeper
darakhtpal   tree-planting grantee
darbari   courtier
desi   indigenous to Indian subcontinent
doab   tract of land between two rivers
faqir   religious mendicant; Muslim ascetic
ghasra   a type of inferior soil
ghee   clarified butter
ghoripal   horse-breeding grantee
gur   unrefined sugar, consisting of consolidated sugarcane juice
gurudawara   Sikh temple
halqa   circle of villages grouped together for administrative purposes
haq   a right
haq abpashi   area proposed for irrigation (popular and erroneous designation)
hithar   riverain lowland
ilaqa   estate; locality
inam   cash allowance for services rendered
jagir   officially granted right to a given tract of land
jatha   band of Sikhs
jhinwar   water carrier (Hindu)
jajmani   relationship between service and landholding castes

kallar
kallar amez } Saltpetre; soils impregnated with saltpetre, but culturable
kalrathi
kamin   village menial
kanal   one-eighth of an acre
kanungo   revenue official who supervises work of *patwaris*
kharaba   failed area of crops
kharif   summer or autumn harvest
killa   one-twenty-fifth of a colony square: 1.1 acres
kisan   peasant; cultivator
kot   reformatory settlement
lambardar   village headman; officially appointed headman of a "village commu-
     nity"
lawaris   without a guardian
maira   a type of light, loamy soil
malikana   fee paid in recognition of proprietary title
mandi   market
marla   an area equal to $\frac{1}{160}$ of an acre
mauza   a colony estate or village
moga   canal watercourse outlet
nai   barber
najaiz   unauthorised
nazarana   payment made to government on acquisition of a colony grant
panchayat   a village assembly or court; body of arbitrators
patti   a subdivision of an estate
pattidar   village shareholder
patwari   village accountant of revenues; record keeper
pir   a holy man; saint (Muslim)
rabi   winter or spring harvest
rais   a notable; rich man; a capitalist grantee
rakh   block of land
sabha   society; organisation
sahukar   professional moneylender; trader
sajjada nashin   shrine keeper (Muslim)
sangh   society; organisation
sanji   an agricultural labourer, receiving payment in kind
sepidari   relationship between service and landholding castes
sarbarah   agent, warden
sarmaya   capital
sarmayadar   one with capital; capitalist
sarshaf   indian rape: an oilseed crop
sarwan   a camel attendant
silladar   regimental system based on principle of joint-stock holdings
sufedposh   a yeoman grantee
surra   a disease peculiar to camels

tabadla   transfer; exchange of land

taccavi   loan by government

tahsil   section, or revenue and administrative subdivision, of a district

tahud khahi   pre-colonial lessees of state land in Montgomery and Multan districts

tarkhan   carpenter

tirni   grazing fee or tax

toria   an oilseed crop

vakil   agent; representative; lawyer

warabandi   system by which the supply of water to canal branches, distributaries, and watercourses is regulated in rotation

warashikni   infringements of *warabandi* schemes by irrigators; taking water out of turn

zail   a group of villages amalgamated for administrative purposes

zaildar   a local notable appointed to the charge of a *zail*

zakhira   a village plantation of trees; nursery

zakhiradar   holder of a colony *zakhira* grant

zamindar   an owner or occupier of land

zilladar   a subordinate official in the Irrigation Department

BIBLIOGRAPHY

GOVERNMENT RECORDS

Board of Revenue, Lahore (Office of the Financial Commissioner, Punjab).

BOR Files in the series: H/251/1-; J/301/1-; 251/1/00/1-; 301/1/00/1-; 601/1/00/1-. Also 61/100; 61/149; 613/6/19/3; and Printed Revenue File No. 74.

Proceedings of the Punjab Government

Punjab Revenue and Agriculture Proceedings, 'A' Files, 1890-1936. India Office Records, London, and Punjab Civil Secretariat, Lahore.
—Also referred to in the years 1880-1899 as Punjab Revenue Proceedings, and in 1933-1936 and Punjab Financial Proceedings.
—Divided into the following branches: Revenue, Irrigation, Agriculture, General, Scarcity.
Punjab Boards and Committees Proceedings (Local Self-Government Department), 'A' Files, 1920-1924. India Office Records, London, and Punjab Civil Secretariat, Lahore.
Punjab Legislative Council Proceedings, 1906-1907 and 1910-1912. India Office Records, London, and Australian National Library, Canberra.

Official Reports and Publications

ASSESSMENT REPORTS (WITH SOURCE)

AR of Lower Sohag Para Colony; in PRAP(R), January 1899, No. 27.
AR of Hafizabad and Khangah Dogran Tahsils, Gujranwala District, in PRAP(R), November 1904, No. 60.
AR of Upper Jhang Branch Circle, Lower Chenab Canal, in PRAP(R), October 1909, No. 81.
AR of Lower Jhang Branch, Circle II, Lower Chenab Canal, in PRAP(R), October 1909, No. 99.
AR of Jhelum Canal (Shahpur), in PRAP(R), October 1909, No. 126.
Revised AR of Upper Jhang Branch Circle, Lower Chenab Canal, in PRAP(R), March 1911, No. 24.
Supplementary AR of Jhang Branch, Circle II, Lower Chenab Canal, in PRAP(R), March 1911, No. 25.
AR of Jhang Branch, Circle III, Lower Chenab Canal, in PRAP(R), March 1911, No. 26.

AR of Gugera Branch, Circle I, Lower Chenab Canal, in PRAP(R), March 1911, No. 27.

AR of Wazirabad Tahsil, Gujranwala District, in PRAP(R), June 1911, No. 30.

Revised AR of Lower Jhelum Canal, Shahpur District, in PRAP(R), January 1912, No. 104.

AR of Gugera Branch, Circle II, Lower Chenab Canal, in PRAP(R), May 1912, No. 24.

AR of Gujranwala Tahsil, Gujranwala District, in PRAP(R), May 1912, No. 73.

AR of Sharakpur Tahsil, Gujranwala District, in PRAP(R), July 1912, No. 10.

AR of Rakh Branch Circle, Chenab Colony, in PRAP(R), April 1913, No. 45.

AR of Gujrat Tahsil, Gujrat District, in PRAP(R), December 1914, No. 22.

AR of Raya Tahsil, Sialkot District, in PRAP(R), April 1914, No. 22.

AR of Kharian Tahsil, Gujrat District, in PRAP(R), December 1914, No. 14.

AR of Pasrur Tahsil, Sialkot District, in PRAP(R), December 1914, No. 36.

AR of Phalia Tahsil, Gujrat District, in PRAP(R), February 1916, No. 24.

AR of Fixed Assessment portions of Bhera, Shahpur and Sargodha Tahsils, Shahpur District, in PRAP(R), March 1916, No. 37.

AR of Jhang Branch Circles, Lyallpur District, in PRAP(R), December 1921, No. 16.

AR of Gugera Branch, Circles I and II, Lyallpur District, in PRAP(R), June 1923, Enclosure No. 2 to No. 35.

AR of Lower Chenab Colony of Jhang District (Lahore, 1923); BOR Library, F 32(5).

AR of Chiniot Tahsil (non-colony portion), Jhang District (Lahore, 1924); BOR Library, F 32(5).

AR of Jhang Tahsil (non-colony portion), Jhang District (Lahore, 1925); BOR Library, F 32(5).

AR of Shorkot Tahsil (non-colony portion), Jhang District (Lahore, 1926); BOR Library, F 32(5).

AR of canal-irrigated tracts of Gujrat and Kharian Tahsils, Gujrat District, in Punjab Financial Proceedings (Revenue), March 1934, Enclosure No. 2 to No. 30.

AR of Montgomery Tahsil, Montgomery District, in Punjab Financial Proceedings (Revenue), May 1934, Enclosure No. 2-A to No. 1.

AR of Okara Tahsil, Montgomery District, in Punjab Financial Proceedings (Revenue), May 1934, No. 3.

AR of Khanewal Tahsil, Multan District, in Punjab Financial Proceedings (Revenue), June 1934, No. 55.

AR of Phalia Tahsil, Gujrat District, in Punjab Financial Proceedings (Revenue), November 1934, No. 130.

AR of Jaranwala Tahsil, Lyallpur District, in Punjab Financial Proceedings (Revenue), Novembere 1936, No. 1.

AR of Lyallpur Tahsil, Lyallpur District, in Punjab Financial Proceedings (Revenue), December 1936, No. 1.

AR of New Extensions Circle of Toba Tek Singh Tahsil, Lyallpur District (Lahore, 1937); BOR Library, F 31.
AR of Samundri Tahsil, Lyallpur District (Lahore, 1937); BOR Library, F 31.

SETTLEMENT REPORTS

Report on the Chenab Colony Settlement (Lahore, 1915).
Report on the Settlement of the Jhang and Gugera Branch Circles of the Lyallpur District, 1920-24 (Lahore, 1924).
Report on the Fourth Revised Settlement of the Gujranwala District, 1923-27 (Lahore, 1927).
Report on the Fourth Regular Settlement of the Jhang District, 1928 (Lahore, 1928).
Report on the Settlement of the canal-irrigated tract of the Gujrat District (Lahore, 1930).
Report on the Settlement of the Lower Bari Doab Colony, 1927-35 (Lahore, 1936).

GAZETTEERS AND MANUALS

Chenab Colony Gazetteer (Lahore, 1904).
Jhang District Gazetteer (Lahore, 1908).
Lahore District Gazetteer (Lahore, 1916).
Shahpur District Gazetteer (Lahore, 1917).
Gujrat District Gazetteer (Lahore, 1921).
Multan District Gazetteer (Lahore, 1923-1924).
Montgomery District Gazetteer (Lahore, 1933).
A Handbook of the Criminal Tribes of the Punjab, compiled by V.P.T. Vivian (Lahore, 1912).
The Criminal Tribes Administration Manual, Punjab (Lahore, 1919).
Punjab Settlement Manual, by J. M. Douie (4th ed., Lahore, 1930).
Punjab Colony Manual, by F. C. Wace (3rd ed., Lahore, 1936).

ANNUAL REPORTS

Punjab Colonies Report, 1892-1940. For the years 1892-1901 the Report was included as an Appendix of the annual *Report on the Land Revenue Administration of the Punjab*.
"Punjab Native Newspaper Reports," 1907-1908, Vol. XX.
Punjab—Public Works Department—Irrigation Branch: Annual Administration Report with Statistical Statements and Accounts, 1905-1906 to 1945-1946.
Report on the Administration of the Criminal Tribes in the Punjab, 1917-1940.
Report on the Land Revenue Administration of the Punjab, 1889-1901.
Report on the Operations of the Department of Agriculture, 1906-1907 to 1940-1941.
Report on Police Administration in the Punjab, 1909-1941.
Report on the Reclamation Department, 1927-1940.

OTHER REPORTS AND PAPERS

First-Third Regular Wages Survey of the Punjab, 1912, 1917, 1922 (Lahore, 1913, 1918, 1923).

Punjab Irrigation Paper No. 12: "On the distribution of water by measurement."

Punjab Irrigation Paper No. 24: "The sale of water for irrigation at volumetric rates."

Punjab Irrigation Paper No. 27: "Further notes on the sale of irrigation water at volumetric rates."

Report of the Camel Browsing Committee, 1911.

Report of the Canal Act Committee, 1940.

Report of the Horse and Mule-breeding Commission, 1900-1901.

Report of the Indian Irrigation Commission, 1901-1903.

Report of the Punjab Colonies Committee, 1907-1908.

Report of the Remount Department Committee on the proposed application of Horse and Mule-breeding conditions on the Lower Bari Doab Canal in the Punjab, 1912.

Report on the Colonisation of the Rakh and Mianali Branches of the Chenab Canal, by F. P. Young (Lahore, 1897).

Colonisation of the Rechna Doab, by Deva Singh (Lahore, n.d.).

Report on Factors Affecting Irrigation in the Punjab from Tubewells, by A.M.R. Montague, 1938.

Report on Questions Relating to the Administration of Criminal and Wandering Tribes in the Punjab (Lahore, 1914).

NEWSPAPERS

Tribune (Lahore), 1906-1907, 1919.

BOOKS AND ARTICLES

Ahmad, Saghir. "Social Stratification in a Punjabi Village." *Contributions to Indian Sociology*, New Series, No. 4 (1970), 105-25.

Alavi, Hamza. "Kinship in West Punjab Villages." *Contributions to Indian Sociology*, New Series, No. 6 (1972), 1-27.

———. "Politics of Dependence: A Village in West Punjab." *South Asian Review*, IV:2 (1971), 111-28.

Ali, Imran. "The Punjab Canal Colonies, 1885-1940." Ph.D. dissertation, Australian National University, 1980.

———. *Punjab Politics in the Decade before Partition*. Lahore, 1975.

———. "Relations between the Muslim League and the Punjab National Unionist Party, 1935-47." *South Asia*, No. 6 (1976), 51-65.

Ali, Tariq. *Pakistan: Military Rule or People's Power?* New York, 1970.

Bath, Slicher van. *The Agrarian History of Western Europe, A.D. 500-1850*. London, 1963.

Barrier, N. G. "The Formulation and Enactment of the Punjab Alienation of Land Bill." *Indian Economic and Social History Review*, II:2 (1965), 145-65.

————. *The Punjab Alienation of Land Bill of 1900* Durham, N.C., 1966.

————. "The Punjab Disturbances of 1907: The Response of the British Government in India to Agrarian Unrest." *Modern Asian Studies*, I:4 (1967), 353-83.

————. "Punjab Politics and the Disturbances of 1907." Ph.D. dissertation, Duke University, 1966.

Beteille, Andre. *Studies in Agrarian Social Structure*. Delhi, 1974.

Bhanga, Indu. *Agrarian System of the Sikhs*. New Delhi, 1978.

Blyn, George. *Agricultural Trends in India, 1891-1947*. Philadelphia, 1966.

Brayne, F. L. *Better Villages*. Bombay, 1937.

Broomfield, John. *Elite conflict in a plural society*. Berkeley and Los Angeles, 1968.

Buckley, R. B. *The Irrigation Works of India*. 2nd ed., London, 1905.

Byres, T. J. "The New Technology, Class Formation and Class Action in the Indian Countryside." *Journal of Peasant Studies*, VIII:4 (1981), 405-54.

Calvert, H. C. *The Wealth and Welfare of the Punjab*. Lahore, 1936.

Chambers, J. D., and G. E. Mingay. *The Agricultural Revolution 1750-1880*. London, 1966.

Cipolla, C. M. (ed.). *The Fontana Economic History of Europe*. Vols. III-IV. London, 1966.

Cross, H. E. *A Note on Surra in Camels for Commandants of Camel Corps*. Lahore, 1914.

Darling, M. L. *The Punjab Peasant in Prosperity and Debt*. 4th ed., London, 1947.

————. *Rusticus Loquitor or the Old Light and the New in the Punjab Village*. London, 1930.

————. *Wisdom and Waste in the Punjab Village*. London, 1934.

Das, Dial. *Vital Statistics of the Punjab, 1901-1940*. Lahore, 1943.

Dewey, C., and A. G. Hopkins (eds.). *The Imperial Impact: Studies in the Economic History of India and Africa*. London, 1978.

Dumont, Louis. *Homo Hierarchicus*. London, 1970.

Dungen, P.H.M. van den. *The Punjab Tradition*. London, 1972.

Eglar, Zekiye. *A Punjabi Village in Pakistan*. New York, 1960.

Farmer, B. H. *Agricultural Colonization in India since Independence*. London, 1974.

Fein, Helen. *Imperial Crime and Punishment*. Honolulu, 1977.

Frykenberg, R. E. (ed.). *Land Control and Social Structure in Indian History*. Madison, Wisc., 1969.

Furneaux, Robert. *Massacre at Amritsar*. London, 1963.

Gilmartin, David. "Religious Leadership and the Pakistan Movement in the Punjab." *Modern Asian Studies*, XIII:3 (1979), 458-517.

Gough, K., and H. P. Sharma (eds.). *Imperialism and Revolution in South Asia*. New York, 1973.

Griffin, L. H., and C. F. Massy. *Chiefs and Families of Note in the Punjab*. 2 vols. Lahore, 1940.

Habib, Irfan. *The Agrarian System of Mughal India*. Bombay, 1963.

Hardiman, David. *Peasant Nationalists of Gujrat, Kheda District, 1917-1934*. Delhi, 1981.

Hasan, S. Nurul. *Thoughts on Agrarian Relations in Mughal India*. New Delhi, 1973.

Heeger, G. A. "The Growth of the Congress Movement in the Punjab, 1920-1940." *Journal of Asian Studies*, XXXI:1 (1972), 39-51.

Ibbetson, D.C.J. *Punjab Castes*. Reprint, Patiala, 1970.

Islam, M. M. "Irrigation and Punjab Agriculture, 1906-1945: Some Preliminary Notes." *South Asia*, New Series, I:1 (1978), 29-37.

Jalal, Ayesha, and Anil Seal. "Alternative to Partition: Muslim Politics Between the Wars." *Modern Asian Studies*, XV:3 (1981), 415-54.

Jeffrey, R. *The Decline of Nayar Dominance*. Brighton, 1976.

Joshi, P. C. "Land Reform and Agrarian Change in India and Pakistan since 1947: I-II. *Journal of Peasant Studies*, I:2-3 (1974), 164-85 and 326-62, respectively.

Kessinger, T. K. *Vilyatpur 1848-1968*. Berkeley and Los Angeles, 1974.

Leigh, M. S. *The Punjab and the War*. Lahore, 1922.

Low, D. A. (ed.). *The Congress and the Raj*. Columbia, Missouri, 1977.

———. *Lion Rampant. Essays in the Study of British Imperialism*. London, 1973.

———. (ed.). *Soundings in Modern South Asian History*. London, 1968.

Mahendru, I. D. *Some Factors Affecting the Price of Wheat in the Punjab*. Lahore, 1937.

Major, A. J. "Return to Empire: The Sikhs and the British in the Punjab 1839-72." Ph.D. dissertation, Australian National University, 1981.

Mason, P. *A Matter of Honour*. London, 1974.

Mayer, A. C. "Pir and *Murshid*: An Aspect of Religious Leadership in West Pakistan." *Middle Eastern Studies*, III:2 (1967), 160-169.

Maynard, John. *Russia in Flux: Before October*. London, 1941.

———. *The Russian Peasant, and Other Studies*. London, 1942.

Michel, A. A. *The Indus Rivers*. New Haven, 1967.

Moore, Barrington. *Social Origins of Dictatorship and Democracy*. London, 1969.

Mukherjee, Mridula. "Some Aspects of Agrarian Structure of Punjab, 1925-47." *Economic and Political Weekly*, XV:26 (1980), A-46 to A-58.

O'Dwyer, Sir Michael. *India as I Knew It, 1885-1925*. London, 1925.

Oren, S. "The Sikhs, Congress and the Unionists in British Punjab, 1937-1945." *Modern Asian Studies*, VIII:3 (1974), 397-418.

Page, David. *Prelude to Partition; The Indian Muslims and the Imperial System of Control, 1920-1932*. Delhi, 1982.

Paustian, P. W. *Canal Irrigation in the Punjab*. New York, 1930.

Preston, S. "Recent Irrigation in the Punjab." IOR, Pamphlets P/T 1,234-44, n.d.

Robinson, Francis. *Separatism amongst Indian Muslims*. London, 1974.

Rose, H. A. (comp.). *A Glossary of the Tribes and Castes of the Punjab and North-West Frontier Province*. 3 vols. Lahore, 1914.

Sandaratne, N. "Landowners and Land Reform in Pakistan." *South Asian Review*, VII:2 (1974), 123-36.

Shah, K. T. *Industrialisation of the Punjab*. Lahore, 1941.

Shanin, T. (ed.). *Peasant Societies*. Middlesex, 1971.

Sharma, S. R. *The Punjab in Ferment*. New Delhi, 1971.

Singh, S. Kartar. *Finance and Marketing of Cultivators' Wheat in the Punjab*. Lahore, 1934.

Stokes, E. *The English Utilitarians and India*. Oxford, 1959.

———. *The Peasant and the Raj*. London, 1978.

Stone, Ian. "Canal Irrigation and Agrarian Change." Cambridge, 1975.

Talbot, I. A. "The Growth of the Muslim League in the Punjab." *Journal of Commonwealth and Comparative Politics*, XX:1 (1982), 5-24.

Tandon, P. *Punjabi Century*. Berkeley and Los Angeles, 1968.

Thorburn, S. S. *Mussalmans and Moneylenders in the Punjab*. Edinburgh, 1886.

———. *The Punjab in Peace and War*. London, 1904.

Trevaskis, H. K. *The Land of the Five Rivers*. Oxford, 1928.

———. *The Punjab of Today*. 2 vols. Lahore, 1931.

Whitcombe, E. M. *Agrarian Conditions in Northern India*. Berkeley and Los Angeles, 1972.

Wikeley, J. M. *Punjabi Mussalmans*. Calcutta, 1915.

Wilson, H. H. *Glossary of Judicial and Revenue Terms*. 2nd ed., Delhi, 1968.

INDEX

9 780691 602356